AspectJ in Action

AspectJ in Action

PRACTICAL ASPECT-ORIENTED PROGRAMMING

RAMNIVAS LADDAD

MANNING

Greenwich
(74° w. long.)

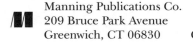

Manning Publications Co.   Copyeditor: Liz Welch
209 Bruce Park Avenue   Typesetter: Denis Dalinnik
Greenwich, CT 06830   Cover designer: Leslie Haimes

ISBN 1-930110-93-6

Printed in the United States of America
1 2 3 4 5 6 7 8 9 10 – VHG – 05 04 03 02

To my late grandfather, Jodhrajji.
You were always there for me.

brief contents

PART 1 UNDERSTANDING AOP AND ASPECTJ 1

    1 ▪ Introduction to AOP   3

    2 ▪ Introducing AspectJ   32

    3 ▪ AspectJ: syntax basics   64

    4 ▪ Advanced AspectJ   100

PART 2 BASIC APPLICATIONS OF ASPECTJ 143

    5 ▪ Monitoring techniques: logging, tracing,
        and profiling   145

    6 ▪ Policy enforcement: system wide contracts   178

    7 ▪ Optimization: pooling and caching   202

PART 3 ADVANCED APPLICATIONS OF ASPECTJ 243

    8 ▪ Design patterns and idioms   245

    9 ▪ Implementing thread safety   286

    10 ▪ Authentication and authorization   323

vii

11 ▪ Transaction management   356

12 ▪ Implementing business rules   391

13 ▪ The next step   425

A ▪ The AspectJ compiler   438

B ▪ Understanding Ant integration   447

▪ resources   455

▪ index   461

contents

preface   xvii

how real is AspectJ?   xix

into the future!   xxi

acknowledgments   xxiii

about this book   xxv

PART 1   UNDERSTANDING AOP AND ASPECTJ 1

---

1 **Introduction to AOP   3**

   1.1   The architect's dilemma   5

   1.2   Evolution of programming methodologies   6

   1.3   Managing system concerns   7

       *Identifying system concerns   8   ▪ A one-dimensional
solution   10   ▪ It's all about modularizing   11*

   1.4   Implementing crosscutting concerns in
nonmodularized systems   14

       *Symptoms of nonmodularization   15   ▪ Implications of
nonmodularization   18   ▪ Introducing AOP   19
A bit of history   20   ▪ The AOP methodology   21*

ix

1.5   Anatomy of an AOP language   22

The AOP language specification   23   ▪ The AOP language implementation   24   ▪ A weaving example   26

1.6   Benefits of AOP   27

1.7   Myths and realities of AOP   29

1.8   Summary   30

2   Introducing AspectJ   32

2.1   AspectJ: a bird's eye view   33

Crosscutting in AspectJ   33   ▪ Crosscutting elements   34

2.2   AspectJ Hello World   37

2.3   AspectJ: under the hood   40

2.4   The join point model   43

Exposed join point categories   44   ▪ Join point demonstration example   50

2.5   Aspects   55

2.6   AspectJ logistics overview   59

The AspectJ compiler   59   ▪ AspectJ browser   60 IDE integration   61

2.7   Summary   62

3   AspectJ: syntax basics   64

3.1   Pointcuts   65

Wildcards and pointcut operators   67   ▪ Signature syntax   68   ▪ Implementing pointcuts   73

3.2   Advice   81

Anatomy of advice   82   ▪ The before advice   83   ▪ The after advice   83   ▪ The around advice   85   ▪ Comparing advice with methods   86   ▪ Passing context from a join point to advice   87 Returning a value from around advice   89   ▪ An example using around advice: failure handling   90   ▪ Context collection example: caching   92

3.3   Static crosscutting   95

Member introduction   95   ▪ Modifying the class hierarchy   96 Introducing compile-time errors and warning   97

3.4   Tips and tricks   98

3.5   Summary   99

4 ***Advanced AspectJ 100***

    4.1   Accessing join point information via reflection   101

        The reflective API   103 ▪ Using reflective APIs   106

    4.2   Aspect precedence   111

        Ordering of advice   114 ▪ Explicit aspect precedence   115
        Aspect inheritance and precedence   117 ▪ Ordering of advice
        in a single aspect   119 ▪ Aspect precedence and member
        introduction   120

    4.3   Aspect association   122

        Default association   123 ▪ Per-object association   125
        Per-control-flow association   128 ▪ Implicit limiting
        of join points   132 ▪ Comparing object association with
        member introduction   134 ▪ Accessing aspect instances   135

    4.4   Exception softening   136

    4.5   Privileged aspects   139

    4.6   Summary   141

PART 2   BASIC APPLICATIONS OF ASPECTJ 143

5 ***Monitoring techniques: logging, tracing, and
profiling 145***

    5.1   Why use AspectJ for logging?   146

        A simple case in point   147 ▪ Logging the conventional
        way   149 ▪ Logging the aspect-oriented way   153

    5.2   What's wrong with conventional logging   154

    5.3   The beauty of AspectJ-based logging   156

    5.4   Developing logging and tracing aspects   156

        Method call tracing   157 ▪ Exceptions logging   163

    5.5   Common logging idioms   167

        Logging the method parameters   168 ▪ Indenting the log
        statements   170 ▪ Aspect precedence   172 ▪ Changing the
        underlying logging mechanism   173 ▪ Using logging in a
        multithreaded environment   173

    5.6   Extending logging for other usage   174

        Testing   174 ▪ Profiling   175

    5.7   Summary   176

6
Policy enforcement: system wide contracts 178

6.1 AspectJ-based policy enforcement overview 179

6.2 The current solution and its challenges 181

6.3 Enforcement using AspectJ 182

Policy enforcement implementation choices 183 ▪ The role of policy enforcement during the product lifecycle 184

6.4 Policy enforcement patterns 185

Detecting the violation of a specific call pattern 185 Implementing flexible access control 187 ▪ Enforcing the best-practices principles 189

6.5 Example: implementing EJB programming restrictions 191

Implementing "no AWT" 193 ▪ Implementing "no nonfinal static field access" 194

6.6 Example: implementing Swing policies 195

Understanding the problem 196 ▪ Detecting the violation 198

6.7 Summary 200

7
Optimization: pooling and caching 202

7.1 The typical case 203

Return, reuse, recycle: The role of resource pooling 205 ▪ Resource pooling issues 206

7.2 Diving into the pool using AspectJ 208

Designing a template aspect 208 ▪ Implementing the template aspect 209

7.3 Example 1: database connection pooling 211

Understanding the database connection pool interface 212 AspectJ-based database connection pooling 213 Implementing the connection pool 216 ▪ Testing our solution 218 ▪ Tweaking the solution 222

7.4 Example 2: thread pooling 223

The echo server 224 ▪ Understanding the thread pool interface 226 ▪ AspectJ-based thread pooling 226 Implementing the thread pool 230 ▪ Testing our solution 231 ▪ Tweaking the solution 234

7.5 Extending pooling concepts to caching 235

AspectJ-based caching: the first version 237 ▪ AspectJ-based caching: the second version 239 ▪ Ideas for further improvements 240

7.6 Summary 241

PART 3 ADVANCED APPLICATIONS OF ASPECTJ 243

8 **Design patterns and idioms 245**

8.1 The worker object creation pattern 247

The current solution 248 ▪ An overview of the worker object creation pattern 249 ▪ The pattern template 249 A summary of the worker object creation pattern 256

8.2 The wormhole pattern 256

The current solution 257 ▪ An overview of the wormhole pattern 257 ▪ The pattern template 258 ▪ A summary of the wormhole pattern 260

8.3 The exception introduction pattern 260

The current solution 261 ▪ An overview of the exception introduction pattern 265 ▪ The pattern template 265 A summary of the exception introduction pattern 269

8.4 The participant pattern 270

Current solutions 271 ▪ An overview of the participant pattern 273 ▪ The pattern template 274 ▪ A summary of the participant pattern 276

8.5 Idioms 277

Avoiding infinite recursion 277 ▪ Nullifying advice 279 Providing empty pointcut definitions 280 ▪ Providing a default interface implementation 281

8.6 Summary 285

9 **Implementing thread safety 286**

9.1 Swing's single-thread rule 287

The rule 288 ▪ The problem 288 ▪ The solution 289

9.2 A test problem 290

9.3 Solution: the conventional way 293

9.4   Solution: the AspectJ way   297

   The first version   298   ▪ The second version   303
   The third version   307

9.5   Improving the solution   311

   Dealing with exceptions   311   ▪ Avoiding the overhead   312

9.6   Improving the responsiveness of UI applications   313

9.7   Modularizing the read-write lock pattern   316

   Implementation: the conventional way   316
   Implementation: the AspectJ way   318

9.8   Summary   321

10   **Authentication and authorization   323**

10.1   Problem overview   324

10.2   A simple banking example   325

10.3   Authentication: the conventional way   329

   Implementing the solution   329   ▪ Testing the solution   331

10.4   Authentication: the AspectJ way   333

   Developing the solution   333   ▪ Testing the solution   336

10.5   Authorization: the conventional way   336

   *Understanding JAAS-based authorization   337   ▪ Developing the
   solution   338   ▪ Testing the solution   342   ▪ Issues with the
   conventional solution   345*

10.6   Authorization: the AspectJ way   346

   Developing the solution   346   ▪ Testing the solution   350

10.7   Fine-tuning the solution   353

   *Using multiple subaspects   353   ▪ Separating authentication
   and authorization   354*

10.8   Summary   354

11   **Transaction management   356**

11.1   Example: a banking system with persistence   358

   Implementing the core concern   358
   Setting up the test scenario   362

11.2   The conventional solution   364

   *Using the same connection object   365   ▪ Committing at
   the top level only   367*

11.3   Developing a simple AspectJ-based solution   368

Implementing the JDBC transaction aspect   368 ▪ Handling legacy system issues   373 ▪ Enabling transaction management for the banking system   374 ▪ Testing the solution   375

11.4   Improving the solution   378

Using the participant pattern   379 ▪ Implementing the JDBC transaction aspect: the second version   382 Testing the solution   385

11.5   Using AspectJ with advanced transaction-management systems   387

11.6   Summary   390

12   ***Implementing business rules   391***

12.1   Using business rules in enterprise applications   392

12.2   An overview of business rule implementation   393

12.3   Current mechanisms   393

12.4   Introducing a solution using AspectJ   394

The template   394

12.5   Example: the banking system   396

Implementing the core business logic   396 ▪ Implementing the first business rule   401 ▪ Implementing the second business rule   403 ▪ Writing a test program   406

12.6   Implementing business rules with a rule engine   411

An overview of the rule engine   412 ▪ Using a rule engine   412 ▪ Modularizing with AspectJ   415

12.7   Example: a banking system with a rule engine   417

A brief overview of Jess (Java Expert System Shell)   417 Specifying rules   418 ▪ Understanding the rule invocation aspect   420

12.8   Summary   423

13   ***The next step   425***

13.1   Applying AspectJ to new problems   426

Talking the talk   426 ▪ Walking the walk   427

13.2 Employing AspectJ in development phases 427

AspectJ in the design phase 428 ▪ *AspectJ in the implementation phase 428* ▪ *AspectJ in the testing phase 431* ▪ *AspectJ in the maintenance phase 432* ▪ *AspectJ in legacy projects 432*

13.3 A word of warning 433

13.4 Evangelizing AspectJ 434

13.5 Parting thoughts 436

A   **The AspectJ compiler 438**

A.1 Downloading and setting up 439

A.2 An overview of the compiler 440

A.3 Compiling source files 441

A.4 Compiling source directories 441

A.5 Weaving into JAR files 442

A.6 Creating aspect libraries 443

A.7 Using aspect libraries 444

A.8 Utilizing incremental compilation mode 444

A.9 Producing useful warnings 446

B   **Understanding Ant integration 447**

B.1 Compiling source files using an Ant task 448

B.2 Weaving into JAR files using an Ant task 451

B.3 Creating aspect libraries using an Ant task 452

B.4 Utilizing aspect libraries using an Ant task 453

B.5 Utilizing incremental compilation using an Ant task 453

resources 455

index 461

preface

I've always felt that implementing a software system is much harder than it needs to be. It is difficult to map requirements to the implementation and then trace the implementation back to the requirements. Although many approaches—such as object-oriented programming, component-oriented programming, and design patterns—help to some extent, none of them satisfactorily addresses the system-level requirements, often referred to as *crosscutting concerns*, that must be included in multiple modules.

I came across AspectJ version 0.3 in 1998 while looking for better ways to architect a Java-based system. AspectJ was an implementation of aspect-oriented programming (AOP), a new methodology that specifically targeted the management of crosscutting concerns. Even though AspectJ was in its infancy, I became fascinated by its potential. The struggle to keep up with all the new advances in the Java and XML world, along with other priorities in my life, prevented me from pursuing it further. Still, exploring AspectJ was always on my to-do list, and I started looking at it again when it was in version 0.8. By then, AspectJ had evolved into a much more powerful language. I started using AspectJ and found that the more I used it, the more I fell in love with it. Today, the current version of AspectJ (1.1)—which this book is based on—has morphed into a mature, robust language.

In early 2002, I wrote a series of articles for *JavaWorld* describing AOP and AspectJ; the book you are holding grew out of that series. From reader responses, I realized that most developers understand that AspectJ can be used to modularize the crosscutting concern of logging, but they struggle to imagine how it may be applied beyond that. Logging, while an important concern, is not something developers lose sleep over. Logging using AspectJ, therefore, is best characterized as a vitamin and not a painkiller; while vitamins are important, often the need for them is not pressing enough to require immediate action. To further complicate the situation, the examples of AOP that are widely available today either repeat the same logging problem or are too abstract to be of immediate practical value.

My mission statement for this book is "to be a key element in bringing AOP and AspectJ into everyday practice." To accomplish this goal, the book not only presents the AspectJ language but also provides practical AspectJ-based solutions to a wide variety of real-world problems. You will find that you can utilize these solutions to quickly reap the benefits of the language. I have tried to use current technologies as the basis for these solutions so that you can readily apply them to your system. This also demonstrates that these latest technologies by themselves are not enough to manage crosscutting concerns, since combined with AspectJ, they provide a better solution. The book also presents a few original design patterns that increase the power of AspectJ significantly.

It is not often that one gets to write about such an exciting new programming methodology and language. I enjoyed writing this book. I hope you will enjoy reading it.

how real is AspectJ?

Can you use AOP and AspectJ *today* and on *real* projects? The answer is yes. People are using AspectJ in real projects for enhancing middleware platforms, monitoring and improving performance, adding security to existing applications, and implementing Enterprise Application Integration (EAI). All these projects have seen impressive results in reducing both the amount of code and the time required to create the products.

AOP is becoming an increasingly popular programming methodology; you can find implementations of AOP for many modern languages. For the Java language, AspectJ is the implementation that has the largest community acceptance. AspectJ is a popular choice for several good reasons. One of its strengths is, and always has been, its pragmatic approach to language design. Instead of allowing the language to get bogged down in theory, AspectJ's developers started with basic AOP support and added new features *only* after people in the field had discussed their practical use extensively. The result was the creation of a simple language that was powerful enough to solve real problems. Another real strength of AspectJ is the tool support that is so crucial to every developer. Let's face it—not many of us write code that runs perfectly the first time, and debugging is an activity on which we spend a good portion of our working life. Since AspectJ is integrated with IDEs such as Eclipse, NetBeans, JBuilder, and Emacs JDEE, you can debug it just like a plain Java program using breakpoints, expression evaluation, and similar techniques.

The recently released version of AspectJ (1.1) has the required maturity that the language and tools need to make it possible to work with large projects. It also features a compiler based on the industry-strength Java compiler that is a part of the Eclipse IDE and used by thousands of projects worldwide. With AspectJ 1.1, it is possible to create closed-source third-party libraries, paving the way for commercial vendors to produce prewritten aspects. AspectJ is now an open source project under eclipse.org. While it always was an open source project, the eclipse.org infrastructure makes it easier for us to participate in the development of the tool. Moreover, with the widespread acceptance of the Eclipse IDE, it sure can't hurt to be associated with a wildly successful project!

Here are ways you can start benefiting from AspectJ right now based on examples in this book. You can bring modularized implementation of resource pooling, thread safety, transaction management, authentication, and authorization to your system just by composing Plain Old Java Objects (POJOs) with "plain old Java services," such as servlets, Java Authentication and Authorization Service (JAAS), and Java Transaction API (JTA). If you are using EJB, which manages many of these concerns, you can still enhance your system by implementing logging and modularizing business rules with AspectJ. Everyone, including those using EJB, can use AspectJ for policy enforcement to ensure correct implementation of applications and avoid costly errors.

So, as you can see, AspectJ is for real! The best way to realize the benefit for yourself is to start using it. Once you do, you will be surprised by its power and versatility, and you will find it to be very programmer-friendly.

into the future!

AOP and AspectJ's influence on software development has just begun. It is going to have an impact on virtually every kind of programming: enterprise applications, desktop clients, real-time systems, and embedded systems.

The examples in this book will give you a preview of how AOP will change the landscape of the enterprise application arena. Currently, EJB is the most common infrastructure technology used to implement an enterprise system. The strength of the EJB specification is in the way it separates the system-level services (such as persistence, transaction management, and authorization) from the application-specific business logic. The weakness of EJB lies in its complexity and the way it ties all the services—some of which you may not need—into one offering: the application server. Further, if you do not like the performance of a service, you have to make hard choices. You may implement the service yourself—in the process mixing the business code with crosscutting logic—or you can replace the current application server with a new one. And we all know how much fun such a replacement is, despite the existence of the standard!

With an AOP-based solution, you will be able to combine various modules, called *aspects*, to create a system that provides just the services you need—no less, no more. You can then individually fine-tune each aspect or even replace it without adversely affecting the other parts of the system. The potential that AOP offers to build your own application server from configurable components, potentially from different vendors, is a far superior alternative in creating a long-lasting and maintainable enterprise system. I expect that the open source community will contribute prewritten aspects that will eventually evolve into a cohesive library. This library will form a foundation on which we can build systems that could replace EJB and similar technologies.

AOP and AspectJ will have an impact on nonenterprise applications as well. The client-side desktop applications will benefit from the clean design and reusability offered by AOP and AspectJ. Implementing concerns such as optimization and thread safety will be a simple matter of including prebuilt aspects. Further, efforts are already under way to apply AspectJ in real-time and embedded systems to realize crosscutting concerns, such as memory management and concurrency control.

Of course, this won't happen overnight; AOP is still new and as with any new methodology, it will take time to be assimilated into the programming community. As this happens, AspectJ will gain widespread acceptance as the powerful language it really is. One thing is for sure—AspectJ's future is bright!

acknowledgments

Although only one name appears on the cover, many people helped behind the scenes. I am humbled by all the support I received in making this book a reality.

Many thanks to the AspectJ team—Gregor Kiczales, Erik Hilsdale, Jim Hugunin, Mik Kersten, and Wes Isberg—for making this book possible by creating such a powerful language and its implementation, replying to email queries, and quickly fixing the reported bugs. A special thanks goes to Mik Kersten for helping with the screenshots.

My sincerest thanks go to Jackie Carter for helping to revise the manuscript. Her technical background and quick grasp of concepts, along with her attention to detail and eye for simplicity and consistency, made this book easy to read and understand. Jackie, you are the best!

Many thanks to Manning's publisher, Marjan Bace, for his commitment to making this a quality book. Marjan's relentless effort in understanding the technology and providing a different perspective on the topic led to many improvements in the book. I'd also like to thank Mary Piergies for managing the production and quickly answering all my queries; Liz Welch for cheerfully going through multiple iterations of copyediting; Tiffany Taylor for meticulously weeding out many hard-to-spot errors during proofreading; and all the helpful people at Manning: Ted Kennedy, Helen Trimes, Denis Dalinnik, Hal Fulton, Lori Piquet, Chris Hillman, Leslie Haimes, Syd Brown, Lee Fitzpatrick, and Susan Capparelle. Also, I'd like to thank Alex Garrett for getting this project started, and Lianna Wlasiuk and Kelly Kwiatkowski for assisting with the initial round of editing.

Thanks to the reviewers, who provided extremely useful feedback that also led to many improvements: Jean Baltus (who served as the technical editor as well), Chris Bartling, Henry Choi, Vlad Ender, Awais Rashid, Arno Schmidmeier, Robert Wenner, and Alan Cameron Wills. All the remaining errors, of course, are mine. Thanks to TheServerSide.com for holding a public review and to the many reviewers, especially Ron Bodkin, Jonathan Cates, Chris Nelson, Jean Safar, and Keith Webster, who gave me useful feedback on chapters posted there.

I'd like to send a big thank-you to all my colleagues at Real-Time Innovations for their support and encouragement.

Thanks go to my family for their love and support over all these years. Thanks to my late father, Ramvallabh, for instilling me with honesty and ethics; my mother, Suraj, for always loving me so much; and my brother, Ramprakash, and sister, Jayashri, for providing the support that I can always count on. Many thanks to my sister-in-law, Vijaya; my brother-in-law, Kamalkishor; my nephew, Prashant; and my nieces, Rakhi and Gauri, for their encouragement. I'd especially like to thank my nephew Ashish for always caring about the book's progress and wishing me the best.

Finally, a special thanks goes to my wife, Kavita, who took care of all the family chores, reviewed the manuscript, and created the illustrations for the book—never complaining about my many broken promises to spend more time with the family. Thanks also to my three-year old son, Shadaj, for accepting that Papa needed to work on the book and could not always play with him—and grabbing me to play once in a while anyway—exactly when I needed to take a break. Looking at your smiling face makes all this effort worthwhile.

about this book

AspectJ in Action is a practical guide to applying AspectJ to real-world problems. I cover a broad spectrum of solutions—from simple examples that address logging and tracing, to complex ones dealing with transactions and security. Regardless of your area of expertise, you are bound to find several examples that you can adapt to the challenges you face in your work.

AspectJ in Action is aimed at intermediate to advanced Java developers. Readers with a background in designing and building large systems will also find a good part of this book useful. While knowledge of object-oriented programming is desirable, I do not assume that you are familiar with aspect-oriented programming or AspectJ. For special topics, I provide sufficient background material and cite resources (both text and online) for those who want to gain an in-depth understanding.

Roadmap

This book is divided into three parts. If you are new to AOP and AspectJ, you should first read part 1 followed by at least a couple of chapters in part 2. Within part 3, you can read chapters in any sequence. If you find that one of the sections specifically addresses your current problem, start using the techniques I present, learn from the experience, and go from there. You can also choose to study all the other chapters and apply hybrid techniques to suit your current needs.

Most chapters in parts 2 and 3 follow a pattern of presenting a conventional solution followed by an AspectJ solution that implements the identical functionality. This pattern provides better understanding of the problem domain, and comparing the two solutions shows the effectiveness of AspectJ.

Part 1 introduces the aspect-oriented programming methodology and the AspectJ language.

Chapter 1 introduces the problems aspect-oriented programming aims to address and explains how it handles them. We discuss the concern decomposition of a system, the classification of concerns, and issues with current implementations of crosscutting concerns. We then show how AOP helps modularize those concerns.

Chapter 2 introduces the AspectJ programming language. We discuss the various language concepts and constructs. The join point model presented in this chapter is the most fundamental concept in AspectJ. We finish the chapter by briefly showing the IDE support for AspectJ.

Chapter 3 gets into the details of the AspectJ language by examining the concepts of pointcuts, advice, the introduction mechanism, and so forth. This chapter provides you with enough information to start writing simple AspectJ programs.

Chapter 4 shows the advanced concepts in AspectJ that you need to understand before you start writing nontrivial AspectJ programs.

Part 2 examines the real-world application of AspectJ using simple constructs.

Chapter 5 introduces logging and monitoring using AspectJ. We show how AspectJ includes logging in a system without touching any of its core modules. You'll also see the ease with which you can switch between different logging APIs.

Chapter 6 shows how to enforce system wide contracts through policy-enforcement aspects. We offer a few simple examples that serve as building blocks. Then we describe an implementation of a UI application and EJB policy enforcement.

Chapter 7 examines how AspectJ can modularize the optimization concerns of pooling and caching. We study a generic template and utilize it to address the concrete challenges of JDBC connection and thread pooling. We finish the chapter with a caching example.

Part 3 examines the advanced application of AspectJ. You must have a good understanding of AspectJ before reading this part of the book.

Chapter 8 introduces a few brand-new AspectJ patterns. We also show a few idioms to avoid certain common pitfalls. Some of these patterns are original contributions from the author. This chapter is required reading before you tackle any of the remaining chapters in part 3, because all of the chapters use one or more of the patterns we present.

Chapter 9 addresses the modularization of thread safety using AspectJ. We specifically address two problems: the thread safety of Swing applications and the read-write lock pattern.

Chapter 10 examines the use of AspectJ for authentication and authorization. We utilize JAAS to implement the underlying authentication and authorization functionality and use AspectJ to achieve modularization.

Chapter 11 explains how AspectJ can separate the transaction concern from the core concern. We examine a JDBC-based as well as a JTA-based transaction.

Chapter 12 shows a novel application of AspectJ—we utilize it to modularize business rule implementations. We discuss AspectJ-based solutions that use plain Java as well as a rule engine (Jess) that evaluates the business rules.

Chapter 13 rounds out the book by showing a pragmatic approach to adopting AspectJ.

The two appendices explain, in detail, how to use the AspectJ compiler and AspectJ/Ant integration. In "Resources," you will find a wealth of information, both text and online, related to AspectJ.

Packages and tools used

The examples in this book use the following external tools and packages. The number in parentheses indicates the version I used for testing—a newer compatible version of these packages should work as well. I will attempt to provide updated source code that you can download from the book's source code download site (see the "Source code" section) whenever significantly newer versions of the packages are released:

- JDK 1.4 (1.4.1_01)—http://java.sun.com/j2se
- AspectJ 1.1 (1.1.0)—http://www.eclipse.org/aspectj
- log4j 1.2 (1.2)—http://jakarta.apache.org/log4j
- J2EE SDK 1.3 (1.3.1)—http://java.sun.com/j2ee
- Doug Lea's Concurrency library (1.3.2)—http://gee.cs.oswego.edu/dl/classes/EDU/oswego/cs/dl/util/concurrent/intro.html
- Jess 6.1 (6.1p2)—http://herzberg.ca.sandia.gov/jess/
- Ant (1.5.1)—http://ant.apache.org/

Source code

The source code for the example applications in this book is freely available from Manning's web site, http://www.manning.com/laddad. Much of the source code is reusable either in its original state or after some customization. The download package contains the source code, instructions on how to obtain the required external packages and set up the test environment, and scripts that automate compiling and running the programs.

Typographical conventions

- *Italic* typeface is used to introduce new terms.
- Courier typeface is used to denote code samples as well as program elements.
- **Courier bold** typeface is used to denote code of special interest.
- Code-line continuations are indicated by ➠.

Author Online

The purchase of *AspectJ in Action* includes free access to a private web forum run by Manning Publications, where you can make comments about the book, ask technical questions, and receive help from the author and from other users. To access the forum and subscribe to it, point your web browser to http://www.manning.com/laddad. This page provides information on how to get on the forum once you are registered, what kind of help is available, and the rules of conduct on the forum.

Manning's commitment to our readers is to provide a venue where a meaningful dialogue between individual readers and between readers and the author can take place. It is not a commitment to any specific amount of participation on the part of the author, whose contribution to the AO remains voluntary (and unpaid). We suggest you try asking the author some challenging questions lest his interest stray!

The Author Online forum and the archives of previous discussions will be accessible from the publisher's web site as long as the book is in print.

About the author

Ramnivas Laddad is a Sun Certified Architect of Java Technology. He has worked with object-oriented systems for over a decade and with aspect-oriented programming for the past three years. He is the author of several articles and papers and co-author of *Professional Java XML* (Wrox Press, 2001). His series of articles on AOP and AspectJ was published in *JavaWorld*. He lives in Sunnyvale, California. Ramnivas can be reached by email at ramnivas@yahoo.com.

About the title

By combining introductions, overviews, and how-to examples, the *In Action* books are designed to help learning *and* remembering. According to research in cognitive science the things people remember are things they discover during self-motivated exploration.

Although no one at Manning is a cognitive scientist, we are convinced that for learning to become permanent it must pass through stages of exploration, play, and, interestingly, retelling of what is being learned. People understand and remember new things, which is to say they master them, only after actively exploring them. Humans learn *in action*. An essential part of an *In Action* guide is that it is example-driven. It encourages the reader to try things out, to play with new code, and explore new ideas.

There is another, more mundane, reason for the title of this book: our readers are busy. They use books to do a job or solve a problem. They need books that allow them to jump in and jump out easily and learn just what they want just when they want it. They need books that aid them *in action*. The books in this series are designed for such readers.

About the cover

The figure on the cover of *AspectJ in Action* is an "Ysleno Moluco," an inhabitant of the Molucan Islands, also known as the Spice Islands, a southwestern province of Indonesia. The illustration is taken from a Spanish compendium of regional dress customs first published in Madrid in 1799.

The title page of the Spanish compendium states:

> *Coleccion general de los Trages que usan actualmente todas las Nacionas del Mundo desubierto, dibujados y grabados con la mayor exactitud por R.M.V.A.R. Obra muy util y en special para los que tienen la del viajero universal*

which we translate, as literally as possible, thus:

General collection of costumes currently used in the nations of the known world, designed and printed with great exactitude by R.M.V.A.R. This work is very useful especially for those who hold themselves to be universal travelers

Although nothing is known of the designers, engravers, and workers who colored this illustration by hand, the "exactitude" of their execution is evident in this drawing. The "Ysleno Moluco" is just one of many figures in this colorful collection. Their diversity speaks vividly of the uniqueness and individuality of the world's towns and regions just 200 years ago. This was a time when the dress codes of two regions separated by a few dozen miles identified people uniquely as belonging to one or the other. The collection brings to life a sense of isolation and distance of that period—and of every other historic period except our own hyperkinetic present.

Dress codes have changed since then and the diversity by region, so rich at the time, has faded away. It is now often hard to tell the inhabitant of one continent from another. Perhaps, trying to view it optimistically, we have traded a cultural and visual diversity for a more varied personal life. Or a more varied and interesting intellectual and technical life.

We at Manning celebrate the inventiveness, the initiative, and the fun of the computer business with book covers based on the rich diversity of regional life of two centuries ago, brought back to life by the pictures from this collection.

Part 1

Understanding AOP and AspectJ

Part 1 of this book introduces aspect-oriented programming (AOP) and the AspectJ language. We discuss the need for a new programming methodology and the way this methodology is realized in AspectJ.

Because AOP is a new methodology, we devote the first chapter to introducing it: why it is needed, and what its core concepts are. The remaining chapters—2 through 4—describe the AspectJ language. First, we present an overview of the language and its concepts, followed by a detailed look at the basic syntax. In chapter 4, we examine the advanced constructs.

You'll find the material in part 1 useful as a reference while reading the rest of the book. If you are new to AOP and AspectJ, we strongly recommend that you read this part first.

Introduction to AOP

This chapter covers

- Understanding crosscutting concerns
- Modularizing crosscutting concerns using AOP
- Understanding AOP languages
- Debunking myths about AOP

Imagine you are an architect designing a house. Your primary concerns involve making good choices for the core features of the house: the design of the foundation, the height of the walls, the pitch of the roof, the location and size of the rooms, and so on. Your secondary concerns are the features shared by many of the core elements, such as the electrical wiring and plumbing. Now envision that you are designing a bridge. While the primary concerns are different—the piers, trusses, beams, and cables, for example—the secondary concerns still include system-wide features such as the electrical wiring.

Software design proceeds in a similar fashion. A software architect, when asked to design something new, first addresses the primary core functionality, which in a business application is the basic business logic. In a banking application, for instance, core modules are designed to manage the banking transactions that each customer makes. In a retail application, the core modules deal with the purchases and inventory management. In both applications, the system-wide concerns involve such features as logging, authorization, persistence, and other elements common to many of the core business modules.

Let's look at another software example. If the architect is designing a robotics application, the core concerns are the motion management and path computation. The concerns that are common to many of the core modules involve features such as logging, remote management, and path optimization. These system-wide concerns that span multiple modules are called *crosscutting concerns*. Aspect-oriented programming (AOP) manages these crosscutting concerns.

While object-oriented programming (OOP) is the most common methodology employed today to manage core concerns, it is not sufficient for many crosscutting concerns, especially in complex applications. As you will see in this chapter, a typical OOP implementation creates a coupling between the core and crosscutting concerns that is undesirable, since the addition of new crosscutting features and even certain modifications to the existing crosscutting functionality require modifying the relevant core modules.

AOP is a new methodology that provides separation of crosscutting concerns by introducing a new unit of modularization—an *aspect*—that crosscuts other modules. With AOP you implement crosscutting concerns in aspects instead of fusing them in the core modules. An *aspect weaver*, which is a compiler-like entity, composes the final system by combining the core and crosscutting modules through a process called *weaving*. The result is that AOP modularizes the crosscutting concerns in a clear-cut fashion, yielding a system architecture that is easier to design, implement, and maintain.

In this opening chapter, we examine the fundamentals of AOP, the problems it addresses, and why *you* need to know about it.

1.1 The architect's dilemma

Perhaps the most commonly asked question in today's software engineering is, How much design is too much? Good system architecture considers present and potential future requirements. Failing to take into account the potential future requirements of a crosscutting nature may eventually require changing many parts of the system or perhaps even reimplementing them. On the other hand, including low-probability requirements may lead to an overdesigned, hard-to-understand, bloated system. There is a demand to create well-designed systems that can meet future needs without compromising quality. Then again, inability to predict the future and time-to-market pressure simply suggests going with what you need today. Further, since requirements are going to change anyway, why bother considering them? I call this underdesign/overdesign issue the *architect's dilemma*.

Understanding the architect's dilemma is crucial in understanding the need for AOP. Otherwise, developers will be likely to wonder, "Couldn't you just have satisfied this requirement by better utilizing the design techniques we currently use?" or "Isn't AOP just patching up bad or inadequate design?" The answer to both questions is no.

Think of your last couple of projects. Ideas about how you could have designed it differently are obvious in hindsight. The question is, could you have made those choices with the information you had *then*? Although in theory the concerns could have been addressed with foresight, even if only partially, in real life it just doesn't work that way.

For example, should an architect consider performance-related requirements in the beginning phases of a project? The usual approach is to build the system, profile it, and retrofit it with optimizations to improve performance. This approach calls for potentially changing many parts of the system using profiling. Further, over time, new bottlenecks may need to be addressed due to changes in usage patterns. The architects of reusable libraries have an even more difficult task because it is a lot harder to imagine all the usage scenarios of a library. Today's fast-changing technology makes it even more difficult since technological changes may make certain design decisions useless. Table 1.1 enumerates the forces on an architect that are at the root of the architect's dilemma.

When software projects turn out to be insufficient for future business requirements, it is common to blame the problem on the design decisions. However,

Table 1.1 Forces behind the architect's dilemma

Benefits of Underdesign	Benefits of Overdesign
Reduced short-term development cost	Better long-term system manageability
Reduced design bloat	Easy to accommodate new requirements
Reduced time-to-market	Improved long-term product quality

what is often believed to be insufficient design effort or design shortcomings may be simply a limitation of the design methodologies used and the language implementation. With current design and implementation techniques, there is a limit to what we can do to produce a system that satisfies the current and potential future requirements in a balanced way, and even that limit may not be acceptable when considering the ever-increasing pressure on time-to-market and quality requirements of feature-rich products.

The architect's dilemma, then, is the perennial problem of achieving balance throughout the software process; you are always aiming for that balance, though you know you can never achieve it. With AOP, as you shall see shortly, you can do better. Throughout this book, you will see many examples of the architect's dilemma and how (and why) AOP is the best available method of addressing it.

One point needs to be made explicitly clear: AOP is not an antidote for bad or insufficient design. In fact, it is very tough to implement crosscutting concerns in a poorly designed core system. You will still need to create a solid core architecture using traditional design methodologies, such as OOP. What AOP offers is not a completely new design process, but an additional means that allows the architect to address future potential requirements without breaking the core system architecture, and to spend less time on crosscutting concerns during the initial design phase, since they can be woven into the system as they are required without compromising the original design.

1.2 *Evolution of programming methodologies*

From machine-level languages to procedural programming to OOP, software engineering has come a long way; we now deal with the problems at a much higher level than we did a few decades back. We no longer worry about the machine instructions but rather view a system as a symbiosis of the collaborating objects. However, even with the current methodologies there is a significant gap between knowing the system goals and implementing them. The current methodologies make initial design and implementation complex and evolution hard to manage. This is ironic given the world we live in, which demands a faster implementation cycle and where the only constant is change.

In the evolutionary view of programming methodology, procedural programming introduced functional abstraction, OOP introduced object abstraction, and now AOP introduces concern abstraction. Currently, OOP is the methodology of choice for most new software development projects. OOP's strength lies in modeling common behavior. However, as we will see shortly and as you may have already experienced, it does not do as good a job in addressing behaviors that span many, often unrelated, modules. AOP fills this void.

1.3 *Managing system concerns*

A *concern* is a specific requirement or consideration that must be addressed in order to satisfy the overall system goal. A *software system* is the realization of a set of concerns. A banking system, for instance, is a realization of the following concerns: customer and account management, interest computation, interbanking transactions, ATM transactions, persistence of all entities, authorization of access to various services, statement generation, customer care, and so on. In addition to system concerns, a software project needs to address process concerns, such as comprehensibility, maintainability, traceability, and ease of evolution.

As we saw in the examples at the beginning of this chapter, a concern can be classified into one of two categories: core concerns capture the central functionality of a module, and crosscutting concerns capture system-level, peripheral requirements that cross multiple modules. A typical enterprise application may need to address crosscutting concerns, such as authentication, logging, resource pooling, administration, performance, storage management, data persistence, security, multithread safety, transaction integrity, error checking, and policy enforcement, to name just a few. All of these concerns crosscut several subsystems. For example, the logging concern affects every significant module in the system, the authorization concern affects every module with access control requirements, and the storage-management concern affects every stateful business object. Figure 1.1 shows how these concerns often interact in a typical application.

This figure shows how the implementation modules in a system each address both system-level and business concerns. This view portrays a system as a composition of multiple concerns that become tangled together by the current implementation techniques; therefore the independence of concerns cannot be maintained.

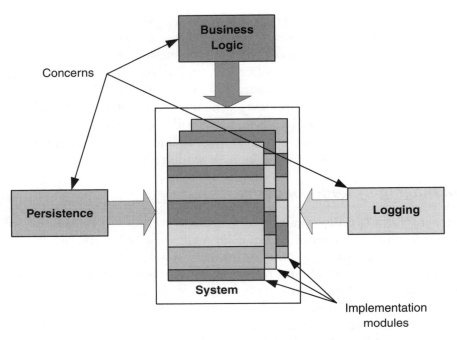

Figure 1.1   Viewing a system as a composition of multiple concerns. Each implementation module addresses some element from each of the concerns the system needs to address.

1.3.1 *Identifying system concerns*

By identifying the core and crosscutting concerns of a system, we can focus on each individual concern separately and reduce the overall complexity of design and implementation. In order to do this, the first step is to decompose the set of requirements by separating them into concerns. Figure 1.2 uses the analogy of a light beam passing through a prism to illustrate the process of decomposing the requirements into a set of concerns. We pass a light beam of requirements through a concern identifier prism and we see each concern separated out. While each requirement initially appears to be a single unit, by applying the concern identification process, we can separate out the individual core and crosscutting concerns that are needed to fulfill the requirement.

Another way of viewing the decomposition of the concerns in a system is to imagine that you are projecting them onto a concern space, which is an N-dimensional space, with each concern forming a dimension in it. Figure 1.3 shows a three-dimensional concern space with the business logic core concern

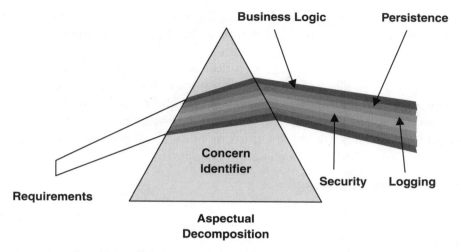

Figure 1.2 Prism/light-beam analogy for concern decomposition. While the requirement initially appears as a single requirement, after passing it through the concern identification mechanism, you can see the constituent concerns separated out.

and the persistence and logging crosscutting concerns as the dimensions. The significance of this kind of system view is it shows us that each concern in this multidimensional space is mutually independent and therefore can evolve without

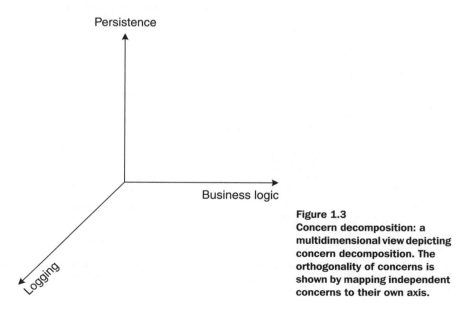

**Figure 1.3
Concern decomposition: a multidimensional view depicting concern decomposition. The orthogonality of concerns is shown by mapping independent concerns to their own axis.**

affecting the rest. For example, changing the persistence requirement from a relational database to an object database should not affect the business logic or security requirements.

Separating and identifying the concerns in a system is an important exercise in the development of a software system, regardless of the methodology used. Once we have done so, we can address each concern independently, making the design task more manageable. The problem arises when we implement the concerns into modules. Ideally, the implementation will preserve the independence of the concerns, but this doesn't always happen.

1.3.2 A one-dimensional solution

Crosscutting concerns, by their nature, span many modules, and current implementation techniques tend to mix them into the individual core modules. To illustrate this, figure 1.4 shows a three-dimensional concern space, whereas the code that implements the concerns is a continuous flow of calls, and in that sense is one-dimensional. Such a mismatch results in an awkward mapping of the concerns to the implementation.

Since the implementation space is one-dimensional, its main focus is usually the implementation of the core concern, and the implementation of the crosscutting concerns is mixed in with it. While we may naturally separate the individual requirements into mutually independent concerns during the design phase, current programming methodologies do not allow us to retain the separation in the implementation phase.

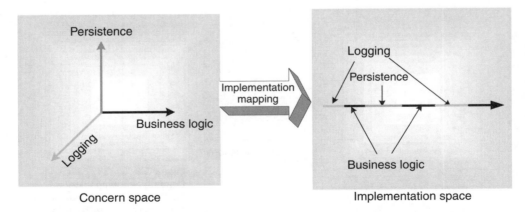

Figure 1.4 **Mapping the N-dimensional concern space using a one-dimensional language. The orthogonality of concerns in the concern space is lost when it is mapped to one-dimensional implementation space.**

1.3.3 *It's all about modularizing*

It's a commonly accepted premise that the best way of dealing with complexity is to simplify it. In software design, the best way of simplifying a complex system is to identify the concerns and then to modularize them. In fact, the OOP methodology was developed as a response to the need to modularize the concerns of a software system. The reality is, though, that although OOP is good at modularizing core concerns, it falls short when it comes to modularizing the crosscutting concerns. The AOP methodology was developed to address that shortfall. In AOP, the crosscutting concerns are modularized by identifying a clear role for each one in the system, implementing each role in its own module, and loosely coupling each module to only a limited number of other modules.

In OOP, the core modules can be loosely coupled through interfaces, but there is no easy way of doing the same for crosscutting concerns. This is because a concern is implemented in two parts: the server-side piece and the client-side piece. (The terms *server* and *client* are used here in the classic OOP sense to mean the objects that are providing a certain set of services and the objects using those services. They should not be confused with the networked client and server.) OOP modularizes the server part quite well in classes and interfaces. However, when the concern is of a crosscutting nature, the client part, consisting of the requests to the server, is spread over all of the clients.

As an example, let's look at a typical implementation of a crosscutting concern in OOP: an authorization module that provides its services through an abstract interface. The use of an interface loosens the coupling between the clients and the implementations of the interface. Clients who use the authorization services through the interface are for the most part oblivious to the exact implementation they are using. Any changes to the implementation they are using will not require any changes to the clients themselves. Likewise, replacing one authorization implementation with another is just a matter of instantiating the right kind of implementation. The result is that one authorization implementation can be switched with another with little or no change to the individual client modules. This configuration, however, still requires that each client have the embedded code to call the API. Such calls will need to be in all the modules requiring authorization and will be mixed in with their core logic.

Figure 1.5 shows how a banking system would implement logging using conventional techniques. Even when using a well-designed logging module that offers an abstract API and hides the details of formatting and streaming the log messages, each client—the accounting module, the ATM module, and the database

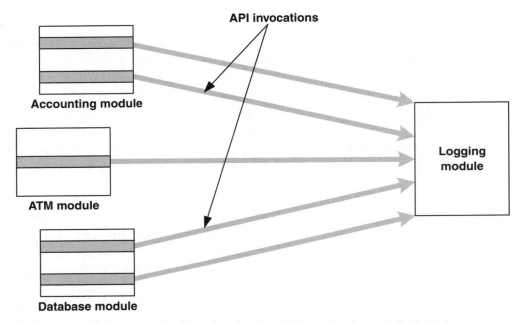

Figure 1.5 **Implementation of a logging concern using conventional techniques: The logging module provides the API for logging. However, the client modules—Accounting, ATM, and Database—each still need to embed the code to invoke the logging API.**

module—still needs the code to invoke the logging API. The overall effect is an undesired tangling between all the modules needing logging and the logging module itself. Each coupling is represented in the figure by a gray arrow.

This is where AOP comes into the picture. Using AOP, none of the core modules will contain calls to logging services—they don't even need to be aware of the presence of logging in the system. Figure 1.6 shows the AOP implementation of the same logging functionality shown in figure 1.5. The logging logic now resides inside the logging module and logging aspect; clients no longer contain any code for logging. The crosscutting logging requirements are now mapped directly to just one module—the logging aspect. With such modularization, any changes to the crosscutting logging requirements affect only the logging aspect, isolating the clients completely. For now, don't worry about the way in which AOP achieves this. That will be explained in section 1.6.

Modularizing crosscutting concerns is so important that there are several techniques to achieve it. For example, the Enterprise JavaBeans (EJB) architecture simplifies creating distributed, server-side applications, and handles the

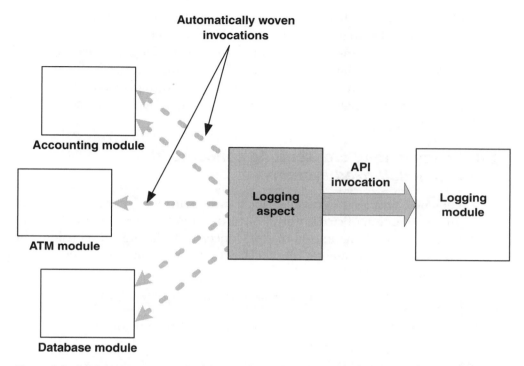

Figure 1.6   Implementation of a logging concern using AOP techniques: The logging aspect defines the interception points needing logging and invokes the logging API upon the execution of those points. The client modules no longer contain any logging-related code.

crosscutting concerns, such as security, administration, performance, and container-managed persistence. Let's look at the crosscutting concern of persistence as it is implemented by EJB. The bean developers focus on the business logic, while the deployment developers focus on the deployment issues, such as mapping the bean data to the database. The bean developers, for the most part, are oblivious to the storage issues. The EJB framework achieves the separation of the persistence concern from the business logic through use of a deployment descriptor—a file in XML format—that specifies how the bean's fields map to database columns. Similarly, the framework separates other crosscutting concerns such as authentication and transaction management by managing their specifications in the deployment descriptor.

Another technique for handling crosscutting concerns is to use dynamic proxies, which provide language support for modularizing the proxy design pattern. Dynamic proxies are complicated and outside the scope of this book; however, this new feature of Java, which has been available since Java Development Kit (JDK) 1.3, offers a reasonable solution to modularize crosscutting concerns, as long as they are simple.

The very existence of frameworks like EJB and language features like dynamic proxies confirms the need for AOP. The advantage of AOP is that it is not limited to a single domain in the way that EJB is limited to distributed server-side computing, and that AOP code is simpler than that of dynamic proxies when they are used alone.

1.4 Implementing crosscutting concerns in nonmodularized systems

Let's now take a more detailed look at the nature of crosscutting concerns. The implementation of crosscutting concerns often becomes complicated by tangling it with the implementation of core concerns. In listing 1.1, consider the following skeleton implementation of a class that encapsulates some business logic in a conventional OOP way.

Listing 1.1 Business logic implementation along with crosscutting concerns

```
public class SomeBusinessClass extends OtherBusinessClass {

    ... Core data members

    ... Log stream                    ❶ Data to support
                                         peripheral concerns
    ... Cache update status

    ... Override methods in the base class

    public void someOperation1(<operation parameters>,
                               <authenticated user>,
                               ...) {
        ... Ensure authorization

        ... Ensure info satisfies contracts

        ... Lock the object to ensure thread-safety

        ... Ensure cache is up-to-date
                                         ❷ Invocation of
        ... Log the start of operation     peripheral
                                           services
        ... Perform the core operation

        ... Log the completion of operation

        ... Unlock the object
```

```
   }

   ... More operations similar to above addressing multiple concerns

   public void save(<persitance storage parameters>) {
      ...
   }

   public void load(<persitance storage parameters>) {
      ...
   }
}
```

❸ Methods to support peripheral services

There are a few observations we can make from this code snippet:

❶ The log stream and cache update status do not seem to be related to the core requirements of this class; they are part of the class only to support the system-level requirements of the logging and caching concerns.

❷ The `someOperation1()` method's implementation seems to be doing a lot more than just the core operation. It is taking care of peripheral concerns: logging, authentication, multithread safety, contract validation, cache management, and so forth.

❸ It is not clear if `save()` and `load()`, which are performing persistence management, should be in the class at all.

A real system would consist of many classes similar to the above. Many would address the same peripheral concerns addressed in this class, such as authorization and logging. Therefore, while we may have had a good understanding of different crosscutting concerns and their separation during the design phase, the implementation paid almost no attention to preserving the separation.

1.4.1 Symptoms of nonmodularization

We can broadly classify the symptoms of nonmodularization into two categories: code tangling and code scattering. If you see these symptoms in your system, it is most likely due to the conventional implementation of crosscutting concerns. Let's take a look at how you can recognize these symptoms.

Code tangling

Code tangling is caused when a module is implemented that handles multiple concerns simultaneously. A developer often considers concerns such as business logic, performance, synchronization, logging, security, and so forth while implementing a module. This leads to the simultaneous presence of elements from

Business logic

Security

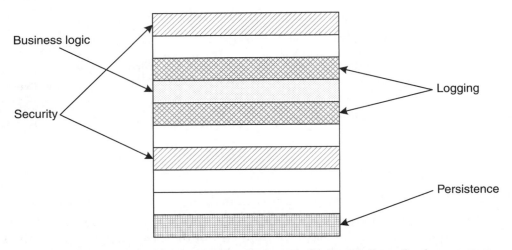

Logging

Persistence

Figure 1.7 **Code tangling caused by multiple simultaneous implementations of various concerns. The figure shows how one module manages a part of multiple concerns.**

each concern's implementation and results in code tangling. Figure 1.7 illustrates code tangling in a module.

In the code snippet for the SomeBusinessClass class in listing 1.1, the method SomeBusinessClass.someOperation1() contains code for authorization, contract enforcement, optimization, and logging, all tangled up with the core operation. Similarly, SomeBusinessClass itself contains operations for persistence management as well as a support structure for logging and cache management, which tangles them with the core state and behavior of the module.

Code scattering

Code scattering is caused when a single issue is implemented in multiple modules. Since crosscutting concerns, by definition, are spread over many modules, related implementations are also scattered over all those modules. For example, in a system using a database, performance concerns may affect all the modules accessing the database.

We can classify the code scattering into two distinct categories: duplicated code blocks and complementary code blocks. The first kind is characterized by repeated code of a nearly identical nature. For example, resource pooling will typically involve adding nearly identical code to multiple modules to fetch a resource from a pool and return the resource back to the pool. Figure 1.8 illustrates the scattered duplicated code blocks.

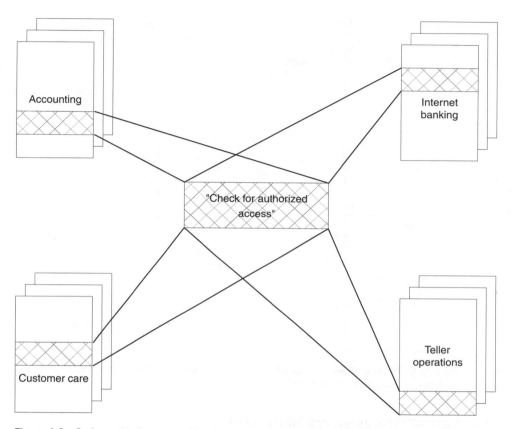

Figure 1.8 Code scattering caused by the need to place nearly identical code blocks in multiple modules to implement a functionality. In this banking system, many modules in the system must embed the code to ensure that only authorized users access the services.

The second kind of code scattering happens when several modules implement complementary parts of the concern. For example, in a conventionally implemented access control system, you will perform authentication in one module, pass the authenticated user to modules that need authorization, and then those modules will perform the required authorization. All these pieces must be carved to fit together perfectly—much like puzzle pieces—to implement the functionality, as shown in figure 1.9.

In figure 1.9, multiple modules include code for authentication logic and access checking; they must work together to correctly implement the authorization. For example, before you can check the credentials of a user (access control), you must have verified that user's authenticity (authentication).

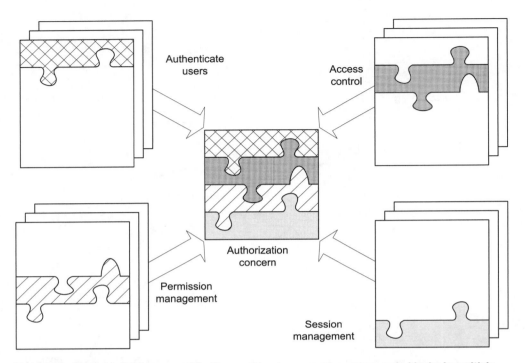

Figure 1.9 Code scattering caused by the need to place complementary code blocks in multiple modules to implement a functionality

1.4.2 *Implications of nonmodularization*

Code tangling and code scattering together impact software design and development in many ways: poor traceability, lower productivity, lower code reuse, poor quality, and harder evolution. While we will discuss each implication separately, they strongly affect one another. For example, poor traceability contributes to lower productivity and poor quality:

- *Poor traceability*—Simultaneous implementation of several concerns obscures the mapping of the concern to its implementation. This causes difficulty in tracing requirements to their implementation, and vice versa. For example, you would have to potentially examine all modules to trace the implementation of an authentication concern.

- *Lower productivity*—Simultaneous implementation of multiple concerns also shifts the focus from the main concern to the peripheral concerns. The lack of focus then leads to lower productivity as developers are sidetracked from their primary objective in order to handle the crosscutting concerns. Further, since different concern implementations may need different skill sets, either several people will have to collaborate on the implementation of a module or the developer implementing the module will need knowledge of each domain. The more concerns you implement together, the lower your probability of focusing on any one thing.

- *Lower code reuse*—If a module is implementing multiple concerns, other systems requiring similar functionality may not be able to readily use the module due to a different set of concerns they might need to implement. Consider a database access module. One project may need one form of authentication to access the database, another project may need a different form, and still another may need no authentication at all. The variation of crosscutting requirements may render an otherwise useful module unusable.

- *Poor quality*—Code tangling makes it more difficult to examine code and spot potential problems, and performing code reviews of such implementations is harder. For example, reviewing the code of a module that implements multiple concerns will require the participation of an expert in each of the concerns. Often not all of them are available at the same time, and the ones who are may not pay sufficient attention to the concerns that are outside their area of expertise.

- *Difficult evolution*—An incomplete perspective and limited resources often result in a design that addresses only current concerns. When future requirements arise, they often require reworking the implementation. Because implementation is not modularized, this may mean modifying many modules. Modifying each subsystem for such changes can lead to inconsistencies. It also requires spending considerable testing effort to ensure that this implementation change does not introduce regression bugs.

All of these problems lead to a search for better approaches to architecture, design, and implementation. Aspect-oriented programming offers one viable solution. In the next section, we introduce you to AOP and give you a little of its history.

1.5 *Introducing AOP*

AOP builds on top of existing methodologies such as OOP and procedural programming, augmenting them with concepts and constructs in order to modularize crosscutting concerns. With AOP, you implement the core concerns using the chosen base methodology. For example, if OOP is the base methodology, you implement core concerns as classes. The aspects in the system encapsulate the crosscutting concerns; they stipulate how the different modules in the system need to be woven together to form the final system.

The most fundamental way that AOP differs from OOP in managing crosscutting concerns is that in AOP, the implementation of each concern is oblivious to the crosscutting behavior being introduced into it. For example, a business logic module is unaware that its operations are being logged or authorized. As a result, the implementation of each individual concern evolves independently.

1.5.1 A bit of history

For years now, many theorists have agreed that the best way to create manageable systems is to identify and separate the system concerns. This general topic is referred to as "separation of concerns" (SOC). In a 1972 paper, David Parnas proposed that the best way to achieve SOC is through modularization—a process of creating modules that hide their decisions from each other. In the ensuing years, researchers have been studying various ways to manage concerns. OOP provided a powerful way to separate core concerns. However, it left something to be desired when it came to crosscutting concerns. Several methodologies—generative programming, meta-programming, reflective programming, compositional filtering, adaptive programming, subject-oriented programming, aspect-oriented programming, and intentional programming—have emerged as possible approaches to modularizing crosscutting concerns. AOP is the most popular among these. To learn more about the other methodologies and their history, see the "Resources" section at the end of this book.

Much of the early work that led to AOP today was done in universities all over the world. Cristina Lopes and Gregor Kiczales of the Palo Alto Research Center (PARC), a subsidiary of Xerox Corporation, were among the early contributors to AOP. Gregor coined the term "AOP" in 1996. He led the team at Xerox that created AspectJ, one of the first practical implementations of AOP, in the late 1990s. Xerox recently transferred the AspectJ project to the open source community at eclipse.org, which will continue to improve and support the project.

AspectJ is an implementation of AOP, just as Java and SmallTalk are implementations of OOP. AspectJ is based on Java, but there are implementations of AOP for other languages, ranging from AspectC for C to Pythius for Python, that apply the same concepts that are in AspectJ to other languages. Further, there are a few Java implementations of AOP other than AspectJ, such as Java Aspect Component (JAC) from AOPSYS. These implementations differ in the ways they express the crosscutting concerns and translate those concerns to form the final system.

1.5.2 *The AOP methodology*

In many ways, developing a system using AOP is similar to developing a system using other methodologies: identify the concerns, implement them, and form the final system by combining them. The AOP research community typically defines these three steps in the following way:

1 *Aspectual decomposition*—In this step, you decompose the requirements to identify crosscutting and core concerns. This step separates core-level concerns from crosscutting, system-level concerns. For example, in the `SomeBusinessClass` example in listing 1.1, we would identify the following concerns: core business logic, logging, cache management, thread safety, contract enforcement, persistence, and authorization. Of these, only the core business logic is the core concern of `SomeBusinessClass`. All other concerns are system wide concerns that will be needed by many other modules and therefore are classified as crosscutting concerns.

2 *Concern implementation*—In this step, you implement each concern *independently*. Using the previous example, developers would implement the business logic unit, logging unit, authorization unit, and so forth. For the core concern of a module, you can utilize procedural or OOP techniques as usual. For example, let's look at authorization. If you are using OOP techniques, you may write an interface for the authorization, a few concrete implementations for it, and perhaps a class to abstract the creation of the authorization implementation used in the system.

     Understand that the term "core" is a relative term. For the authorization module itself, the core concern would be mapping users to credentials and determining if those credentials are sufficient to access an authorized service. However, for the business logic module, the authorization concern would be a peripheral concern and so would not be implemented in the module at this time.

3 *Aspectual recomposition*—In this step, you specify the recomposition rules by creating modularization units, or *aspects*. The actual process of recomposition, also known as weaving or integrating, uses this information to compose the final system. For our example, you would specify, in the language provided by the AOP implementation, that each operation must first ensure that the client has been authorized before it proceeds with the business logic.

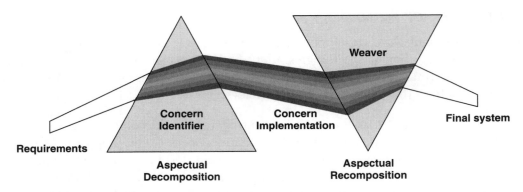

Figure 1.10 AOP development stages. In the first stage, you decompose the system requirements into individual concerns and implement them independently. The weaver takes these implementations and combines them together to form the final system.

Remember the analogy of a light beam passing through a prism that we used in figure 1.2 to illustrate the process of decomposing the requirements into a set of concerns? That illustrated the first step of aspectual decomposition. Figure 1.10 shows the same prism analogy, only now we have added the steps of concern implementation and aspectual recomposition. Notice that the object that is responsible for integrating the concerns after they have been implemented is called the *weaver*. We will talk more about the weaver in section 1.6.

The fundamental change that AOP brings is the preservation of the mutual independence of the individual concerns when they are implemented. The implementation can then be easily mapped back to the corresponding concerns, resulting in a system that is simpler to understand, easier to implement, and more adaptable to change.

1.6 Anatomy of an AOP language

The AOP methodology is just that—a methodology. In order to be of any use in the real world, it must be implemented, or realized. As with any methodology, it can be implemented in various ways. For example, one realization of the OOP methodology specification consists of the Java language and tools such as the compiler. In a similar manner, each realization of AOP involves specifying a language and offering tools to work with that language. Like any other programming methodology, an AOP implementation consists of two parts:

- The language specification describes the language constructs and syntax that will be used to realize both the logic of the core concerns and the weaving of the crosscutting concerns.

- The language implementation verifies the code's adherence to the language specification and translates the code into an executable form. This is commonly accomplished by a compiler or an interpreter.

1.6.1 The AOP language specification

Any realization of AOP must have a language that will be used to implement the individual concerns and a language that will be used to implement the rules for weaving the concern implementations together. Let's take a closer look at these two processes.

Implementation of concerns

As in other methodologies, the concerns of a system are implemented into modules that contain the data and behavior needed to provide their services. For example, a module that implements the core part of the caching concern will maintain a collection of cached objects, manage the validity of the cached object, and ensure bounded memory consumption. To implement both the core and crosscutting concerns, we normally use standard languages such as C, C++, and Java.

Weaving rules specification

Weaving rules specify how to integrate the implemented concerns in order to form the final system. For example, once the core part of the logging concern has been implemented in a module, you need to introduce logging into the system. The weaving rule in this case specifies the log points, the information to be logged, and so forth. The system then uses these rules to correctly invoke the logging calls from the specified operations. The power of AOP comes from the economical way in which the weaving rules can be expressed. For instance, in this logging example, you can specify that all the public operations in the system will be logged in just a few lines of code. This is much more succinct than actually modifying each public operation to add logging code.

Weaving rules can be very general or very specific in the ways they interact with the core modules. For example, in the previous logging example, the weaving rules did not need to mention any specific classes or operation in the system; they were just woven into the entire system. On the other end of the spectrum, a weaving rule may specify that a business rule that is to be applied to several modules may only be applied to specific operations, such as the credit and debit operations in an `Account` class. The specificity of the weaving rules determines the amount of coupling between the aspect and core logic once the weaving rules have been applied.

The language used for specifying weaving rules could be a natural extension of that language or something entirely different. For example, an AOP implementation using Java as the base language might introduce new extensions that blend well with the core Java language, or it could use a separate XML-based language to express weaving rules.

1.6.2 *The AOP language implementation*

The AOP language implementation performs two logical steps: It first combines the individual concerns using the weaving rules, and then it converts the resulting information into executable code. The process that combines the individual concerns according to the weaving rules is called *weaving* and the processor doing this job is called a *weaver*.

Weaving

Weaving is the process of composing the system from individual core modules by following the weaving rules. In essence, the weaving rules determine the final form of the system. The weaving rules are defined in aspects that are separate entities from the individual core modules. This separation makes it possible to change the woven system simply by providing alternative weaving rules in the aspects.

One way to look at the implementation of the weaving specification is to compare it to event-based programming. In event-based programming, the system fires events to notify interested parties of important incidents and the system responds to those events by executing appropriate action. In AOP, the program is woven with logic to "fire" *virtual* events and "respond" to the events with an action that corresponds to the crosscutting concern it is implementing. The result is the effective weaving of those actions into the places that generated the events. Note, however, an important difference: Unlike event-based programming, there is no explicit creation and firing of events and as such you won't see any code related to them. The mere execution of a part of the program constitutes the virtual event generation.

The weaver

The weaver, the actual processor that does the weaving, can be implemented in various ways. A simple way is through source-to-source translation. Here, source

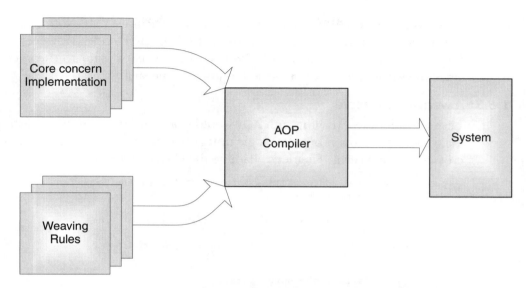

Figure 1.11 **An AOP language implementation that provides a weaver in the form of a compiler. The compiler takes the implementation of the core and crosscutting concerns and weaves them together to form the final system. In a Java-based AOP implementation, the core concern implementation would be Java source files and class files and the system would be a set of class files.**

code modules for individual classes and aspects are preprocessed by the aspect compiler to produce woven source code. The aspect compiler then feeds this converted code to the base language compiler to produce the final executable code. Using this approach, a Java-based AOP implementation converts individual source input files into woven Java source code and then lets the Java compiler convert it into the byte code. Note that regardless of the approach taken, the weaver does not modify the original source code.

Another approach could be that the source code would first be compiled into class files using the base language compiler. The class files would then be fed to the aspect compiler, which would weave the aspects into the class files to produce woven class files. Figure 1.11 shows a schematic of a compiler-based AOP language implementation.

Other implementations would be similar, but with the location and the process of the weaving changed appropriately. For example, if the implementation of AOP is Java-based, a special class loader could be used to perform the weaving operation. Such an implementation will first load the byte code for the aspects, weave them into the classes as they are being loaded, and supply those woven versions of the classes to the underlying virtual machine (VM). Note that you will still need to compile the aspects to create their byte code. However, you no longer have to weave them with the rest of the classes prior to the execution, since the weaving is now performed in just-in-time style.

1.6.3 A weaving example

Let's consider how weaving with AOP would work with the example in listing 1.1. We'll look at the main business logic unit as well as the implementation of a few crosscutting concerns. First let's examine the class containing the core logic:

```
public class SomeBusinessClass extends OtherBusinessClass {
    ... Core data members

    ... Override methods in the base class

    public void someOperation1(<operation parameters>,
                              ...) {

        ... Perform the core operation

    }

    ... More operations similar to above

}
```

Compare this class with the one in listing 1.1: All the data and method members, method parameters, and code to perform crosscutting—the ancillary concerns—have been removed and only the core business logic remains.

Now let's apply a crosscutting concern, using logging as an example. Let's assume that we have the following interface to abstract the logging implementation. The first step is to create an appropriate implementation of this interface so that calls to it can be woven into SomeBusinessClass:

```
public interface Logger {
    public void log(String message);
}
```

Now that we have the logging class, we need to create the weaving rules that tell the system what to do with it. The weaving rules are expressed here in natural language. The programmatic equivalent of these rules go into an aspect:

Logging Aspect:
Rule 1: Create a logger object.
Rule 2: Log the beginning of each public operation.
Rule 3: Log the completion of each public operation.

When the compiler or the VM combines `SomeBusinessClass`, which contains the core logic, with the aspect containing the weaving rules, the result is an implementation that is equivalent to the following:

```
public class SomeBusinessClass extends OtherBusinessClass {
    ... Core data members

    ... Override methods in the base class

    Logger _logger = ...


    public void someOperation1(<operation parameters>,
                      ...) {

       _logger.log("Starting someOperation1");

       ... Perform the core operation

       _logger.log("Completed someOperation1");
    }
    ... More operations similar to above
    ... Each public operation will be similarly
    ... woven in with log statements


}
```

Rule I—creating a logger object

Woven in automatically

Rule 2—logging the beginning of the operation

Woven in automatically

Rule 3—logging the completion of the operation

Woven in automatically

You can now see that the woven code contains the calls to the `log()` method as was prescribed by the weaving rules. Similarly, you can take care of the remaining crosscutting concerns by having an implementation for each of them, and weaving rules to specify the interaction between the individual concerns. Because multiple crosscutting concerns are affecting a module, you will also have to specify the order in which the concerns should be woven. We now have a clear separation of individual concerns and we avoid code tangling. We also no longer have code scattering because the specification of weaving resides only in the aspect that contains the weaving rules.

1.7 Benefits of AOP

Critics of AOP often talk about the difficulty of understanding it. And indeed AOP takes some time, patience, and practice to master. However, the main reason behind the difficulty is simply the newness of the methodology. After all, when was the last time a brand-new programming methodology was accepted without its share of adaptation resistance? AOP demands thinking about the system design and implementation in a new way. The benefits of AOP actually far outweigh the perceived costs. Among these benefits are:

- *Cleaner responsibilities of the individual module*—AOP allows a module to take responsibility only for its core concern; a module is no longer liable for other crosscutting concerns. For example, a module accessing a database is no longer responsible for pooling database connections as well. This results in cleaner assignments of responsibilities, leading to improved traceability.

- *Higher modularization*—AOP provides a mechanism to address each concern separately with minimal coupling. This results in modularized implementation even in the presence of crosscutting concerns. Such implementation results in a system with much less duplicated code. Because the implementation of each concern is separate, it also helps avoid code clutter. Modularized implementation results in an easier-to-understand and easier-to-maintain system.

- *Easier system evolution*—AOP modularizes the individual aspects and makes core modules oblivious to the aspects. Adding a new functionality is now a matter of including a new aspect and requires no change to the core modules. Further, when we add a new core module to the system, the existing aspects crosscut it, helping to create a coherent evolution. The overall effect is a faster response to new requirements.

- *Late binding of design decisions*—Recall the architect's dilemma we discussed previously: the architect is faced with underdesign/overdesign issues. With AOP, the architect can delay making design decisions for future requirements because it is possible to implement those as separate aspects. Architects can now focus on the current core requirements of the system. New requirements of a crosscutting nature can be handled by creating new aspects. Further, AOP works in harmony with one of the most popular trends of Extreme Programming (XP) by supporting the practice of "You aren't gonna need it" (YAGNI). This is a result of the observation that implementing a feature just because you may need it in the future often results in wasted effort because you won't actually need it. Now with AOP, you can practice YAGNI, and if you do need functionality later, you can implement it without system wide modifications.

- *More code reuse*—The key to greater code reuse is a more loosely coupled implementation. Because AOP implements each aspect as a separate module, each module is more loosely coupled than equivalent conventional implementations. In particular, core modules aren't aware of each other—only the weaving rule specification modules are aware of any coupling. By simply changing the weaving specification instead of multiple core modules, you can change the system configuration. For example, a database module can be used with a different logging implementation without change to either of the modules.

- *Improved time-to-market*—Late binding of design decisions allows a much faster design cycle. Cleaner separation of responsibilities allows better matching of the module to the developer's skills, leading to improved productivity. More code reuse leads to reduced development time. Easier evolution allows a quicker response to new requirements. All of these lead to systems that are faster to develop and deploy.

- *Reduced costs of feature implementation*—By avoiding the cost of modifying many modules to implement a crosscutting concern, AOP makes it cheaper to implement the crosscutting feature. By allowing each implementer to focus more on the concern of the module and make the most of his or her expertise, the cost of the core requirement's implementation is also reduced. The end effect is a cheaper overall feature implementation.

1.8 Myths and realities of AOP

Although AOP has grown in popularity in recent years, it is still often perceived as difficult to implement and hard to learn. Let's examine some common assumptions about AOP, and whether or not they are true:

- *The program flow in an AOP-based system is hard to follow*: True. This is actually a step in the right direction! Given the limited number of concerns our brain can deal with simultaneously, we can either worry about the order in which instructions are executed or how the functionality is implemented at a higher level. AOP is not the first time we are giving up the control of a detailed and understandable program flow. In OOP too, polymorphic methods make analyzing program flow a complex task. Even in procedural languages such as C, if you use function pointers, the program flow is not static and requires some effort to be understood.

- *AOP doesn't solve any new problems:* True. AOP is not about providing solutions to yet unsolved problems; it is about solving the problems in a better way, with much less effort and with improved maintainability. You can solve problems with any methodology and language, and the only difference is the complexity of the solution. In fact, there is nothing that cannot be implemented with machine code.

- *AOP promotes sloppy design:* False. An aspect-oriented solution is not the cure for sloppy programs. AOP merely provides new ways to solve problems in areas where procedural and OOP naturally fall short. In fact, AOP requires a good design of core concerns and makes it easy to achieve an overall clean design goal.

- *AOP is nice, but a nice abstract OOP interface is all you need:* False. This issue stems from the problem with the way crosscutting concerns are implemented using OOP. The technique in OOP is to use an abstract API and swap implementations underneath without the need to modify the clients of the API. While a clean OO interface simplifies the subsystems, it still requires you to call that API from all the places that use it. A well-abstracted API absolutely helps—in OOP and AOP—but the interface is no substitute for AOP.

- *The AOP compiler simply patches the core implementation:* False. Patching is a process of fixing the implementation without fixing the underlying problem and results in making the overall system hard to understand. The patching process tends to be unrestricted in terms of the kind of modifications that are permitted. AOP, on the other hand, provides a methodological approach permitting only modifications that improve comprehensibility and traceability.

- *AOP breaks the encapsulation:* True, but only in a systematic and controlled way. In object-oriented programming, a class encapsulates all the behavior. The weaving added by AOP, however, removes this level of control from the class. In this sense, AOP offers considerable power, and it can work wonders if you utilize the power correctly.

- *AOP will replace OOP:* False. Core concerns will continue to be implemented in OOP (or even procedural programming). AOP simply adds a few additional concepts to OOP, just as OOP adds to procedural programming. However, AOP will change the way we use OOP and procedural languages for implementing crosscutting concerns. A few currently used design patterns and idioms that specifically address the problems of crosscutting concerns will lose their importance. Further, crosscutting concerns will receive a lot less attention during the initial design phase.

1.9 Summary

The most fundamental principle in software engineering is that the separation of concerns leads to a system that is simpler to understand and easier to maintain. Various methodologies and frameworks exist to support this principle in some form. For instance, with OOP, by separating interfaces from their implementation, you can modularize the core concerns well. However, for crosscutting concerns, OOP forces the core modules to embed the crosscutting concern's logic. While the crosscutting concerns themselves are independent of each other, the use of OOP leads to an implementation that no longer preserves the independence in implementation.

The current most common response to the difficulties of crosscutting concerns is to develop new domain-specific solutions, such as the EJB specification for enterprise server-side development. While these solutions do modularize certain crosscutting concerns within the specific domain, their usefulness is restricted to that domain. The cost of using these pre-wired solutions is reflected in the time and effort that is required to learn each new technology that, in the end, is useful only within its own limited scope.

Aspect-oriented programming will change this by modularizing crosscutting concerns in a generic and methodical fashion. With AOP, crosscutting concerns are modularized by encapsulating them in a new unit called an aspect. Core concerns no longer embed the crosscutting concern's logic, and all the associated complexity of the crosscutting concerns is isolated into the aspects. AOP marks the beginning of new ways of dealing with a software system by viewing it as a composition of mutually independent concerns. By building on the top of existing programming methodologies, it preserves the investment in knowledge gained over the last few decades. In the short-term future, it is highly likely that we will see AOP-based solutions providing powerful alternatives to domain-specific solutions. For enterprise-level server-side development, for example, you will be creating make-your-own frameworks by incorporating loosely coupled, prewritten, reusable aspects. You can then get exactly the functionality you need in your application—no more, no less.

AOP, being a brand-new methodology, is not the easiest to understand. The learning curve involved is similar to transitioning from procedural to OOP. The payoff, however, is tremendous. Most developers who are exposed to AOP are amazed by its power once they get over the initial learning curve.

In the next three chapters, we will study a specific implementation of AOP for Java—AspectJ. The rest of the book shows specific examples that use AspectJ to solve real problems. If you are not yet convinced of the power of AOP, those examples will most definitely convince you.

Introducing AspectJ

This chapter covers

- AspectJ language overview
- AspectJ "Hello, world!"
- The join point model
- The aspect construct

AspectJ is a general-purpose, aspect-oriented extension to the Java programming language. Given that AspectJ is an extension to Java, every valid Java program is also a valid AspectJ program. An AspectJ compiler produces class files that conform to the Java byte-code specification, allowing any compliant Java virtual machine (VM) to execute those class files. By using Java as the base language, AspectJ passes on all the benefits of Java and makes it easy for Java programmers to understand the AspectJ language.

AspectJ consists of two parts: the language specification and the language implementation. The language specification part defines the language in which you write the code; with AspectJ, you implement the core concerns using the Java programming language, and you use the extensions provided by AspectJ to implement the weaving of crosscutting concerns. The language implementation part provides tools for compiling, debugging, and integrating with popular integrated development environments (IDEs).

In this chapter, we introduce you to the core concepts that will get you started with AspectJ. The next chapter will delve more deeply into the syntax of AspectJ. Together, the two chapters should give you enough information to start writing simple code in order to see the benefits that AspectJ offers. Chapter 4 will introduce more advanced concepts. These three chapters also serve as reference material for part 2 of this book.

2.1 AspectJ: a bird's eye view

In chapter 1, we introduced the AOP concept of weaving the crosscutting concerns into the core logic using weaving rules. Weaving rules specify "what" action to perform "when" certain points in the execution of the program are encountered. In the AspectJ implementation of AOP, the AspectJ compiler uses the modules containing the weaving rules, which address the crosscutting concerns, to add new behavior into the modules that address the core concerns—all without making any modifications to the core modules' source code; the weaving occurs only in the byte code that the compiler produces.

2.1.1 Crosscutting in AspectJ

In AspectJ, the implementation of the weaving rules by the compiler is called crosscutting; the weaving rules *cut across* multiple modules in a systematic way in order to modularize the crosscutting concerns. AspectJ defines two types of crosscutting: *static* crosscutting and *dynamic* crosscutting.

Dynamic crosscutting

Dynamic crosscutting is the weaving of new behavior into the execution of a program. Most of the crosscutting that happens in AspectJ is dynamic. Dynamic crosscutting augments or even replaces the core program execution flow in a way that cuts across modules, thus modifying the system behavior. For example, if you want to specify that a certain action be executed before the execution of certain methods or exception handlers in a set of classes, you can just specify the weaving points and the action to take upon reaching those points in a separate module.

Static crosscutting

Static crosscutting is the weaving of modifications into the static structure—the classes, interfaces, and aspects—of the system. By itself, it does not modify the execution behavior of the system. The most common function of static crosscutting is to support the implementation of dynamic crosscutting. For instance, you may want to add new data and methods to classes and interfaces in order to define class-specific states and behaviors that can be used in dynamic crosscutting actions. Another use of static crosscutting is to declare compile-time warnings and errors across multiple modules.

2.1.2 Crosscutting elements

AspectJ uses extensions to the Java programming language to specify the weaving rules for the dynamic and static crosscutting. The extensions are designed in such a way that a Java programmer should feel at home while using them. The AspectJ extensions use the following constructs to specify the weaving rules programmatically; they are the building blocks that form the modules that express the crosscutting concern's implementation. While we introduce them in this section, each construct will be discussed in depth in the following sections of this and the next chapter.

Join point

A *join point* is an identifiable point in the execution of a program. It could be a call to a method or an assignment to a member of an object. In AspectJ, everything revolves around join points, since they are the places where the crosscutting actions are woven in. Let's look at some join points in this code snippet:

```
public class Account {

    ...
```

```
    void credit(float amount) {
        _balance += amount;
    }
}
```

The join points in the `Account` class include the execution of the `credit()` method and the access to the `_balance` instance member.

Pointcut

A *pointcut* is a program construct that selects join points and collects context at those points. For example, a pointcut can select a join point that is a call to a method, and it could also capture the method's context, such as the target object on which the method was called and the method's arguments.

We can write a pointcut that will capture the execution of the `credit()` method in the `Account` class shown earlier:

```
execution(void Account.credit(float))
```

To understand the difference between a join point and pointcut, think of pointcuts as specifying the weaving rules and join points as situations satisfying those rules.

Advice

Advice is the code to be executed at a join point that has been selected by a pointcut. Advice can execute before, after, or around the join point. Around advice can modify the execution of the code that is at the join point, it can replace it, or it can even bypass it. Using an advice, we can log a message before executing the code at certain join points that are spread across several modules. The body of advice is much like a method body—it encapsulates the logic to be executed upon reaching a join point.

Using the earlier pointcut, we can write advice that will print a message before the execution of the `credit()` method in the `Account` class:

```
before() : execution(void Account.credit(float)) {
    System.out.println("About to perform credit operation");
}
```

Pointcuts and advice together form the dynamic crosscutting rules. While the pointcuts identify the required join points, the advice completes the picture by providing the actions that will occur at the join points.

Introduction

The *introduction* is a static crosscutting instruction that introduces changes to the classes, interfaces, and aspects of the system. It makes static changes to the modules that do not directly affect their behavior. For example, you can add a method or field to a class.

The following introduction declares the `Account` class to implement the `BankingEntity` interface:

```
declare parents: Account implements BankingEntity;
```

Compile-time declaration

The *compile-time declaration* is a static crosscutting instruction that allows you to add compile-time warnings and errors upon detecting certain usage patterns. For example, you can declare that it is an error to call any Abstract Window Toolkit (AWT) code from an EJB.

The following declaration causes the compiler to issue a warning if any part of the system calls the `save()` method in the `Persistence` class. Note the use of the `call()` pointcut to capture a method call:

```
declare warning : call(void Persistence.save(Object))
    : "Consider using Persistence.saveOptimized()";
```

Aspect

The *aspect* is the central unit of AspectJ, in the same way that a class is the central unit in Java. It contains the code that expresses the weaving rules for both dynamic and static crosscutting. Pointcuts, advice, introductions, and declarations are combined in an aspect. In addition to the AspectJ elements, aspects can contain data, methods, and nested class members, just like a normal Java class.

We can merge all the code examples from this section together in an aspect as follows:

```
public aspect ExampleAspect {
    before() : execution(void Account.credit(float)) {
        System.out.println("About to perform credit operation");
    }

    declare parents: Account implements BankingEntity;

    declare warning : call(void Persistence.save(Object))
        : "Consider using Persistence.saveOptimized()";
}
```

Let's take a look at how this all functions together. When you're designing a crosscutting behavior, the first thing you need to do is identify the join points at which you want to augment or modify the behavior, and then you design what that new behavior will be. To implement this design, you first write an aspect that serves as a module to contain the overall implementation. Then, within the aspect, you write pointcuts to capture the desired join points. Finally, you create advice for each pointcut and encode within its body the action that needs to happen upon reaching the join points. For certain kinds of advice, you may use static crosscutting to support the implementation.

For example, consider an e-commerce implementation where you want to write an aspect to log the execution of all public methods. First, you create the aspect that will encapsulate the logging crosscutting concern. You then write a pointcut in the aspect to capture all join points for the public operations in the desired set of classes. Finally, in the aspect, you write an advice to this pointcut and, within its body, you print a logging statement. If you wanted to keep some logging-specific state in the logged classes, such as the number of method executions in each class, you could use a static introduction within the aspect to add an integer data member to all classes being logged. The advice could then update and read this integer field and print it to the logging stream.

So far we have looked at simple code snippets. In the next section we will see the first working example of AspectJ that we can compile and run.

2.2 AspectJ Hello World

Let's begin our journey into the details of AspectJ by writing a simple application. This code introduces a few AspectJ concepts and gives you a feel for the language. Don't worry if you don't understand it all now. We will be discussing all of these concepts in the following sections and the next chapter. Let's start by creating a class, as shown in listing 2.1, which contains two methods that will print messages.

Listing 2.1   MessageCommunicator.java

```java
public class MessageCommunicator {
    public static void deliver(String message) {
        System.out.println(message);
    }

    public static void deliver(String person, String message) {
        System.out.print(person + ", " + message);
    }
}
```

The MessageCommunicator class has two methods: one to deliver a general message and the other to deliver a message to a specified person. Next let's write a simple class to test the functionality of the MessageCommunicator class, as shown in listing 2.2.

Listing 2.2   Test.java

```java
public class Test {
    public static void main(String[] args) {
        MessageCommunicator.deliver("Wanna learn AspectJ?");
        MessageCommunicator.deliver("Harry", "having fun?");
    }
}
```

When we compile the MessageCommunicator and the Test class together and run the Test program, we see the following output. Since every valid Java program is a valid AspectJ program, you can use the AspectJ compiler (ajc) to compile the classes much as you would do with a Java compiler such as javac:

```
> ajc MessageCommunicator.java Test.java
> java Test
Wanna learn AspectJ?
Harry, having fun?
```

Without changing even a single line of code in the MessageCommunicator class, we could enhance its functionality by adding an aspect to the system. Let's add an implementation for the crosscutting concern of manners, as shown in listing 2.3. Before delivering any message, we would like to say "Hello!"

Listing 2.3   MannersAspect.java

```java
public aspect MannersAspect {          ❶  Aspect declaration
    pointcut deliverMessage()
        : call(* MessageCommunicator.deliver(..));      ❷  Pointcut
                                                           declaration

    before() : deliverMessage() {       ❸  Advice
        System.out.print("Hello! ");
    }
}
```

Now let's compile our classes along with the aspect. Note that ajc needs all input files to be provided together so that it can produce class files that have the aspects woven in. Now when we run the program, we see the following output:

```
> ajc MessageCommunicator.java MannersAspect.java Test.java
> java Test
Hello! Wanna learn AspectJ?
Hello! Harry, having fun?
```

Let's understand the magic this new aspect and ajc perform. The Manners-Aspect.java file declares the `MannersAspect` aspect:

❶ The declaration of an aspect is similar to a class declaration.

❷ The aspect defines a pointcut `deliverMessage()` that captures calls to all the methods named `deliver()` in the `MessageCommunicator` class. The * indicates that we don't care about the return type, and the .. inside parentheses after `deliver` specifies that we don't care about the number of arguments or their types either. In our example, the pointcut would capture calls to both of the overloaded versions of `deliver()` in the `MessageCommunicator` class.

❸ Then we define a piece of advice to execute before reaching the `deliverMessage()` pointcut. The `before()` part indicates that the advice should run prior to the execution of the advised join point—in our case, prior to calling any `MessageCommunicator.deliver()` method. In the advice, we simply print a message "Hello!" without a linefeed.

With the aspect now present in the system, each time that `MessageCommunicator.deliver()` is executed, the advice code that prints "Hello!" will execute before the method.

Let's play some more and add another aspect to the system. This time, we will use a language-appropriate salutation. In Hindi, the suffix "ji" is often added to a person's name to show respect—much like appending "san" in Japanese. We will make this modification to the person's name whenever a message is delivered to that person, as shown in listing 2.4.

Listing 2.4 HindiSalutationAspect.java

```
public aspect HindiSalutationAspect {          Pointcut to capture
    pointcut sayToPerson(String person)        the deliver() method  ❶
        : call(* MessageCommunicator.deliver(String, String))
        && args(person, String);

    void around(String person) : sayToPerson(person) {   ❷  Advice to the
        proceed(person + "-ji");  ❸ Advice body               pointcut
    }
}
```

When we compile our classes with both `MannersAspect` and `HindiSalutation-Aspect` and run the `Test` class, we see the following output:

```
> ajc MessageCommunicator.java MannersAspect.java
    HindiSalutationAspect.java Test.java
> java Test
Hello! Wanna learn AspectJ?
Hello! Harry-ji, having fun?
```

Let's take a closer look at the `HindiSalutationAspect` aspect:

❶ The pointcut captures all the join points that are making a call to the `Message-Communicator.deliver()` method that take two arguments. Since our goal is to append "-ji" to a person's name, we will need to capture the `person` argument. The `args()` part does just that; the first parameter to it specifies that the first argument to the method be made available as a variable `person`. The second parameter specifies that the second argument (the message) does not need to be captured, but must be of type String. It does so by specifying type "String" for the second argument, instead of the `person` argument.

❷ To alter the person's name in output (by appending "-ji"), we need to execute the original operation with a changed argument. We cannot achieve this by using the `before()` advice as that would simply execute additional code before the advised operation. We have to modify the advised operation's argument instead. We therefore need the around advice to this join point, since it can execute the original operation with an altered context.

❸ This is the advice body. `proceed()` is an AspectJ keyword that tells the captured join point to execute. We capture the original argument, append "-ji" to it, and then pass it on to `proceed()`. The result is the invocation of the `MessageCommunicator.deliver()` method with the altered argument.

By now, you must be wondering how AspectJ performs its magic. In the next section, we'll take a quick look at how the source files are compiled into the byte code.

2.3 AspectJ: under the hood

Since the byte code produced by the AspectJ compiler must run on any compliant Java VM, it must adhere to the Java byte-code specification. This means any crosscutting element must be mapped to one of the Java constructs. In this section, we outline how the different elements in an AspectJ program are mapped to pure Java byte code. Note that the discussion that follows presents a simplified view of how AspectJ code is transformed into pure Java byte code. Further, the details of the woven code will vary depending on the compiler version and the compiler options.

Here are the typical ways that the AspectJ compiler maps various crosscutting elements to pure Java:

- Aspects are mapped to classes, with each data member and method becoming the members of the class representing the aspect.

- Advice is usually mapped to one or more methods. The calls to these methods are then inserted into the join points matching the pointcut specified within the advice. Advice may also be mapped to code that is directly inserted inside an advised join point.

- Pointcuts are intermediate elements that instruct how advice is woven and usually aren't mapped to any program element, but they may have auxiliary methods to help perform matching at runtime.

- Introductions are mapped by making the required modification, such as adding the introduced fields to the target classes.

- Compile-time warnings and errors have no effect on byte code. They simply cause the compiler to print warnings or abort the compilation when producing an error.

In light of this information, let's see how the `MannersAspect` (listing 2.3) would look if the weaving process produced pure Java code at the source code level. Note that in actuality, the AspectJ compiler produces byte code and not the Java code as shown here. We're showing you this code only to give you an idea of the source code that would be roughly equivalent to the byte code produced. Also, some of the details that are beyond the scope of this discussion have been omitted.

First, let's examine the code in a class that would be equivalent to the aspect itself:

```
public class MannersAspect {
    public static MannersAspect aspectInstance;

    public final void before0$ajc() {
        System.out.print("Hello! ");
    }

    static {
        MannersAspect.aspectInstance = new MannersAspect();
    }
}
```

`MannersAspect` is mapped to a class of the same name. The static block of the aspect ensures that the aspect instance is created as soon as the `MannersAspect` class is loaded into the system—typically during the execution of some code that refers to the aspect. The before advice is mapped to the `before0$ajc()` method whose body is identical to the advice body. The synthesized method name for the advice, such as before0$ajc(), is purely for internal purposes.

Now let's see the equivalent code for the MessageCommunicator class, after it has been aspected by MannersAspect:

```
public class MessageCommunicator {
    public static void deliver(String message) {
        MannersAspect.aspectInstance.before0$ajc();
        System.out.println(message);
    }

    public static void deliver(String person, String message) {
        MannersAspect.aspectInstance.before0$ajc();
        System.out.print(person + ", " + message);
    }
}
```

Recall that the deliverMessage() pointcut in MannersAspect is defined to capture both of the overloaded deliver() methods in MessageCommunicator. To show the effect of advice to the join points captured by deliverMessage(), the identical modification must be made to both methods. Accordingly, we see that the MannersAspect.aspectInstance.before0$ajc() call is made from both methods.

The resulting code looks simple because MannersAspect itself is simple. For complex aspects, the woven code is accordingly complex.

CAUTION Thinking about the language semantics in terms of the transformed code helps in taking the mystery out of AspectJ. It also makes you appreciate the hard work that the AspectJ compiler is performing—and the hard work that you no longer need to perform! However, such thinking has inherent within it the danger of bogging down too much in the details of the transformed code. A better approach is to start thinking in terms of language semantics instead of transformation.

Now that you are familiar with the basic flavor of the AspectJ programming language, let's jump into the details. In the rest of this chapter, we examine the join point model and aspects, followed by a brief description of the AspectJ implementation. In chapter 3, we look at the syntax of AspectJ code as it is used in pointcuts, advice, and introductions.

2.4 *The join point model*

The join point is the most fundamental concept in AspectJ. A join point is any identifiable execution point in a system. A call to a method is a join point, and so is a method's execution. Even an assignment to a variable or a return statement is a join point. In addition, the following are all join points: an object construction, a conditional check, a comparison, an exception handler, and even for, while, and do/while loops. In AspectJ, the join points are the places where we can interject the crosscutting actions; therefore, it is necessary to understand the join point model in order to specify the weaving rules using pointcuts and advice.

Not all of the join points in a system are available for your use. The join points that you can select in pointcuts are called *exposed* join points. In order to prevent implementation-dependent or unstable crosscutting, AspectJ deliberately exposes only a subset of all the possible join points in the system. AspectJ, for example, does not expose for loops because you can easily change a for loop to a while loop that functions in the same manner. If such a change were to be made, all of the advice to the join point for the for loop would no longer be valid since the loop would no longer exist. Some of the join points exposed by AspectJ include method calls and execution, object instantiation, field access, and exception handlers. The exposed join points in the system are the only possible places in the code where we can augment or alter the main program execution.

All join points also have a context associated with them. For example, a call to a join point in a method has the caller object, the target object, and the arguments of the method available as the context. Similarly, the exception handler join point would have the current object and the thrown exception as the context. As we will see in chapter 3, certain pointcuts can capture this context and pass it to advice to be used in the advice body to make decisions based on the context. For example, a pointcut capturing a join point in a debit() method in the Account class may collect the amount to be debited as context so that advice to the join points can check it against the minimum balance requirement.

In figure 2.1, the UML sequence diagram shows a graphical representation of join points in an ATM transaction example, which illustrates some of the places where you could introduce a new or alternative crosscutting behavior.

In the sequence diagram, we see several join points that are encountered when an ATM object invokes a debit() method on an Account object. The first join point is the call to the debit() method itself. During the execution of the debit() method, the join points for the execution of the getBalance() and setBalance() methods are encountered, and so on. Method calls aren't the only join

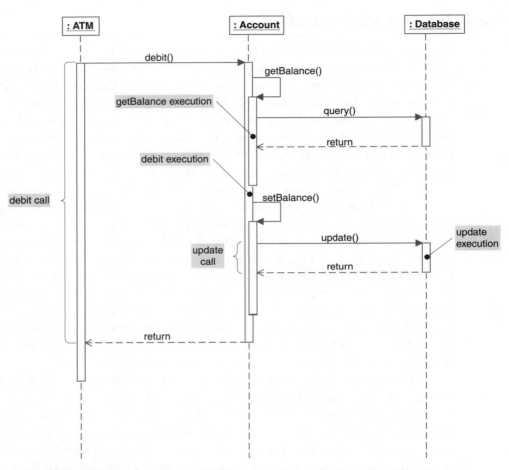

Figure 2.1   Join points in a program execution. Method calls and execution are some of the most commonly used join points. (Not all the join points in the sequence diagram are shown in the figure.)

points in the diagram; an assignment to a member of a class—in this case, the _balance of the Account class—is also a join point. We can write advice to perform an action at each of these join points. For example, the execution of set-Balance() could detect and flag a minimum-balance rule violation.

2.4.1 *Exposed join point categories*

AspectJ exposes several categories of join points. It is very important to have a clear understanding of these categories so that you can capture the join points effectively when you do your crosscutting. In addition, it is important to know the scope of the join points—that is, what code each join point encompasses—so that when you write advice for that join point, it is applied to the proper place. The following list details the categories of the join points exposed by AspectJ and their semantics. In the next chapter, we will show you how to use various pointcut constructs to capture these join points.

Method join points

There are two types of join points that AspectJ exposes for each method: execution and call join points. The execution join point is on the method body itself, whereas the call join points are on other parts of the program, which are usually the methods that are calling this method. Since in well-written software each method performs a well-defined behavior, these join points represent the most useful points at which to weave in crosscutting behavior. Therefore, these join points are perhaps the most commonly used join points.

The method execution join point encompasses the execution of all the code within the body of the method itself. The following code shows an example of the method execution join point for the `debit()` method:

```
public class Account {

    ...

    public void debit(float amount)
        throws InsufficientBalanceException {
        if (_balance < amount) {
            throw new InsufficientBalanceException(
                "Total balance not sufficient");
        } else {
            _balance -= amount;
        }
    }
}
```

debit() method execution join point

In this code snippet, the join point for the execution of the `debit()` method is the whole method body. This means that we can write advice for this join point to be applied before, after, and around the body.

The method call join point occurs at the places where this method is being invoked. The following code shows an example of the method call join point for the `debit()` method:

```
Account account = ...;
account.debit(100);
```

debit() method call join point

In this code, the call join point is the call to the `debit()` method. Note that the code that forms the arguments is not a part of the join point. For example, if the `debit()` method is called in the statement `account.debit(Currency.round(100.2345))`, the call `Currency.round(100.2345)` is not part of the `debit()` method call join point.

For most purposes, the difference between the execution and call join points does not matter. However, at times you need to be careful about which method join point you use. For example, consider a situation in which you need to advise the `debit()` method in the `Account` class from another class. If you want the compiler to weave the `Account` class, you will use an execution join point. Otherwise, if you want the compiler to affect only the caller class, you will use a call join point. Additionally, there are various compiler options that control the weaving scope. These options are discussed in appendix A.

Constructor join points

The exposed join points on a constructor are much like method join points, except they represent the execution and invocation of the creation logic of an object. The execution join point is on the constructor itself, whereas the call join point is at the point where the creation logic is invoked. A typical use of these join points is in advice that affects the construction of objects. For example, you could advise the join points at the creation of certain classes to bypass the actual creation and recycle a previously created object.

The constructor execution join point encompasses the execution of the code within the body of a constructor for an object that is being created. This code shows an example of the constructor execution join point for the `Account` class:

```
public class Account {
    ...

    public Account(int accountNumber) {          Account constructor
        _accountNumber = accountNumber;   ←──┘   execution
    }

    ...
}
```

Similar to the method execution join point, the execution join point for the `Account(int)` constructor encompasses the whole constructor body.

The constructor call join points represent the points in other methods that invoke the creation of an object. The following code shows an example of a constructor call join point for the `Account` object:

```
Account account = new Account(199);
```

In this code, the constructor call join point is the call to the constructor. Just like the method call join point, any code to form the arguments to a constructor, such as method calls to get the arguments, will not be part of the constructor call join point.

The discussion of choosing an execution or a call join point for a method applies to constructor join points equally well.

Field access join points

The join points for field access capture the read and write access to an instance or class member of a class. Note that only access to the *data member* of a class or aspect is exposed in AspectJ. In other words, join points corresponding to access to local variables in a method are not exposed.

The field read access join point captures the read access to an instance or class member of a class. A typical usage of these join points is in advice to ensure that objects are correctly initialized before their use. The following code snippet shows a field read access join point in `Account`:

```
public class Account {

    int _accountNumber;

    ...

    public String toString() {
        return "Account: "
            + _accountNumber        <──┐  Read access
            + ...                           join point
    }

    ...

}
```

In this code snippet, a join point for a field's read access encompasses reading the field as a part of creating the string representation of an object in the `toString()` method.

The field write access join point captures the modification to an instance or class member of a class. These join points are typically used to enforce constraints, such as ensuring the field is within a range of valid values. The following code snippet shows a field write access join point in `Account`:

```
public class Account {

    int _accountNumber;
```

```
public Account(int accountNumber) {
    _accountNumber = accountNumber;        ◁──┐ Write access
}                                              join point

...

}
```

In this code snippet, a join point for a field's write access encompasses an assignment to _accountNumber in the constructor.

Exception handler execution join points

The exception handler execution join points represent the handler block of an exception type. Think of these join points as the catch blocks associated with an exception type. These join points are useful in enforcing certain policies regarding exception handling. This code shows the execution join points:

```
try {
    account.debit(amount);
} catch (InsufficientBalanceException ex) {
    postMessage(ex);                                      Exception
    OverdraftManager.applyOverdraftProtection(account,    handler join
                                              amount);    point
}
```

In this snippet, the exception handler join point encompasses the whole catch block—in this case, the invocation of logging and overdraft protection logic.

Class initialization join points

The class initialization join points represent the loading of a class, including the initialization of the static portion. These join points are used to perform class-level crosscutting, such as the initialization of class (static) variables. This code shows the class initialization join points:

```
public class Account {

    ...

    static {
        try {
            System.loadLibrary("accounting");     Account class
        } catch (UnsatisfiedLinkError error) {    initialization
            ... deal with the error
        }
    }

    ...

}
```

The class initialization join point in this code snippet encompasses a call to the `System.loadLibary()` method and the try/catch block surrounding it. If there were multiple static blocks, the join point will include all of those as well. Note that this join point is present even when you do not have an explicit static block. Such join points still represent the loading of the class and can be used to weave class load-time actions.

Object initialization join points

The object initialization join points capture the initialization of an object starting from the return of a parent class's constructor until the end of the first called constructor. While class initialization join points are encountered when a class loader loads a class, object initialization occurs when an object is created. Typically, these join points are used in advice that needs to perform certain additional object initialization. This code shows the object initialization join points:

```
public class SavingsAccount extends Account {
    ...

    public SavingsAccount(int accountNumber, boolean isOverdraft) {
        super(accountNumber);
        _isOverdraft = isOverdraft;                    ◁┐
    }                                                   │ Object
                                                        │ initialization
    public SavingsAccount(int accountNumber) {          │ join points
        this(accountNumber, false);                    ◁┘
    }

    ...
}
```

In this code snippet, if the first constructor is called, the object initialization join point encompasses the assignment to the `_isOverdraft` instance member and not the `super()`. If the second constructor is invoked, the call to `this()` and the assignment in the first constructor form the join point.

Object pre-initialization join points

The object pre-initialization join point is rarely used. It encompasses the passage from the constructor that was called first to the beginning of its parent constructor. Practically, it encompasses calls made while forming arguments to the `super()` call in the constructor. This code shows the object pre-initialization join points:

```
public class SavingsAccount extends Account {
    ...
```

```
        public SavingsAccount(int accountNumber) {
            super(accountNumber,
                    AccountManager.internalId(accountNumber)
                    );                                              ◁───┐  Object pre-
            _type = AccountConstants.SAVINGS;                           │  initialization
        }                                                              │  join point

        ...

    }
```

In this code snippet, the object pre-initialization encompasses a call to the
`AccountManager.internalId(accountNumber)` method only—and *not* the entire
`super()` call.

Advice execution join points

The advice execution join point is a recent addition to the AspectJ language. It
encompasses the execution of every advice in the system. This join point's usage
is not yet fully established. Such join points may be used to advise an advice for
purposes such as profiling the advice itself. This code shows the advice execution
join point:

```
    public aspect MannersAspect {

        before() : deliverMessage() {
            System.out.print("Hello! ");          ├─┐
        }                                           │
    }                                               │   Advice
                                                    │   execution
    public aspect LoggingAspect {                   │   join point
        after() : loggedOperations() {              │
            ...                                     │
            _logger.log(...);                       ├─┘
            ...
        }

    }
```

In this code snippet, the advice execution join points encompasses the before
and after advice in `MannersAspect` and `LoggingAspect`.

2.4.2 Join point demonstration example

Let's create an example to help solidify our understanding of important join
points by printing out the join points that are encountered as the code is executed. First, we will set up a simple class structure with an `Account` class and its
subclass `SavingsAccount`. This inheritance helps us understand the join points
occurring in the method and constructor invocation between the base and

derived classes. In this example, we need to jump ahead a little and use some simple AspectJ constructs—pointcuts and advice—which we will explain in detail in chapter 3.

The `Account` class in listing 2.5 represents a simplified version of a bank account. It contains methods for performing the debit and credit operations as well as getting and setting the account balance.

Listing 2.5 Account.java

```java
public abstract class Account {
    private float _balance;
    private int _accountNumber;

    public Account(int accountNumber) {
        _accountNumber = accountNumber;
    }

    public void credit(float amount) {
        setBalance(getBalance() + amount);
    }

    public void debit(float amount)
        throws InsufficientBalanceException {
        float balance = getBalance();
        if (balance < amount) {
            throw new InsufficientBalanceException(
                "Total balance not sufficient");
        } else {
            setBalance(balance - amount);
        }
    }

    public float getBalance() {
        return _balance;
    }

    public void setBalance(float balance) {
        _balance = balance;
    }
}
```

The `debit()` method of the `Account` class declares that it may throw `InsufficientBalanceException` when the account balance is not sufficient to perform the operation. Listing 2.6 shows the implementation of this exception.

Listing 2.6   InsufficientBalanceException.java

```java
class InsufficientBalanceException extends Exception {
    public InsufficientBalanceException(String message) {
        super(message);
    }
}
```

The `SavingsAccount` class is a specialization of the `Account` class that represents the savings account. In our example in listing 2.7, it serves to show that the join point for classes is connected with the inheritance relationship.

Listing 2.7   SavingsAccount.java

```java
public class SavingsAccount extends Account {
    public SavingsAccount(int accountNumber) {
        super(accountNumber);
    }
}
```

Listing 2.8 is a simple test program that will cause the execution of the join points.

Listing 2.8   Test.java

```java
public class Test {
    public static void main(String[] args)
        throws InsufficientBalanceException {
        SavingsAccount account = new SavingsAccount(12456);
        account.credit(100);
        account.debit(50);
    }
}
```

Next, let's write a simple tracing aspect, shown in listing 2.9, that prints the information for all join points as the code executes. Since we have not officially discussed the details of the pointcut, we will use only a `within()` pointcut along with a negation operator to capture all the join points occurring outside the aspect itself. (You'll learn more about the `within()` pointcut in the next chapter.) The before and after advice prints the information about the join points captured by the `tracePoints()` pointcut. We also use a special variable—`this-JoinPoint`—that is available in each advice body; `thisJoinPoint` is a special object that contains information about the join point. It will be discussed in depth in chapter 4.

Listing 2.9   JoinPointTraceAspect.java

```
public aspect JoinPointTraceAspect {                              ❶ The
    private int _callDepth = -1;                                    capturing
                                                                    of trace
    pointcut tracePoints() : !within(JoinPointTraceAspect);  ◁───┘ points

    before() : tracePoints() {
        _callDepth++;                                   ❷ Before
        print("Before",  thisJoinPoint);                  advice
    }

    after() : tracePoints() {
        print("After",  thisJoinPoint);                 ❸ After
        _callDepth--;                                     advice
    }

    private void print(String prefix, Object message) {
        for(int i = 0, spaces = _callDepth * 2; i < spaces; i++) {
            System.out.print(" ");
        }
        System.out.println(prefix + ": " + message);
    }
}
```

---

❶ We captured all the join points occurring outside the body of the aspect itself. The `!within(JoinPointTraceAspect)` method captures all the calls, the execution, the set, the get, and so forth outside the `JoinPointTraceAspect`. Such exclusion, a common idiom, is discussed in detail in chapter 8. For now, just know that it prevents infinite recursion.

❷ The before advice runs just before the execution of each advised join point. The call depth is the level in the execution stack of method calls. We use the call depth to get the indentation effect by printing additional spaces corresponding to the call depth before each print statement; this helps us to better understand the output. In the advice body, we increment the call depth to indicate that we are going one level deeper into the call stack. Then we print the `thisJoinPoint` object, which contains the text representation of the captured join point.

❸ The after advice runs just after the execution of each advised join point. For the call depth, we perform the opposite action to the one we did in the before advice, since we are now going one level up in the call stack. Just as in the before advice, we print the `thisJoinPoint` object.

When we compile all the classes and the tracing aspect and run the Test class, we get the following output:

```
> ajc Account.java SavingsAccount.java
  ➡ InsufficientBalanceException.java JoinPointTraceAspect.java
  ➡ Test.java
> java Test
Before: staticinitialization(Test.<clinit>)
After: staticinitialization(Test.<clinit>)
Before: execution(void Test.main(String[]))
  Before: call(SavingsAccount(int))
    Before: staticinitialization(Account.<clinit>)
    After: staticinitialization(Account.<clinit>)
    Before: staticinitialization(SavingsAccount.<clinit>)
    After: staticinitialization(SavingsAccount.<clinit>)
    Before: preinitialization(SavingsAccount(int))
    After: preinitialization(SavingsAccount(int))
    Before: preinitialization(Account(int))
    After: preinitialization(Account(int))
    Before: initialization(Account(int))
      Before: execution(Account(int))
        Before: set(int Account._accountNumber)
        After: set(int Account._accountNumber)
      After: execution(Account(int))
    After: initialization(Account(int))
    Before: initialization(SavingsAccount(int))
      Before: execution(SavingsAccount(int))
      After: execution(SavingsAccount(int))
    After: initialization(SavingsAccount(int))
  After: call(SavingsAccount(int))
  Before: call(void Account.credit(float))
    Before: execution(void Account.credit(float))
      Before: call(float Account.getBalance())
        Before: execution(float Account.getBalance())
          Before: get(float Account._balance)
          After: get(float Account._balance)
        After: execution(float Account.getBalance())
      After: call(float Account.getBalance())
      Before: call(void Account.setBalance(float))
        Before: execution(void Account.setBalance(float))
          Before: set(float Account._balance)
          After: set(float Account._balance)
        After: execution(void Account.setBalance(float))
      After: call(void Account.setBalance(float))
    After: execution(void Account.credit(float))
  After: call(void Account.credit(float))
  Before: call(void Account.debit(float))
    Before: execution(void Account.debit(float))
      Before: call(float Account.getBalance())
        Before: execution(float Account.getBalance())
```

```
        Before: get(float Account._balance)
         After: get(float Account._balance)
       After: execution(float Account.getBalance())
     After: call(float Account.getBalance())
     Before: call(void Account.setBalance(float))
       Before: execution(void Account.setBalance(float))
         Before: set(float Account._balance)
          After: set(float Account._balance)
       After: execution(void Account.setBalance(float))
     After: call(void Account.setBalance(float))
   After: execution(void Account.debit(float))
 After: call(void Account.debit(float))
After: execution(void Test.main(String[]))
```

Here are some keys to interpreting this output, and also to mapping the trace output to the parts of the program flow that caused the execution of these join points:

- The output lines that contain `staticinitialization()` show class-level initialization that occurs when a class gets loaded. The `<clinit>` part of the output indicates the class initialization.

- The output lines that contain `execution()` and `call()` show the execution and call join points of a method or a constructor.

- The output lines that contain `get()` and `set()` show the read and write field access join points.

You can take this code as a base and play with it to gain a better understanding of the join point model.

2.5 *Aspects*

Let's take a closer look at aspects. To recap what we learned in section 2.1.2, aspects are class-like entities that are the basic units for implementing aspect-oriented crosscutting concerns. The AspectJ compiler takes the rules specified in each aspect in the system and uses them to modify the behavior of the core modules in a crosscutting manner.

As you can see here, an aspect declaration looks very much like a class declaration:

```
[access specification] aspect <AspectName>
    [extends class-or-aspect-name]
    [implements interface-list]
    [<association-specifier>(Pointcut)]  {
    ... aspect body
}
```

The keyword `aspect` declares that the element being defined is an aspect. Each aspect has a name to enable the other parts of the program to refer to it and its elements using that name. Aspects may also have an access specification, extend another aspect or a class, and implement interfaces. For now, ignore the optional `[<association-specifier>(Pointcut)]` part; we will discuss it in chapter 4 in section 4.3.

The body of the aspect contains the code that expresses the crosscutting rules. Advice, introductions, and compile-time declarations can only be defined within aspects. Pointcuts, however, may be defined within classes and interfaces as well as in aspects. The pointcuts in an aspect may have access specifiers, and they may also be declared abstract. Advice, introductions, and compile-declarations cannot be declared abstract and cannot have access specifiers.

Since the simplest way to look at aspects is to see them as analogous to classes in Java, let's look at the similarities and differences between aspects and classes. Aspects are similar to classes in the following ways:

- *Aspects can include data members and methods.*

  The data members and methods inside aspects function in the same way they do in classes. For instance, the crosscutting concern could manage its state using the data members, whereas the methods could implement behavior that supports the crosscutting concern's implementation, or they could simply be utility methods. Aspects may also include constructors. However, if a concrete aspect includes a constructor, it must be a no-argument constructor to allow the system to instantiate the aspect.

- *Aspects can have access specifications.*

  The access specifier of an aspect governs its visibility following the same rules as classes and interfaces. Top-level aspects can have only public or packaged (specified by omitting the access specifier) access. Nested aspects, like nested classes, can have public, private, protected, or packaged access specifiers. The following aspect, for example, does not specify the access, which means that it has packaged or "friendly" access; it can be accessed by other objects in the package in which it is declared:

```
aspect OverdraftProtection {
    ...
}
```

- *Aspects can declare themselves to be abstract.*

  With abstract aspects, you can create reusable units of crosscutting by deferring some of the implementation details to the concrete subaspects. An abstract aspect can mark any pointcut or method as abstract, which allows a base aspect to implement the crosscutting logic without needing the exact details that only a system-specific aspect can provide. Note that an abstract aspect by itself does not cause any weaving to occur; you must provide concrete subaspects to do so.

  An aspect that contains any abstract pointcut or method must declare itself as an abstract aspect. In this respect, aspects resemble classes. Any subaspect of an abstract aspect that does not define every abstract pointcut and method in the base aspect, or that adds additional abstract pointcuts or methods, must also declare itself abstract.

  The following example shows an abstract aspect that contains an abstract pointcut and an abstract method:

```
public abstract aspect AbstractLogging {

    public abstract pointcut logPoints();      <— Abstract pointcut

    public abstract Logger getLogger();        <— Abstract method

    before() : logPoints() {    <— Advice to abstract pointcut
        getLogger().log(Level.INFO, "Before: " + thisJoinPoint);   <—
    }                                                                    Use of the
}                                                                        abstract
                                                                         method
```

  In this aspect, the `logPoints()` pointcut is declared abstract in order to let subaspects provide a definition for it. Similarly, the abstract method `getLogger()` defers providing the logger object to subaspects. The advice that logs the message uses both these abstract entities to perform its task. The net effect is that the logging logic is embedded in the advice, while each subaspect will fill in the details of the log points and the log object. In the following discussion, we will see how a concrete aspect provides a definition for abstract pointcuts and methods.

- *Aspects can extend classes and abstract aspects, as well as implement interfaces.*

  As we saw in the previous section, extending an abstract aspect is a very useful mechanism that allows us to reuse prewritten aspects. These abstract aspects implement the bulk of the logic, but they contain abstract pointcuts and methods to defer the implementation of the specific details to the concrete subaspects. Although AspectJ allows an aspect to also extend a class and to implement interfaces, it is uncommon to do so in practice.

In the previous example, we looked at an abstract aspect called `Abstract-Logging`. The following concrete aspect extends the `AbstractLogging` aspect and provides definitions for its abstract pointcut and method that are suitable for a banking system:

```
public aspect BankLogging extends AbstractLogging {

    public pointcut logPoints()            │ Pointcut
        : call(* banking..*(..));           │ definition

    public Logger getLogger() {            │ Method
        return Logger.getLogger("banking"); │ definition
    }
}
```

In this aspect, we have defined the `logPoints()` pointcut to capture all calls to all methods in classes that are part of the `banking` root package. The `getLogger()` method implementation returns the logger that is specific to the banking system. You can have many such subaspects, each providing the required definitions. The result is that the code in the base aspect is shared, while the subaspects can provide the application-specific details.

■ *Aspects can be embedded inside classes and interfaces as nested aspects.*

You embed aspects into classes and interfaces when the aspect's implementation is intimately tied to its enclosing class or interface. Since the aspect resides in the same source file, this simplifies the modifications required for the aspect's implementation when the enclosing entity changes.

Despite their similarities, aspects are not classes. Here are some of the ways that aspects are different from classes:

■ *Aspects cannot be directly instantiated.*

It is the system that instantiates the aspect *objects* appropriately. In other words, you never use "new" to create an object for an aspect. AspectJ doesn't guarantee anything except that the object will be instantiated at or before you use it. Further, it is possible that in some cases, the system won't instantiate an object for an aspect at all!

By default, an aspect is associated with the virtual machine—only one instance will be created for the whole system. However, there are ways to associate aspects with a set of objects and join points, and have multiple instances in the system. We will study aspect association in detail in chapter 4.

- *Aspects cannot inherit from concrete aspects.*

   Although aspects can inherit from abstract aspects, they cannot inherit from concrete aspects. The reason for this limit is to reduce complexity. For example, with this rule in place, the AspectJ compiler considers only the concrete aspects for the purpose of weaving. If subaspects of a concrete aspect were allowed, the language would have to specify how such subaspects interact with the weaving specified by their base aspect. In practice, this restriction usually does not pose any significant problem.

- *Aspects can be marked as privileged.*

   Aspects can have an access specifier of privileged. This gives them access to the private members of the classes they are crosscutting. We will learn more about this in chapter 4.

Now that we have examined the purpose and characteristics of aspects, we are almost ready to turn our attention to the pointcuts and advice that we write within those aspects to implement crosscutting. But before we delve into the details of the code in chapter 3, let's review the logistics of the AspectJ language implementation.

2.6 AspectJ logistics overview

AspectJ offers a complete set of tools ranging from a compiler to integrated development environment (IDE) support. Let's look at each of these tools in more detail.

2.6.1 The AspectJ compiler

The compiler is the central piece of the AspectJ language implementation. It combines the different Java and aspect source files and JARs (containing the byte-code form of classes, interfaces, and aspects) together to produce woven class files or JAR files as output. The input can be in the form of pure Java classes, pure aspects, or a mix. The system that is created by the AspectJ compiler contains only pure Java byte code and therefore can run on any conformant VM. Figure 2.2 shows an overview of the compiler logistics.

   In AspectJ, the weaving process is carried out during the compilation phase. The AspectJ compiler processes the source and byte code for the core concerns and the programmatic expression of the weaving rules in the aspects. It then applies the rules to all the modules and creates output class files or a JAR file. Appendix A provides the compilation logistics in detail.

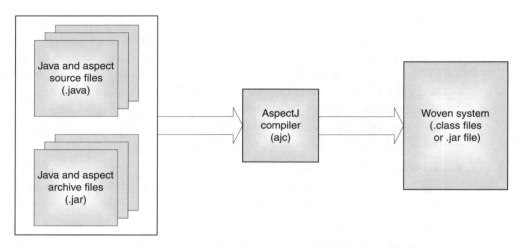

Figure 2.2   The AspectJ compiler takes input in various forms and creates a woven system. The output produced by the compiler complies with the Java byte-code specification and therefore can run on any compliant Java VM.

In the future, AspectJ has plans to support runtime weaving, in which the weaving will take place as the classes are loaded in the virtual machine. Most likely, the implementation of this just-in-time weaving will be a special class loader.

2.6.2 AspectJ browser

AspectJ provides a standalone tool, ajbrowser, which is an aspect-aware source browser that shows how weaving rules affect different parts of program. For instance, it shows how advice applies to various places in an application. Figure 2.3 shows how the relationship between various elements in a program is displayed by ajbrowser. The view offered by ajbrowser is useful in understanding the effect of a crosscutting construct on different modules. It is also useful as a debugging tool, to help you verify that your constructs crosscut the desired parts of the system.

If you are using an IDE with AspectJ integration, you won't need to use ajbrowser very much, since the IDEs offer a superset of its functionality. IDEs not only offer the view of the crosscutting structure, but also all the features you would expect of an IDE, such as integrated debugging and project management.

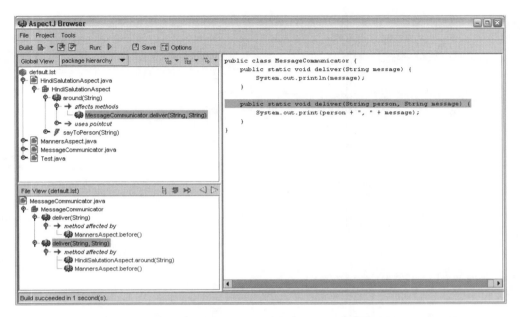

Figure 2.3   A typical session with AspectJ's source browser, ajbrowser. The tool shows how a crosscutting element affects different parts of an application. Similarly, it shows the reverse relationship: how a part of program is affected by crosscutting elements. This tool is useful if you aren't using any IDEs that have integration with AspectJ.

2.6.3   *IDE integration*

IDE support offers an integrated approach to editing, compiling, executing, and debugging tasks. AspectJ eases the development process by providing integration with popular IDEs, including Eclipse, Forte, NetBeans, JBuilder, and Emacs JDEE. The integration with the IDEs is achieved through plug-ins for each IDE. See "Resources" at the end of this book for information on where you can download the plug-in for the IDE of your choice. Using these integrations, you can edit, compile, and debug your project in the same way you would work with a project written only in Java. Figure 2.4 shows how our HelloWorld example would look in the Eclipse IDE.

In figure 2.4, we see that the IDE shows the standard views, along with the crosscutting view of the system. This view is nearly identical to that shown in ajbrowser in figure 2.3. It shows how an advice applies to different parts of the code. This is a useful debugging tool when you have applied advice to a method but you do not see any effect.

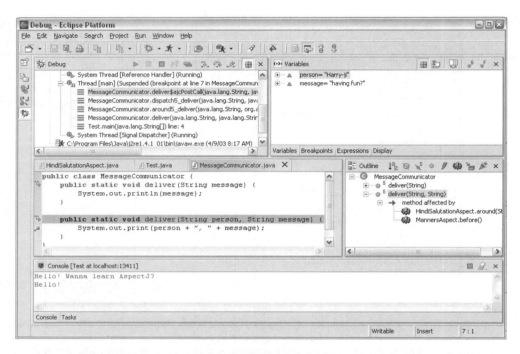

Figure 2.4 Developing applications using Eclipse-AspectJ integration. The overall feel for editing, building, and debugging is like a pure Java project. The IDE also shows how crosscutting elements affect the various parts of the system. The integrations with other IDEs, such as NetBeans and JBuilder, offer essentially the same functionality.

2.7 *Summary*

AspectJ adds a few new concepts to Java, creating a powerful language that includes ease of learning and modularization of crosscutting concerns, all while retaining the benefits of Java, such as platform independency. Simply by learning the concepts, a Java programmer can benefit from the AOP paradigm right away. Aspects allow the separation of crosscutting actions from the core modules. You can then add new functionality without changing any code in the core modules, and without them even being aware of it.

Aspect-oriented programming in AspectJ is simple: choose where you want to crosscut, choose the kind of action you need to perform the task, and programmatically specify both of them. The AspectJ language exposes the necessary join points in a Java program. Pointcuts let you choose the join points you want to affect, and advice allows you to specify the action at those join points. The static crosscutting mechanism enables you to modify the static structure of the system in a way that affects multiple modules. AspectJ complements—and doesn't compete with—Java. By utilizing its power to modularize the crosscutting concerns, Java programmers no longer need to recode multiple modules when implementing or changing a crosscutting concern.

In this chapter, we studied the core AspectJ concepts. The next chapter introduces the basic AspectJ syntax that will enable you to start writing simple programs.

AspectJ: syntax basics

This chapter covers

- Pointcuts and advice
- Static crosscutting
- Simple examples that put it all together

In chapter 2, we presented a high-level view of the AspectJ programming language and introduced the concepts of aspects and join points. In this chapter, we continue with a more detailed discussion of the constructs of pointcuts and advice, their syntax, and their usages. We also examine a few simple programs that will help strengthen your understanding of the AspectJ constructs. Then we discuss static crosscutting. After reading this chapter, you should be able to start writing short programs in AspectJ.

Although the AspectJ syntax may feel somewhat complex in the beginning, once you understand the basic form, it's quite natural for a seasoned Java programmer: An aspect looks like a class, a pointcut looks like a method declaration, and an advice looks like a method implementation. Rest assured that the AspectJ syntax is actually a lot easier than it appears.

3.1 Pointcuts

Pointcuts capture, or identify, join points in the program flow. Once you capture the join points, you can specify weaving rules involving those join points—such as taking a certain action before or after the execution of the join points. In addition to matching join points, certain pointcuts can expose the context at the matched join point; the actions can then use that context to implement crosscutting functionality.

A pointcut designator identifies the pointcut either by name or by an expression. The terms *pointcut* and *pointcut designator* are often used interchangeably. You can declare a pointcut inside an aspect, a class, or an interface. As with data and methods, you can use an access specifier (public, private, and so forth) to restrict access to it.

In AspectJ, pointcuts can be either *anonymous* or *named*. Anonymous pointcuts, like anonymous classes, are defined at the place of their usage, such as a part of advice, or at the time of the definition of another pointcut. Named pointcuts are elements that can be referenced from multiple places, making them reusable.

Named pointcuts use the following syntax:

```
[access specifier] pointcut pointcut-name([args]) : pointcut-definition
```

Notice that the name of the pointcut is at the left of the colon and the pointcut definition is at the right. The pointcut definition is the syntax that identifies the join points where you want to insert some action. You can then specify what that action is in advice, and tie the action to the pointcut there. (We discuss advice in section 3.2.) Pointcuts are also used in static crosscutting to declare compile-time

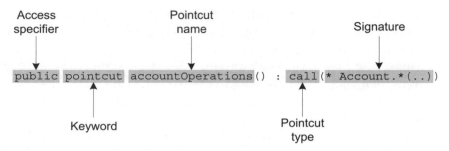

Figure 3.1 Defining a named pointcut. A named pointcut is defined using the `pointcut` keyword and has a name. The part after the colon defines the captured join points using the pointcut type and signature.

errors and warnings (discussed in section 3.3.3) as well as to soften exceptions thrown by captured join points (see section 4.4).

Let's look at an example of a pointcut named `accountOperations()` in figure 3.1 that will capture calls to all the methods in an `Account` class.

You can then use the named pointcut in advice as follows:

```
before() : accountOperations() {
    ... advice body
}
```

An anonymous pointcut, on the other hand, is a pointcut expression that is defined at the point of its usage. Since an anonymous pointcut cannot be referenced from any place other than where it is defined, you cannot reuse such a pointcut. Consequently, in practice, you should avoid using anonymous pointcuts when the pointcut code is complicated. Anonymous pointcuts can be specified as a part of advice, as follows:

```
advice-specification : pointcut-definition
```

For example, the previous example of a named pointcut and advice could all be replaced just by advice that includes an anonymous pointcut, like this:

```
before() : call(* Account.*(..)) {
    ... advice body
}
```

You can also use an anonymous pointcut as part of another pointcut. For example, the following pointcut uses an anonymous `within()` pointcut to limit the join points captured by calls to `accountOperations()` that are made from classes with `banking` as the root package:

```
pointcut internalAccountOperations()
    : accountOperations() && within(banking..*);
```

Anonymous pointcuts may be used in a similar manner as a part of static crosscutting.

Regardless of whether a pointcut is named or anonymous, its functionality is expressed in the pointcut definition, which contains the syntax that identifies the join points. In the following sections, we examine this syntax and learn how pointcuts are constructed.

NOTE   There is a special form of named pointcut that omits the colon and the pointcut definition following it. Such a pointcut does not match any join point in the system. For example, the following pointcut will capture no join point:

```
pointcut threadSafeOperation();
```

We will discuss the use of this form in section 8.5.3.

3.1.1 *Wildcards and pointcut operators*

Given that crosscutting concerns, by definition, span multiple modules and apply to multiple join points in a system, the language must provide an economical way to capture the required join points. AspectJ utilizes a wildcard-based syntax to construct the pointcuts in order to capture join points that share common characteristics.

Three wildcard notations are available in AspectJ:

- `*` denotes any number of characters except the period.

- `..` denotes any number of characters including any number of periods.

- `+` denotes any subclass or subinterface of a given type.

Just like in Java, where unary and binary operators are used to form complex conditional expressions composed of simpler conditional expressions, AspectJ provides a unary negation operator (`!`) and two binary operators (`||` and `&&`) to form complex matching rules by combining simple pointcuts:

- *Unary operator*—AspectJ supports only one unary operation—`!` (the negation)—that allows the matching of all join points *except* those specified by the pointcut. For example, we used `!within(JoinPointTraceAspect)` in the tracing example in listing 2.9 to exclude all the join points occurring inside the `JoinPointTraceAspect`'s body.

- *Binary operators*—AspectJ offers `||` and `&&` to combine pointcuts. Combining two pointcuts with the `||` operator causes the selection of join points that match either of the pointcuts, whereas combining them with the `&&` operator causes the selection of join points matching both the pointcuts.

The precedence between these operators is the same as in plain Java. AspectJ also allows the use of parentheses with the unary and binary operators to override the default operator precedence and make the code more legible.

3.1.2 Signature syntax

In Java, the classes, interfaces, methods, and fields all have signatures. You use these signatures in pointcuts to specify the places where you want to capture join points. For example, in the following pointcut, we are capturing all the calls to the `credit()` method of the `Account` class:

```
pointcut creditOperations() : call(void Account.credit(float));
```

When we specify patterns that will match these signatures in pointcuts, we refer to them as *signature patterns*. At times, a pointcut will specify a join point using one particular signature, but often it identifies join points specified by multiple signatures that are grouped together using matching patterns. In this section, we first examine three kinds of signature patterns in AspectJ—type, method, and field—and we then see how they are used in pointcut definitions in section 3.1.3.

Pointcuts that use the wildcards `*`, `..`, and `+` in order to capture join points that share common characteristics in their signatures are called *property-based pointcuts*. We have already seen an example of a signature that uses `*` and `..` in figure 3.1. Note that these wildcards have different usages in the type, method, and field signatures. We will point out these usages as we discuss the signatures and how they are matched.

Type signature patterns

The term *type* collectively refers to classes, interfaces, and primitive types. In AspectJ, type also refers to aspects. A type signature pattern in a pointcut specifies the join points in a type, or a set of types, at which you want to perform some crosscutting action. For a set of types, it can use wildcards, unary, and binary operators. The `*` wildcard is used in a type signature pattern to specify a part of the class, interface, or package name. The wildcard `..` is used to denote all direct and indirect subpackages. The `+` wildcard is used to denote a subtype (subclass or subinterface).

For example, the following signature matches `JComponent` and all its direct and indirect subclasses, such as `JTable`, `JTree`, `JButton`, and so on:

```
javax.swing.JComponent+
```

The `javax.swing.JComponent` portion matches the class `JComponent` in the `javax.swing` package. The `+` following it specifies that the signature will match all the subclasses of `javax.swing.JComponent` as well.

Let's look at a few examples. Note that when packages are not explicitly specified, the types are matched against the imported packages and the package to which the defining aspect or class belongs. Table 3.1 shows simple examples of matching type signatures.

Table 3.1 Examples of type signatures

Signature Pattern	Matched Types
`Account`	Type of name `Account`.
`*Account`	Types with a name ending with `Account` such as `SavingsAccount` and `CheckingAccount`.
`java.*.Date`	Type `Date` in any of the direct subpackages of the `java` package, such as `java.util.Date` and `java.sql.Date`.
`java..*`	Any type inside the `java` package or all of its direct subpackages, such as `java.awt` and `java.util`, as well as indirect subpackages, such as `java.awt.event` and `java.util.logging`.
`javax..*Model+`	All the types in the `javax` package or its direct and indirect subpackages that have a name ending in `Model` and their subtypes. This signature would match `TableModel`, `TreeModel`, and so forth, and all their subtypes.

In table 3.2, we combine type signatures with unary and binary operators.

Table 3.2 Examples of a combined type signature using unary and binary operators

Signature Pattern	Matched Types
`!Vector`	All types other than `Vector`.
`Vector || Hashtable`	`Vector` or `Hashtable` type.
`javax..*Model ||` `javax.swing.text.Document`	All types in the `javax` package or its direct and indirect subpackages that have a name ending with `Model` or `javax.swing.text.Document`.
`java.util.RandomAccess+` `&& java.util.List+`	All types that implement both the specified interfaces. This signature, for example, will match `java.util.ArrayList` since it implements both the interfaces.

Although certain pointcut definitions use only a type signature pattern by itself to designate all join points in all types that match the pattern, type signature patterns are also used within the method, constructor, and field signature patterns to further refine the selection of join points. In figure 3.1, the pointcut uses the `Account` type signature as a part of the method signature—`* Account.*(..)`. For example, if you want to identify all method call join points in a set of classes, you specify a pointcut that includes a signature pattern matching all of the type signatures of the classes, as well as the method call itself. Let's take a look at how that works.

Method and constructor signature patterns

These kinds of signature patterns allow the pointcuts to identify call and execution join points in methods that match the signature patterns. Method and constructor signatures need to specify the name, the return type (for methods only), the declaring type, the argument types, and modifiers. For example, an `add()` method in a `Collection` interface that takes an `Object` argument and returns a `boolean` would have this signature:

```
public boolean Collection.add(Object)
```

The type signature patterns used in this example are `boolean`, `Collection`, and `Object`. The portion before the return value contains modifiers, such as the access specification (`public`, `private`, and so on), `static`, or `final`. These modifiers are optional, and the matching process will ignore the unspecified modifiers. For instance, unless the `final` modifier is specified, both final and nonfinal methods that match the rest of the signature will be selected. The modifiers can also be used with the negation operator to specify matching with all but the specified modifier. For example, `!final` will match all nonfinal methods.

When a type is used in the method signature for declaring classes, interfaces, return types, arguments, and declared exceptions, you can specify the type signature discussed in tables 3.1 and 3.2 in place of specifying exact types.

Please note that in method signatures, the wildcard `..` is used to denote any type and number of arguments taken by a method. Table 3.3 shows examples of matching method signatures.

Table 3.3   Examples of method signatures

Signature Pattern	Matched Methods
`public void Collection.clear()`	The method `clear()` in the `Collection` class that has `public` access, returns `void`, and takes no arguments.
`public void Account.debit(float) throws InsufficientBalanceException`	The public method `debit()` in the `Account` class that returns `void`, takes a single `float` argument, and declares that it can throw `InsufficientBalanceException`.

Table 3.3 Examples of method signatures *(continued)*

Signature Pattern	Matched Methods
`public void Account.set*(*)`	All public methods in the `Account` class with a name starting with `set` and taking a single argument of any type.
`public void Account.*()`	All public methods in the `Account` class that return `void` and take no arguments.
`public * Account.*()`	All public methods in the `Account` class that take no arguments and return any type.
`public * Account.*(..)`	All public methods in the `Account` class taking any number and type of arguments.
`* Account.*(..)`	All methods in the `Account` class. This will even match methods with `private` access.
`!public * Account.*(..)`	All methods with nonpublic access in the `Account` class. This will match the methods with `private`, default, and `protected` access.
`public static void Test.main(String[] args)`	The `static main()` method of a `Test` class with public access.
`* Account+.*(..)`	All methods in the `Account` class or its subclasses. This will match any new method introduced in `Account`'s subclasses.
`* java.io.Reader.read(..)`	Any `read()` method in the `Reader` class irrespective of type and number of arguments to the method. In this case, it will match `read()`, `read(char[])`, and `read(char[], int, int)`.
`* java.io.Reader.read(char[],..)`	Any `read()` method in the `Reader` class irrespective of type and number of arguments to the method as long as the first argument type is `char[]`. In this case, it will match `read(char[])` and `read(char[], int, int)`, but not `read()`.
`* javax..*.add*Listener(Event-Listener+)`	Any method whose name starts with `add` and ends in `Listener` in the `javax` package or any of the direct and indirect subpackages that take one argument of type `EventListener` or its subtype. For example, it will match `TableModel.addTableModelListener(Table-ModelListener)`.
`* *.*(..) throws Remote-Exception`	Any method that declares it can throw `RemoteException`.

A constructor signature is similar to a method signature, except for two differences. First, because constructors do not have a return value, there is no return value specification required or allowed. Second, because constructors do not have names as regular methods do, new is substituted for the method name in a signature. Let's consider a few examples of constructor signatures in table 3.4.

Table 3.4 Examples of constructor signatures

Signature Pattern	Matched Constructors
`public Account.new()`	A public constructor of the `Account` class taking no arguments.
`public Account.new(int)`	A public constructor of the `Account` class taking a single integer argument.
`public Account.new(..)`	All public constructors of the `Account` class taking any number and type of arguments.
`public Account+.new(..)`	Any public constructor of the `Account` class or its subclasses.
`public *Account.new(..)`	Any public constructor of classes with names ending with `Account`. This will match all the public constructors of the `SavingsAccount` and `CheckingAccount` classes.
`public Account.new(..) throws InvalidAccountNumberException`	Any public constructors of the `Account` class that declare they can throw `InvalidAccountNumberException`.

Field signature patterns

Much like the method signature, the field signature allows you to designate a member field. You can then use the field signatures to capture join points corresponding to read or write access to the specified fields. A field signature must specify the field's type, the declaring type, and the modifiers. Just as in method and constructor signatures, you can use type signature patterns to specify the types. For example, this designates a public integer field x in the Rectangle class:

```
public int java.awt.Rectangle.x
```

Let's dive straight into a few examples in table 3.5.

Table 3.5 Examples of field signatures

Signature Pattern	Matched Fields
`private float Account._balance`	Private field `_balance` of the `Account` class
`* Account.*`	All fields of the `Account` class regardless of an access modifier, type, or name

Table 3.5 Examples of field signatures *(continued)*

Signature Pattern	Matched Fields
`!public static * banking..*.*`	All nonpublic `static` fields of `banking` and its direct and indirect subpackages
`public !final *.*`	Nonfinal public fields of any class

Now that you understand the syntax of the signatures, let's see how to put them together into pointcuts.

3.1.3 Implementing pointcuts

Let's recap: Pointcuts are program constructs that capture a set of exposed join points by matching certain characteristics. Although a pointcut can specify a single join point in a system, the power of pointcuts comes from the economical way they match a set of join points.

There are two ways that pointcut designators match join points in AspectJ. The first way captures join points based on the category to which they belong. Recall from the discussion in section 2.4.1 that join points can be grouped into categories that represent the kind of join points they are, such as method call join points, method execution join points, field get join points, exception handler join points, and so forth. The pointcuts that map directly to these categories or *kinds* of exposed join points are referred as *kinded* pointcuts.

The second way that pointcut designators match join points is when they are used to capture join points based on matching the circumstances under which they occur, such as control flow, lexical scope, and conditional checks. These pointcuts capture join points in any category as long as they match the prescribed condition. Some of the pointcuts of this type also allow the collection of context at the captured join points. Let's take a more in-depth look at each of these types of pointcuts.

Kinded pointcuts

Kinded pointcuts follow a specific syntax to capture each kind of exposed join point in AspectJ. Once you understand the categories of exposed join points, as discussed in section 2.4.1, you will find that understanding kinded pointcuts is simple—all you need is their syntax. Table 3.6 shows the syntax for each of the kinded pointcuts.

When you understand the pointcut syntax in table 3.6 and the signature syntax as described in section 3.1.2, you will be able to write kinded pointcuts that

Table 3.6   Mapping of exposed join points to pointcut designators

Join Point Category	Pointcut Syntax
Method execution	`execution(MethodSignature)`
Method call	`call(MethodSignature)`
Constructor execution	`execution(ConstructorSignature)`
Constructor call	`call(ConstructorSignature)`
Class initialization	`staticinitialization(TypeSignature)`
Field read access	`get(FieldSignature)`
Field write access	`set(FieldSignature)`
Exception handler execution	`handler(TypeSignature)`
Object initialization	`initialization(ConstructorSignature)`
Object pre-initialization	`preinitialization(ConstructorSignature)`
Advice execution	`adviceexecution()`

capture the weaving points in the system. Once you express the pointcuts in this fashion, you can use them as a part of dynamic crosscutting in the advice construct as well as in static crosscutting constructs. For example, to capture all public methods in the `Account` class, you use a `call()` pointcut along with one of the signatures in table 3.3 to encode the pointcut as follows:

```
call(public * Account.*())
```

Similarly, to capture all write accesses to a `private _balance` field of type `float` in the `Account` class, you would use a `set()` pointcut with the signature described in table 3.3 to encode the pointcut as follows:

```
set(private float Account._balance)
```

Let's take a quick look at an example of how a pointcut is used in static crosscutting. In the following snippet, we declare that calling the `Logger.log()` method will result in a compile-time warning. The pointcut `call(void Logger.log(..))` is a kinded pointcut of the method call category type. We will discuss the compile-time error and warning declaration in section 3.3.3:

```
declare warning : call(void Logger.log(..))
    : "Consider Logger.logp() instead";
```

Now that we've examined the kinded pointcuts, let's look at the other type of pointcut—the ones that capture join points based on specified conditions regardless of the kind of join point it is. This type of pointcut offers a powerful way to capture certain complex weaving rules.

Control-flow based pointcuts

These pointcuts capture join points based on the control flow of join points captured by another pointcut. The control flow of a join point defines the flow of the program instructions that occur as a result of the invocation of the join point. Think of control flow as similar to a call stack. For example, the `Account.debit()` method calls `Account.getBalance()` as a part of its execution; the call and the execution of `Account.getBalance()` is said to have occurred in the `Account.debit()` method's control flow, and therefore it has occurred in the control flow of the join point for the method. In a similar manner, it captures other methods, field access, and exception handler join points within the control flow of the method's join point.

A control-flow pointcut always specifies another pointcut as its argument. There are two control-flow pointcuts. The first pointcut is expressed as `cflow(Pointcut)`, and it captures all the join points in the control flow of the specified pointcut, including the join points matching the pointcut itself. The second pointcut is expressed as `cflowbelow(Pointcut)`, and it excludes the join points in the specified pointcut. Table 3.7 shows some examples of the usage of control-flow based pointcuts.

Table 3.7 Examples of control-flow based pointcuts

Pointcut	Description
`cflow(call(* Account.debit(..))`	All the join points in the control flow of any `debit()` method in `Account` that is called, including the call to the `debit()` method itself
`cflowbelow(call(* Account.debit(..))`	All the join points in the control flow of any `debit()` method in `Account` that is called, but excluding the call to the `debit()` method itself
`cflow(transactedOperations())`	All the join points in the control flow of the join points captured by the `transactedOperations()` pointcut
`cflowbelow(execution(Account.new(..))`	All the join points in the control flow of any of the `Account`'s constructor execution, excluding the constructor execution itself
`cflow(staticinitializer(BankingDatabase))`	All the join points in the control flow occurring during the class initialization of the `BankingDatabase` class

The sequence diagram in figure 3.2 shows the graphical representation of the `cflow()` and `cflowbelow()` pointcuts. Here, the area encompassing the captured join points is superimposed on a sequence diagram that shows an

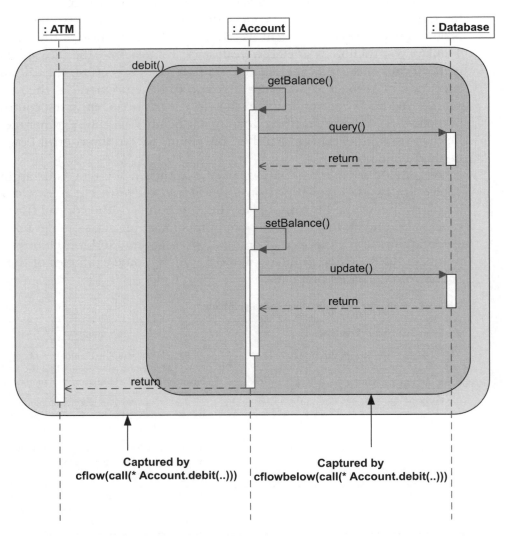

Figure 3.2 Control-flow based pointcuts capture every join point occurring in the control flow of join points matching the specified pointcut. The `cflow()` pointcut includes the matched join point itself, thus encompassing all join points occurring inside the outer box, whereas `cflowbelow()` excludes that join point and thus captures only join points inside the inner box.

`Account.debit()` method that is called by an ATM object. The difference between the matching performed by the `cflow()` and `cflowbelow()` pointcuts is also depicted.

One common usage of `cflowbelow()` is to select nonrecursive calls. For example, `transactedOperations() && !cflowbelow(transactedOperations())` will select the methods that are not already in the context of another method captured by the `transactedOperations()` pointcut.

Lexical-structure based pointcuts

A lexical scope is a segment of source code. It refers to the scope of the code as it was written, as opposed to the scope of the code when it is being executed, which is the dynamic scope. Lexical-structure based pointcuts capture join points occurring inside a lexical scope of specified classes, aspects, and methods. There are two pointcuts in this category: `within()` and `withincode()`. The `within()` pointcuts take the form of `within(TypePattern)` and are used to capture all the join points within the body of the specified classes and aspects, as well as any nested classes. The `withincode()` pointcuts take the form of either `within-code(MethodSignature)` or `withincode(ConstructorSignature)` and are used to capture all the join points inside a lexical structure of a constructor or a method, including any local classes in them. Table 3.8 shows some examples of the usage of lexical-structure based pointcuts.

Table 3.8   Examples of lexical-structure based pointcuts

Pointcut	Natural Language Description
`within(Account)`	Any join point inside the `Account` class's lexical scope
`within(Account+)`	Any join point inside the lexical scope of the `Account` class and its subclasses
`withincode(* Account.debit(..))`	Any join point inside the lexical scope of any `debit()` method of the `Account` class
`withincode(* *Account.get-Balance(..))`	Any join point inside the lexical scope of the `getBalance()` method in classes whose name ends in `Account`

One common usage of the `within()` pointcut is to exclude the join points in the aspect itself. For example, the following pointcut excludes the join points corresponding to the calls to all print methods in the `java.io.PrintStream` class that occur inside the `TraceAspect` itself:

```
call(* java.io.PrintStream.print*(..)) && !within(TraceAspect)
```

Execution object pointcuts

These pointcuts match the join points based on the types of the objects at execution time. The pointcuts capture join points that match either the type `this`, which is the current object, or the `target` object, which is the object on which the method is being called. Accordingly, there are two execution object pointcut designators: `this()` and `target()`. In addition to matching the join points, these pointcuts are used to collect the context at the specified join point.

The `this()` pointcut takes the form `this(Type or ObjectIdentifier)`; it matches all join points that have a `this` object associated with them that is of the specified type or the specified *ObjectIdentifier*'s type. In other words, if you specify *Type*, it will match the join points where the expression `this instanceof <Type>` is true. The form of this pointcut that specifies *ObjectIdentifier* is used to collect the `this` object. If you need to match without collecting context, you will use the form that uses *Type*, but if you need to collect the context, you will use the form that uses *ObjectIdentifier*. We discuss context collection in section 3.2.6.

The `target()` pointcut is similar to the `this()` pointcut, but uses the target of the join point instead of `this`. The `target()` pointcut is normally used with a method call join point, and the target object is the one on which the method is invoked. A `target()` pointcut takes the form `target(Type or ObjectIdentifier)`. Table 3.9 shows some examples of the usage of execution object pointcuts.

Table 3.9 Examples of execution object pointcuts

Pointcut	Natural Language Description
`this(Account)`	All join points where `this` is `instanceof Account`. This will match all join points like methods calls and field assignments where the current execution object is `Account`, or its subclass, for example, `SavingsAccount`.
`target(Account)`	All the join points where the object on which the method called is `instanceof Account`. This will match all join points where the target object is `Account`, or its subclass, for example, `SavingsAccount`.

Note that unlike most other pointcuts that take the *TypePattern* argument, `this()` and `target()` pointcuts take *Type* as their argument. So, you cannot use the `*` or `..` wildcard while specifying a type. You don't need to use the `+` wildcard since subtypes that match are already captured by Java inheritance without `+`; adding `+` will not make any difference.

Because static methods do not have the `this` object associated with them, the `this()` pointcut will not match the execution of such a method. Similarly, because static methods are not invoked on a object, the `target()` pointcut will not match calls to such a method.

There are a few important differences in the way matching is performed between `within()` and `this()`: The former will match when the object in the lexical scope matches the type specified in the pointcut, whereas the latter will match when the current execution object is of a type that is specified in the pointcut or its subclass. The code snippet that follows shows the difference between the two pointcuts. We have a `SavingsAccount` class that extends the `Account` class. The `Account` class also contains a nested class: `Helper`. The join points that will be captured by `within(Account)` and `this(Account)` are annotated.

```
public class Account {

    ...                                              Captured by
                                                     within(Account)
    public void debit(float amount)
        throws InsufficientBalanceException {        Captured by
        ...                                          this(Account)
    }

    private static class Helper {            Captured by
        ...                                  within(Account)
    }
}

public class SavingsAccount extends Account {
             Captured by
    ...      this(Account)

}
```

In this example, `within(Account)` will match all join points inside the definition of the `Account` class, including any nested classes, but no join points inside its subclasses, such as `SavingsAccount`. On the other hand, `this(Account)` will match all join points inside the definition of the `Account` class as well as `SavingsAccount`, but will exclude any join points inside either class's nested classes. You can match all the join points in subclasses of a type while excluding the type itself by using the `this(Type) && !within(Type)` idiom. Another difference between the two pointcuts is their context collection capability: `within()` cannot collect any context, but `this()` can.

Also note that the two pointcuts `call(* Account.*(..))` and `call(* *.*(..)) && this(Account)` won't capture the same join points. The first one will pick up all the instance and static methods defined in the `Account` class and all the parent classes in the inheritance hierarchy, whereas the latter will pick up the same instance methods and any methods in the subclasses of the `Account` class, but none of the static methods.

Argument pointcuts

These pointcuts capture join points based on the argument type of a join point. For method and constructor join points, the arguments are simply the method and constructor arguments. For exception handler join points, the handled exception object is considered an argument, whereas for field write access join points, the new value to be set is considered the argument for the join point. Argument-based pointcuts take the form of `args(`*TypePattern* `or` *ObjectIdentifier*`, ..)`.

Similar to execution object pointcuts, these pointcuts can be used to capture the context, but again more will be said about this in section 3.2.6. Table 3.10 shows some examples of the usage of argument pointcuts.

Table 3.10   Examples of argument pointcuts

Pointcut	Natural Language Description
`args(String,..,` `int)`	All the join points in all methods where the first argument is of type `String` and the last argument is of type `int`.
`args(Remote-` `Exception)`	All the join points with a single argument of type `RemoteException`. It would match a method taking a single `RemoteException` argument, a field write access setting a value of type `RemoteException`, or an exception handler of type `RemoteException`.

Conditional check pointcuts

This pointcut captures join points based on some conditional check at the join point. It takes the form of `if(`*BooleanExpression*`)`. Table 3.11 shows some examples of the usage of conditional check pointcuts.

Table 3.11   Examples of conditional check pointcuts

Pointcut	Natural Language Description
`if(System.currentTimeMillis() >` `triggerTime)`	All the join points occurring after the current time has crossed the `triggerTime` value.
`if(circle.getRadius() < 5)`	All the join points where the `circle`'s radius is smaller than 5. The `circle` object must be a context collected by the other parts of the pointcut. See section 3.2.6 for details about the context-collection mechanism.

We now have completed the overview of all the pointcuts supported in AspectJ. In the next section, we study the dynamic crosscutting concept of advice. Writing an advice entails first specifying a pointcut and then defining the action to be taken at the join points captured by the pointcut. Later, in section 3.3, we discuss using pointcuts for static crosscutting.

3.2 Advice

Advice is the action and decision part of the crosscutting puzzle. It helps you define "what to do." Advice is a method-like construct that provides a way to express crosscutting action at the join points that are captured by a pointcut. The three kinds of advice are as follows:

- *Before advice* executes prior to the join point.
- *After advice* executes following the join point.
- *Around advice* surrounds the join point's execution. This advice is special in that it has the ability to bypass execution, continue the original execution, or cause execution with an altered context.

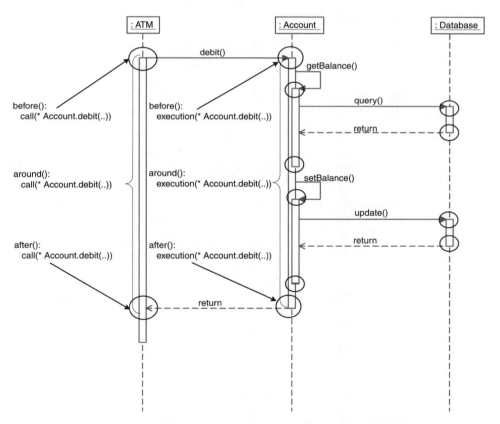

Figure 3.3   Various points in a program flow where you can advise the join point (not all possible points are shown). Each circle represents an opportunity for before or after advice. The passage between the matching circles on each lifeline represents an opportunity for around advice.

Join points exposed by AspectJ are the only points where you apply an advice. Figure 3.3 shows various join points in an execution sequence at which you can introduce a new behavior via advice.

3.2.1 *Anatomy of advice*

Let's look at the general syntactical structure of an advice. We will study the details of each kind of advice—before, after, and around—in subsequent sections. An advice can be broken into three parts: the advice declaration, the point-cut specification, and the advice body. Let's look at two examples of these three parts. Both examples will use the following named pointcut:

```
pointcut connectionOperation(Connection connection)
    : call(* Connection.*(..) throws SQLException)
      && target(connection);
```

This named pointcut consists of two anonymous pointcuts. The method call pointcut captures calls to any method of the `Connection` class that takes any argument and returns any type. The `target()` pointcut captures the `target` object of the method calls. Now let's look at an example of before and around advice using the named pointcut:

```
before(Connection connection):        ❶ Advice declaration
    connectionOperation (connection) {    ❷ Pointcut specification
    System.out.println("Performing operation on " + connection);    ❸
}

Object around(Connection connection) throws SQLException    ❶
    : connectionOperation (connection) {    ❷
    System.out.println("Operation " + thisJoinPoint
                       + " on " + connection
                       + " started at "
                       + System.currentTimeMillis());

    proceed(connection);                            ❸ Advice
                                                      body
    System.out.println("Operation " + thisJoinPoint
                       + " on " + connection
                       + " completed at "
                       + System.currentTimeMillis());
}
```

❶ The part before the colon is the advice declaration, which specifies when the advice executes relative to the captured join point—before, after, or around it. The advice declaration also specifies the context information available to the advice body, such as the execution object and arguments, which the advice body can use to perform its logic in the same way a method would use its parameters. It also specifies any checked exceptions thrown by the advice.

❷ The part after the colon is the pointcut; the advice executes whenever a join point matching the pointcut is encountered. In our case, we use the named pointcut, `connectionOperation()`, in the advice to log join points captured by the pointcut.

❸ Just like a method body, the advice body contains the actions to execute and is within the {}. In the example, the before advice body prints the context collected by the pointcut, whereas the around advice prints the start and completion time of each connection operation. `thisJoinPoint` is a special variable available in each join point. We will study its details in the next chapter, section 4.1. In around advice, the `proceed()` statement is a special syntax to carry out the captured operation that we examine in section 3.2.4.

Let's take a closer look at each type of advice.

3.2.2 *The before advice*

The before advice executes before the execution of the captured join point. In the following code snippet, the advice performs authentication prior to the execution of any method in the `Account` class:

```
before() : call(* Account.*(..)) {
    ... authenticate the user
}
```

If you throw an exception in the before advice, the captured operation won't execute. For example, if the authentication logic in the previous advice throws an exception, the method in `Account` that is being advised won't execute. The before advice is typically used for performing pre-operation tasks, such as policy enforcement, logging, and authentication.

3.2.3 *The after advice*

The after advice executes after the execution of a join point. Since it is often important to distinguish between normal returns from a join point and those that throw an exception, AspectJ offers three variations of after advice: after returning normally, after returning by throwing an exception, and returning either way. The following code snippet shows the basic form for after advice that returns either way:

```
after() : call(* Account.*(..)) {
    ... log the return from operation
}
```

The previous advice will be executed after any call to any method in the Account class, regardless of how it returns—normally or by throwing an exception. Note that an after advice may be used not just with methods but with any other kind of join point. For example, you could advise a constructor invocation, field write-access, exception handler, and so forth.

It is often desirable to apply an advice only after a successful completion of captured join points. AspectJ offers "after returning" advice that is executed after the successful execution of join points. The following code shows the form for after returning advice:

```
after() returning : call(* Account.*(..)) {
    ... log the successful completion
}
```

This advice will be executed after the successful completion of a call to any method in the Account class. If a captured method throws an exception, the advice will not be executed. AspectJ offers a variation of the after returning advice that will capture the return value. It has the following syntax:

```
after() returning(<ReturnType returnObject>)
```

You can use this form of the after returning advice when you want to capture the object that is returned by the advised join point so that you can use its context in the advice. Note that unless you want to capture the context, you don't need to supply the parentheses following returning. See section 3.2.6 for more details on collecting the return object as context.

Similar to after returning advice, AspectJ offers "after throwing" advice, except such advice is executed only when the advised join point throws an exception. This is the form for after advice that returns after throwing an exception:

```
after() throwing : call(* Account.*(..)) {
    ... log the failure
}
```

This advice will be executed after a call to any method in the Account class that throws an exception. If a method returns normally, the advice will not be executed. Similar to the variation in the after returning advice, AspectJ offers a variation of the after throwing advice that will capture the thrown exception object. The advice has the following syntax:

```
after() throwing (<ExceptionType exceptionObject>)
```

You can use this form of the after throwing advice when you want to capture the exception that is thrown by the advised method so that you can use it to make decisions in the advice. See section 3.2.6 for more details on capturing the exception object.

3.2.4 *The around advice*

The around advice surrounds the join point. It has the ability to bypass the execution of the captured join point completely, or to execute the join point with the same or different arguments. It may also execute the captured join points multiple times, each with different arguments. Some typical uses of this advice are to perform additional execution before and after the advised join point, to bypass the original operation and perform some other logic in place of it, or to surround the operation with a try/catch block to perform an exception-handling policy.

If within the around advice you want to execute the operation that is at the join point, you must use a special keyword—proceed()—in the body of the advice. Unless you call proceed(), the captured join point will be bypassed. When using proceed(), you can pass the context collected by the advice, if any, as the arguments to the captured operation or you can pass completely different arguments. The important thing to remember is that you must pass the same number and types of arguments as collected by the advice. Since proceed() causes the execution of the captured operation, it returns the same value returned by the captured operation. For example, while in an advice to a method that returns a float value, invoking proceed() will return the same float value as the captured method. We will study the details of returning a value from an around advice in section 3.2.7.

In the following snippet, the around advice invokes proceed() with a try/catch block to handle exceptions. This snippet also captures the context of the operation's target object and argument. We discuss that part in section 3.2.6:

```
void around(Account account, float amount)
    throws InsufficientBalanceException :
    call(* Account.debit(float) throws InsufficientBalanceException)
    && target(account)
    && args(amount) {
    try {
        proceed(account, amount);
    } catch (InsufficientBalanceException ex) {
        ... overdraft protection logic
    }
}
```

In the previous advice, the advised join point is the call to the Account.debit() method that throws InsufficientBalanceException. We capture the Account object and the amount using the `target()` and `args()` pointcuts. In the body of the advice, we surround the call to `proceed()` with a try/catch block, with the catch block performing overdraft protection logic. The result is that when the advice is executed, it in turn executes the captured method using `proceed()`. If an exception is thrown, the catch block executes the overdraft protection logic using the context that it captured in the `target()` and `args()` pointcuts.

3.2.5 *Comparing advice with methods*

As you can see, the advice declaration part looks much like a method signature. Although it does not have a name, it takes arguments and may declare that it can throw exceptions. The arguments form the context that the advice body can use to perform its logic, just like in a method. The before and after advice cannot return anything, while the around advice does and therefore has a return type. The pointcut specification part uses named or anonymous pointcuts to capture the join points to be advised. The body of advice looks just like a method body except for the special keyword `proceed()` that is available in the around advice.

By now, you might be thinking that advice looks an awful lot like methods. Let's contrast the two here. Like methods, advice:

- Follows access control rules to access members from other types and aspects
- Declares that it can throw checked exceptions
- Can refer to the aspect instance using `this`

Unlike methods, however, advice:

- Does not have a name
- Cannot be called directly (it's the system's job to execute it)
- Does not have an access specifier (this makes sense because you cannot directly call advice anyway)
- Has access to a few special variables besides `this` that carry information about the captured join point: `thisJoinPoint`, `thisJoinPointStaticPart`, and `thisEnclosingJoinpointStaticPart` (we examine these variables in chapter 4)

One way to think of advice is that it overrides the captured join points, and in fact, the exception declaration rules for advice actually do follow the Java specification for overridden methods. Like overridden methods, advice:

- Cannot declare that it may throw a checked exception that is not already declared by the captured join point. For example, when your aspect is implementing persistence, you are not allowed to declare that the advice may throw SQLException unless the method that was captured by the join point already declares that it throws it.

- May omit a few exceptions declared by the captured join points.
- May declare that it can throw more specific exceptions than those declared by the captured join points.

Chapter 4 discusses the issue of dealing with additional checked exceptions in more depth and shows a pattern for addressing the common situations.

3.2.6 *Passing context from a join point to advice*

Advice implementations often require access to data at the join point. For example, to log certain operations, advice needs information about the method and arguments of the operation. This information is called *context*. Pointcuts, therefore, need to expose the context at the point of execution so it can be passed to the advice implementation. AspectJ provides the this(), target(), and args() pointcuts to collect the context. You'll recall that there are two ways to specify each of these pointcuts: by using the type of the objects or by using *ObjectIdentifier*, which simply is the name of the object. When context needs to be passed to the advice, you use the form of the pointcuts that use *ObjectIdentifier*.

In a pointcut, the object identifiers for the collected objects must be specified in the first part of the advice—the part before the colon—in much the same way you would specify method arguments. For example, in figure 3.4, the anonymous pointcut in the before advice collects all the arguments to the method executions associated with it.

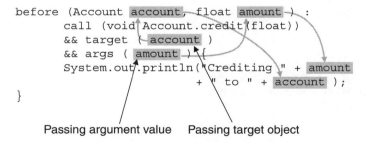

Passing argument value   Passing target object

Figure 3.4   Passing an executing object and an argument context from the join point to the advice body. The target object in this case is captured using the `target()` pointcut, whereas the argument value is captured using the `args()` pointcut. The current execution object can be captured in the same way using `this()` instead of `target()`.

Figure 3.4 shows the context being passed between an anonymous pointcut and the advice. The `target()` pointcut collects the objects on which the `credit()` method is being invoked, whereas the `args()` pointcut captures the argument to the method. The part of the advice before the colon specifies the type and name for each of the captured arguments. The body of the advice uses the collected context in the same way that the body of a method would use the parameters passed to it. The object identifiers in the previous code snippet are `account` and `amount`.

When you use named pointcuts, those pointcuts themselves must collect the context and pass it to the advice. Figure 3.5 shows the collection of the same information as in figure 3.4, but uses named pointcuts to capture the context and make it available to the advice.

The code in figure 3.5 is functionally identical to that in 3.4, but unlike figure 3.4, we use a named pointcut. The pointcut `creditOperation()`, besides matching join points, collects the context so that the advice can use it. We collect the target object and the argument to the `credit()` operation. Note that the pointcut itself declares the type and name of each collected element, much like a method call. In the advice to this pointcut, the first part before the colon is unchanged from figure 3.4. The pointcut definition simply uses the earlier defined pointcut. Note how the names of the arguments in the first part of the advice match those in the pointcut definition.

Let's look at some more examples of passing context. In figure 3.6, an after returning advice captures the return value of a method.

```
pointcut creditOperation(Account account, float amount ) :
    call (void Account.credit(float))
        && target ( account )
        && args ( amount );


before (Account account, float amount ) :
    creditOperation(account, amount ) {
        System.out.println("Crediting " + amount
                            + " to " + account );
}
```

Figure 3.5 Passing an executing object and an argument captured by a named pointcut. This code snippet is functionally equivalent to figure 3.4, but achieves it using a named pointcut. For the advice to access the join point's context, the pointcut itself must collect the context, as opposed to the advice collecting the context when using anonymous pointcuts.

```
after() returning(Connection  conn ) :
     call(Connection DriverManager.getConnection(..)) {
     System.out.println("Obtained database connection: "
                         +  conn );
}
```

Passing return object

Figure 3.6 Passing a return object context to an advice body. The return object is captured in `returning()` by specifying the type and object ID.

```
after() throwing (RemoteException  ex )
     : call(* *.*(..) throws RemoteException) {
     System.out.println("Exception " +  ex
     + " while executing "
     +  thisJoinPoint );
}
```

Accessing special variable   Passing exception object

Figure 3.7 Passing a thrown exception to an advice body. The exception object is captured in `throwing()` by specifying the type and object ID. The special variables such as `thisJoinPoint` are accessed in a similar manner to `this` inside an instance method.

In figure 3.6, we capture the return value of `DriverManager.getConnection()` by specifying the type and the name of the return object in the `returning()` part of the advice specification. We can use the return object in the advice body just like any other collected context. In this example, the advice simply prints the return value.

In figure 3.7, we capture the exception object thrown by any method that declares that it can throw `RemoteException` by specifying the type and name of the exception to the `throwing()` part of the advice specification. Much like the return value and any other context, we can use this exception object in the advice body.

Note that `thisJoinPoint` is a special type of variable that carries join point context information. We will look at these types of variables in detail in chapter 4.

3.2.7 *Returning a value from around advice*

Each around advice must declare a return value (which could be `void`). It is typical to declare the return type to match the return type of the join points that are being advised. For example, if a set of methods that are each returning an integer were advised, you would declare the advice to return an integer. For a field-read join point, you would match the advice's return type to the accessed field's type.

Invoking `proceed()` returns the value returned by the join point. Unless you need to manipulate the returned value, around advice will simply return the value that was returned by the `proceed()` statement within it. If you do not invoke `proceed()`, you will still have to return a value appropriate for the advice's logic.

There are cases when an around advice applies to join points with different return types. For example, if you advise all the methods needing transaction support, the return values of all those methods are likely to be different. To resolve such situations, the around advice may declare its return value as `Object`. In those cases, if around returns a primitive type after it calls `proceed()`, the primitive type is wrapped in its corresponding wrapper type and performs the opposite, unwrapping after returning from the advice. For instance, if a join point returns an integer and the advice declares that it will return `Object`, the integer value will be wrapped in an `Integer` object and it will be returned from the advice. When such a value is assigned, the object is first unwrapped to an integer. Similarly, if a join point returns a non-primitive type, appropriate typecasts are performed before the return value is assigned. The scheme of returning the `Object` type works even when a captured join point returns a `void` type.

3.2.8 *An example using around advice: failure handling*

Let's look at an example that uses around advice to handle system failures. In a distributed environment, dealing with a network failure is often an important task. If the network is down, clients often reattempt operations. In the following example, we examine how an aspect with around advice can implement the functionality to handle a network failure.

In listing 3.1, we simulate the network and other failures by simply making the method throw an exception randomly.

Listing 3.1   RemoteService.java

```java
import java.rmi.RemoteException;

public class RemoteService {
    public static int getReply() throws RemoteException {
        if(Math.random() > 0.25) {
            throw new RemoteException("Simulated failure occurred");
        }
        System.out.println("Replying");
        return 5;
    }
}
```

The `getReply()` method simulates the service offered. By checking against a randomly generated number, it simulates a failure resulting in an exception (statistically, the method will fail approximately 75 percent of the time—a really high failure rate!). When it does not fail, it prints a message and returns 5.

Next let's write a simple client (listing 3.2) that invokes the only method in `RemoteService`.

Listing 3.2   RemoteClient.java

```java
public class RemoteClient {
    public static void main(String[] args) throws Exception {
        int retVal = RemoteService.getReply();
        System.out.println("Reply is " + retVal);
    }
}
```

Now let's write an aspect to handle failures by reattempting the operation three times before giving up and propagating the failure to the caller (listing 3.3).

Listing 3.3   FailureHandlingAspect.java

```java
import java.rmi.RemoteException;

public aspect FailureHandlingAspect {
    final int MAX_RETRIES = 3;

    Object around() throws RemoteException        ❶  Method part
        : call(* RemoteService.get*(..) throws RemoteException) {   of advice
        int retry = 0;
        while(true){                                              Pointcut  ❷
            try{                                                  (anonymous)
                return proceed();                                 part of advice
            } catch(RemoteException ex){
                System.out.println("Encountered " + ex);   ❸  Execution of
                if (++retry > MAX_RETRIES) {                     captured
                    throw ex;                                    join point
                }
                System.out.println("\tRetrying...");
            }
        }
    }
}
```

❶ We declare that the around advice will return `Object` to accommodate the potential different return value types in the captured join points. We also declare that it may throw `RemoteException` to allow the propagating of any exception thrown by the execution of captured join points.

❷ The pointcut part of the advice uses an anonymous pointcut to capture all the getter methods in `RemoteService` that throw `RemoteException`.

❸ We simply return the value returned by the invocation of `proceed()`. Although the join point is returning an integer, AspectJ will take care of wrapping and unwrapping the logic.

When we compile and run the program, we get output similar to the following:

```
> ajc RemoteService.java RemoteClient.java FailureHandlingAspect.java
> java RemoteClient
Encountered java.rmi.RemoteException: Simulated failure occurred
        Retrying...
Encountered java.rmi.RemoteException: Simulated failure occurred
        Retrying...
Replying
Reply is 5
```

The output shows a few failures, retries, and eventual success. (Your output may be a little different due to the randomness introduced.) It also shows the correct assignment to the `retVal` member in the `RemoteClient` class, even though the advice returned the `Object` type.

3.2.9 *Context collection example: caching*

The goal of this example is to understand how to collect context in arguments, execution objects, and return values. First, we write a method for a simple factorial computation, and then we write an aspect to cache the computed value for later use. We want to insert a result into the cache for values passed on to only nonrecursive calls (to limit the amount of caching). Before any calls to the `factorial()` method, including the recursive ones, we check the cache and print the value if a precomputed value is found. Otherwise, we proceed with the normal computation flow. Let's start with creating the factorial computation in listing 3.4.

> **Listing 3.4 TestFactorial.java: factorial computation**

```
import java.util.*;

public class TestFactorial {
    public static void main(String[] args) {
        System.out.println("Result: " + factorial(5) + "\n");
        System.out.println("Result: " + factorial(10) + "\n");
        System.out.println("Result: " + factorial(15) + "\n");
```

```
        System.out.println("Result: " + factorial(15) + "\n");
    }

    public static long factorial(int n) {
        if (n == 0) {
            return 1;
        } else {
            return n * factorial(n-1);
        }
    }
}
```

Now let's write the aspect to optimize the factorial computation by caching the computed value for later use, as shown in listing 3.5.

Listing 3.5   OptimizeFactorialAspect.java: aspect for caching results

```
import java.util.*;

public aspect OptimizeFactorialAspect {
    pointcut factorialOperation(int n) :           ❶ Capturing context
        call(long *.factorial(int)) && args(n);       using args()

    pointcut topLevelFactorialOperation(int n) :   ❷ Capturing context
        factorialOperation(n)                         from another
        && !cflowbelow(factorialOperation(int));      pointcut

    private Map _factorialCache = new HashMap();   ❸ Using pointcut's
                                                      context
    before(int n) : topLevelFactorialOperation(n) {  ◁─┐
        System.out.println("Seeking factorial for " + n);
    }
                                                   ❹ Returning primitive
                                                      from around advice
    long around(int n) : factorialOperation(n) {   ◁─┘
        Object cachedValue = _factorialCache.get(new Integer(n));
        if (cachedValue != null) {
            System.out.println("Found cached value for " + n
                                + ": " + cachedValue);
            return ((Long)cachedValue).longValue();
        }
        return proceed(n);   ❺ Passing along context
    }                           to proceed()

    after(int n) returning(long result)   ❻ Capturing
        : topLevelFactorialOperation(n) {     return value
        _factorialCache.put(new Integer(n), new Long(result));
    }
}
```

❶ The `factorialOperation()` pointcut captures all calls to the `factorial()` method. It also collects the argument to the method.

❷ The `topLevelFactorialOperation()` pointcut captures all nonrecursive calls to the `factorial()` method. It captures the context available in any `factorialOperation()` pointcut it uses. See figure 3.5 for a graphical representation of capturing context using named pointcuts.

❸ The before advice logs the nonrecursive `factorial()` method invocation. In the log message, it uses the collected context.

❹ The around advice to any `factorial()` method invocation also uses the context. It declares that it will return a `long` matching the return type of the advised join point.

❺ The around advice passes the captured context to `proceed()`. Recall that the number and type of arguments to `proceed()` must match the advice itself.

❻ The after returning advice collects the return value by specifying its type and identifier in the `returning()` part. It then uses the return value as well as the context collected from the join point to update the cache.

When we compile and run the code, we get the following output:

```
> ajc TestFactorial.java OptimizeFactorialAspect.java
> java TestFactorial
Seeking factorial for 5
Result: 120

Seeking factorial for 10
Found cached value for 5: 120
Result: 3628800

Seeking factorial for 15
Found cached value for 10: 3628800
Result: 1307674368000

Seeking factorial for 15
Found cached value for 15: 1307674368000
Result: 1307674368000
```

As soon as a cached value is found, the factorial computation uses that value instead of continuing with the recursive computation. For example, while computing a factorial for 15, the computation uses a pre-cached factorial value for 10.

NOTE It seems that you could simply modify the `Test.factorial()` method to insert code for caching optimization, especially since only one method needs to be modified. However, such an implementation will tangle the optimization logic with factorial computation logic. With conventional refactoring techniques, you can limit the inserted code to a few lines. Using an aspect, you refactor the caching completely out of the core factorial computation code. You can now modify the caching strategy without even touching the `factorial()` method.

3.3 *Static crosscutting*

In AOP, we often find that in addition to affecting dynamic behavior using advice, it is necessary for aspects to affect the static structure in a crosscutting manner. While dynamic crosscutting modifies the execution behavior of the program, static crosscutting modifies the static structure of the types—the classes, interfaces, and other aspects—and their compile-time behavior. There are four broad classifications of static crosscutting: member introduction, type-hierarchy modification, compile-time error and warning declaration, and exception softening. In this section, we study the first three kinds. Understanding exception softening requires additional design considerations for effective use, and we will visit that along with other similar topics in chapter 4.

3.3.1 *Member introduction*

Aspects often need to introduce data members and methods into the aspected classes. For example, in a banking system, implementing a minimum balance rule may require additional data members corresponding to a minimum balance and a method for computing the available balance. AspectJ provides a mechanism called *introduction* to introduce such members into the specified classes and interfaces in a crosscutting manner.

The code snippet in listing 3.6 introduces the `_minimumBalance` field and the `getAvailableBalance()` method to the `Account` class. The after advice sets the minimum balance in `SavingsAccount` to 25.

Listing 3.6 MinimumBalanceRuleAspect.java

```
public aspect MinimumBalanceRuleAspect {                    Introducing a data
    private float Account._minimumBalance;          ⊲─┘     member

    public float Account.getAvailableBalance() {
        return getBalance() - _minimumBalance;             Introducing a
    }                                                      method

    after(Account account) :
        execution(SavingsAccount.new(..)) && this(account) {
        account._minimumBalance = 25;        ⊲─┐  Using the introduced
    }                                           data member
```

```
before(Account account, float amount)
    throws InsufficientBalanceException :
    execution(* Account.debit())
    && this(account)  && args(amount) {
    if (account.getAvailableBalance() < amount) {     ◁──┐ Using the introduced
        throw new InsufficientBalanceException(            │ method
            "Insufficient available balance");
    }
  }
}
```

In the aspect in listing 3.6, we introduce a member `_minimumBalance` of type `float` into the `Account` class. Note that introduced members can be marked with an access specifier, as we have marked `_minimumBalance` with private access. The access rules are interpreted with respect to the aspect doing the introduction. For example, the members marked `private` are accessible only from the introducing aspect.

You can also introduce data members and methods with implementation into *interfaces*; this will provide a default behavior to the implementing classes. As long as the introduced behavior suffices for your implementation needs, this prevents the duplication of code in each class, since the introduction of the data members and methods effectively adds the behavior to each implementing class. In chapter 8, we will look more closely at doing this.

3.3.2 *Modifying the class hierarchy*

A crosscutting implementation often needs to affect a set of classes or interfaces that share a common base type so that certain advice and aspects will work only through the API offered by the base type. The advice and aspects will then be dependent only on the base type instead of application-specific classes and interfaces. For example, a cache-management aspect may declare certain classes to implement the `Cacheable` interface. The advice in the aspect then can work only through the `Cacheable` interface. The result of such an arrangement is the decoupling of the aspect from the application-specific class, thus making the aspect more reusable. With AspectJ, you can modify the inheritance hierarchy of existing classes to declare a superclass and interfaces of an existing class or interface as long as it does not violate Java inheritance rules. The forms for such a declaration are:

```
declare parents : [ChildTypePattern] implements [InterfaceList];
```

and

```
declare parents : [ChildTypePattern] extends [Class or InterfaceList];
```

For example, the following aspect declares that all classes and interfaces in the `entities` package that have the `banking` package as the root are to implement the `Identifiable` interface:

```
aspect AccountTrackingAspect {
    declare parents : banking..entities.* implements Identifiable;

    ... tracking advices
}
```

The declaration of parents must follow the regular Java object hierarchy rules. For example, you cannot declare a class to be the parent of an interface. Similarly, you cannot declare parents in such a way that it will result in multiple inheritance.

3.3.3 *Introducing compile-time errors and warning*

AspectJ provides a static crosscutting mechanism to declare compile-time errors and warnings based on certain usage patterns. With this mechanism, you can implement behavior similar to the #error and #warning preprocessor directives supported by some C/C++ preprocessors, and you can also implement even more complex and powerful directives.

The declare error construct provides a way to declare a compile-time error when the compiler detects the presence of a join point matching a given pointcut. The compiler then issues an error, prints the given message for each detected usage, and aborts the compilation process:

```
declare error : <pointcut> : <message>;
```

Similarly, the declare warning construct provides a way to declare a compile-time warning, but does not abort the compilation process:

```
declare warning : <pointcut> : <message>;
```

Note that since these declarations affects compile-time behavior, you must use only *statically* determinable pointcuts in the declarations. In other words, the pointcuts that use dynamic context to select the matching join points—`this()`, `target()`, `args()`, `if()`, `cflow()`, and `cflowbelow()`—cannot be used for such a declaration.

A typical use of these constructs is to enforce rules, such as prohibiting calls to certain unsupported methods, or issuing a warning about such calls. The following code example causes the AspectJ compiler to produce a compile-time error if the join point matching the `callToUnsafeCode()` pointcut is found anywhere in the code that is being compiled:

```
declare error : callToUnsafeCode()
  : "This third-party code is known to result in crash";
```

The following code is similar, except it produces a compile-time warning instead of an error:

```
declare warning : callToBlockingOperations()
  : "Please ensure you are not calling this from AWT thread";
```

We have more examples of how to use compile-time errors and warnings for policy enforcement in chapter 6.

3.4 *Tips and tricks*

Here are some things to keep in mind as you are learning AspectJ. These simple tips will make your aspects simpler and more efficient:

- *Understand the difference between the AspectJ compiler and a Java compiler*—One of the most common misconceptions that first-time users have is that an AspectJ compiler works just like a Java compiler. However, unlike a Java compiler, which can compile either individual files or a set of files together without any significant difference, the AspectJ complier must compile all of the related classes and aspects at the same time. This means that you need to pass all the source files to the compiler together. The latest compiler version has additional options for weaving these files into JAR files. With those options, you also need to pass all JAR files together into a single invocation of the compiler. See appendix A for more details.

- *Use a consistent naming convention*—To get the maximum benefit from a wildcard-pointcut, it is important that you follow a naming convention consistently. For example, if you follow the convention of naming all the methods changing the state of an object to start with set, then you can capture all the state-change methods using set*. A consistent package structure with the right granularity will help capture all the classes inside a package tree.

- *Use after returning when appropriate*—When designing the after advice, consider using after returning instead of after, as long as you don't need to capture an exception-throwing case. The implementation for the after advice without returning needs to use a try/catch block. There is a cost associated with such a try/catch block that you can avoid by using an after returning advice.

- *Don't be misled by &&*—The natural language reading of pointcuts using && often misleads developers who are new to AspectJ. For example, the pointcut `publicMethods() && privateMethods()` won't match any method even though the natural reading would suggest "public *and* private methods." This is because a method can have either private access or public access, but not both. The solution is simple: use `||` instead to match public *or* private methods.

Chapter 8 presents a set of idioms that will help you avoid potential troubles as you begin using AspectJ.

3.5 *Summary*

AspectJ introduces AOP programming to Java by adding constructs to support dynamic and static crosscutting. Dynamic crosscutting modifies the behavior of the modules, while static crosscutting modifies the structure of the modules. Dynamic crosscutting consists of pointcut and advice constructs. AspectJ exposes the join points in a system through pointcuts. The support of wildcard matching in pointcuts offers a powerful yet simple way to capture join points without knowing the full details. The advice constructs provide a way to express actions at the desired join points. Static crosscutting, which can be used alone or in support of dynamic crosscutting, includes the constructs of member introduction, type hierarchy modification, and compile-time declarations. The overall result is a simple and programmer-friendly language supporting AOP in Java. At this point, if you haven't already done so, you may want to download and install the AspectJ compiler and tools. Appendix A explains where to find the compiler and how to install it.

Together, this chapter and the previous one should get you started on AspectJ, but for complex programs, you will need to learn a few more concepts, such as exception softening and aspect association. We present these concepts and more in the next chapter.

Advanced AspectJ

This chapter covers

- Using reflection support to access join point information
- Using aspect precedence to coordinate multiple aspects
- Creating reusable aspects with aspect association
- Exception softening and privileged aspects

The core concepts presented earlier equipped you with basic AspectJ constructs so that you can begin to implement crosscutting functionality in your system. For complex applications involving the creation of reusable aspects and the use of multiple aspects, you will need advanced AspectJ concepts and constructs to provide you with additional options for design and implementation.

This chapter introduces more advanced features of AspectJ, such as aspect precedence and aspect association. Unlike the earlier chapters, where concepts build on top of one another, this chapter contains a collection of constructs that each stand alone.

4.1 *Accessing join point information via reflection*

Reflective support in AspectJ provides programmatic access to the static and dynamic information associated with the join points. For example, using reflection, you can access the name of the currently advised method as well as the argument objects to that method. The dynamic context that can be captured using reflective support is similar to that captured using `this()`, `target()`, and `args()` pointcuts—only the mechanism to obtain the information is different. The most common use of this reflective information is in aspects that implement logging and similar functionaliy. We have already used simple reflective support to write the `JoinPointTraceAspect` in chapter 2. In this section, we examine the details of reflective support.

NOTE   While you can always use reflection to obtain the dynamic context, the preferred way is to use the `this()`, `target()`, and `args()` pointcuts. The reflective way of accessing information has poor performance, lacks static type checking, and is cumbersome to use. However, there are times when you need to use reflection because you need to access dynamic context and little information is available or required about the advised join points. For instance, you cannot easily use an `args()` pointcut to capture arguments for all logged methods, since each method may take a different number and type of arguments. Further, the logging aspect's advice doesn't need to care about the type of the argument objects because the only interaction of the logging aspect with those objects is to print them.

AspectJ provides reflective access by making three special objects available in each advice body: `thisJoinPoint`, `thisJoinPointStaticPart`, and `thisEnclosing-JoinPointStaticPart`. These objects are much like the special variable `this` that is available in each instance method in Java to provide access to the execution object. The information contained in these three objects is of two types: *dynamic* information and *static* information:

- Dynamic information consists of the kind of information that changes with each invocation of the same join points. For example, two different calls to the method `Account.debit()` will probably have different account objects and debit amounts.

- Static information is information that does not change between the multiple executions. For example, the name and source location of a method remain the same during different invocations of the method.

Each join point provides one object that contains dynamic information and two objects that contain static information about the join point and its enclosing join point. Let's examine the information in each of these special objects. We will examine the API to access the information from these objects in section 4.1.1:

- *thisJoinPoint*—This object of type `JoinPoint` contains the dynamic information of the advised join point. It gives access to the target object, the execution object, and the method arguments. It also provides access to the static information for the join point, using the `getStaticPart()` method. You use `thisJoinPoint` when you need dynamic information related to the join point. For example, if you want to log the execution object and method arguments, you would use the `thisJoinPoint` object.

- *thisJoinPointStaticPart*—This object of type `JoinPoint.StaticPart` contains the static information about the advised join point. It gives access to the source location, the kind (method-call, method-execution, field-set, field-get, and so forth), and the signature of the join point. You use `this-JoinPointStaticPart` when you need the structural context of the join point, such as its name, kind, source location, and so forth. For example, if you need to log the name of the methods that are executed, you would use the `thisJoinPointStaticPart` object.

- *thisEnclosingJoinPointStaticPart*—This object of type `JoinPoint.StaticPart` contains the static information about the enclosing join point, which is also refered to as the enclosing context. The enclosing context of a join point depends on the kind of join point. For example, for a method-call join point, the enclosing join point is the execution of the caller method, whereas for an exception-handler join point, the enclosing join point is the method that surrounds the catch block. You use the `thisEn-`

`closingJoinPointStaticPart` object when you need the context information of the join point's enclosing context. For example, while logging an exception, you can log the enclosing context information as well.

4.1.1 *The reflective API*

The reflective API in AspectJ is a set of interfaces that together form the programmatic access to the join point information. These interfaces provide access to dynamic information, static information, and various join point signatures. In this section, we examine these interfaces and their relationship with each other. Figure 4.1 shows the structural relationship between the interfaces of the reflective API in a UML class diagram.

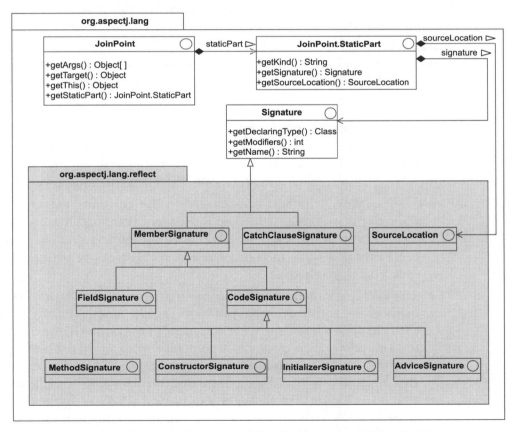

Figure 4.1 The structural relationship among various interfaces supporting reflection

The package `org.aspectj.lang` contains three interfaces and a subpackage. These modules provide support to access all of the join point's information. The `JoinPoint` interface models dynamic information associated with an advised join point. A `JoinPoint` object also contains an object of type `Join-Point.StaticPart` that can be accessed through the method `getStaticPart()`. This object provides access to the join point's static information. This static information consists of the join point's "kind," signature, and source code location. A `JoinPoint.StaticPart` object is composed of a `String` object (that represents the "kind"), a `Signature` object, and a `SourceLocation` object. The `Signature` object provides access to the join point's signature, and the `SourceLocation` object provides access to the join point's source-code location. The subpackage `org.aspectj.lang.reflect` contains interfaces for various join point signatures connected through an inheritance relationship, as well as the `Source-Location` interface.

NOTE   The purpose of the API discussion in this section is to give an overview. For more detailed information, refer to the AspectJ API documentation.

The org.aspectj.lang.JoinPoint interface

This interface provides access to the dynamic information associated with the currently advised join point. It specifies methods for obtaining the currently executing object, target object, and arguments, as well as the static information:

- The `getThis()` method gives access to the currently executing object, whereas the `getTarget()` method is used for obtaining the target object for a called join point. The `getThis()` method returns `null` for join points occurring in a static method, whereas `getTarget()` returns `null` for the calls to static methods.

- The `getArgs()` method gives access to arguments for the join point. For method and constructor join points, `getArgs()` simply returns an array of each element referring to each argument in the order they are supplied to the join point. Each primitive argument is wrapped in the corresponding wrapper type. For example, an `int` argument will be wrapped inside an `Integer` object. For field-set join points, the new value of the field is available in `getArgs()`. For field-get join points, `getArgs()` returns an empty array, since there is no argument for the operation. Similarly, for handler execution, `getArgs()` returns the exception object.

Besides providing access to the dynamic information, the JoinPoint interface offers direct access to the static information of the advised join point. There are two ways to obtain the static information through the thisJoinPoint variable of type JoinPoint:

- By using direct methods (getKind(), getSignature(), and getSourceLocation()) with the thisJoinPoint object. The next section discusses these methods since they are also defined in the JoinPoint.StaticPart interface, where they perform identical tasks.

- Through the object obtained with getStaticPart(), which contains the same information as thisJoinPointStaticPart.

The org.aspectj.lang.JoinPoint.StaticPart interface

This interface allows the API to access the static information associated with the currently advised join point. It specifies methods to obtain the kind of join point, the join point signature, and the source location information corresponding to code for the join point:

- The method getKind() returns the kind of join point. The method returns a string such as "method-call", "method-execution", or "field-set" that indicates the kind of the advised join point. The JoinPoint interface defines one constant for each of the available kinds of join points.

- The method getSignature() returns a Signature object for the executing join point. Depending on the nature of the join point, it can be an instance of one of the subinterfaces shown in figure 4.1. While the base Signature interface allows access to common information such as the name, the declaring type, and so forth, you will have to cast the object obtained through getSignature() to a subinterface if you need finer information (the type of method argument, its return type, its exception, and so on).

- The method getSourceLocation(), which returns a SourceLocation object, allows access to the source location information corresponding to the join point. The SourceLocation interface contains a method for accessing the source filename, line number, and so forth.

Each of the JoinPoint, JoinPoint.StaticPart, and Signature interfaces specifies three methods for obtaining string representation of the object with varied descriptiveness: toString() (which suffices for most debug logging needs), toLongString(), and toShortString().

> **NOTE**   The `thisJoinPoint` object is allocated every time an advice is executed to capture the current dynamic context, whereas the `thisJoinPoint-StaticPart` is allocated only once per join point during the execution of a program. Therefore, using dynamic information is expensive compare to static information. You should be aware of this fact while designing aspects such as logging.
>
> Also note that the static information obtained through both `this-JoinPoint.getStaticPart()` and `thisJoinPointStaticPart` is the same. In many situations, such as low-overhead logging and profiling, you need to gather only static, and not dynamic, information about the join point. In those cases, you should use the `thisJoinPointStatic-Part` object directly instead of the object obtained through `thisJoin-Point.getStaticPart()`. The first method does not require allocation of a separate object (`thisJoinPoint`) for each join point execution and thus is a lot more efficient.

4.1.2   Using reflective APIs

To demonstrate the use of reflective APIs, let's modify the simple tracing aspect that we wrote in chapter 2. If you recall, `JoinPointTraceAspect` used simple reflective support to print the information for all the join points as the code in the classes executed. We will use the same unmodified classes, `Account`, `Insufficient-BalanceException`, and `SavingsAccount`, from listings 2.5, 2.6, and 2.7. The abstract `Account` class provides the methods for debiting, crediting, and querying the account balance. The `SavingsAccount` class extends `Account` to a savings account. We will modify the versions of the `Test` class (from listing 2.8) and `Join-PointTraceAspect` (from listing 2.9) so that our new example will use the reflection API to log detailed messages that show information not only about the methods invoked, but also about the objects involved in each method invocation.

To limit the output, we first remove the call to the `debit()` method in the `Test` program as shown in listing 4.1.

Listing 4.1   Test.java

```
public class Test {
    public static void main(String[] args) {
        SavingsAccount account = new SavingsAccount(12456);
        account.credit(100);
    }
}
```

Now let's modify the `JoinPointTraceAspect` aspect, as shown in listing 4.2. Instead of printing the string representation of `thisJoinPoint` that showed only the signature and kind of the join point, we want it to print the join point's dynamic information, which is the `this` object, the target object, and the arguments at the join point, as well as its static information, which consists of the signature, the kind, and the source location of the join point in the before advice. We will also limit the trace join points for the purpose of limiting the output.

Listing 4.2 JoinPointTraceAspect.java

```
import org.aspectj.lang.*;
import org.aspectj.lang.reflect.*;

public aspect JoinPointTraceAspect {
    private int _indent = -1;

    pointcut tracePoints() :                              Defining trace    ❶
        !within(JoinPointTraceAspect)                     join points
        && !call(*.new(..)) && !execution(*.new(..))
        && !initialization(*.new(..)) && !staticinitialization(*);

    before() : tracePoints() {
        _indent++;
        println("========= " + thisJoinPoint + " ===========");
        println("Dynamic join point information:");
        printDynamicJoinPointInfo(thisJoinPoint);
        println("Static join point information:");
        printStaticJoinPointInfo(thisJoinPointStaticPart);
        println("Enclosing join point information:");
        printStaticJoinPointInfo(thisEnclosingJoinPointStaticPart);
    }
                                                          Obtaining         ❷
    after() : tracePoints() {                             reflective
        _indent--;                                        access objects
    }

    private void printDynamicJoinPointInfo(JoinPoint joinPoint) {
        println("This: " + joinPoint.getThis() +
                " Target: " + joinPoint.getTarget());
        StringBuffer argStr = new StringBuffer("Args: ");
        Object[] args = joinPoint.getArgs();
        for (int length = args.length, i = 0; i < length; ++i) {
            argStr.append(" [" + i + "] = " + args[i]);
        }                                                 Printing          ❸
        println(argStr);                                  dynamic
    }                                                     information
```

```
private void printStaticJoinPointInfo(
    JoinPoint.StaticPart joinPointStaticPart) {
    println("Signature: " + joinPointStaticPart.getSignature()
            + " Kind: " + joinPointStaticPart.getKind());
    SourceLocation sl = joinPointStaticPart.getSourceLocation();
    println("Source location: " +
            sl.getFileName() + ":" + sl.getLine());
}

private void println(Object message) {
    for (int i = 0, spaces = _indent * 2; i < spaces; ++i) {
        System.out.print(" ");
    }
    System.out.println(message);
}
}
```

Printing static information ➍

➊ The `tracePoints()` pointcut excludes the join points inside the aspect itself by using the `!within()` pointcut. Without the pointcut, the method calls within the advice in the aspect will get advised. When the advice executes for the first method, it will encounter a method call inside itself, and the advice will be called again. This will begin the infinite recursion. To limit the trace output, we also exclude the join points for the call and execution of constructors as well as object and class initialization.

➋ The advice body passes the reflective objects to the helper methods to print information contained in them.

➌ The `printDynamicJoinPointInfo()` method prints the dynamic information passed in the argument object. We first print the current execution object and the method target object by using `getThis()` and `getTarget()`, respectively. Note that `getThis()` will return `null` for the static method execution, whereas `getTarget()` will return `null` for the static method call. The `getArgs()` method returns an object array with each primitive argument wrapped in a corresponding type. For example, our float argument is wrapped in a `Float` object.

➍ The `printStaticJoinPointInfo()` method prints static information passed in the argument object. We print the signature of the join point and the kind of join point. We also print the source location information obtained through `getSourceLocation()`, returning a `SourceLocation` object that contains such information as the source file, the declaring class, and the line number.

When we run the program, we see the following output. You can see how `getThis()`, `getTarget()`, and `getArgs()` behave for different kinds of join points:

```
> ajc *.java
> java Test
========= execution(void Test.main(String[])) ===========
Dynamic join point information:
This: null Target: null
Args:   [0] = [Ljava.lang.String;@1eed786
Static join point information:
Signature: void Test.main(String[]) Kind: method-execution
Source location: Test.java:3
Enclosing join point information:
Signature: void Test.main(String[]) Kind: method-execution
Source location: Test.java:3
  ========= preinitialization(SavingsAccount(int)) ===========
  Dynamic join point information:
  This: null Target: null
  Args:   [0] = 12456
  Static join point information:
  Signature: SavingsAccount(int) Kind: preinitialization
  Source location: SavingsAccount.java:5
  Enclosing join point information:
  Signature: SavingsAccount(int) Kind: preinitialization
  Source location: SavingsAccount.java:5
  ========= preinitialization(Account(int)) ===========
  Dynamic join point information:
  This: null Target: null
  Args:   [0] = 12456
  Static join point information:
  Signature: Account(int) Kind: preinitialization
  Source location: Account.java:7
  Enclosing join point information:
  Signature: Account(int) Kind: preinitialization
  Source location: Account.java:7
  ========= set(int Account._accountNumber) ===========
  Dynamic join point information:
  This: SavingsAccount@1ad086a Target: SavingsAccount@1ad086a
  Args:   [0] = 12456
  Static join point information:
  Signature: int Account._accountNumber Kind: field-set
  Source location: Account.java:8
  Enclosing join point information:
  Signature: Account(int) Kind: constructor-execution
  Source location: Account.java:8
  ========= call(void Account.credit(float)) ===========
  Dynamic join point information:
  This: null Target: SavingsAccount@1ad086a
  Args:   [0] = 100.0
  Static join point information:
  Signature: void Account.credit(float) Kind: method-call
  Source location: Test.java:4
  Enclosing join point information:
  Signature: void Test.main(String[]) Kind: method-execution
```

```
Source location: Test.java:3
  ========= execution(void Account.credit(float)) ===========
  Dynamic join point information:
  This: SavingsAccount@1ad086a Target: SavingsAccount@1ad086a
  Args:  [0] = 100.0
  Static join point information:
  Signature: void Account.credit(float) Kind: method-execution
  Source location: Account.java:12
  Enclosing join point information:
  Signature: void Account.credit(float) Kind: method-execution
  Source location: Account.java:12
     ========= call(float Account.getBalance()) ===========
     Dynamic join point information:
     This: SavingsAccount@1ad086a Target: SavingsAccount@1ad086a
     Args:
     Static join point information:
     Signature: float Account.getBalance() Kind: method-call
     Source location: Account.java:12
     Enclosing join point information:
     Signature: void Account.credit(float) Kind: method-execution
     Source location: Account.java:12
       ========= execution(float Account.getBalance()) ===========
       Dynamic join point information:
       This: SavingsAccount@1ad086a Target: SavingsAccount@1ad086a
       Args:
       Static join point information:
       Signature: float Account.getBalance() Kind: method-execution
       Source location: Account.java:26
       Enclosing join point information:
       Signature: float Account.getBalance() Kind: method-execution
       Source location: Account.java:26
          ========= get(float Account._balance) ===========
          Dynamic join point information:
          This: SavingsAccount@1ad086a Target: SavingsAccount@1ad086a
          Args:
          Static join point information:
          Signature: float Account._balance Kind: field-get
          Source location: Account.java:26
          Enclosing join point information:
          Signature: float Account.getBalance() Kind: method-execution
          Source location: Account.java:26
     ========= call(void Account.setBalance(float)) ===========
     Dynamic join point information:
     This: SavingsAccount@1ad086a Target: SavingsAccount@1ad086a
     Args:  [0] = 100.0
     Static join point information:
     Signature: void Account.setBalance(float) Kind: method-call
     Source location: Account.java:12
     Enclosing join point information:
     Signature: void Account.credit(float) Kind: method-execution
     Source location: Account.java:12
```

```
========= execution(void Account.setBalance(float)) ===========
Dynamic join point information:
This: SavingsAccount@1ad086a Target: SavingsAccount@1ad086a
Args:   [0] = 100.0
Static join point information:
Signature: void Account.setBalance(float) Kind: method-execution
Source location: Account.java:30
Enclosing join point information:
Signature: void Account.setBalance(float) Kind: method-execution
Source location: Account.java:30
   ========= set(float Account._balance) ===========
   Dynamic join point information:
   This: SavingsAccount@1ad086a Target: SavingsAccount@1ad086a
   Args:   [0] = 100.0
   Static join point information:
   Signature: float Account._balance Kind: field-set
   Source location: Account.java:30
   Enclosing join point information:
   Signature: void Account.setBalance(float) Kind: method-execution
   Source location: Account.java:30
```

Notice in the output that `getThis()` returns `null` for method calls from the `main()` method. This is because it will return `null` for join points in a static method, as we mentioned in ❸ of the discussion of listing 4.2.

In a similar manner, you can build a quick logging functionality to get insight into the program flow of your system. The use of dynamic information can enhance your understanding of the system execution by logging the object and parameter with each join point along with the static information. In chapter 5, we provide a more detailed description of logging. In chapter 10, we use reflective information for creating authorization permission objects.

4.2 Aspect precedence

When a system includes multiple aspects, it's possible that advice in more than one aspect applies to a join point. In such situations, it may be important to control the order in which the advice is applied. To understand the need for controlling the advice execution order, let's look at the example in listing 4.3. Consider a class representing a home, with the methods of entering and exiting the home.

Listing 4.3 Home.java

```java
public class Home {
    public void enter() {
        System.out.println("Entering");
    }
```

```
    public void exit() {
        System.out.println("Exiting");
    }
}
```

Now let's create a security aspect (listing 4.4) consisting of advice for engaging the security system in the home when you exit and disengaging it when you enter.

Listing 4.4   HomeSecurityAspect.java

```
public aspect HomeSecurityAspect {
    before() : call(void Home.exit()) {
        System.out.println("Engaging");
    }

    after() : call(void Home.enter()) {
        System.out.println("Disengaging");
    }
}
```

Another aspect (listing 4.5) handles conserving energy by switching the lights off before you leave the home and switching them on after you enter.

Listing 4.5   SaveEnergyAspect.java

```
public aspect SaveEnergyAspect {
    before() : call(void Home.exit()) {
        System.out.println("Switching off lights");
    }

    after() : call(void Home.enter()) {
        System.out.println("Switching on lights");
    }
}
```

Now let's create a simple test (listing 4.6) to see the effects of multiple advice on a join point.

Listing 4.6   TestHome.java: a simple test to see the effect of multiple advice on a join point

```
public class TestHome {
    public static void main(String[] args) {
        Home home = new Home();

        home.exit();
```

```
        System.out.println();

        home.enter();
    }
}
```

Now when we compile these files together and execute the `Test` program, we see the following output:[1]

```
> ajc Home.java TestHome.java
    HomeSecurityAspect.java SaveEnergyAspect.java
> java TestHome
Switching off lights
Engaging
Exiting

Entering
Disengaging
Switching on lights
```

The exhibited behavior may not be desirable, considering that switching lights off prior to securing the home may make you fumble in the dark. Also, trying to disarm the security system without the lights on upon entry may cause similar troubles, and any delay in disarming the system may result in calling security. So the preferred sequence when entering the home is *enter-switch on lights-disarm*, and while exiting, *arm-switch off lights-exit*. From the implementation perspective, we would like:

1 The before advice in `SaveEnergyAspect` to run before the `HomeSecurity-Aspect` before advice

2 The after advice in `SaveEnergyAspect` to run after the `HomeSecurityAspect` after advice

In the next sections, we will study the rules and ways to control precedence. Later we will apply this information to the previous problem to show how you can achieve the correct advice ordering.

---

[1] It is possible to get output that is different from that shown here, depending on several factors, including the version of the AspectJ compiler you are using. The actual output may match the desired output. Such matching, however, is purely accidental, since the precedence is arbitrarily determined unless you specify the advice precedence.

4.2.1 *Ordering of advice*

As you have just seen, with multiple aspects present in a system, pieces of advice in the different aspects can often apply to a single join point. When this happens, AspectJ uses the following precedence rules to determine the order in which the advice is applied. Later, we will see how to control precedence:

- The aspect with higher precedence executes its before advice on a join point *before* the one with lower precedence.
- The aspect with higher precedence executes its after advice on a join point *after* the one with lower precedence.
- The around advice in the higher-precedence aspect encloses the around advice in the lower-precedence aspect. This kind of arrangement allows the higher-precedence aspect to control whether the lower-precedence advice will run at all by controlling the call to `proceed()`. In fact, if the higher-precedence aspect does not call `proceed()` in its advice body, not only will the lower-precedence aspects not execute, but the advised join point also will not be executed.

Figure 4.2 illustrates the precedence rules.

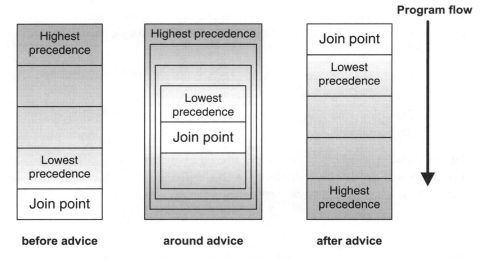

before advice   **around advice**   **after advice**

Figure 4.2   Ordering the execution of advice and join points. The darker areas represent the higher-precedence advice. The around advice could be thought of as the higher-precedence advice running the lower-precedence advice in a nested manner.

WARNING In the absence of any special precedence control, the order in which the advice is applied is unpredictable.

4.2.2 *Explicit aspect precedence*

It is often necessary to change the precedence of advice as it is applied to a join point. AspectJ provides a construct—declare precedence—for controlling aspect precedence. The declare precedence construct must be specified inside an aspect. The construct takes the following form:

```
declare precedence : TypePattern1, TypePattern2, ..;
```

The result of this kind of declaration is that aspects matching the type pattern on the left dominate the ones on the right, thus taking a higher precedence. In this example, the precedence of `TypePattern1` is higher than the precedence of `TypePattern2`. Precedence ordering considers only the concrete aspects when matching the type pattern and ignores all the abstract aspects. By controlling the aspect precedence, you can control the order in which advice is applied to a pointcut. For example, the following declaration causes `AuthenticationAspect` to dominate `AuthorizationAspect`:

```
declare precedence : AuthenticationAspect, AuthorizationAspect;
```

Let's use this declaration to correct the precedence between `HomeSecurityAspect` and `SaveEnergyAspect` in the `Home` class example. Since we want to run the before advice to arm before the before advice to switch off the lights, and the after advice to disarm after the after advice to switch on the lights, we need `Home-SecurityAspect` to dominate `SaveEnergyAspect`. We achieve this goal by writing another aspect (listing 4.7) that declares the correct and explicit precedence between the two.

> **Listing 4.7 HomeSystemCoordinationAspect.java**

```
public aspect HomeSystemCoordinationAspect {
    declare precedence: HomeSecurityAspect, SaveEnergyAspect;
}
```

Now when we compile our code and run the test program we see the following output:

```
> ajc Home.java TestHome.java
    ➡ HomeSecurityAspect.java SaveEnergyAspect.java
    ➡ HomeSystemCoordinationAspect.java
> java TestHome
Engaging
Switching off lights
Exiting

Entering
Switching on lights
Disengaging
```

This is exactly what we wanted. We could have added the declare precedence clause in either `HomeSecurityAspect` or `SaveEnergyAspect` and gotten the same result. However, this kind of modification would require the creation of an undesirable coupling between the two.

Let's examine more examples of the declare precedence clause to better understand it. Since the clause expects a list of *TypePatterns*, we can use wildcards in aspect names. The following declaration causes all aspects whose names start with `Auth`, such as `AuthenticationAspect` and `AuthorizationAspect`, to dominate the `PoolingAspect`:

```
declare precedence : Auth*, PoolingAspect;
```

In this declaration, however, the precedence between two aspects starting with `Auth` is unspecified. If controlling the precedence between two such aspects is important, you will need to specify both aspects in the desired order.

Since declare precedence takes a type list, you can specify a sequence of domination. For example, the following declaration causes aspects whose names start with `Auth` to dominate both `PoolingAspect` and `LoggingAspect`, while also causing `PoolingAspect` to dominate `LoggingAspect`:

```
declare precedence : Auth*, PoolingAspect, LoggingAspect;
```

It is common for certain aspects to dominate all other aspects. You can use a `*` wildcard to indicate such an intention. The following declaration causes `AuthenticationAspect` to dominate all the remaining aspects in the system:

```
declare precedence : AuthenticationAspect, *;
```

It is also common for certain aspects to be dominated by all other aspects. You can use a wildcard to achieve this as well. The following declaration causes `CachingAspect` to have the lowest precedence:

```
declare precedence : *, CachingAspect;
```

It is an error if a single declare precedence clause causes circular dependency in the ordering of aspect precedence. The following declaration will produce a compile-time error since `Auth*` will match `AuthenticationAspect`, causing a circular dependency:

```
declare precedence : Auth*, PoolingAspect, AuthenticationAspect;
```

However, it *is* legal to specify a circular dependency causing precedence in two different clauses. You can use this to enforce that two different, potentially conflicting or redundant aspects, such as two pooling aspects, share no join points. You will get a compile-time error if the two aspects in question share a join point. The following declarations will *not* produce an error unless `PoolingAspect` and `AuthenticationAspect` share a join point:

```
declare precedence : AuthenticationAspect, PoolingAspect;
declare precedence : PoolingAspect, AuthenticationAspect;
```

You can include a declare precedence clause inside any aspect. A common usage idiom is to add such clauses to a separate coordination aspect (such as the one we used in the previous `HomeSystemCoordinationAspect` example) so that aspects themselves are unaware of each other and need no modification to the core aspects. Such a separation is particularly important for third-party, off-the-shelf aspects where you may not have the control over source files you would need to add such clauses. Separating precedence control also avoids the tangling of the core functionality in the precedence relationship with other aspects. The following snippet shows the use of a separate precedence-coordinating aspect in a banking system:

```
aspect BankingAspectCoordinator {
    declare precedence : Auth*, PoolingAspect, LoggingAspect;
}
```

The precedence control offered by AspectJ is simple yet powerful, and is immensely helpful for a complex system. You can now create multiple aspects independently as well as use aspects developed by others without requiring modifications to any other aspect.

4.2.3 *Aspect inheritance and precedence*

Besides explicitly controlling aspect precedence using the declare precedence construct, AspectJ implicitly determines the precedence of two aspects related by a base-derived aspect relationship. The rule is simple: If the inheritance relates two aspects, the derived aspect implicitly dominates the base aspect. Here's an example to illustrate this rule. In listing 4.8, the TestPrecedence class sets up the scenario to test the precedence in aspect inheritance by calling the perform() method from the main() method:

Listing 4.8   TestPrecedence.java

```
public class TestPrecedence {
    public static void main(String[] args) {
        TestPrecedence test = new TestPrecedence();
        test.perform();
    }

    public void perform() {
        System.out.println("<performing/>");
    }
}
```

In listing 4.9, the abstract aspect SecurityAspect advises the perform() method in the TestPrecedence class. The advice simply prints a message.

Listing 4.9   SecurityAspect.java

```
public abstract aspect SecurityAspect {
    public pointcut performCall() :
        call(* TestPrecedence.perform());

    before() : performCall() {
        System.out.println("<SecurityAspect:check/>");
    }
}
```

In listing 4.10, the aspect ExtendedSecurityAspect uses SecurityAspect as the base aspect. It too advises the perform() method in the TestPrecedence class and prints a message.

Listing 4.10   ExtendedSecurityAspect.java

```
public aspect ExtendedSecurityAspect extends SecurityAspect {
    before() : performCall() {
        System.out.println("<ExtendedSecurityAspect:check/>");
    }
}
```

Now when we compile the class with the aspects, we get the following output. You can observe that the before advice of the derived class was executed before that of the base class:

```
> ajc *.java
> java TestPrecedence
<ExtendedSecurityAspect:check/>
<SecurityAspect:check/>
<performing/>
```

WARNING   Since only concrete aspects in the declare precedence clause are designated for precedence ordering, the declaration of a base aspect (which is always abstract) to dominate a child has *no* effect. For example, adding the following clause in the system has no effect:

```
declare precedence : SecurityAspect, ExtendedSecurityAspect;
```

4.2.4 *Ordering of advice in a single aspect*

It is also possible to have multiple pieces of advice in one aspect that you want to apply to a pointcut. Since the advice resides in the same aspect, aspect precedence rules can no longer apply. In such cases, the advice that appears first lexically inside the aspect executes first. Note that the only way to control precedence between multiple advice in an aspect is to arrange them lexically. Let's illustrate this rule through a simple example (listing 4.11) that shows both the effect of the precedence rule and its interaction between different types of advice. Chapter 10 presents a real-world example in which understanding interadvice precedence is important in authentication and authorization aspects.

> **Listing 4.11 InterAdvicePrecedenceAspect.java: testing advice ordering in a single aspect**

```
public aspect InterAdvicePrecedenceAspect {
    public pointcut performCall() : call(* TestPrecedence.perform());

    after() returning : performCall() {
        System.out.println("<after1/>");
    }

    before() : performCall() {
        System.out.println("<before1/>");
    }

    void around() : performCall() {
        System.out.println("<around>");
        proceed();
```

```
        System.out.println("</around>");
    }

    before() : performCall() {
        System.out.println("<before2/>");
    }
}
```

After compiling the aspect with the same `TestPrecedence` class in listing 4.8, when we run the code we get this output:

```
> ajc *.java
> java TestPrecedence
<before1/>
<around>
<before2/>
<performing/>
<after1/>
</around>
```

The output shows that:

1 The first before advice is followed by around advice due to their lexical ordering.

2 The second before advice runs after the around advice starts executing, but *before* executing the captured join point. Note that, regardless of precedence, all before advice for a join point must execute before the captured join point itself.

3 The after advice executes *before* completing the around advice, since it has higher precedence than the around advice. Note that the earliest an after advice can run is *after* the join point's execution.

4.2.5 *Aspect precedence and member introduction*

In rare cases, when multiple aspects introduce data members with the same name or methods with the same signature, the members introduced by the aspect with the higher precedence will be retained and the matching members introduced by other aspects will be eliminated. For example, if you have introduced a method and its implementation in one aspect, and another implementation for the same method in another aspect, only the dominating aspect's implementation will survive. The same is true for data members. If two aspects introduce a member with the same name, type, and initial value, only the member from the dominating aspect will survive.

Listing 4.12 illustrates the effect of aspect precedence on member introduction. Compile these two aspects with `TestPrecedence.java` from listing 4.8. Running the test program will show that the dominating aspect's data and method win over the members of the other aspect.

Listing 4.12   SecurityAspect.java

```
public aspect SecurityAspect {
    private String TestPrecedence._id          Introducing
        = "SecurityAspect:id";                  data

    private void TestPrecedence.printId() {              Introducing
        System.out.println(                              method
            "<SecurityAspect:performSecurityCheck id=" + _id + "/>");
    }

    public pointcut performCall() : call(* TestPrecedence.perform());

    before(TestPrecedence test) : performCall() && target(test) {
        System.out.println("<SecurityAspect:before/>");
        System.out.println(test._id);    <— Printing introduced data
        test.printId();         <—┐ Invoking introduced
    }                              method
}
```

`SecurityAspect` introduces a data member and a method in the `TestPrecedence` class. It also invokes the introduced method as well as prints the value of the introduced member in the before advice to test the effect.

In listing 4.13, the `TrackingAspect` aspect introduces the same-named data and a same-named method as the `SecurityAspect` aspect. However, it uses a different initial value for the data member and a different body for the method.

Listing 4.13   TrackingAspect.java

```
public aspect TrackingAspect {                            Introducing
    private String TestPrecedence._id = "TrackingAspect:id";  <—┘ data

    private void TestPrecedence.printId() {
        System.out.println(
            "<TrackingAspect:performTracking id=" + _id + "/>");  Introducing
    }                                                             method
}
```

Let's also add the following precedence-coordinating aspect (listing 4.14).

> **Listing 4.14   SystemAspectCoordinator.java**

```
aspect SystemAspectCoordinator {
    declare precedence : SecurityAspect, TrackingAspect;
}
```

When we compile all the files and run the `TestPrecedence` class, we see this output:

```
> ajc *.java
> java TestPrecedence
<SecurityAspect:before/>
SecurityAspect:id
<SecurityAspect:performSecurityCheck id=SecurityAspect:id/>
<performing/>
```

As you can see, the initial value and method implementation introduced by the dominating `SecurityAspect` override the same in `TrackingAspect`.

4.3 *Aspect association*

By default, only one instance of an aspect exists in a virtual machine (VM)—much like a singleton class. All the entities inside the VM then share the state of such an aspect. For example, all objects share a resource pool inside a pooling aspect. Usually, this kind of sharing is fine and even desirable. However, there are situations, especially when creating reusable aspects, where you want to associate the aspect's state with an individual object or control flow.

The aspect associations can be classified into three categories:

- Per virtual machine (default)
- Per object
- Per control-flow association

You can specify a nondefault association by modifying the aspect declaration that takes the following form:

```
aspect <AspectName> [<association-specifier>(<Pointcut>)]  {
    ... aspect body
}
```

Note the part in bold. This optional aspect association specification determines how the aspect is associated with respect to the join points captured by the specified pointcut.

4.3.1 *Default association*

Default association is in effect when you do not include an association specification in the aspect declaration. All the aspects you have seen so far in this book are of this type. This type of association creates one instance of the aspect for the VM, thus making its state shared. To understand aspect creation, let's create an aspect for the banking-related `Account` class (listing 2.5, chapter 2), which provided a simple API for crediting and debiting amounts for an account. Later, we will modify this aspect to show the other kinds of associations: per object and per control flow.

For our discussion of aspect association in this section, let's create an aspect, `AssociationDemoAspect`. Listing 4.15 shows the default association aspect that illustrates when an aspect instance is created. We will also use the `Account` class developed in listing 2.5 in chapter 2. The aspect logs a message in its constructor to designate its creation. Then it prints the aspect's instance and the aspected object.

Listing 4.15 AssociationDemoAspect.java: using default association

```
public aspect AssociationDemoAspect {
    public AssociationDemoAspect() {
        System.out.println("Creating aspect instance");    ❶ Aspect
    }                                                          constructor

    pointcut accountOperationExecution(Account account)    ❷ Account
        : (execution(* Account.credit(..))                     operation
          || execution(* Account.debit(..)))                   pointcut
          && this(account);

    before(Account account)
        : accountOperationExecution(account) {
        System.out.println("JoinPoint: " + thisJoinPointStaticPart
                        + "\n\taspect: " + this
                        + "\n\tobject: " + account);       ❸
    }                                        Advice that prints the aspect
}                                                and account instance
```

❶ We print a simple message in the aspect constructor to keep track of when the aspect instance is created.

❷ The `accountOperationExecution()` pointcut captures the execution of the `credit()` and `debit()` methods in the `Account` class. It also captures the `Account` object using the `this()` pointcut so that we can print it in the advice.

❸ The advice to `accountOperationExecution()` prints the static context of the captured join point, the aspect instance, and the `Account` object captured by the
pointcut. Note that when used from advice, the object `this` refers to the instance
of an aspect and not the execution object at a join point.

Next let's write a simple test program (listing 4.16) that creates two `Account`
objects and calls methods on them.

> **Listing 4.16   TestAssociation.java: testing associations**

```
public class TestAssociation {
    public static void main(String[] args) throws Exception {
        SavingsAccount account1 = new SavingsAccount(12245);
        SavingsAccount account2 = new SavingsAccount(67890);
        account1.credit(100);
        account1.debit(100);

        account2.credit(100);
        account2.debit(100);
    }
}
```

When we compile the classes and run the `TestAssociation` program, we see output similar to the following:

```
> ajc *.java
> java TestAssociation
Creating aspect instance
JoinPoint: execution(void Account.credit(float))          Aspect instance
        aspect: AssociationDemoAspect@187aeca             creation
        object: SavingsAccount@e48e1b
JoinPoint: execution(void Account.debit(float))
        aspect: AssociationDemoAspect@187aeca
        object: SavingsAccount@e48e1b
JoinPoint: execution(void Account.credit(float))
        aspect: AssociationDemoAspect@187aeca
        object: SavingsAccount@12dacd1
JoinPoint: execution(void Account.debit(float))
        aspect: AssociationDemoAspect@187aeca
        object: SavingsAccount@12dacd1
```

The output shows that only one instance of the aspect is created, and that
instance is available to all advice in the aspect.

4.3.2 *Per-object association*

Oftentimes, reusable base aspects need to keep some per-object state consisting of the data that is associated with each object, without having sufficient information about the type of objects that will participate in the static crosscutting mechanism of member introduction. Consider a cache-management aspect that needs to track the last access time for each object in the cache so that it can remove from the cache objects that are not accessed for a long duration. Since such cache management is a reusable concept, we want to create a reusable base aspect. By associating a separate aspect instance with each object under cache management and by keeping the field definition for the last accessed time inside the base aspect, we can track the required information for each cache-managed object.

The per-object association feature lets us associate a new aspect instance with an execution or target object by using a pointcut. In the following snippet, a new aspect instance is associated with each new execution object using perthis(), which matches the abstract access() pointcut:

```
public abstract aspect CacheManagementAspect perthis(access()) {

    ... aspect's state - instance members such as the last accessed time

    abstract pointcut access();

    ... advice to access() pointcut to update the last accessed time

    ... advice using the aspect's state
}
```

As an example, we can enable cache management in a banking application by simply creating a subaspect that provides a definition for the abstract access() pointcut:

```
public aspect BankingCacheManagementAspect extends CacheManagementAspect {
    pointcut access() : execution(* banking..Account+.*(..))
                        || execution(* banking..Customer+.*(..));
}
```

Now whenever a join point that is captured by the access() pointcut executes (such as the debit() method), and the execution object is not previously associated with a BankingCacheManagementAspect instance, a new instance of the aspect is created and associated with the execution object. The same scenario will take place with Customer objects as well. Effectively, the aspect's state now forms a part of each execution object's state. The advice in the base and derived aspects may then use the state of the aspect as if it were the cached object's state.

With per-object associations, an aspect instance is associated with each object matching the association specification. You can specify two kinds of per-object associations:

- perthis()—Associates a separate aspect instance with the execution object (this) for the join point matching the pointcut specified inside perthis()
- pertarget()—Associates a separate aspect instance with the target object for the join point matching the pointcut specified inside pertarget()

With object associations, the aspect instance is created when executing a join point of a matching object for the first time. Once an association is created between an object and an instance of the declaring aspect, the association is good for the lifetime of the object. Specifically, executing another matching join point on the same object does not create a new aspect with the object. Figure 4.3 illustrates object association using a UML sequence diagram.

To illustrate, let's modify the aspect AssociationDemoAspect. Listing 4.17 shows the use of the perthis() association with the accountOperationExecution pointcut.

Listing 4.17   AssociationDemoAspect.java: with `perthis()` association

```
public aspect AssociationDemoAspect
    perthis(accountOperationExecution(Account)) {

    public AssociationDemoAspect() {
        System.out.println("Creating aspect instance");
    }

    pointcut accountOperationExecution(Account account)
        : (execution(* Account.credit(..))
          || execution(* Account.debit(..)))
          && this(account);

    before(Account account)
        : accountOperationExecution(account) {
        System.out.println("JoinPoint: " + thisJoinPointStaticPart
                        + "\n\taspect: " + this
                        + "\n\tobject: " + account);
    }
}
```

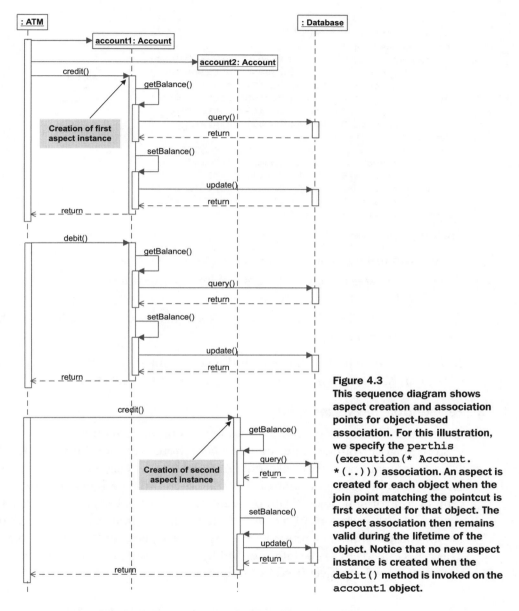

Figure 4.3
This sequence diagram shows aspect creation and association points for object-based association. For this illustration, we specify the `perthis (execution(* Account. *(..)))` association. An aspect is created for each object when the join point matching the pointcut is first executed for that object. The aspect association then remains valid during the lifetime of the object. Notice that no new aspect instance is created when the `debit()` method is invoked on the `account1` object.

Now when we compile this using the modified aspect and run the test program, we get following output:

```
> ajc *.java
> java TestAssociation
Creating aspect instance
JoinPoint: execution(void Account.credit(float))
        aspect: AssociationDemoAspect@e48e1b
        object: SavingsAccount@12dacd1
JoinPoint: execution(void Account.debit(float))
        aspect: AssociationDemoAspect@e48e1b
        object: SavingsAccount@12dacd1
Creating aspect instance
JoinPoint: execution(void Account.credit(float))
        aspect: AssociationDemoAspect@1ad086a
        object: SavingsAccount@10385c1
JoinPoint: execution(void Account.debit(float))
        aspect: AssociationDemoAspect@1ad086a
        object: SavingsAccount@10385c1
```

Aspect instance creation

The output shows:

1 Two instances of `AssociationDemoAspect` are created.

2 Each aspect is created right before the execution of the first join point with each `Account` object.

3 In each advice body, the same aspect instance is available for each join point on an object.

To associate an aspect instance with the target object for a matching join point instead of the execution object, you use `pertarget()` instead of `perthis()`.

4.3.3 *Per-control-flow association*

As with per-object association, you sometimes need per-control-flow association to store per-control-flow states in implementations. You can think of control flow as a conceptual object that encapsulates the thread of execution encompassing a given join point. The per-control-flow state then is data associated with this conceptual control-flow object. With per-control-flow association, an aspect instance is associated with each control flow matching the association specification. Consider the following snippet of a reusable base aspect providing transaction management. This aspect needs to store states needed by the transaction management, such as a JDBC connection object used by all operations:

```
public abstract
    aspect TransactionManagementAspect percflow(transacted()) {

    ... aspect state:
    ...     instance members such as the connection object used
```

```
      abstract pointcut transacted();

      ... advice using the aspect state
}
```

We can then introduce a transaction management capability in a banking application by extending this aspect and providing a definition for the abstract `transacted()` pointcut:

```
public aspect BankingTransactionManagementAspect
    extends TransactionManagementAspect {

    pointcut transacted() : execution(* banking..Account+.*(..))
                          || execution(* banking..Customer+.*(..));
}
```

In this aspect, we introduced transaction management into a banking system by simply specifying the operations that need transaction management support in the definition of the abstract pointcut `transacted()`. This will capture the execution of appropriate methods in banking-related classes. The bulk of transaction management logic resides in the reusable base `Transaction-ManagementAspect` aspect.

There are a few ways to achieve the goal of creating reusable aspects that need to keep some per-control-flow state without using a control-flow-based association. For example, you could use a thread-specific storage such as `ThreadLocal` to manage the control flow's state. In many cases, however, using an aspect association creates a simpler implementation.

You can specify two kinds of per-control-flow object associations:

- `percflow()`—Associates a separate aspect instance with the control flow at the join point matching the pointcut specified inside `percflow()`
- `percflowbelow()`—Associates a separate aspect instance with the control flow below the join point matching the pointcut specified inside `percflowbelow()`

Much like the `perthis` and `pertarget` cases, once an association is made between a control flow and an aspect instance, it continues to exist for the lifetime of that control flow. Figure 4.4 illustrates the effect of control-flow-based association.

In figure 4.4, we consider an aspect that associates the aspect instance with the control flow of join points that match the execution of any method in the `Account` class. We see that six aspect instances are created—one each for the top-level `credit()` and `debit()` executions, and two each for `getBalance()` and `setBalance()`, which are called from the `credit()` and `debit()` methods. Each aspect instance continues to exist until its join point's execution completes.

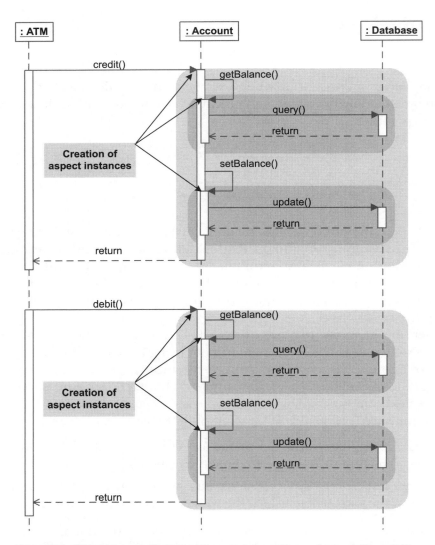

Figure 4.4 This sequence diagram shows aspect creation and association points for control-flow-based associations. In this illustration, we show the `percflow(execution(* Account.*(..)))` association. An aspect is created as soon as each matching control flow is entered for the first time. The aspect association then remains valid during the lifetime of the control flow. Each gray area indicates the scope of the aspect instance that was created upon entering the area.

To better understand control-flow-based association, let's modify `Associa-tionDemoAspect` again. We will also modify the pointcut in the before advice to include the `setBalance()` execution, as shown in listing 4.18.

Listing 4.18 AssociationDemoAspect.java: with `percflow()` association

```
public aspect AssociationDemoAspect
    percflow(accountOperationExecution(Account)) {

    public AssociationDemoAspect() {
        System.out.println("Creating aspect instance");
    }

    pointcut accountOperationExecution(Account account)
        : (execution(* Account.credit(..))
            || execution(* Account.debit(..)))
            && this(account);

    before(Account account)
        : accountOperationExecution(account)
        || (execution(* Account.setBalance(..)) && this(account)) {
        System.out.println("JoinPoint: " + thisJoinPointStaticPart
                            + "\n\taspect: " + this
                            + "\n\tobject: " + account);
    }
}
```

When we compile the aspect with the `TestAssociation` class and run the program, we see output similar to the following:

```
> ajc *.java
> java TestAssociation
Creating aspect instance
JoinPoint: execution(void Account.credit(float))
        aspect: AssociationDemoAspect@10385c1
        object: SavingsAccount@42719c
JoinPoint: execution(void Account.setBalance(float))
        aspect: AssociationDemoAspect@10385c1
        object: SavingsAccount@42719c
Creating aspect instance
JoinPoint: execution(void Account.debit(float))
        aspect: AssociationDemoAspect@30c221
        object: SavingsAccount@42719c
JoinPoint: execution(void Account.setBalance(float))
        aspect: AssociationDemoAspect@30c221
        object: SavingsAccount@42719c
```

**Aspect
instance
creation**

```
Creating aspect instance
JoinPoint: execution(void Account.credit(float))
       aspect: AssociationDemoAspect@119298d
       object: SavingsAccount@f72617
JoinPoint: execution(void Account.setBalance(float))
       aspect: AssociationDemoAspect@119298d
       object: SavingsAccount@f72617
Creating aspect instance
JoinPoint: execution(void Account.debit(float))
       aspect: AssociationDemoAspect@1e5e2c3
       object: SavingsAccount@f72617
JoinPoint: execution(void Account.setBalance(float))
       aspect: AssociationDemoAspect@1e5e2c3
       object: SavingsAccount@f72617
```

Aspect instance creation

We now see that:

1. Four instances of the aspect are created, two corresponding to `credit()` and two corresponding to the `debit()` method executions initiated by the `TestAssociation` class. Each execution of the `credit()` and `debit()` methods called from the `TestAssociation` class resulted in a new control flow matching the join point specified in the aspect association pointcut, resulting in a new aspect instance being created.

2. Each instance is created just before the execution of the `credit()` and `debit()` methods, since a new control flow matching the pointcut specified starts with their execution.

3. The `setBalance()` method that is called from the control flow of `debit()` and `credit()` is associated with the same aspect as its caller. Because the `setBalance()` method falls in the control flow of `debit()` and `credit()`, the instance created for the caller continues to be associated with any method called by this caller. Note that if we include the `setBalance()` method in the `accountOperationExecution()` pointcut, it will result in the creation of a new aspect instance upon each execution of the `set-Balance()` method, similar to the aspect instances shown in figure 4.4.

4.3.4 *Implicit limiting of join points*

Using the per-object or per-control-flow association has the side effect of implicitly limiting the advice in the aspect to only join points that match the scope of an aspect instance. The *scope* of an aspect instance is the set of join points that have an aspect instance associated with them. For example, for the `percflow()` association, the scope of an aspect instance is all the join points occurring inside the control flow of the specified pointcut. This means that even if a pointcut specified for an advice matches a join point, the advice to that join point won't apply unless the join point also matches the scope of the aspect. This side effect often surprises developers when they refactor an aspect to create reusable parts and need to use `per-` associations.

The aspect association implies that advice in an aspect will apply to join points only if:

- For `perthis()` associations, the join point's execution object matches the aspect instance's associated object.

- For `pertarget()` associations, the join point's target object matches the aspect's associated object.

- For `percflow()` associations, the join point is in the control flow of the aspect's associated control flow.

- For `percflowbelow()` associations, the join point is below the control flow of the aspect's associated control flow.

A simple example, shown in listing 4.19, might illustrate this concept better.

Listing 4.19   TestAssociationScope.java

```java
public class TestAssociationScope {
    public static void main(String[] args) {
        A a = new A();
        a.m();
    }
}

class A {
    public void m() {
        B b = new B();
        b.m();
    }
}

class B {
    public void m() {
    }
}

aspect TestAspect {
    before() : !within(TestAspect) {
        System.out.println(thisJoinPoint);
    }
}
```

When we compile and run this program, we see logging of each executed join point:

```
> ajc *.java
> java TestAssociationScope
staticinitialization(TestAssociationScope.<clinit>)
execution(void TestAssociationScope.main(String[]))
call(A())
staticinitialization(A.<clinit>)
preinitialization(A())
initialization(A())
execution(A())
call(void A.m())
execution(void A.m())
call(B())
staticinitialization(B.<clinit>)
preinitialization(B())
initialization(B())
execution(B())
call(void B.m())
execution(void B.m())
```

Now let's modify `TestAspect` to use the `perthis()` association.

```
aspect TestAspect perthis(execution(void A.*())) {
    before() : !within(TestAspect) {
        System.out.println(thisJoinPoint);
    }
}
```

When we compile and run this again, we see that only the methods that match the `execution(void A.*())` pointcut are advised:

```
> ajc *.java
> java TestAssociationScope
execution(void A.m())
call(B())
call(void B.m())
```

4.3.5 *Comparing object association with member introduction*

It is possible to avoid using the `perthis()`/`pertarget()` association with a judicious use of static crosscutting using introduced fields. In that case, instead of keeping the state in an aspect, you introduce that state to the object being aspected. This kind of modification often leads to simpler design. For example, consider this aspect, which associates an aspect instance with each `Account` object. The aspect's state—`_minimumBalance`—effectively becomes part of the `Account` object's state:

```
public aspect MinimumBalanceAspect perthis(this(Account)) {
    private float _minimumBalance;

    ... methods and advice using _minimumBalance
}
```

Now if we want to use member introduction instead of association, we can change the aspect in the following way:

```
public aspect MinimumBalanceAspect {
    private float Account._minimumBalance;

    ... methods and advice using _minimumBalance
}
```

In this snippet, we use the member introduction mechanism to associate a new member—_minimumBalance—with each `Account` object. The result is identical in both snippets—a new state is associated with each `Account` object.

Certain reusable aspects, such as cache management, that need to work with diverse types of objects may not have any common shared type. For example, `Customer` and `Account` probably have no class or interface common to their inheritance hierarchy. Therefore, to introduce a state, you will first need to specify a common type using a declare parent. For example, you can declare the interface `Cacheable` to be a parent type of `Account` and `Customer`. Then you may introduce the required state to `Cacheable`. This way, you get the same effect as per-object association using a simple introduction mechanism.

Developing reusable aspects using introduction instead of per-object association can get tricky. The main reason is that a reusable base aspect, unaware of the application-specific classes, cannot use the declare parents construct to specify a common type. While you can get around this issue by using a complex design, per-object association can offer an elegant alternative solution. When you're using per-object associations, the base aspect includes an abstract pointcut that associates the aspect with the object at the matching join points. Then, all that a derived aspect needs to do is provide a definition for that pointcut so that it captures join points whose associated objects need additional per-object state. Chapter 9 (section 9.7.2) provides a concrete example of the simplification of a reusable aspect using per-object association.

The choice between use of per-object association and member introduction is a balance between elegance and simplicity. Experience is usually the best guide.

4.3.6 *Accessing aspect instances*

Aspect instances are created automatically by the system according to the association specification. To access their state from outside the aspect, however, you will need to get its instance. For example, in a profiling aspect that collects duration for the execution of profiled methods, typically you would keep the profile data inside the profile aspect. When you need to retrieve this data, say from another thread that will print the latest profile information, you have to get the aspect instance first. For all types of aspect associations, you can get the aspect instance using the static method `aspectOf()` that is available for each aspect. The method returns an instance of the aspect. For a profiler case, we could retrieve the data as follows:

```
Map profileData = ProfilerAspect.aspectOf().getProfileData();
```

If the `getProfileData()` method were static (which would require data returned to be marked static), we could directly access the data using `Profiler-Aspect.getProfileData()` irrespective of the association specification. In certain cases, such as when using third-party aspects or aspects with a class as a base, it may not be possible to mark certain members static due to other design considerations. In any case, marking a certain state static for easy access may not be a good practice and may prevent reusability through the use of different aspect associations.

Each aspect contains two static methods—`aspectOf()` to obtain the associated aspect instance and `hasAspect()` to check if an instance is associated. For aspects with default and control-flow association, both these methods take no arguments, whereas for aspects with per-object association, these methods take one argument of type `Object` to specify the object for which the associated aspect instance is sought. In all cases, the `aspectOf()` method returns the instance of an aspect if one is associated; otherwise, it throws a `NoAspectBoundException`. The method `hasAspect()` returns true if an aspect instance is associated; otherwise, it returns false. Note that since an aspect instance with a control-flow-based association lives only during the control flow (or below, for `percflowbelow()`), you can get the aspect instance only in the control flow associated with the aspect.

4.4 *Exception softening*

Java specifies two categories of exceptions that can be thrown by a method: checked and unchecked exceptions. When an exception is checked, callers must deal with it either by catching the exception or by declaring that they can throw it. Unchecked exceptions, which can be either `RuntimeException` or `Error`, do not need to be dealt with explicitly. Exception softening allows checked exceptions thrown by specified pointcuts to be treated as unchecked ones. Softening eliminates the need to either catch the exception or declare it in the caller's method specification.

The softening feature helps to modularize the crosscutting concerns of exception handling. For example, you can soften a RemoteException thrown in a Remote Method Invocation (RMI)-based system to avoid handling the exception at each level. This may be a useful strategy in some situations. For instance, if you know that you are using local objects of RMI-capable classes that won't throw any RemoteException, you can soften those exceptions.

To soften exceptions, you use the declare soft construct that takes the following form:

```
declare soft : <ExceptionTypePattern> : <pointcut>;
```

If a method is throwing more than one checked exception, you will have to individually soften each one. In listing 4.20, the aspect declares the softening of an exception thrown by the TestSoftening.perform() method. The method now behaves as if it is throwing an org.aspectj.lang.SoftException, which extends RuntimeException.

Listing 4.20 TestSoftening.java: code for testing the effect of softening an exception

```
import java.rmi.RemoteException;

public class TestSoftening {
    public static void main(String[] args) {
        TestSoftening test = new TestSoftening();
        test.perform();
    }

    public void perform() throws RemoteException {
        throw new RemoteException();
    }
}
```

Compiling the TestSoftening class will result in a compiler error, since main() neither catches the exception nor declares that it is throwing that exception:

```
> ajc TestSoftening.java
F:\aspectj-book\ch04\section4.4\TestSoftening.java:6
   Unhandled exception type RemoteException
test.perform();
^^^^^^^^^^^^^^
```

Listing 4.21 shows SofteningTestAspect, which softens the RemoteException thrown by the join point that corresponds to the call to the TestSoftening.perform() method.

Listing 4.21   Softening aspect

```
import java.rmi.RemoteException;

public aspect SofteningTestAspect {
    declare soft : RemoteException : call(void TestSoftening.perform());
}
```

By softening the exception, we can compile the code without errors. When we run the program, we see a call stack due to a thrown `SoftException`:

```
> ajc TestSoftening.java SofteningTestAspect.java
> java TestSoftening
Exception in thread "main" org.aspectj.lang.SoftException
        at TestSoftening.main(TestSoftening.java:6)
```

An aspect declaring an exception for a join point wraps the join point execution in a try/catch block. The catch block catches the original exception, and the throw block throws a `SoftException` that wraps the original exception. This means that in listing 4.21, if we were to specify `execution` instead of `call` in the pointcut, the compiler would still give us a compiler error for the unhandled exception. To illustrate this, let's look at the code in listings 4.20 and 4.21 again. First let's see that compiling `TestSoftening` together with `SofteningTestAspect` results in a woven `TestSoftening` class that looks like the following:

```
import java.rmi.RemoteException;

public class TestSoftening {
    public static void main(String[] args) {
        TestSoftening test = new TestSoftening();
        try {
            test.perform();
        } catch (RemoteException ex) {
            throw new SoftException(ex);
        }
    }

    public void perform() throws RemoteException {
        throw new RemoteException();
    }
}
```

The portion marked in bold shows the effective code that was inserted due to `SofteningTestAspect`. As you see, the `RemoteException` is now caught by the `main()` method, which throws a `SoftException` wrapping the caught exception. Since the `SoftException` is an unchecked exception, `main()` no longer needs to declare that it can throw it.

Now, instead of the aspect in listing 4.20, let's apply the following aspect (which softens the exception at an `execution` pointcut rather than a `call` pointcut) to the original `TestSoftening` class:

```
public aspect SofteningTestAspect {
    declare soft : RemoteException : execution(void TestSoftening.perform());
}
```

Compiling this aspect with the `TestSoftening` class will result in woven code that looks like this:

```
import java.rmi.RemoteException;

public class TestSoftening {
    public static void main(String[] args) {
        TestSoftening test = new TestSoftening();
        test.perform();
    }

    public void perform() throws RemoteException {
        try {
            throw new RemoteException();
        } catch (RemoteException ex) {
            throw new SoftException(ex);
        }
    }
}
```

Here too, the portion marked in bold is the result of effective code added in the process of weaving. Since we have specified the softening of the execution of the `perform()` method, the try/catch is added to the `perform()` method itself. Note that although `perform()` would now never throw a `RemoteException`, its specification has not been altered, and therefore the compiler will complain that the `RemoteException` that may be thrown by `perform()` must be caught or declared to be thrown.

Exception softening is a quick way to avoid tangling the concern of exception handling with the core logic. But be careful about overusing this, because it can lead to masking off checked exceptions that you actually should handle in the normal way by making a conscious decision to handle the exception or propagate it to the caller. We will look at another pattern to handle exceptions in chapter 8.

4.5 *Privileged aspects*

For the most part, aspects have the same standard Java access-control rules as classes. For example, an aspect normally cannot access any private members of other classes. This is usually sufficient and, in fact, desirable on most occasions.

However, in a few situations, an aspect may need to access certain data members or operations that are not exposed to outsiders. You can gain such access by marking the aspect "privileged."

Let's see how this works in the following example. The TestPrivileged class (listing 4.22) contains two private data members.

Listing 4.22   TestPrivileged.java

```
public class TestPrivileged {
    private static int _lastId = 0;
    private int _id;

    public static void main(String[] args) {
        TestPrivileged test = new TestPrivileged();
        test.method1();
    }

    public TestPrivileged() {
        _id = _lastId++;
    }

    public void method1() {
        System.out.println("TestPrivileged.method1");
    }
}
```

Consider a situation where PrivilegeTestAspect (listing 4.23) needs to access the class's private data member to perform its logic.

Listing 4.23   PrivilegeTestAspect.java

```
public aspect PrivilegeTestAspect {
    before(TestPrivileged callee) : call(void TestPrivileged.method1())
                                    && target(callee) {
        System.out.println("<PrivilegeTestAspect:before objectId=\""
                            + callee._id + "\"");
    }
}
```

If we tried to compile this code, we would get a compiler error for accessing the TestPrivileged class's private member _id:

```
> ajc *.java
F:\aspectj-book\ch04\section4.5\PrivilegeTestAspect.java:7
```

```
The field callee._id is not visible
+ callee._id + "\"");
  ^^^^^^^^^^
```

```
1 error
```

If, however, we mark the aspect as privileged (as follows), the code compiles without error and behaves as expected:

```
privileged public aspect PrivilegeTestAspect {
   ...
}
```

Now with the privileged aspect, we could access the internal state of a class without changing the class.

WARNING   Privileged aspects have access to implementation details. Therefore, exercise restraint while using this feature. If the classes change their implementation—which they are legitimately entitled to do—the aspect accessing such implementation details will need to be changed as well.

4.6 *Summary*

Einstein said, "Keep things as simple as possible, but no simpler." The AspectJ concepts and constructs presented in this and the previous chapter are consistent with this advice. You can start writing crosscutting implementations of moderate complexity without using the advanced concepts presented in this chapter; however, you may eventually face situations that require the use of these more advanced constructs to simplify your implementation significantly.

The reflection support in AspectJ provides access to the join point's static and dynamic information through a small number of interfaces. This information can be used in logging to gain more insight into the system's inner workings. The dynamic and static information together can produce an enriched log output with a simple logging aspect.

Aspect-precedence control and aspect-association choices help manage complexity in systems that have a large number of aspects. As you begin to realize the benefits of aspect-oriented programming, you may find that you are implementing more aspects to handle typical crosscutting concerns that affect the same parts of the system, such as authorization and transaction management. Aspect precedence will help you coordinate these aspects so that they function correctly. The design and implementation of off-the-shelf reusable aspects will also benefit from the aspect-association feature. Developers will now be able to create reusable aspects more effectively while knowing only minimal information about the target systems.

Using the privileged aspect feature will help in handling situations where you need to access the private members of classes. In this case, though, it is perhaps more important to understand the negative implications of using this technique.

These concepts, along with the ones presented in the earlier chapters, complete our introduction to the AspectJ language. Now that you have an understanding of the concepts and constructs in AspectJ, we are ready to dive into practical examples in areas such as logging, resource pooling, and authorization. The material presented in this and the two previous chapters will serve as a reference for you while reading the remainder of the book.

Part 2

Basic applications of AspectJ

Part 2 puts the knowledge you gained in the first part to practical use. The reason we chose the examples in these chapters is the simplicity of the AspectJ constructs used, and that they can be of benefit even if your organization has not yet fully embraced AspectJ. These examples demonstrate how you can use AspectJ to improve your personal productivity during the development phase. You can take out these aspects when you deploy your system without affecting the correctness of the core system. Of course, as we explain, you may continue using these aspects in the deployed system and gain a lot more benefits. The aspects in these examples are also sometimes referred to as *developmental* aspects.

We begin by examining a classic application of AspectJ: logging. Then we modularize the system wide policy-enforcement concern using AspectJ to create a safety net that ensures you won't get into trouble by violating programming policies. Finally, we deal with the optimization concern by using resource pooling and caching. The real benefit of optimization comes if you use these aspects in a deployment situation. However, you may simply use them to understand the bottlenecks in your application and to determine if and where pooling or caching is needed. Later, if you find that using AspectJ in your deployed application is not an option, you may hand-code those optimizations.

Monitoring techniques: logging, tracing, and profiling

This chapter covers
- Noninvasive logging using AspectJ
- Comparisons between AspectJ-based and conventional logging
- Logging idioms
- Extending logging for other purposes

Logging is one of the most common techniques that we use to understand a system's behavior. In its simplest form, logging prints messages describing the operations performed. For example, in a banking system, you would log each account transaction with information such as the nature of the transaction, the account number, and the transaction amount. During the development cycle, logging plays a role similar to a debugger. It is also usually the only reasonable choice for debugging distributed programs. By examining the log, a developer can spot unexpected system behavior and correct it. A log also helps the developer see the interaction between different parts of a system in order to detect exactly where the problem might be. Likewise, in fully deployed systems, logging acts as a diagnostic assistant for finding the root cause of the problem.

Currently used mechanisms implement logging along with the operation's core logic, which is tangled with the logging statements. Further, changing the logging strategy often requires changing many modules. Since logging is a crosscutting concern, AOP and AspectJ can help modularize it. With AspectJ, you can implement the logging mechanism independent of the core logic. AspectJ simplifies the logging task by modularizing its implementation and obviating the need to change many source files when requirements change. AspectJ not only saves a ton of code, but also establishes centralized control, consistency, and efficiency.

Implementing logging with AspectJ—a safe and relatively simple task—is a good way to learn AOP and AspectJ and to introduce it into your organization. The next time you encounter some unexpected problem that occurs infrequently, you can use AspectJ-based logging to easily monitor the operation log and isolate the problem. Once the problem is fixed, you can just as easily remove logging. In this chapter, we demonstrate how you'd use AspectJ in implementing logging. The solution presented here builds on the standard logging APIs. Throughout the book, you will see how logging aspects are used to reveal the inner workings of the solutions.

5.1 Why use AspectJ for logging?

Although we already have a few good logging toolkits, such as the standard Java logging introduced in JDK 1.4 and log4j, we still have to write log statements everywhere we need logging—and it is not a trivial task. In the next few sections, we will consider a simple example that will allow us to examine both conventional and AspectJ-based logging. We will first study the conventional solution using logging toolkits. This will help you understand the AspectJ-based solution we will present next, since it also uses these logging toolkits.

5.1.1 *A simple case in point*

Consider this simple example of shopping-cart functionality. For brevity's sake, we will implement only a handful of classes, enough to allow us to look at various facets of the logging concern. The Item class, in listing 5.1, models a shopping item that can be purchased. The Item class has methods for querying its identifier and price as well as for getting its string representation.

Listing 5.1 The Item class: models an item that can be purchased

```java
public class Item {
    private String _id;
    private float _price;

    public Item(String id, float price) {
        _id = id;
        _price = price;
    }

    public String getID() {
        return _id;
    }

    public float getPrice() {
        return _price;
    }

    public String toString() {
        return "Item: " + _id;
    }
}
```

Next, the ShoppingCart class, shown in listing 5.2, contains a list and allows us to add and remove items.

Listing 5.2 The ShoppingCart class: models a shopping cart

```java
import java.util.*;

public class ShoppingCart {
    private List _items = new Vector();

    public void addItem(Item item) {
        _items.add(item);
    }

    public void removeItem(Item item) {
```

```
        _items.remove(item);
    }

    public void empty() {
        _items.clear();
    }

    public float totalValue() {
        // unimplemented... free!
        return 0;
    }
}
```

The Inventory class, in listing 5.3, models items in the stock. The class contains methods for adding and removing items.

Listing 5.3   The Inventory class: models the shop inventory

```
import java.util.*;

public class Inventory {
    private List _items = new Vector();

    public void addItem(Item item) {
        _items.add(item);
    }

    public void removeItem(Item item) {
        _items.remove(item);
    }
}
```

The next class, ShoppingCartOperator, shown in listing 5.4, is a service class that ensures that inventory is kept up-to-date when items are added to or removed from a shopping cart. This class allows us to examine logging needs for nested operations.

Listing 5.4   ShoppingCartOperator: manages the shopping cart

```
public class ShoppingCartOperator {
    public static void addShoppingCartItem(ShoppingCart sc,
                                           Inventory inventory,
                                           Item item) {

        inventory.removeItem(item);
        sc.addItem(item);
    }
```

```
public static void removeShoppingCartItem(ShoppingCart sc,
                                          Inventory inventory,
                                          Item item) {
    sc.removeItem(item);
    inventory.addItem(item);
}
```
}

Finally, we implement a class for testing the functionality. As you can see in listing 5.5, we simply add several items to the inventory and then add a few of those items to a shopping cart.

Listing 5.5 A test class

```
public class Test {
    public static void main(String[] args) {
        Inventory inventory = new Inventory();
        Item item1 = new Item("1", 30);
        Item item2 = new Item("2", 31);
        Item item3 = new Item("3", 32);

        inventory.addItem(item1);
        inventory.addItem(item2);
        inventory.addItem(item3);

        ShoppingCart sc = new ShoppingCart();
        ShoppingCartOperator.addShoppingCartItem(sc, inventory, item1);
        ShoppingCartOperator.addShoppingCartItem(sc, inventory, item2);
    }
}
```

This collection of classes allows us to understand various logging scenarios and requirements. As with typical software systems in the initial stages, this example contains no logging—it is only in later stages that logging becomes an important concern. Now let's look at logging as it would be implemented in the conventional way; later we will see how it is implemented in AspectJ.

5.1.2 *Logging the conventional way*

To truly appreciate the advantages offered by AspectJ, let's consider implementing logging without AspectJ. Since logging is such a common requirement, APIs and libraries are available that let us perform logging consistently. Notable examples are the standard Java logging API and log4j from Apache. These toolkits provide an efficient and abstract access to the underlying logging mechanics.

They enable us to easily switch between console, socket stream, native event logging, and so forth. In addition, they allow sophisticated formatting of log messages, including the XML format. These toolkits further allow the hierarchy of logger objects and offer an easy control over the information logged.

Although these logging APIs are a significant improvement over the use of `System.out.println()` or other homegrown solutions, in the complete perspective, they provide only a part of the answer. To illustrate the additional work needed on our part, let's look at how we can add logging to the shopping cart example in section 5.1.1, using the standard Java logging API.

NOTE   When using the standard Java logging kit, we use `Logger.logp()` instead of `Logger.log()` because of an inherent problem associated with the latter. The `log()` method deduces the caller class and method by examining the call stack. With the presence of an optimizing compiler and hotspot/JIT-enabled virtual machine, the deduced caller may be an incorrect one. The same problem exists with the log4j toolkit as well (with %C, %M, %F, %L, or a combined %l layout pattern). The performance hit from using the call stack for deducing a caller is also significant. The cost involves obtaining the call stack and parsing its contents—not a trivial job. See the toolkit documentation for more details.

First, we instrument each method of the `Item` class to log the entry into it. We choose to log each method at the `Level.INFO` level because we are simply writing informational entries to the log when we enter the methods. In listing 5.6, we change the `Item` class by adding code to obtain the logger object and log each method.

Listing 5.6   The `Item` class with logging enabled

```
import java.util.logging.*;

public class Item {
    private String _id;
    private float _price;
    static Logger _logger = Logger.getLogger("trace");

    public Item(String id, float price) {
        _id = id;
        _price = price;
    }

    public String getID() {
```

```
        _logger.logp(Level.INFO, "Item", "getID", "Entering");
        return _id;
    }

    public float getPrice() {
        _logger.logp(Level.INFO, "Item", "getPrice", "Entering");
        return _price;
    }

    public String toString() {
        _logger.logp(Level.INFO, "Item", "toString", "Entering");
        return "Item: " + _id;
    }
}
```

Next, similar to what we've done with the `Item` class, we instrument logging into the `ShoppingCart` class's methods, as shown in listing 5.7. As you can see, the changes needed for logging in both classes are the same in that every method needs to make an additional call to the `logp()` method.

Listing 5.7   The `ShoppingCart` class with logging enabled

```
import java.util.*;
import java.util.logging.*;

public class ShoppingCart {
    static Logger _logger = Logger.getLogger("trace");

    private List _items = new Vector();

    public void addItem(Item item) {
        _logger.logp(Level.INFO,
                     "ShoppingCart", "addItem", "Entering");
        _items.add(item);
    }

    public void removeItem(Item item) {
        _logger.logp(Level.INFO,
                     "ShoppingCart", "removeItem", "Entering");
        _items.remove(item);
    }

    public void empty() {
        _logger.logp(Level.INFO,
                     "ShoppingCart", "empty", "Entering");
        _items.clear();
    }
```

```
      public float totalValue() {
          _logger.logp(Level.INFO,
                        "ShoppingCart", "totalValue", "Entering");
          // unimplemented... free!
          return 0;
      }
  }
```

Because the logging instrumentation for the Inventory and ShoppingCartOperator classes is very similar, we will not show the listings for those classes here.

Finally, we change the Test class to obtain the logger object and log the action of entering the Test class's only method, main(), as shown in listing 5.8.

Listing 5.8   The Test class with logging enabled

```
import java.util.logging.*;

public class Test {
    static Logger _logger = Logger.getLogger("trace");

    public static void main(String[] args) {
        _logger.logp(Level.INFO,
                      "Test", "main", "Entering");

        Inventory inventory = new Inventory();
        Item item1 = new Item("1", 30);
        Item item2 = new Item("2", 31);
        Item item3 = new Item("3", 32);

        inventory.addItem(item1);
        inventory.addItem(item2);
        inventory.addItem(item3);

        ShoppingCart sc = new ShoppingCart();
        ShoppingCartOperator.addShoppingCartItem(sc, inventory, item1);
        ShoppingCartOperator.addShoppingCartItem(sc, inventory, item2);

    }
}
```

We now have an implementation with an entry for each method to be logged, using the standard Java logging toolkit. When you compile the classes and run the program, you get output similar to this:

```
> ajc *.java
> java Test
```

```
Mar 30, 2003 12:14:20 AM Test main
INFO: Entering
Mar 30, 2003 12:14:20 AM Inventory addItem
INFO: Entering
Mar 30, 2003 12:14:20 AM Inventory addItem
INFO: Entering
Mar 30, 2003 12:14:20 AM Inventory addItem
INFO: Entering
Mar 30, 2003 12:14:20 AM ShoppingCartOperator addShoppingCartItem
INFO: Entering
Mar 30, 2003 12:14:20 AM Inventory removeItem
INFO: Entering
Mar 30, 2003 12:14:20 AM ShoppingCart addItem
INFO: Entering
Mar 30, 2003 12:14:20 AM ShoppingCartOperator addShoppingCartItem
INFO: Entering
Mar 30, 2003 12:14:20 AM Inventory removeItem
INFO: Entering
Mar 30, 2003 12:14:20 AM ShoppingCart addItem
INFO: Entering
```

This was quite a task, right? Granted, the job was mostly mechanical. You probably copied and pasted code and modified the arguments to `logp()` methods. We hope you did a perfect job of changing each argument correctly; if not, you'll end up with a logging message that is inconsistent with the operation being performed. Now consider how long it would take to introduce logging in a real system with hundreds of classes. How sure could you be that the methods would log the right information?

5.1.3 *Logging the aspect-oriented way*

Now let's use AspectJ to introduce the logging functionality into each method in all the classes in the original example. As you will see, with AspectJ-based logging, we don't have to modify our classes. All we need to do is add the aspect in listing 5.9 to our system, and compile it with the classes (from listings 5.1 through 5.5) using the AspectJ compiler. That's it! We now have tons of output to impress our colleagues.

> **Listing 5.9   TraceAspect performing the same job**

```
import java.util.logging.*;
import org.aspectj.lang.*;

public aspect TraceAspect {
    private Logger _logger = Logger.getLogger("trace");

    pointcut traceMethods()
        : execution(* *.*(..)) && !within(TraceAspect);
```

```
    before() : traceMethods() {
        Signature sig = thisJoinPointStaticPart.getSignature();
        _logger.logp(Level.INFO, sig.getDeclaringType().getName(),
                    sig.getName(), "Entering");
    }
}
```

When we compile this aspect together with the shopping cart classes and run the test program, we get output similar to this:

```
> ajc *.java
> java Test
Mar 30, 2003 12:16:15 AM Test main
INFO: Entering
Mar 30, 2003 12:16:16 AM Inventory addItem
INFO: Entering
Mar 30, 2003 12:16:16 AM Inventory addItem
INFO: Entering
Mar 30, 2003 12:16:16 AM Inventory addItem
INFO: Entering
Mar 30, 2003 12:16:16 AM ShoppingCartOperator addShoppingCartItem
INFO: Entering
Mar 30, 2003 12:16:16 AM Inventory removeItem
INFO: Entering
Mar 30, 2003 12:16:16 AM ShoppingCart addItem
INFO: Entering
Mar 30, 2003 12:16:16 AM ShoppingCartOperator addShoppingCartItem
INFO: Entering
Mar 30, 2003 12:16:16 AM Inventory removeItem
INFO: Entering
Mar 30, 2003 12:16:16 AM ShoppingCart addItem
INFO: Entering
```

Observe the sheer amount of code we saved with AspectJ! Such modularization is possible because of AOP and AspectJ's support for programming crosscutting concerns. However, saved coding effort is not the only benefit of using AspectJ. Later in this chapter, we will explore all the details of logging using AspectJ and the benefits it offers.

5.2 *What's wrong with conventional logging*

Now that you have seen logging using conventional and AspectJ-based techniques, let's look at the shortcomings of conventional solutions. Figure 5.1 illustrates the overall schematic of current logging solutions. Every place that needs to log an event needs to *explicitly* invoke a call to the log() method of an appropriate logger.

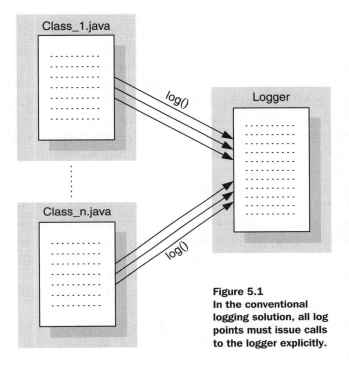

**Figure 5.1
In the conventional
logging solution, all log
points must issue calls
to the logger explicitly.**

As you can see, the logging calls will be all over the core modules. When a new module is added to the system, all of its methods that need logging must be instrumented. Such instrumentation is *invasive,* causing the tangling of the core concerns with the logging concern. Further, if you ever happen to change the logging toolkit to a different API, you need to revisit every logging statement and modify it.

Consistency is the single most important requirement of logging. It means that if the logging specification requires that certain kinds of operations be logged, then the implementation must log *every* invocation of those operations. When things go wrong in a system, doubting the logging consistency is probably the last thing you want to do. Missed logging calls can make output hard to understand and sometimes useless. Achieving consistency using conventional logging is a lofty goal, and while systems can attain it initially, it requires continuing vigilance to keep it so. For example, if you add new classes to the system or new methods in existing classes, you must ensure that they implement logging that matches the current logging strategy.

5.3 *The beauty of AspectJ-based logging*

Although logging APIs solve quite a few problems, as you have just seen they also leave some gaps. The limitations are not a result of the logging APIs or their implementations; rather, they stem from the fundamental limitations of object-oriented programming, which require embedding the logging invocations in each module. AOP and AspectJ overcome those limitations. AspectJ easily implements the invocation of logging statements from all the log points. The beauty is that you do not need to actually instrument any log points; writing an aspect does it automatically. Further, since there is a central place to control logging operations, you achieve consistency easily.

The most fundamental difference between conventional logging and AspectJ-based logging is modularization of the logging concern. Instead of writing modules that implement core concepts in addition to invoking logging operations, with AspectJ you write a few aspects that advise the execution of the operations in the core modules to perform the logging. That way, the core modules do not carry any logging-related code. By modularizing, you separate the logging concern from the core concerns.

The solution presented here builds on available logging toolkits. For the final act of logging, you can use any of the toolkits available. AspectJ comes into the picture to intercept the operations, collect the context, and form a message to pass on to the underlying logging system. Note that you do not have to use a special-purpose logging toolkit to perform logging; using `System.out` and `System.err` or any print stream is a legitimate choice, although perhaps a poor one. Figure 5.2 shows the overview of AspectJ-based logging.

With AspectJ-based logging, the logger aspect separates the core modules and the logger object. Instead of the core modules' embedding the `log()` method invocations in their source code, the logger aspect weaves the logging invocations into the core modules when they are needed. AspectJ-based logging reverses the dependency between the core modules and the logger; it is the aspect that encodes how the operations in the core modules are logged instead of each core module deciding for itself.

5.4 *Developing logging and tracing aspects*

Tracing is a special form of logging where the entry and/or exit of selected methods are logged. Tracing is useful during the development phase in order to understand system behavior, especially when a debugger is not an option, either

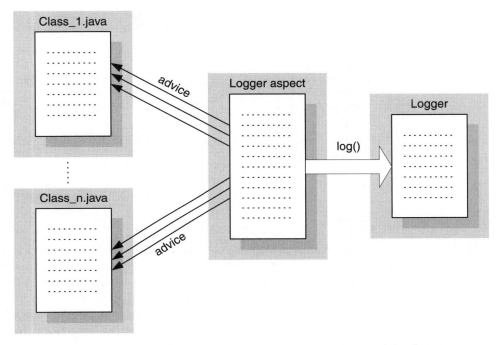

Figure 5.2   An overall schematic of AspectJ-based logging. Compare this with figure 5.1. Specifically note the reversal of arrows to Class_1.java and Class_n.java.

due to the speed at which the activities occur or due to the distributed nature of the application. In this section, we will examine method tracing and exception logging. We will also use these examples to show how you can accomplish the task using different logging toolkits. These snippets will enable you to try logging for your own system.

5.4.1 *Method call tracing*

Let's develop an aspect that will enable tracing method calls in any system. Simply compile this aspect with the rest of the code and you will see the logging of every method call. No changes will be needed in any of your classes. Our first version, in listing 5.10, uses System.out as the logging stream.

Listing 5.10 Tracing methods: the first version, using `System.out` as the logging stream

```
import org.aspectj.lang.*;

public aspect TraceAspectV1 {
    pointcut traceMethods()
        : (execution(* *.*(..))
        || execution(*.new(..))) && !within(TraceAspectV1);

    before() : traceMethods() {
        Signature sig = thisJoinPointStaticPart.getSignature();
        System.out.println("Entering ["
                        + sig.getDeclaringType().getName() + "."
                        + sig.getName() + "]");
    }
}
```

❶ **Traced methods pointcut**

❷ **Log advice**

❶ The `traceMethods()` pointcut captures the calls to methods that need tracing—in our case, it will be all the methods in the system. The `!within(TraceAspectV1)` part helps us avoid recursion caused by tracing method calls in the aspect itself. Once we compile the aspect along with the core modules, a log message will print to `System.out` before any method is executed. We could also, if required, easily produce a log message after the method execution by adding an after advice.

❷ We use `thisJoinPointStaticPart` to get information about the method captured by the pointcut. The method `getSignature()` on `thisJoinPointStaticPart` returns the signature of the captured method. We use this object to get the name of the class and method to form and print the log message. Note that we could have used `thisJoinPoint`, but using `thisJoinPointStaticPart` instead gives better performance using fewer resources, and in our case, the information contained in it is sufficient. See chapter 4 for detailed information about using reflection in an advice body.

When we run this aspect with our shopping cart example, we get the following output:

```
> ajc *.java
> java Test
Entering [Test.main]
Entering [Inventory.<init>]
Entering [Item.<init>]
Entering [Item.<init>]
Entering [Item.<init>]
Entering [Inventory.addItem]
Entering [Inventory.addItem]
Entering [Inventory.addItem]
Entering [ShoppingCart.<init>]
```

```
Entering [ShoppingCartOperator.addShoppingCartItem]
Entering [Inventory.removeItem]
Entering [ShoppingCart.addItem]
Entering [ShoppingCartOperator.addShoppingCartItem]
Entering [Inventory.removeItem]
Entering [ShoppingCart.addItem]
```

Typically, you will want to limit the list of traced methods to make log output more understandable and avoid degrading the performance. We can achieve this goal by simply modifying the `traceMethods()` pointcut to limit the tracing to certain packages, classes, or methods with a particular signature, as shown in the following snippet:

```
pointcut traceMethods()
    : (execution(* com.manning.model..*.*(..))
       || execution(com.manning.model..*.new(..))
       || execution(* com.manning.ui.*.*(..))
       || execution(com.manning.ui.*.new(..))
       || execution(* com.manning.util.ComplexComputation.*(..))
       || execution(com.manning.util.ComplexComputation.new(..))
       || execution(* com.manning.database.Database.set*(..)))
    && !within(TraceAspectV1);
```

This modified pointcut ensures that only calls to the methods in the following packages get traced: methods in `com.manning.model` and its subpackages (note the `..` between `model` and `*`), methods in the `com.manning.ui` package but not its subpackages, methods in the `com.manning.util.ComplexComputation` class, and methods with a name starting in `set` in `com.manning.database.Database`. (See chapter 3, tables 3.3 and 3.4, for more information on using wildcards to capture methods and constructors.) In a similar way, you may use `within()` and `within-code()` pointcuts to limit logging for join points occurring in the lexical scope of classes and methods. The `cflow()` and `cflowbelow()` pointcuts are useful when you want to perform logging only for the operations invoked from a certain subsystem. The control-flow based pointcuts are also useful in limiting logging to only the top-level operation in a recursive call stack.

Now let's modify the aspect to use the standard Java logging toolkit so that we can use the features it offers, such as the ability to dynamically modify the logging level. Note that we can introduce such a change to the whole system by modifying just a few lines in one aspect. Without AspectJ, we would have to modify every log statement in the system. In listing 5.11, we show how you can use the standard logging toolkit to perform logging that is identical in functionality to that in listing 5.10.

Listing 5.11 Tracing methods: the second version, using the standard logging toolkit

```
import java.util.logging.*;
import org.aspectj.lang.*;

public aspect TraceAspectV2 {                               Obtaining
    private Logger _logger = Logger.getLogger("trace");     the logger
                                                            object
    TraceAspectV2() {
        _logger.setLevel(Level.ALL);            Initializing the
    }                                           log level

    pointcut traceMethods()
        : (execution(* *.*(..))
            || execution(*.new(..))) && !within(TraceAspectV2);

    before() : traceMethods() {
        if (_logger.isLoggable(Level.INFO)) {
            Signature sig = thisJoinPointStaticPart.getSignature();
            _logger.logp(Level.INFO,
                    sig.getDeclaringType().getName(),
                    sig.getName(),              Using logging
                    "Entering");                methods
        }
    }
}
```

The aspect in listing 5.11 contains a logger object, and the constructor sets its logging level to an initial value. This logging level is only the initial level; any part of the system can later get hold of the "trace" logger object using `Logger.getLogger("trace")` and modify its level. Therefore, before we perform the actual logging, advice to the `traceMethods()` pointcut first checks if the current logging level is such that the `logp()` method call will result in a log message. It does this by calling `isLoggable()`. The check for the log level is needed for performance reasons only. It ensures that we do not perform a wasteful operation in assembling the log message if the message will not be logged. To perform the actual logging, we invoke the `logp()` method on the logger object with the appropriate log message and caller information.

In section 5.1.2, we discussed why we want to use the `logp()` method to log messages instead of `log()`. Another reason to use `logp()` is that calling the `log()` method would cause the logging kit to deduce that the caller is the advice instead of the advised method. This happens because the `log()` method uses the call stack to infer the caller. In this example, the actual caller is the advice, but we want the *real* caller of the logged method (that triggered the advice) to be shown in the log message and not the advice—which just happens to be the caller due to the addition of the logger aspect.

We have a robust mechanism in AspectJ that addresses all these issues. It is the thisJoinPointStaticPart object, which contains information about the captured join point's class, method, precise source location, and so forth. The compiler creates this information at compile time, and neither compiler optimization nor the presence of the JIT/hotspot virtual machine alters this information. We use the information contained in thisJoinPointStaticPart to obtain the method and class name of the logged method. Please refer to chapter 4 (section 4.1) for more details on using thisJoinPointStaticPart.

Compiling this aspect with the shopping cart source code and running the Test class results in output similar to this:

```
> ajc *.java
> java Test
Mar 30, 2003 12:56:18 AM Test main
INFO: Entering
Mar 30, 2003 12:56:18 AM Inventory <init>
INFO: Entering
Mar 30, 2003 12:56:18 AM Item <init>
INFO: Entering
Mar 30, 2003 12:56:18 AM Item <init>
INFO: Entering
Mar 30, 2003 12:56:18 AM Item <init>
INFO: Entering
Mar 30, 2003 12:56:18 AM Inventory addItem
INFO: Entering
Mar 30, 2003 12:56:18 AM Inventory addItem
INFO: Entering
Mar 30, 2003 12:56:18 AM Inventory addItem
INFO: Entering
Mar 30, 2003 12:56:18 AM ShoppingCart <init>
INFO: Entering
Mar 30, 2003 12:56:18 AM ShoppingCartOperator addShoppingCartItem
INFO: Entering
Mar 30, 2003 12:56:18 AM Inventory removeItem
INFO: Entering
Mar 30, 2003 12:56:18 AM ShoppingCart addItem
INFO: Entering
Mar 30, 2003 12:56:18 AM ShoppingCartOperator addShoppingCartItem
INFO: Entering
Mar 30, 2003 12:56:18 AM Inventory removeItem
INFO: Entering
Mar 30, 2003 12:56:18 AM ShoppingCart addItem
INFO: Entering
```

The output shows a message being logged as soon as the execution of the program enters each method and constructor in the system. The toolkit also prints a timestamp corresponding to each of the logged messages.

Finally, let's modify our aspect to use the log4j toolkit from Apache. This example, like the earlier one, shows how easy it is to switch from one logging toolkit to another when you use AspectJ for logging. Listing 5.12 shows the same logging functionality implemented using the log4j logging toolkit instead of the standard Java logging toolkit.

Listing 5.12 Tracing methods: the third version, using the log4j toolkit

```
import org.apache.log4j.*;
import org.aspectj.lang.*;

public aspect TraceAspectV3 {
    Logger _logger = Logger.getLogger("trace");

    TraceAspectV3() {
        _logger.setLevel(Level.ALL);
    }

    pointcut traceMethods()
        : (execution(* *.*(..))
           || execution(*.new(..))) && !within(TraceAspectV3);

    before() : traceMethods() {
        if (_logger.isEnabledFor(Level.INFO)) {
            Signature sig = thisJoinPointStaticPart.getSignature();
            _logger.log(Level.INFO,
                        "Entering ["
                        + sig.getDeclaringType().getName() + "."
                        + sig.getName() + "]");
        }
    }
}
```

The API for both toolkits is the same for the most part. Therefore, we need to change only a few statements from our earlier version (the changes appear in bold in the listing). Note that log4j does not have a `logp()` method; instead, the `log()` method, along with the use of properties file, offers the equivalent functionality. We encode the caller information in the message that is passed as an argument to the `log()` method call. log4j requires a properties file that specifies the information to be logged and the format for each log message. For the purpose of this test, we used the following properties file (log4j.properties) to configure log4j:

```
log4j.rootCategory=DEBUG, dest1
log4j.appender.dest1=org.apache.log4j.ConsoleAppender
log4j.appender.dest1.layout=org.apache.log4j.PatternLayout
```

When we compile the aspect in listing 5.12 with the rest of our classes and run the Test class, we see the following output:

```
> ajc *.java
> java Test
Entering [Test.main]
Entering [Inventory.<init>]
Entering [Item.<init>]
Entering [Item.<init>]
Entering [Item.<init>]
Entering [Inventory.addItem]
Entering [Inventory.addItem]
Entering [Inventory.addItem]
Entering [ShoppingCart.<init>]
Entering [ShoppingCartOperator.addShoppingCartItem]
Entering [Inventory.removeItem]
Entering [ShoppingCart.addItem]
Entering [ShoppingCartOperator.addShoppingCartItem]
Entering [Inventory.removeItem]
Entering [ShoppingCart.addItem]
```

The output is similar to that using the standard Java logging toolkit. You can control the information being logged, such as the addition of a timestamp or the format of the log messages, by modifying the properties file. Please refer to the log4j documentation for more details.

5.4.2 *Exceptions logging*

Because exception throwing is usually considered an important event in the system, logging such occurrences is typically desirable. Exception logging is an extension of the tracing concept, except the focus is on exceptional conditions in a program rather than execution of methods. The conventional way to log exceptions is to surround the interesting parts of code with a try/catch block and instrument each catch block with a log statement. With AspectJ, it is possible to log exceptions thrown by a method without any modification to the original code.

In this section, we develop an aspect that enables the logging of thrown exceptions in the system. As in the earlier section, we later modify the aspect to use standard Java logging and log4j toolkit. Let's begin with listing 5.13. This aspect can log any method in the system that is returned by throwing an exception. The version in listing 5.13 uses the good old System.err as the logging stream.

Listing 5.13   Logging exception: the first version, using `System.err` as the logging stream

```
import org.aspectj.lang.*;

public aspect ExceptionLoggerAspectV1 {
    pointcut exceptionLogMethods()
        : call(* *.*(..)) &&
          !within(ExceptionLoggerAspectV1);

    after() throwing(Throwable ex) : exceptionLogMethods() {
        Signature sig = thisJoinPointStaticPart.getSignature();
        System.err.println("Exception logger aspect ["
                           + sig.getDeclaringType().getName() + "."
                           + sig.getName() + "]");
        ex.printStackTrace(System.err);
    }
}
```

❶ **Traced method pointcut**

❷ **Advice that logs any exception thrown**

❶ The `exceptionLogMethods()` pointcut captures all the methods that need exception logging. Here, we are defining this as a call to any method in the system. You can modify this pointcut to include a subset of methods, as described in section 5.4.1.

❷ The after throwing advice collects the thrown object as context. The advice uses `thisJoinPointStaticPart` to log the information about captured join points. Finally, it prints the stack trace of the thrown exception.

Let's write a simple program (listing 5.14) to test our aspect.

Listing 5.14   TestException.java: a program that tests exception logging

```
public class TestException {
    public static void main(String[] args) {
        perform();
    }

    public static void perform() {
        Object nullObj = null;
        nullObj.toString();
    }
}
```

When we compile the `TestException` class along with `ExceptionLoggerAspectV1` and run the test program, we get the following output:

```
> ajc *.java
> java TestException
Exception logger aspect [java.lang.Object.toString]
```

```
java.lang.NullPointerException
        at TestException.perform(TestException.java:8)
        at TestException.main(TestException.java:3)
Exception logger aspect [TestException.perform]
java.lang.NullPointerException
        at TestException.perform(TestException.java:8)
        at TestException.main(TestException.java:3)
Exception in thread "main" java.lang.NullPointerException
        at TestException.perform(TestException.java:8)
        at TestException.main(TestException.java:3)
```

The output shows that `NullPointerException`, which was thrown due to calling the `toString()` method on a null object inside the `perform()` method, is logged. Since this exception isn't caught by the `perform()` method, the exception is propagated to the caller. The resulting exception thrown by `perform()` is also logged by our aspect.

Since you are more likely to use one of the available logging toolkits, listing 5.15 shows the second version of the same aspect, this time using the standard Java logging toolkit. The portions in bold reflect changes compared to listing 5.14.

Listing 5.15 Logging exception: second version, using Java's standard logging toolkit

```java
import java.util.logging.*;
import org.aspectj.lang.*;

public aspect ExceptionLoggerAspectV2 {
    Logger _logger = Logger.getLogger("exceptions");

    ExceptionLoggerAspectV2() {
        _logger.setLevel(Level.ALL);
    }

    pointcut exceptionLogMethods()
        : call(* *.*(..))  && !within(ExceptionLoggerAspectV2);

    after() throwing(Throwable ex) : exceptionLogMethods() {
        if (_logger.isLoggable(Level.WARNING)) {
            Signature sig = thisJoinPointStaticPart.getSignature();
            _logger.logp(Level.WARNING,
                        sig.getDeclaringType().getName(),
                        sig.getName(),
                        "Exception logger aspect", ex);
        }
    }
}
```

The aspect in listing 5.15 is similar to the one in listing 5.13. We log the exception using the `Logger.logp()` method that takes a `Throwable` object as an argument. As you can see in the listing, to switch from `System.err` to the standard Java logging toolkit we only need to modify the aspect. When we compile the `TestException` class with the aspect in listing 5.15 and run the test program, we get the following output:

```
> ajc *.java
> java TestException
Feb 26, 2003 12:05:19 AM java.lang.Object toString
WARNING: Exception logger aspect
java.lang.NullPointerException
        at TestException.perform(TestException.java:8)
        at TestException.main(TestException.java:3)
Feb 26, 2003 12:05:19 AM TestException perform
WARNING: Exception logger aspect
java.lang.NullPointerException
        at TestException.perform(TestException.java:8)
        at TestException.main(TestException.java:3)
Exception in thread "main" java.lang.NullPointerException
        at TestException.perform(TestException.java:8)
        at TestException.main(TestException.java:3)
```

The output is similar to that using `System.err` except for the addition of timestamps and the formatting of the message.

Finally, let's modify our aspect to use the log4j toolkit, since it is another logging toolkit available for your use. Listing 5.16 shows that changing the underlying logging toolkit is easy with AspectJ. The portions in bold indicate changes compared to listing 5.15.

Listing 5.16   Logging exception: third version, using the log4j toolkit

```java
import org.apache.log4j.*;
import org.aspectj.lang.*;

public aspect ExceptionLoggerAspectV3 {
    Logger _logger = Logger.getLogger("exceptions");

    ExceptionLoggerAspectV3() {
        _logger.setLevel(Level.ALL);
    }

    pointcut exceptionLogMethods()
        : call(* *.*(..)) && !within(ExceptionLoggerAspectV3);

    after() throwing(Throwable ex) : exceptionLogMethods() {
        if (_logger.isEnabledFor(Level.ERROR)) {
            Signature sig = thisJoinPointStaticPart.getSignature();
            _logger.log(Level.ERROR,
                    "Exception logger aspect ["
```

```
                            + sig.getDeclaringType().getName() + "."
                            + sig.getName() + "]", ex);
              }
          }
      }
```

All we needed to modify from listing 5.15 was the advice for using the equivalent API for log4j instead of the standard Java logging toolkit's API. When we compile `TestException` with this aspect and run the test program, we get the following output, which is similar to the output from the aspects using `System.err` and the standard Java logging toolkit (we use the same log4j.properties from section 5.4.1):

```
> ajc *.java
> java TestException
Exception logger aspect [java.lang.Object.toString]
java.lang.NullPointerException
        at TestException.perform(TestException.java:8)
        at TestException.main(TestException.java:3)
Exception logger aspect [TestException.perform]
java.lang.NullPointerException
        at TestException.perform(TestException.java:8)
        at TestException.main(TestException.java:3)
Exception in thread "main" java.lang.NullPointerException
        at TestException.perform(TestException.java:8)
        at TestException.main(TestException.java:3)
```

These examples show how writing a simple aspect can ensure consistent logging and how noninvasive it is to change the underlying toolkit. The modularization of the crosscutting concern of logging helps solve one part of the architect's dilemma discussed in chapter 1; you no longer have to make an upfront decision about the logging toolkit and logging strategy. This is important because even if you make such a decision in the beginning, you may have to change your mind if a new technology that better suits your needs becomes available. With AspectJ, such a change in toolkits necessitates only local changes to the logging aspects, leaving the rest of your system intact.

5.5 *Common logging idioms*

Idioms are solutions to simple, recurring problems. While developing a logging solution, you will encounter a few common issues, such as logging the operation's context, beautifying the output for human consumption, considering the precedence for other aspects, and changing the logging toolkit. In this section, we discuss common idioms that should guide you in your attempts to introduce logging in your system.

5.5.1 *Logging the method parameters*

Often, you not only want to log the method calls but also the invoked object and
the method parameters. Implementing this requirement is easily accomplished
by using the `thisJoinPoint` reference. In each advice body, a special `thisJoin-
Point` object is available that contains the information about the captured join
point and its associated context.

The aspect in listing 5.17 modifies the `TraceAspectV1`'s before advice to also
log the method parameters.

Listing 5.17   TraceAspectV1.java: modified to log method parameters

```java
import org.aspectj.lang.*;

public aspect TraceAspectV1 {                                    Augment
    pointcut traceMethods()                                      pointcut
        : (execution(* *.*(..))                              that avoids
        || execution(*.new(..))) && !within(TraceAspectV1);     infinite
                                                                recursion
    before() : traceMethods()&& !execution(String *.toString()){   ◄──┘
        Signature sig = thisJoinPointStaticPart.getSignature();

        System.err.println("Entering ["
                        + sig.getDeclaringType().getName() + "."
                        + sig.getName() + "]"
                        + createParameterMessage(thisJoinPoint));
    }
                                            Formatting of the log message
    private String createParameterMessage(JoinPoint joinPoint) {   ◄──┘
        StringBuffer paramBuffer = new StringBuffer("\n\t[This: ");
        paramBuffer.append(joinPoint.getThis());

        Object[] arguments = joinPoint.getArgs();
        paramBuffer.append("]\n\t[Args: (");
        for (int length = arguments.length, i = 0; i < length; ++i) {
            Object argument = arguments[i];
            paramBuffer.append(argument);
            if (i != length-1) {
                paramBuffer.append(',');
            }
        }
        paramBuffer.append(")]");
        return paramBuffer.toString();
    }
}
```

❶ We use the `!execution(String *.toString())` pointcut to avoid the recursion that will be caused by the execution of the `toString()` methods. Without this pointcut, the logger will prepare the parameter string in `createParameter-Message()` when it calls `toString()` for each object. However, when `toString()` executes, it first attempts to log the operation, and the logger will prepare a parameter string for it again when it calls `toString()` on the same object, and so on, causing an infinite recursion. By avoiding the join points for `toString()` execution, we avoid infinite recursion, leading to a stack overflow. Note that the `!within(TraceAspectV1)` pointcut is not sufficient here because it will only capture the *calls* to `toString()` methods; the execution of the methods will still be advised.

❷ The `createParameterMessage()` helper method returns a formatted string containing the object and arguments.

Now when we compile the classes in our shopping cart example with this aspect and execute the `Test` class, the output of logging includes the invoked object and the method parameters, similar to this output:

```
> ajc *.java
> java Test
Entering [Test.main]
        [This: null]
        [Args: ([Ljava.lang.String;@1eed786)]
Entering [Inventory.<init>]
        [This: Inventory@e48e1b]
        [Args: ()]
Entering [Item.<init>]
        [This: Item: null]
        [Args: (1,30.0)]
Entering [Item.<init>]
        [This: Item: null]
        [Args: (2,31.0)]
Entering [Item.<init>]
        [This: Item: null]
        [Args: (3,32.0)]
Entering [Inventory.addItem]
        [This: Inventory@e48e1b]
        [Args: (Item: 1)]
Entering [Inventory.addItem]
        [This: Inventory@e48e1b]
        [Args: (Item: 2)]
Entering [Inventory.addItem]
        [This: Inventory@e48e1b]
        [Args: (Item: 3)]
Entering [ShoppingCart.<init>]
        [This: ShoppingCart@30c221]
        [Args: ()]
```

```
Entering [ShoppingCartOperator.addShoppingCartItem]
        [This: null]
        [Args: (ShoppingCart@30c221,Inventory@e48e1b,Item: 1)]
Entering [Inventory.removeItem]
        [This: Inventory@e48e1b]
        [Args: (Item: 1)]
Entering [ShoppingCart.addItem]
        [This: ShoppingCart@30c221]
        [Args: (Item: 1)]
Entering [ShoppingCartOperator.addShoppingCartItem]
        [This: null]
        [Args: (ShoppingCart@30c221,Inventory@e48e1b,Item: 2)]
Entering [Inventory.removeItem]
        [This: Inventory@e48e1b]
        [Args: (Item: 2)]
Entering [ShoppingCart.addItem]
        [This: ShoppingCart@30c221]
        [Args: (Item: 2)
```

NOTE TO STANDARD JAVA LOGGING KIT USERS	You cannot easily log the method arguments if you use the version of the `Logger.logp()` method that takes an arbitrary `Object` array as an argument. The reason is that the method requires that you supply the message in the format specified by the `MessageFormat` class. You can implement this if you know the method argument types, position, and count. However, this is not very practical for a general-purpose logging scheme. The solution, therefore, is to build your own message that contains the argument information before you pass it to the logger object.

5.5.2 *Indenting the log statements*

With nested operations, it is desirable that the logging mimic the operation depth. For stream output, this usually means indenting the log messages based on their depth in the transaction. Without such information, the output is hard to decipher.

The basic idea behind implementing the indentation functionality is simple: keep a state corresponding to the call depth of the currently executing operation and prefix each log message with spaces proportionate to the call depth. The concrete implementation of this idea can be implemented in various ways. You have already seen one way in chapter 2, listing 2.9. In this section, we examine another implementation that offers the advantage of reusability.

The abstract aspect shown in listing 5.18 encapsulates the indentation functionality. By simply extending this aspect, a logging aspect can introduce the indentation effect.

Listing 5.18 IndentedLogging.java: a reusable base aspect to get indentation behavior

```java
package logging;

public abstract aspect IndentedLogging {
    protected int _indentationLevel = 0;

    protected abstract pointcut loggedOperations();

    before() : loggedOperations() {
        _indentationLevel++;
    }

    after() : loggedOperations() {
        _indentationLevel--;
    }

    before() : call(* java.io.PrintStream.println(..))
        && within(IndentedLogging+) {
        for (int i = 0, spaces = _indentationLevel * 4;
            i < spaces; ++i) {
            System.out.print(" ");
        }
    }
}
```

The `IndentedLogging` aspect declares an abstract pointcut, `loggedOperations()`, that the subaspects should define to capture the operations they are logging. The `IndentedLogging` aspect simply increments the indentation level before executing the join points captured by `loggedOperations()` and decrements after their execution. By providing a before advice to the `java.io.PrintStream.println()` method and appending spaces corresponding to the indentation level to the `System.out` stream, we get the indentation effect. If you are using a logging kit instead of `System.out`, you will want to modify this advice, perhaps replacing it with an around advice, to get the indentation effect.

Now let's change the aspect, `TraceAspectV1`, from listing 5.10 so that the log output will be indented. Listing 5.19 modifies the aspect by making it a subaspect of `IndentedLogging` that indents the log messages according to the call depth.

Listing 5.19 TraceAspectV4.java: adding the indentation effect to the log

```java
import org.aspectj.lang.*;

import logging.*;

public aspect TraceAspectV4 extends IndentedLogging {
```

```
     protected pointcut loggedOperations()
         : (execution(* *.*(..))
           || execution(*.new(..))) && !within(IndentedLogging+);

     before() : loggedOperations() {
         Signature sig = thisJoinPointStaticPart.getSignature();
         System.out.println("Entering ["
                             + sig.getDeclaringType().getName() + "."
                             + sig.getName() + "]");
     }
 }
```

In addition to extending the abstract aspect `IndentedLogging`, the aspect in listing 5.19 renames the `tracedMethods()` pointcut to `loggedOperations()` to match the abstract pointcut in `IndentedLogging`.

When we compile all the classes and aspects together and run the test program, we get the following output:

```
> ajc *.java logging\IndentedLogging.java
> java Test
Entering [Test.main]
    Entering [Inventory.<init>]
    Entering [Item.<init>]
    Entering [Item.<init>]
    Entering [Item.<init>]
    Entering [Inventory.addItem]
    Entering [Inventory.addItem]
    Entering [Inventory.addItem]
    Entering [ShoppingCart.<init>]
    Entering [ShoppingCartOperator.addShoppingCartItem]
        Entering [Inventory.removeItem]
        Entering [ShoppingCart.addItem]
    Entering [ShoppingCartOperator.addShoppingCartItem]
        Entering [Inventory.removeItem]
        Entering [ShoppingCart.addItem]
```

By simply extending a reusable aspect, we have the required indentation effort. You will see additional examples of the `IndentedLogging` aspect in part 3.

5.5.3 *Aspect precedence*

Generally, you want the logging aspects to have the highest precedence. This way, the logging aspect's before advice executes before any of the other aspects' before advice, and the logging aspect's after advice executes after the other aspects' after advice. You can implement this requirement by making the logging aspects dominate all other aspects by using the following construct:

```
declare precedence LoggingAspect, *;
```

If multiple logging aspects are present and if they dominate all other aspects, the precedence between the logging aspects themselves is not determined. If such precedence between logging aspects is important to your system, you can make certain logging aspects dominate other specific logging aspects. However, this can get complex. A better solution is to design the logging aspects so that only one logging aspect advises each join point. In practice, you rarely need such precise control over the logging aspect precedence.

5.5.4 *Changing the underlying logging mechanism*

In most situations, you will be using just one logging API. However, in certain situations you may need to support multiple underlying logging APIs. One common situation calling for such support is during the development of components, when you may need to support the possibility of multiple logging packages.

The simplest solution is to use a wrapper logging toolkit such as the Jakarta Commons Logging toolkit (see http://jakarta.apache.org/commons/logging.html). This kit provides an abstract logging API and delegates the actual logging to standard Java logging toolkit, log4j, or `System.out`.

The other solution is to separate the definition of logging join points and the advice to those join points. You can then write multiple aspects advising the join points in a toolkit-specific manner. In building the system, you can then include the aspects of the required toolkit. Any changes to the definition of logging join points are isolated from the logging toolkit implementation.

Yet another choice is to use around advice to bridge between multiple APIs. With such a style, you advise each invocation of the source logging method and bypass it with the call to the target logging kit. You need only one such bridge for all of the projects. However, this approach is more complex, and you should not consider it as your first choice.

5.5.5 *Using logging in a multithreaded environment*

If a logger is shared among multiple threads, the log messages from each thread will be intertwined, making the output difficult to analyze. A simple solution is to keep a logger associated with each thread object. There are many ways to manage this association. One way is to keep the logger in a thread-specific storage provided by the `ThreadLocal` class. In the logging advice, you first check for a logger object associated with the current thread. If no such logger is present, you create a new one and make the association. In either case, you use the thread-specific logger to log the messages.

You must take special care to ensure that loggers corresponding to a defunct thread do not loiter around. If you use thread-local storage, when the thread terminates, the associated logger no longer has a strong reference to reach it (unless some other part of the system also keeps a reference to it), and it becomes a candidate for garbage collection. In other cases, you could advise the thread termination join point to make the logger a candidate for garbage collection.

5.6 Extending logging for other usage

With very little modification, the basic logging mechanism can be used for other purposes, such as testing, profiling, recovering lost data, and logging user actions. AspectJ-based solutions for such requirements offer essentially the same benefits that we discussed for logging: modularization, noninvasiveness, ease of evolution, and ease of understanding. Let's look at a couple of other ways you can extend the basic logging mechanism.

5.6.1 Testing

One way to ensure the accuracy of programs is to use regression testing, in which the testing apparatus checks for the preservation of the output of a specified set of input across all iterations of a module's evolution. You provide a set of input that covers a sufficient range of possible options. Each time you test the program, you use this same input, and the output is expected to be the same. With AspectJ, you can log the output as well as the intermediate steps that have been taken while performing the operation. Then you can compare the actual log with the expected log to check for the preservation of the system behavior.

Reproducing bugs is often a hard task—you see a bug, but you do not know what actions led to it. Often, the least-suspected step is the cause of the bug. During the QA phase, you can enable the system to log the steps that are followed during testing. When a bug appears, you can get a much better idea about the cause of the bug by looking at the log of the operations performed prior to encountering the bug. In the final shipped product, you can simply remove the logging aspect by excluding it from the final build. Of course, you can implement all this functionality using traditional techniques, which require embedding logging into each module.

5.6.2 *Profiling*

Profiling a system means collecting the information about the time spent by each operation in the system. By extending the core AspectJ-based logging concepts, you can create profiling functionality without needing invasive changes.

The conventional profiling solutions often depend on using specific tools, and they sometimes need to execute the applications in a special VM in order to gather the profile data. These requirements make profiling practical only in the implementation phase, and it is seldom used in a deployed situation. With AspectJ-based profiling, you can use profiling in the deployed system as well, without the need for any special tools or VM, just by embedding the profiling logic in separate aspects. A typical profiling process often needs to gradually focus on certain parts of the system to gather more detailed timing information. The modular, plug-and-play approach of AspectJ adds noninvasive modification to the focus of profiling by limiting the modification to only the profiling aspect. For example, you can change the list of classes and methods that will be profiled by modifying the pointcuts in the profile aspect.

A simple way to implement profiling is to augment the invocation timestamp of each log message. You will need to provide both before and after advice to the profiled methods and log their invocation time. Although you could also use an around advice, using both before and after advice is often cheaper due to the cost associated with the creation of the around advice and the unwrapping of the return value. You can use the call depth idea presented in section 5.5.2 to ensure the correct matching of the entry and exit log statements. You can write a log analyzer to extract and process the log information to provide the profiling data, such as the duration of the execution of the methods and the number of invocations of the methods.

An alternative approach to using timestamped logging messages for the purpose of profiling is to keep the profile data in memory. Under this scheme, you save the profile information inside an object, typically a map, in the profile aspect. Since a `thisJoinPointStaticPart` object is the same to all the invocations of a join point, you may use it as the key for the profile data map and store the profile information that is associated with the join point. The map's values contain typical profile data, such as the cumulative average, the longest and shortest duration, and the invocation count. In the before and after advice, instead of logging the timing information to an output stream, you can update the profile data held inside the map. Periodically, or in response to some request, the profiling aspect supplies the data to interested parties. As with the other logging-based aspects, you can choose to exclude it in the final shipped product without making any system wide changes.

You can also extend AspectJ-based profiling functionality to implement modular dynamic service-level monitoring. For example, let's say that you are using some third-party services such as credit-card approval processing over the Internet. You may have an agreement that provides you with certain performance guarantees. You can collect the time before and after each invocation of the services. When the service gets near or below the agreed level, you can alert the provider as well as use the information to collect penalties, if the agreement so specifies. If you are on the other side—the provider of such services—you can use the profile information to create alerts when the level of service approaches the agreed level. Such alerts may help you fix the problem before it becomes critical.

Overall, AspectJ-based logging provides a simple way to introduce profiling and other related functionality to your system without needing a full commitment to the continued use of AspectJ. Try it during the development phase. Start getting the benefits. If you want to use it in the deployed system, great—you continue to get the benefits of profiling in the deployed system. If, however, you do not want aspects in your deployed system yet, you just need to exclude the aspects during the final build. You still had the benefit of AspectJ-based profiling during development and the almost zero-cost option to continue/discontinue its usage in the deployed system.

5.7 *Summary*

Software professionals and management often look for a "killer application," one that is so well suited that it makes adopting a new technology worthwhile despite the risks. The reason behind this conservative approach is to balance the considerable investment associated with any new technology against the benefits it offers. A killer application supposedly provides enough benefits to outweigh the risks. However, such applications are hard to find. Add to that the difficulty in measuring largely qualitative benefits, such as productivity improvements, cleaner design, ease of evolution, and improved quality. Such qualitative benefits make proving the benefits of a new approach to a skeptic very challenging. The more practical approach is to find ways to reduce the investment involved with the new technology. If you can achieve such reduction, you no longer have to wait until you see a big bonanza of benefits.

AspectJ-based logging is a low-investment, low-risk way to begin using AspectJ. The aspects and idioms presented in this chapter may be all that you need to start your logging adventure. Logging aspects also offer a unique plug-and-play nature. If this chapter convinced you of the benefits of using AspectJ for logging, you may start out by simply using it for debugging and tracing. Later, you can demonstrate to your team the benefits you have experienced, which may lead them to use AspectJ as well. At any point, including during the final shipment, you can exclude the AspectJ and logging aspects. The overall effect is that you can start using AspectJ with minimal risk.

Once you commit to AspectJ-based logging, you will start seeing even more benefits. You can use AspectJ-based solutions for core logging tasks that go beyond debugging and tracing. Implementation of such logging concerns is now nicely modularized. This solution leads to increased flexibility, improved accuracy, and better consistency. It saves you from the laborious and boring task of writing nearly identical log statements in code all over your system. The use of AspectJ also makes the job of choosing logging toolkits an easy task. You can start with any one that you are familiar with, and feel comfortable that changing the choice later on will require modifying only a few statements.

Therefore, while not a killer application, logging just may be the perfect way to introduce AspectJ to yourself and your organization.

Policy enforcement:
system wide contracts

6

This chapter covers
■ Understanding AspectJ policy enforcement patterns
■ Enforcing EJB programming restrictions using AspectJ
■ Enforcing Swing policies using AspectJ

Imagine a situation where you are convinced that public access to a data member of a class is not a good idea. Or you have just finished reading the Enterprise JavaBeans (EJB) specification and realize that the specification prohibits calling the Abstract Window Toolkit (AWT) methods from a bean. Clearly, you would like to ensure that the projects you work on do not violate certain principles and restrictions. What are your choices? You could send email messages to your team asking them to check for these violations, or you could add this information to a knowledge base. But these solutions are hard to maintain. Even if you somehow manage to fix any violations, perhaps through regular code reviews, what if you start a new project with a new team? Educate them again? OK, you get the point.

Policy enforcement is a mechanism for ensuring that system components follow certain programming practices, comply with specified rules, and meet the assumptions. For example, say you want to enforce that EJBs do not call AWT code. If there is no enforcement, the error may go undetected during development and show up only in the deployed system. How would you enforce this policy today? Probably you won't enforce it at all. Policy enforcement is a good concept without a good implementation mechanism.

AOP/AspectJ provides a way of enforcing policies that requires little human diligence and ensures a continual enforcement. This chapter presents an aspect-oriented solution that illustrates how you can detect violations by simply compiling your code along with a few prewritten aspects. You can also reuse those aspects and apply them to other projects without incurring any additional development cost. Policy enforcement with AspectJ falls in the developmental aspect category. You can include these aspects during the development phase to help detect policy violations, and for deployment, you can exclude them without affecting the core system behavior. This can be part of an incremental adaptation of AspectJ; you don't have to commit to using AspectJ in the deployed system in order to get the benefits from it.

6.1 AspectJ-based policy enforcement overview

Using policy enforcement and AspectJ relieves you from relying totally on developers' diligence. Consider the issue of `log()` versus `logp()` (see chapter 5, section 5.1.2). During your initial encounter with logging toolkits, you may not have recognized the inefficiency problem associated with using `log()`. Now when you do realize that you should use `logp()`, how do you enforce it? With AspectJ, it becomes a matter of writing a simple aspect such as the following:

```
import java.util.logging.*;

public aspect DetectLogUsage {
    declare warning : call(void Logger.log(..))
        : "Consider Logger.logp() instead";
}
```

Now when you compile this aspect along with the rest of your classes, you get warnings like this one:

```
F:\aspectj-book\ch06\section6.1\Test.java:12
   Consider Logger.logp() instead

1 warning
```

Once this aspect is added to your project's build facility (such as a makefile or an Ant build file), you never have to remind your team members to avoid using `log()`; the aspect will do the job for you.

Figure 6.1 shows the overall scheme of policy enforcement using AspectJ. The policy-enforcement concerns are implemented as aspects that identify any violation by the core concern implementation.

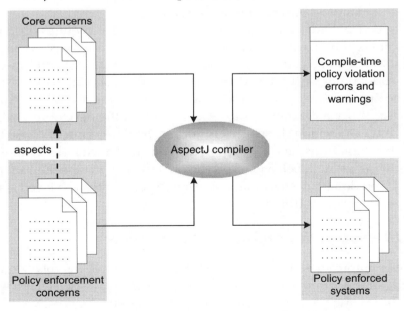

Figure 6.1 The overall scheme of policy enforcement using AspectJ. Aspects implementing policy enforcement are compiled together with the core concern implementation. The policies are enforced in two ways: compile-time errors and warnings and auditing of the violations during runtime.

The solution presented in this chapter opens a new possibility for application frameworks and library creators. Instead of (or in addition to) shipping the documentation specifying the restrictions, such products can now ship aspects capturing parts of the specification along with their framework. Developers using the framework can detect most violations at compile time by simply including the aspects in their build system. The aspects detect other violations at runtime with a clear message indicating where things went wrong. Aspects, since they are program constructs, also serve as precise documents themselves. These aspects will then watch the users "over their shoulder" to check if the assumptions made by the library developers are indeed satisfied. Avoiding incorrect usages will lead to a better quality application based on those libraries and frameworks, resulting in higher user satisfaction.

6.2 *The current solution and its challenges*

So, if enforcing policies is so beneficial, why don't we do it more often? Sure, everybody talks about contract enforcement and implementing best practices, but few implement systematic enforcement. The most common mechanisms used today are documentation, training, and code reviews. The fundamental problem is that these mechanisms are expensive, time-consuming, and still error-prone. Let's take a brief look at a few current solutions and the problems associated with each:

- *Documenting the restrictions*—Perhaps the most popular way of enforcing policies is documenting usage restrictions. These documents of the "watch out" flavor are fine for a small piece of software or for software with few restrictions. For complex software, however, this is an error-prone approach.

- *Embedding policy-enforcement code*—Including code to enforce the policies and checking the fulfillment of assumptions is another common way to implement policy enforcement. Implementing policy enforcement in this way is cumbersome, considering the magnitude of effort required for system-wide enforcement logic instrumentation. Further, the "policies along with the core concepts" approach does not offer any enforcement for the parts of the system that do not implement such checks.

- *Using violation-detection tools*—For a popular framework such as EJB, it is possible that either the application server vendor or a third party will provide a tool that performs policy enforcements. You can then pass your code through such a tool and check for the violations. An EJB compiler could also instrument code, perhaps optionally to catch runtime violations.

When such tools are available, they usually do a good job. For other situations, however, you are pretty much on your own.

The problems with most of these solutions are:

- *Lack of reusability*—Because their implementations do not carry over from one project to another, this means implementing such enforcement all over again. Most programmers do not like to perform repetitive activities.

- *Tangling of policy code with the core logic*—Policy enforcement, being a system-wide concern, crosscuts multiple modules. The code for policy-enforcement concerns is tangled with the core-concern implementation, causing confusion between the two. It may not be clear from the code if a check performs some core requirement or policy enforcement.

- *Policy code scattering*—Because policy code is scattered all over the modules, if you need to change a policy you must modify *every* module. In addition, when you create new modules, you must remember to code all the policies. This makes consistent implementation a difficult task.

- *Cumbersome implementation*—Current policy-enforcement implementation results in significant work—both initially and during maintenance. The amount of work often outweighs the benefit obtained.

Because of these issues, most systems include little policy-enforcement logic in a systematic way, if they include any at all. Code reviews are usually a substitute for policy enforcement. Although such reviews have a definite place in the software-development process, using them for mundane tasks like simple policy checks is wasteful. Code reviews should instead focus on the subtler nuances of implementation.

To sum up, current mechanisms make policy enforcement inelegant and expensive to implement. Therefore, the failure of policy enforcement lies in the way it is implemented, not in its concepts.

6.3 *Enforcement using AspectJ*

Fundamentally, policy enforcement requires flagging conditions that violate certain principles and assumptions, such as accessing the state of a class in a thread-unsafe way or from nonfriendly classes. The detection and correction of these conditions ensure the quality of the overall system. Policy enforcement using AspectJ involves creating a few aspects that detect all usages that are in violation of the required policies.

You can use many of the aspects developed in this chapter directly without any modifications at all. This reusability makes aspects-based policy enforcement highly cost-effective.

6.3.1 *Policy enforcement implementation choices*

You have two choices for implementing policies: compile-time checking and runtime checking. Each kind of enforcement has its appropriate usages and limitations; AspectJ helps with both types. In this section, we study the implementation of both compile-time checking and runtime checking.

Compile-time enforcement

Compile-time checking implies performing policy-violation checks during the compilation phase. Compile-time checks are very powerful—they allow you to perform checks even before running the system. In strongly typed languages such as Java and C++, compilers already perform certain compile-time checking, such as type matching, access control, and so forth. With AspectJ, you can take such checking to a new level; you can specify custom checks. Now the compiler is your best friend; it can save you from a potentially time-consuming bug-fix cycle.

While its early detection capability is powerful, compile-time checking has limitations on the kinds of checks that it can perform. Certain kinds of behavior can be checked only during the execution of a program. For example, checking for ranges in values of certain arguments can be performed only at runtime.

Implementing compile-time enforcement involves the use of declare error and declare warning constructs. These mechanisms provide a way to detect the usage of a specified pointcut during the compilation phase and issue an error or a warning. One important thing to note is that the pointcuts used in this kind of declaration must be statically determinable pointcuts. This means you cannot use constructs such as `cflow()` for this purpose. You can learn more about these constructs in chapter 3.

Runtime enforcement

In contrast to compile-time checking, runtime checking is performed during system execution. In languages such as Java, the VMs already perform certain runtime checks, such as cast-correctness and null-reference access checks. Runtime policy enforcement is a similar idea except that the constraints expressed are custom specified.

Upon detecting a policy violation at runtime, the usual approach is to log the violation along with the context under which it occurred. In case the system malfunctions, the logs may offer insight to potential precursors. Even without malfunctions, periodically examining the logs can provide useful information to developers so that they can avoid potential problems in the next release—a sort of built-in QA.

Runtime enforcement involves verifying the policies using AspectJ's dynamic crosscutting constructs. For instance, you can write advice to detect the violation of Swing's thread-safety rule and print a message. Since such checking detects the violations after the fact, logging for auditing purposes is usually the best option. For certain major violations, it may be desirable to let the system shut down gracefully to avoid further damage. The choice of action ultimately depends on the nature of the violation.

NOTE Why issue warnings when you can fix it? In many situations, it is possible to fix policy violations using AspectJ instead of issuing warnings or errors at either runtime or compile time. However, fixing the problem will force you to include the aspects in the deployed system, and that will remove the choice of not using AspectJ in the deployed system. If you want to preserve that choice, it is important that the policy enforcements do not change the core program behavior in any way. They should simply add notifications to inform you of policy violations.

6.3.2 *The role of policy enforcement during the product lifecycle*

Policy enforcement has different roles in different parts of the product lifecycle. In this section, we examine how an AspectJ-based solution helps realize those roles.

During the development phase, AspectJ-based policy enforcement helps by immediately flagging policy violations. During this phase, you also develop your own policies. You should strive to develop reusable, general-purpose policies so that you can carry them to other projects. Policies also help in training developers who are new to a technology—acting as a kind of mentor.

For internal testing, you should keep your build configuration the same as the development build configuration by including policy-enforcement aspects. Then the policy-violation logs produced during testing can help developers fix the problems.

During the maintenance phase too, you should keep the build configuration identical to the development build. Policy-enforcement aspects can then ensure that the modifications and new code do not violate the existing policies, because the aspects will catch the compile-time violations during the compilation phase and the runtime violations during the testing of the new functionality. Essentially, these policies serve as a constant, automatic code review.

In a deployed system, you can choose whether to include the policy-enforcement aspects or exclude them; the decision depends largely on your comfort level with AspectJ. If included, those aspects serve as a logging mechanism for a post-analysis of the violations encountered within the deployed application. One reason you may want to remove policy-enforcement aspects is to avoid any performance penalties associated with the policy checks in the critical paths.

If you are planning to remove policy enforcement because you do not want to use AspectJ in a deployed system, you should pay particular attention to two issues when you create your aspects: First, ensure that you separate pure Java code from aspects so that you can easily remove the aspects and compile the rest of the code without using the AspectJ compiler. In particular, you should avoid putting nested aspects inside classes (we will look at an example of a nested aspect in section 6.4.2) by putting the enforcement aspects into separate source files. Second, be careful that your policy-enforcement aspects do not change the core system behavior in any way. Otherwise, your deployed system's behavior will be different from that of the tested system.

6.4 *Policy enforcement patterns*

With a few typical patterns, you can implement policy enforcement using AspectJ. In this section, we introduce a set of examples to illustrate these patterns. These examples then serve as building blocks that you can use to create polices for specific kinds of applications, such as EJB-based and Swing-based systems.

6.4.1 *Detecting the violation of a specific call pattern*

Consider a situation where, after learning about the logging kits, you have decided that using `System.out` or `System.err` is a poor way to perform logging. You may convey this to your team, and you may do a fine job the first time by simply searching through your code base for *System.out* or *System.err* and replacing those instances with a logging toolkit such as log4j. The problem, however, is that a few months later, some developer, perhaps a new person on your team, starts using `System.out`. Until you perform another search, it will go undetected.

Using AspectJ, we can write a simple aspect, shown in listing 6.1, that will spot the calls to `System.out.println()` and `System.err.println()` at compile time, and issue appropriate warnings. If we include this simple aspect in our build system, it will catch any violations immediately.

Listing 6.1 **An aspect that detects usage of** System.out **or** System.err

```
aspect DetectSystemOutErrorUsage {
    declare warning : get(* System.out) || get(* System.err)
    : "Consider Logger.logp() instead";
}
```

Our aspect, per se, does not detect call to methods such as System.out.println().
We instead simply detect access to out or err members in the System class and
presume that the code is accessing these fields for printing a message. This
makes it possible to detect violations at compile time itself. When we compile our
code, we get a warning for each access to such fields:

```
F:\aspectj-book\ch06\section6.4.1\Test.java:7
➡ Consider Logger.logp() instead
F:\aspectj-book\ch06\section6.4.1\Test.java:9
➡ Consider Logger.logp() instead

2 warnings
```

We can specify when this warning should be issued by identifying only a selected
set of packages or classes in the within() pointcut. We can combine multiple
within() pointcuts to specify a precise control:

```
declare warning : (get(* System.out) || get(* System.err))
        && within(com.manning.ui..*)
    : "Consider Logger.log() instead";
```

In this code, we are specifying that the violation detection should be limited only
to all subpackages of the com.manning.ui package.

After a reasonable period of issuing warnings, you can mark such usage as an
error by simply changing declare warning to declare error, as shown in the following snippet. Now the aspects will force the developer to fix the problem
immediately. Be sure to inform your team members before you make such a
change, so as not to catch them by surprise!

```
declare error : get(* System.out) || get(* System.err)
    : "Consider Logger.log() instead";
```

You can extend this usage to detect many such violations. This solution is a lot
more powerful than just using the @deprecation JavaDoc tag. First, the AspectJ
way of implementing such usage-pattern violations modularizes the policy control; there is only one aspect that controls the enforcement as opposed to changing JavaDoc comments for each method. Compared to @deprecated, which
allows only execution-side control, the AspectJ-based solution offers caller-side

control by enabling you to specify that certain selected clients will get the error or warning. With deprecation mechanisms, all you can implement is a global mandate (which you can implement using AspectJ as well). Finally, it provides an easy way to switch from compile-time warnings to hard errors.

6.4.2 *Implementing flexible access control*

Access control is a kind of enforcement that limits the access to certain functionality. Consider the shopping cart example in chapter 5. It appears that the programmer intended to allow the manipulation of the ShoppingCart class only through the ShoppingCartOperator class, which ensures correct inventory updates. However, what is there to prevent direct access to a ShoppingCart object? Leaving the situation as it is downgrades the programmer's "intention" to a programmer's "wish." Java's access control mechanism simply isn't enough in this case. What we need here is a way to implement access control that will disallow calls to certain operations on a ShoppingCart object from anywhere except in ShoppingCartOperator. With AspectJ, writing a simple aspect such as the one in listing 6.2 ensures the intended access control.

Listing 6.2   ShoppingCartAccessAspect.java: enforcing access control

```
public aspect ShoppingCartAccessAspect {
    declare error
        : (call(* ShoppingCart.add*(..))
           || call(* ShoppingCart.remove*(..))
           || call(* ShoppingCart.empty(..)))
        && !within(ShoppingCartOperator)
        : "Illegal manipulation to ShoppingCart;\n
              only ShoppingCartOperator may perform such operations";
}
```

Compiling this aspect along with the rest of the code will detect any illegal access and issue a compile-time error like this:

```
F:\aspectj-book\ch06\section6.4.2\v1\Test.java:16
    Illegal manipulation to ShoppingCart;
    only ShoppingCartOperator may perform such operations

1 error
```

With pure Java, this type of complex access control—allowing communication only between collaborating classes—is not possible. Consider, for example, the implementation of a factory pattern to create objects of a Product class. You want only the factory to create the `Product` objects. With Java's access-control mechanism, the best you can do is force the `Product` class and the factory class to reside in the same package and assign package access to the `Product` class's constructors. This is over-restrictive and, in some cases, impossible to implement. For example, if the factory is in a package and the `Product` class is in a subpackage, it is not possible to implement the pattern correctly. Further, other classes in the same package can freely create `Product` objects. The usual solution is to simply let the `Product` class's constructors have public access and document the restriction. If a developer misses this documentation, you are out of luck.

AspectJ enforcements can define access control in far more precise terms than those offered by the standard Java access specifiers of public, protected, package (default), and private. For package access, for example, Java offers only two categories: the owner package and other packages. However, you may need to define access at a much finer package granularity—such as user interface, networking, and database—so that you can control which packages can access a certain class or method.

With AspectJ, you can implement and enforce the needed access control properly. The usage is similar to `friend` access in C++. With AspectJ, you can implement friend-functionality in Java as well as far more powerful types of access control. For instance, let's go back to the previous discussion of the factory pattern that creates `Product` objects. In listing 6.3, the `Product` class contains a nested aspect that implements the policy that only `ProductFactory` can create `Product` objects.

> **Listing 6.3 The `Product` class, with an aspect that controls its creation**

```
public class Product {
    public Product() {
        // constructor implementation
    }

    // product methods

    static aspect FlagNonFactoryCreation {
        declare error
            : call(Product.new(..))
              && !within(ProductFactory+)
            : "Only ProductFactory can create Product";
    }
}
```

The nested aspect declares that invoking any of the `Product` class's constructors from any class other than `ProductFactory` or one of its subclasses will result in a compile-time error:

```
F:\aspectj-book\ch06\section6.4.2\factory\Test.java:5
➥ Only ProductFactory can create Product

1 error
```

We could further restrict the access to only `ProductFactory`'s `createProduct()` methods simply by replacing the `within()` pointcut with a `withincode()`. See chapter 3, table 3.8, for more details on the `withincode()` pointcut.

```
declare error
    : call(Product.new(..))
        && !withincode(Product ProductFactory.createProduct(..))
    : "Only ProductFactory.createProduct() can create Product";
```

Now if we call a constructor of the `Product` class from anywhere other than any `createProduct()` method in `ProductFactory` or its subclass, we will get a compile-time error.

Note that we are using a nested aspect, `FlagNonFactoryCreation`, to implement the access control in our example. If you have adopted AspectJ as your project's programming language, this is often a better approach since it tightly connects the enforced class and enforcing aspect. Such tight coupling allows you to update the enforcement aspect when the implementation of the access-controlled class changes. However, when you use this approach, you lose the choice of compiling the project with a pure Java compiler for deployment builds. If such a choice is important to you, you should move the aspect to a separate file that can be excluded from the final build.

Our examples have shown implementing precise access control using AspectJ. You can use this pattern for implementing the access control that is suitable for your purposes.

6.4.3 *Enforcing the best-practices principles*

Over the years, the programming community in general, and most likely you and your team specifically, have developed a few best-practices techniques. We use these techniques to protect ourselves against potential problems that may not be easy to spot otherwise. With experience, the list of best-practices techniques, as well as your confidence in their utility, grows. Policy-enforcement techniques can detect violations of these best practices. Since best practices are simply programming idioms and patterns to help avert potential trouble, their violation may not always be an immediate issue. It may be perfectly fine to violate them as long as you understand what you are doing. Policy enforcement for best practices, therefore, simply warns developers of potential traps instead of issuing hard errors. For example, even though one of the basic object-oriented principles is to not expose the implementation, such exposure will not cause any observable problems immediately. However, over time you will start to see that such exposure will lead to brittle systems; flagging such violations will help you make an informed choice.

Minimally, the rule against exposing internal implementation translates to assigning a nonpublic access to any (nonfinal) members. Although this principle is commonly accepted, its enforcement still relies on education and code reviews. Reviews usually involve searching through the code base either manually or with a tool. Maybe, with effort, you can initially fix all such violations, but after a time some developer forgets this principle and adds a public field. Such a violation of your policy will go undetected until another review or, worse, another bug. The reason for the lack of better enforcement of this policy is that it is a crosscutting concern—every part of the code has to adhere to it. In listing 6.4, the aspect warns the developer about using public access to any nonfinal field.

Listing 6.4 An aspect that detects public access to members

```
aspect DetectPublicAccessMembers {
    declare warning :
        get(public !final * *) || set(public * *) :
         "Please consider using nonpublic access";
}
```

The aspect, per se, does not detect the presence of public fields in a class. However, it detects read or write access to any such field. The pointcut `get(public !final * *)` captures read access to any nonfinal public field of any class. The use of `!final` prevents the code from issuing warnings for access to final fields, which usually isn't considered bad practice. Similarly, the pointcut `set(public * *)` captures all write access to any public field of any class. In case of write access, we have omitted `!final`, because Java's access check will take care of issuing an error for writing to a final field.

Now when the developer compiles this aspect along with the rest of classes, he will get warnings similar to the following:

```
F:\aspectj-book\ch06\section6.4.3\Test.java:7
    Please consider using nonpublic access
```

```
F:\aspectj-book\ch06\section6.4.3\Test.java:21
➡ Please consider using nonpublic access
```

```
2 warnings
```

The developer can then assign appropriate nonpublic access control to the field and may introduce getter and/or setter methods. The next time someone writes code that uses access to a public field, this aspect will catch the violation immediately.

Try this aspect in your own system; you might get some surprises.

6.5 Example: implementing EJB programming restrictions

The EJB specification imposes several programming restrictions on a bean. For example, it does not allow you to make AWT operations, directly work with networking resources, or use thread-synchronization primitives from a bean. These restrictions ensure that application servers can utilize nodes in a server cluster without any behavioral change in the system. Since most of these situations occur during user-heavy loads, you may not run into these situations during the development phase, and failure may occur only in real deployment situations and stress testing. Please refer to section 24.1.2 of the EJB 2.0 specification for more details.[1]

Our way to detect EJB violations, like most of the solutions presented in this book, works in a plug-and-play style and is reusable. Simply compiling your code with the aspect in listing 6.5 gets you the benefit. You can use AspectJ to catch violations at compile time and runtime in a nonintrusive manner, as we discussed in section 6.3.1. So now let's dive straight into an aspect. Listing 6.5 shows an EJB policy-enforcement aspect that enforces two rules: no AWT code from EJBs and no nonfinal static field access.

> **Listing 6.5 DetectEJBViolations.java: ensuring EJB policy enforcement**

```
import javax.ejb.*;

public aspect DetectEJBViolations {
    pointcut uiCalls() : call(* java.awt.*+.*(..));

    declare error : uiCalls() && within(EnterpriseBean+)
            : "UI calls are not allowed from EJB beans.\n
                ➡ See EJB 2.0 specification section 24.1.2";
```

---

[1] For information on EJB antipatterns, please refer to Bruce Tate et al, *Bitter EJB* (Greenwich, CT: Manning, 2003).

```
before() : uiCalls() && cflow(call(* EnterpriseBean+.*(..))) {
    System.out.println("Detected call to AWT from enterprise bean");
    System.out.println("See EJB 2.0 specification section 24.1.2");
    Thread.dumpStack();
}

// Similar implementation of other programming restrictions:
// Socket, file i/o, native library loading, keyboard input
// thread methods access, reflection etc.

pointcut staticMemberAccess() :
    set(static * EnterpriseBean+.*);

declare error : staticMemberAccess()
    : "EJBs are not allowed to have nonfinal static variables.\n
        ➡ See EJB 2.0 specification section 24.1.2";
}
```

If you are involved in development using EJB, you can use the aspect in listing 6.5 as a template and extend it for other restrictions. Once you have the enforcement aspects ready, you can compile them along with your other classes and watch how much time it saves you in the laborious task of reviewing the code, and how it ensures better quality for your deployed system. Either you will see violations (and then you can fix the problems) or you will see no violations (and you can feel more confident about your code).

As an example, consider listing 6.6, which violates some of the EJB programming restrictions.

Listing 6.6   ViolationBean.java: a bean that violates the EJB rules

```
package customer;

import javax.ejb.*;
import javax.naming.*;

public abstract class ViolationBean implements EntityBean {
    private static int _subscriptionCount = 0;

    // ...

    public void addSubscription (String subscriptionKey) {
        try {
            Context ic = new InitialContext();
            // ...
        } catch (Exception ex) {
            javax.swing.JOptionPane.showMessageDialog(null,
                "Exception while adding subscription");
```

```
        ex.printStackTrace();
    }
    _subscriptionCount++;
}

// ...
}
```

When we compile the `ViolationBean` class along with the `DetectEJBViolations` aspect, we get the following output:

```
> ajc DetectEJBViolations.java customer\*.java
F:\aspectj-book\ch06\section6.5\customer\ViolationBean.java:7
  EJBs are not allowed to have non-final static variables.
 See EJB 2.0 specification section 24.1.2
F:\aspectj-book\ch06\section6.5\customer\ViolationBean.java:14
  UI calls are not allowed from EJB beans.
 See EJB 2.0 specification section 24.1.2
F:\aspectj-book\ch06\section6.5\customer\ViolationBean.java:18
  EJBs are not allowed to have non-final static variables.
 See EJB 2.0 specification section 24.1.2

3 errors
```

Let's now get into the details of how the `DetectEJBViolations` aspect implements various enforcement policies. In the next two sections, we look at each of the enforced policies separately.

6.5.1 *Implementing "no AWT"*

The first EJB restriction we will examine disallows calls to AWT methods. In the following code snippet, we use a pointcut to capture join points that correspond to calls to AWT methods, and declare the occurrence of any such join point in any subclass of `EnterpriseBean` to be an error:

```
pointcut uiCalls() : call(* java.awt..*+.*(..));

declare error : uiCalls() && within(EnterpriseBean+)
      : "UI calls are not allowed from EJB beans.
         See EJB 2.0 specification section 24.1.2";
```

This code simply says:

> If a call to any method in any class extending any class in `java.awt` or its subpackage is made from within any class implementing `javax.ejb.EnterpriseBean`, declare it an error.

This is probably over-restrictive because it is OK to access classes such as `java.awt.Rectangle`. Nevertheless, we would rather err on the side of safety. It is easy to later exclude a few classes from restrictions by modifying the `uiCalls()` pointcut to not capture the join points for the classes to be excluded. When the aspect detects a violation, it prints a message like the following:

```
F:\aspectj-book\ch06\section6.5\customer\ViolationBean.java:16
   UI calls are not allowed from EJB beans.
See EJB 2.0 specification section 24.1.2
```

However, what if we do not call code in AWT directly, but rather through another class? First, we should try to enumerate all the classes and packages that make UI calls and include those classes in the `uiCalls()` pointcut. This way, we will catch any violations at compile time and will not have to wait until we run the system for problems to occur. As a last resort, we can add the following advice in the aspect to check whether any of the methods' control flow led to a call in AWT. Bear in mind, however, that this advice may not always catch the violations, since the code path leading to the violating calls may not be executed in a particular test sequence:

```
before() : uiCalls() && cflow(call(* EnterpriseBean+.*(..))) {
    System.out.println("Detected call to AWT from enterprise bean");
    System.out.println("See EJB 2.0 specification section 24.1.2");
    Thread.dumpStack();
}
```

In a similar fashion, you can implement other restrictions, such as no calls to `Thread`'s methods, socket creation, `System.in` access, native library loading, or reflection use. For each such restriction, you will need to provide a pointcut definition to capture the join points corresponding to the restricted operations. You will also need to include a declare error clause for those pointcuts. To capture indirect calls, you will have to advise the join point occurring in the control flow of the bean method and log the violation.

6.5.2 *Implementing "no nonfinal static field access"*

Another EJB programming restriction disallows the use of nonfinal static fields by a bean. This ensures the correctness of those fields when a bean moves from one VM to another. With AspectJ, you can indirectly capture this restriction by capturing write access to such fields. This solution does not implement the policy in exact terms, but it implements the spirit of it. The following snippet defines a pointcut that will capture write access to any static field in any subclass of `EnterpriseBean` and declare the access to be an error:

```
pointcut staticMemberAccess() :
    set(static * EnterpriseBean+.*);

declare error : staticMemberAccess()
    : "EJBs are not allowed to have nonfinal static variables.
        ➥ See EJB 2.0 specification section 24.1.2";
```

When the AspectJ compiler detects a write access to a static field, it gives a compile-time error, as follows:

```
F:\aspectj-book\ch06\section6.5\customer\ViolationBean.java:7
➥ EJBs are not allowed to have nonfinal static variables.
See EJB 2.0 specification section 24.1.2
F:\aspectj-book\ch06\section6.5\customer\ViolationBean.java:20
➥ EJBs are not allowed to have nonfinal static variables.
See EJB 2.0 specification section 24.1.2
```

The output shows that compiling the aspect with the rest of the system results in compile-time errors upon discovering that a nonfinal static variable is being modified. The developer is then forced to address the problem (which may involve a simple fix or may require design modifications) before the system can be compiled without errors again.

Note that if a developer forgets to mark a static field as final, and if she never modifies that field, not even initializing it, then that field behaves as a final field, since its value is never changed. You need not be concerned about such "actually final" fields since their value will remain the same throughout the lifecycle of the bean and will not affect the system when a bean moves from one VM to another.

Now that you understand how to enforce EJB policies with the `DetectEJBViolations.java` aspect, you can compile it with your EJB classes and watch it go to work. With such an aspect watching your project all the time, you can be sure that all the restrictions captured by the enforcement aspect will no longer be present in your system. It will also ensure the quality of your code. Since the enforcement aspect does all the heavy work, you can focus your code reviews on more complex issues, such as optimization or business logic.

6.6 *Example: implementing Swing policies*

Because Swing is a single-threaded library, its correct usage requires accessing or modifying any state of the Swing components only from the AWT event-dispatching thread.[2] Swing's single-thread rule is a contract between the Swing components

---

[2] Please refer to http://java.sun.com/docs/books/tutorial/uiswing/overview/threads.html if you are not already familiar with Swing's thread-safety rule and ways to ensure adherence to it.

and the user of those components. The methods `invokeLater()` and `invokeAnd-Wait()` in `java.awt.EventQueue` (or `javax.swing.SwingUtilities`) provide a way to route calls through the event-dispatching thread.

In this section, we examine a way to detect these violations. In chapter 9, we will implement a way to use aspects to automatically fix the problem.

6.6.1 *Understanding the problem*

First, let's look at a simple program in listing 6.7 that illustrates a violation of this policy.

Listing 6.7 Test code violating the policy

```java
import java.awt.*;
import javax.swing.*;
import javax.swing.table.*;

public class Test extends JFrame {
    public static void main(String[] args) {
        Test appFrame = new Test();
        appFrame.setDefaultCloseOperation(JFrame.EXIT_ON_CLOSE);

        DefaultTableModel tableModel = new DefaultTableModel(4,2);
        JTable table = new JTable(tableModel);

        appFrame.getContentPane().add(table);

        appFrame.pack();
        appFrame.setVisible(true);

        System.out.println("Frame is now visible");

        tableModel.setValueAt("[0,0]", 0, 0);
        tableModel.removeRow(2);
    }
}
```

The two lines in bold violate the rule requiring that, once the components are put onto the screen (using `pack()` and `setVisible()`), any access or modification must take place only from the event-dispatching thread by calling either `invoke-Later()` or `invokeAndWait()` in the main thread. In our case, we are calling the `setValueAt()` and `removeRow()` methods on the table model. In practice, this type of violation will occur as a result of calls made from another user thread, such as a thread reading data from a network or database.

The solution for this problem is to wrap the operation performed in a class implementing `Runnable` and then use `EventQueue.invokeLater()` or `Event-Queue.invokeAndWait()` to route the operation through the event-dispatching thread. Note, as of JDK 1.3, the same-named methods in the class `Swing-Utilities` are simply a wrapper around the `EventQueue` class's methods. Listings 6.8 and 6.9 show the classes needed to set the value of a table cell and remove a table row, respectively. You would use these classes instead of the highlighted method calls in listing 6.7. Using these classes along with `Event-Queue.invokeLater()` or `EventQueue.invokeAndWait()` ensures thread-safe access. Listing 6.8 implements the `Runnable` interface for setting the values in `TableModel` in a thread-safe way.

Listing 6.8 An example of a class that sets the value of a table cell

```java
import javax.swing.table.*;

public class TableValueSetter implements Runnable {
    TableModel _model;
    Object _value;
    int _row;
    int _column;

    public TableValueSetter(TableModel model, Object value,
                            int row, int column) {
        _model = model;
        _value = value;
        _row = row;
        _column = column;
    }

    public void run() {
        _model.setValueAt(_value, _row, _column);
    }
}
```

The `TableValueSetter` class's constructor takes all the parameters needed to invoke the operation. The `run()` method simply invokes the `setValueAt()` method using those parameters. Similarly, `TableRowRemover` in listing 6.9 implements `Runnable` to allow the routing of `DefaultTableModel.removeRow()`.

Listing 6.9 An example of a class that removes a table row

```
import javax.swing.table.*;

public class TableRowRemover implements Runnable {
    DefaultTableModel _model;
    int _row;

    public TableRowRemover(DefaultTableModel model, int row) {
        _model = model;
        _row = row;
    }

    public void run() {
        _model.removeRow(_row);
    }
}
```

The developer will need to use these classes in conjunction with Event-Queue.invokeLater() or EventQueue.invokeAndWait(). Note that you will need to implement a class for each operation or combination of operations. For example, you will need a class for adding a row, adding a column, and so on. However, this requirement is present even when you don't use an AspectJ-based solution. Once you have these classes implemented, you need to ensure that *every* part of the code uses these classes. For example, you should replace the last two lines in the Test class with the following lines:

```
EventQueue.invokeLater(new TableValueSetter(tableModel,
                                          "[0,0]", 0, 0));
EventQueue.invokeLater(new TableRowRemover(tableModel, 2));
```

6.6.2 *Detecting the violation*

We will now develop a dynamic checking aspect to catch any violation of Swing's single-thread rule. The fundamental idea is quite simple: check if any call accessing a Swing component's state is called through a thread other than the event-dispatching thread. In listing 6.10, DetectSwingSingleThreadRuleViolationAspect flags the call to the Swing component's methods from a nonevent-dispatching thread.

Listing 6.10 An aspect that detects the Swing single-thread rule

```
import java.awt.*;
import javax.swing.JComponent;
```

```
public aspect DetectSwingSingleThreadRuleViolationAspect {
    pointcut viewMethodCalls()
        : call(* javax..JComponent+.*(..));
```
❶ **Calls to UI component methods**

```
    pointcut modelMethodCalls()
        : call(* javax..*Model+.*(..))
        || call(* javax.swing.text.Document+.*(..));
```
❷ **Calls to UI model methods**

```
    pointcut uiMethodCalls()
        : viewMethodCalls() || modelMethodCalls();
```
❸ **Calls to UI methods**

```
    before() : uiMethodCalls() && if(!EventQueue.isDispatchThread()) {
        System.err.println(
            "Violation: Swing method called from nonAWT thread"
            + "\nCalled method: "
            + thisJoinPointStaticPart.getSignature()
            + "\nCaller: "
            + thisEnclosingJoinPointStaticPart.getSignature()
            + "\nSource location: "
            + thisJoinPointStaticPart.getSourceLocation()
            + "\nThread: " + Thread.currentThread()
            + "\nChange code to use EventQueue.invokeLater() "
            + "or EventQueue.invokeAndWait()\n");
    }
}
```
❹ **Advice that flags violations**

The aspect `DetectSwingSingleThreadRuleViolationAspect` defines a pointcut `uiMethodCalls()` and advises it to check whether the caller thread of the captured join points is the event-dispatching thread. Let's examine the aspect in more detail:

❶ The pointcut `viewMethodCalls()`, which captures the method invocations on a view object, is defined as a call to any method of `JComponent` or its subclasses.

❷ The pointcut `modelMethodCalls()`, which captures operations on a model, is defined as a call to any method of any class with a name ending in `Model` or its subclasses. We also capture the call to `javax.swing.text.Document` or its subclass, since our property-based pointcut that requires the name to end in `Model` would not capture its methods. By the way, notice the importance of following a consistent naming convention; if you name all your models ending in `Model`, then capturing join points based on name becomes easy.

❸ The pointcut `uiMethodCalls()` combines the `viewMethodCalls()` and `modelMethodCalls()` pointcuts to capture all the method calls that are involved in Swing's thread-safety rule. We could have defined the `uiMethodCalls()` to directly capture all the required methods calls, but the refactoring helps improve the overall understanding.

4 In the advice to the `uiMethodCalls()` pointcut, if any join points are found that have not been called from the event-dispatching thread, a message will be logged with the information about the call, the caller method, and the caller thread. This will help the developer analyze the root cause of the problem. In practice, instead of simply printing a message onto a console, you will want to log it into some file; there is little point in telling the user that your program did something wrong.

When we compile the classes and aspect together and run the test program, we get the following output:

```
> ajc *.java
> java Test
Frame is now visible
Violation: Swing method called from nonAWT thread
Called method: void javax.swing.table.DefaultTableModel.
      setValueAt(Object, int, int)
Caller: void Test.main(String[])
Source location: Test.java:20
Thread: Thread[main,5,main]
Change code to use EventQueue.invokeLater()
      or EventQueue.invokeAndWait()

Violation: Swing method called from nonAWT thread
Called method: void javax.swing.table.DefaultTableModel.
      removeRow(int)
Caller: void Test.main(String[])
Source location: Test.java:21
Thread: Thread[main,5,main]
Change code to use EventQueue.invokeLater()
      or EventQueue.invokeAndWait()
```

We see from the output that both the violations that accessed the Swing component from the main thread are flagged by `DetectSwingSingleThreadRuleViolation-Aspect`.

6.7 *Summary*

As you introduce AspectJ to your project, one of the problems you may face is resistance to committing to AOP and AspectJ. People will demand proof that AspectJ indeed is worth the effort. This could become a Catch-22 situation—you can't show its usefulness to your project because you can't use it, and you won't be able to use it unless you show its usefulness. Well, policy enforcement offers you a way to overcome this issue. Even if your organization or team isn't yet committed to AspectJ, you can still use AspectJ-based enforcement to improve your personal productivity. Then you can show what you have gained to others. If that convinces your colleagues of the benefits that AspectJ offers, very well. Otherwise, continue using the aspects in your own development world and simply exclude them in the shipment builds. The plug-and-play nature of policy-enforcement aspects provides you an opportunity to play with AspectJ without requiring a full commitment.

Start with the aspects presented in this chapter. The next time you encounter a novel programming wisdom or best practice, consider writing an enforcement aspect encapsulating the knowledge. Over time, you will have a repository of policy-enforcement aspects that will help you in all your projects. When you start using a new framework, you can create policy-enforcement aspects specifically targeted to the framework. If you are in a mentoring role, you can provide your aspects to your team. You will then no longer have to sit down and repeat the policies with each team member.

AspectJ offers a simple and yet powerful way of implementing system wide policy-enforcement concerns. The policy-enforcement aspects you develop are reusable, lowering your per-project development cost. These aspects use the AspectJ compiler to enforce as many policies as possible at compile time and use dynamic crosscutting to understand the runtime violations in more detail. With such aspects in place, you are assured of better-quality code and you can spend your time on more "exciting" issues. Note, though, that the mechanisms presented here do not substitute for code reviews. However, with policy enforcement in place, the code reviews can focus on the subtler nuances of the implementations.

Once you start enforcing policies in a significant way by using AspectJ, you will find AspectJ to be your best friend; it always watches you, reminds you of common pitfalls, and lets you spend time on the more creative aspects of life (yes, pun intended).

Optimization: pooling and caching

7

This chapter covers

- Resource pooling template
- Database connection pooling
- Thread pooling
- XSLT stylesheet caching

Resource pooling—the recycling of resources that are expensive to create and discard—is one of the most common techniques for improving system performance. Without resource pooling, systems spend a good amount of time creating and destroying resources. The conventional methods of resource pooling require that you explicitly code the pooling logic within each module that deals with the creation and destruction of resources. Since many modules may be performing those tasks, this approach can be cumbersome. Further, a resource pooling feature may need tuning at various times during its evolution, and if it is a part of a reusable subsystem, tuning may be needed in each system in which it is implemented because usage patterns will differ. The conventional solution requires modifications to all affected modules in such cases, making it a crosscutting concern. AOP can help modularize this crosscutting concern by encapsulating the pooling logic in an aspect.

This chapter examines aspect-oriented resource pooling techniques. First we will create a template to demonstrate a plug-and-play style of resource pooling, and then we will add examples that implement database connection and thread pooling based on that template. Using the generic template, you should be able to extend the idea to other kinds of resources, such as JMS or TCP/IP connection objects. Since caching is closely related to resource pooling, we will also introduce AspectJ-based caching by using an example of caching XSLT stylesheet transformer objects.

7.1 *The typical case*

The simplest method of resource usage is to create a resource when there is a need for it, utilize it, and then dispose of it when it is no longer needed. The following snippet shows a skeleton example of resource usage that does not use any resource pooling:

```
Resource resource
    = new Resource(<resource_creation_parameters>);
// or
// Resource resource
//  = resourceFactory.createResource(<resource_creation_parameters>);


...
// use the resource object
...

resource.dispose();
```

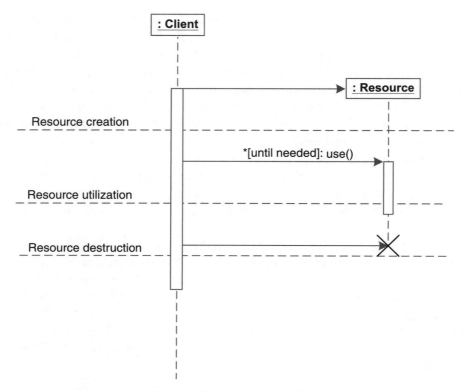

Figure 7.1 Typical resource usage in the absence of any pooling. You create resources just in time to serve the requests, use them, and dispose of them after their usage. Any subsequent use requires creating a new resource.

Figure 7.1 shows a sequence diagram for the same scheme of creating, using, and destroying a resource.

This usage pattern has a simple resource lifecycle—create-use-dispose—and it works fine with resources that are inexpensive to create and discard. However, certain kinds of resources, such as database connections, socket connections, and threads, are time-consuming to create and discard. With a simple database operation such as querying the existence of a certain record, for example, the creation and destruction of a database connection may take a few seconds, whereas the operation itself may take only a few milliseconds. Resource pooling becomes particularly important for such resources, where the overhead of creating and disposing of the resource may far outweigh the time required to actually perform the core task.

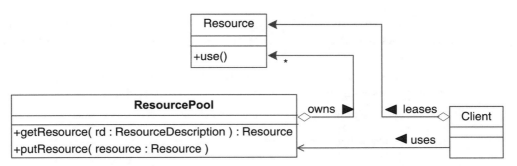

Figure 7.2 **The structure of a resource pool, resource, and client. The resource pool owns the resources in it, and the client leases a resource from it.**

7.1.1 *Return, reuse, recycle: The role of resource pooling*

Resource pooling is used to keep the resources around instead of discarding them. Many resources with significant creation time can be recycled. When you need the resource again, instead of creating a new one, simply reuse an earlier one. For example, in a database application, instead of creating and destroying the connection when you need to perform a set of operations, you could obtain an existing connection object from a connection pool. You would also return the connection to the pool after using it, instead of destroying it.

Figure 7.2 shows the typical static structure of a system that uses resource pooling. For the basic implementation of a resource pool, you need two things:

- A method of obtaining the required resources from a pool
- A way to relinquish a resource to the pool once you no longer need it

Listing 7.1 shows a typical resource pool API that provides the basic functionality of obtaining a resource and then releasing it back to the pool.

Listing 7.1 A typical resource pool interface

```
public interface ResourcePool {
    public Resource getResource(ResourceDescription rd);

    public boolean putResource(Resource r);
}
```

The getResource() method attempts to obtain a resource with a description that matches the ResourceDescription argument. If there is no matching resource, this method returns `null`. The `putResource()` method puts resource `r` into the resource pool. If the pool cannot accept the resource, it should indicate so by returning `false`.

Let's consider a way we could use this interface for resource pooling. The following snippet shows a typical usage of a resource pool to obtain and release resources:

```
// resPool object of type ResourcePool is constructed elsewhere
Resource resource
    = resPool.getResource(rd);
if (resource == null) {
    resource
        = resourceFactory.createResource(rd);
}

...
// use resource object
...

if (resPool.putResource(resource) == false) {
    resource.dispose();
}
```

When a client needs a resource, it first attempts to obtain one from the resource pool by using `getResource()` to look for a resource with the description `rd`. If the pool cannot provide a matching resource, the client falls back to the normal mechanism and creates a new resource either directly or through a factory. The client then uses either the resource obtained from the pool or the freshly created one. When the client is finished with the resource, instead of releasing it, the client returns it to the resource pool. That way, when a resource is needed the next time, the pool can provide it. If the pool does not accept a resource, the client calls `dispose()` to discard the resource.

Figure 7.3 depicts the scenario from the earlier snippet in a sequence diagram.

In summary, resource pools provide a way for you to recycle resources—which means you avoid the cost of creating and destroying a new resource every time you need one. The result is improved overall system performance.

7.1.2 *Resource pooling issues*

When resource pooling is implemented in conventional ways, it leads to several problems common to a crosscutting concern. You are undoubtedly familiar with the issues of code tangling and scattering by now, so let's examine a couple of other issues in a bit more detail:

- *Space/time tradeoff*—While resource pooling reduces the time it takes to obtain a new resource, this benefit comes at a cost; the pooled resources

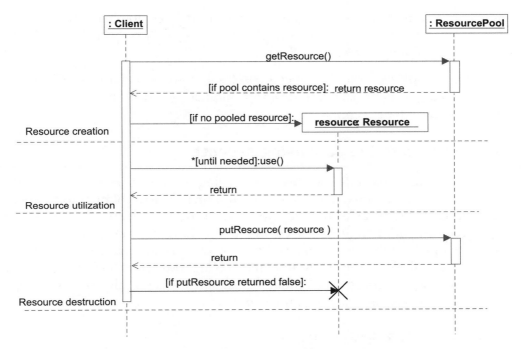

Figure 7.3 **Typical interaction of resource usage in a resource pooling scheme**

consume extra memory and other system resources. This is known as a *space/time tradeoff*. A system designer must enable resource pooling only for the modules where the benefit of improved speed outweighs the cost of extra space. However, such details are seldom known during the initial design phase. During the product lifecycle, subsystems may need to switch resource pooling off and on in certain modules, depending on their usage patterns. It is also often desirable to replace one pool implementation with another to better match the requirements of the system. With conventional pooling techniques, either of these scenarios may require changing most or all of the modules that use pooling.

- *Need for upfront decision making*—Whether to introduce resource pooling early on is the architect's dilemma. On one hand, using a simple scheme that does not involve resource pooling may lead to a faster development cycle. On the other hand, introducing resource pooling later may be too invasive. Further, the need for resource pooling may not be evident until after the completed system has been profiled. The current pooling solutions mandate choosing between an early decision to use pooling or implementing time-consuming code changes throughout the system when pooling is later introduced.

As you will see next, the AspectJ-based solution offers all the benefits of resource pooling without having to deal with these issues—you can then have your cake and eat it too.

7.2 Diving into the pool using AspectJ

The goal of AspectJ-based resource pooling is to create an aspect that transforms the simple resource usage template in listing 7.1 to a solution that uses pooling in the least invasive manner possible. In particular, the solution should not require any change on the client side, making it possible to add, remove, or modify the resource pooling without any system-wide changes. In a way, with this plug-and-play approach to resource pooling, you can dive right in without making a big splash. In this section, we examine a solution that builds on top of any available resource pooling implementation.

7.2.1 Designing a template aspect

The overall scheme for the resource pooling aspect is quite simple. All you need to do is create an aspect that advises the resource creation and destruction pointcuts with resource pooling logic.

We will develop a template to help you understand the solution at an abstract level without getting bogged down in resource-specific details. You can use this template as the basis for AspectJ-based pooling of any kind of resource by simply mapping elements in the template to the actual participating entities. For example, you can replace `Resource` in the template with `Connection` to introduce database connection pooling. Figure 7.4 shows the overall relationship between the resource pooling aspect and the rest of the system.

The participating entities in this solution are the same as the ones in the conventional solution: `Resource`, `ResourcePool`, and `ResourceDescription`. For participating join points, we are mainly interested in two pointcuts: one to capture resource creation and one to capture resource destruction. The first pointcut captures the join points at which we want to get a resource from the pool instead of creating it. Such a pointcut typically captures calls to constructors or creation methods of the resource factory. The second pointcut captures the resource destruction join points so that we can try to return the resource to the pool

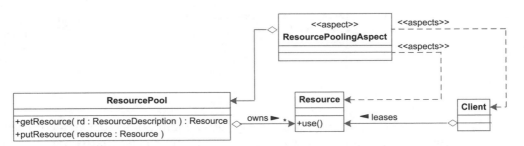

Figure 7.4 The relationship between all entities participating in resource pooling in a system. The `ResourcePoolingAspect` applies to all clients that create or dispose resources. (We show only one client for simplicity.)

instead of destroying it. Such a pointcut typically captures the calls to the methods in the resource class that release the resource.

7.2.2 *Implementing the template aspect*

Let's take a closer look at the implementation of the resource-pooling template. First, we revisit the sequence diagram in figure 7.1 that depicted the resource usage without pooling and identify the join points that need to be advised to introduce pooling. Figure 7.5 shows the pointcuts and the advice needed at the join points captured by the pointcuts.

The template of the resource pooling aspect in listing 7.2 advises the resource creation and destruction join points to use resource pooling.

Listing 7.2 The template of the resource pooling aspect

```
public aspect ResourcePoolingAspect {
    private ResourcePool _rpool = new ResourcePoolImpl();

    pointcut resourceCreation(ResourceDescription rd)          ❶ Pointcut capturing
        : <creation-pointcut-definition>;                         resource creation
                                                                   join points

    pointcut resourceDestruction(Resource r)                   Pointcut capturing resource
        : <destruction-pointcut-definition>;                   ❷ destruction join points

    Resource around(ResourceDescription rd) : resourceCreation(rd) {
        Resource resource = _rpool.getResource(rd);
        if (resource == null) {
            resource = proceed(rd);
                                                                      Advice  ❸
        }                                                            resource
        return resource;                                          creation join
    }                                                                points
```

```
        void around(Resource r) : resourceDestruction(r) {
            if (! _rpool.putResource(r)) {
                proceed(r);
            }
        }
    }
```

❹ Advice resource destruction join points

❶ The pointcut `resourceCreation()` captures all join points that create the resource. Typically, it captures constructors of the resource class that is being created or the creation methods of the factories for the resource. The pooling mechanism in step 3 must identify the desired resource it wants to obtain from the pool. To

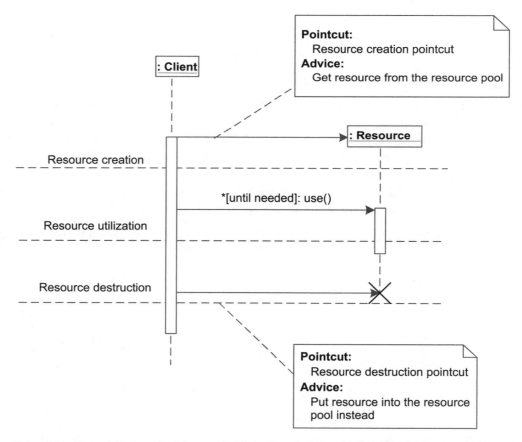

Figure 7.5 The pointcuts and advice needed to realize resource pooling. This diagram resembles figure 7.1, except that it superimposes the information for concern-weaving elements. We show only one client classifier role for simplicity.

facilitate this, the pointcut also collects the context at the join point, rd, that identifies the resource that is to be created.

❷ The pointcut resourceDestruction() captures all join points that discard the resource. Typically, it captures methods like close() on resources. Since the resources that need pooling tend to be expensive, it is common to have an explicit method to release the resource rather than rely on a garbage collector to do it. This join point also collects the context at the join point, r, that identifies the resource that is to be released so that the pool can acquire it.

❸ The around advice to the resourceCreation() pointcut first attempts to obtain a resource matching the given description from the pool. If a matching resource cannot be obtained from the pool, the proceed() statement causes the normal creation logic to be executed. It finally returns the resource object.

❹ The around advice to the resourceDestruction() pointcut first attempts to put the resource back in the pool. If the pool does not accept it for some reason (for example, adding the resource would exceed the pool's capacity), the proceed() statement causes the normal destruction logic to be executed.

This template implementation for resource pooling should enable you to understand the core issues associated with generic resource pooling. This will help you understand the concrete implementations for database and thread pooling as we focus more on the resource-specific issues in the next sections.

7.3 *Example 1: database connection pooling*

The need for database connection pooling is so common that JDBC 2.0 provides a standard way to do it. With the JDBC-based solution, you simply create and dispose of database connections in the normal way and the driver will, behind the scenes, take care of connection pooling. The solution, for the most part, works fine. However, you are dependent on the database driver for the implementation of resource pooling. If you determine that the pooling feature of the driver you are using is not acceptable, you have to replace the whole driver with another one. Such a complete change may not be satisfactory; for instance, the original driver may provide better performance than the new one. The problem lies in the coupling between the database connectivity and the resource pooling concern. With an AspectJ-based solution, we can separate these two concerns so that they will be able to evolve independently.

In this section, we look at a concrete example of database connection pooling. We base our solution in JDBC1.0 (it works fine with higher versions as well).

7.3.1 *Understanding the database connection pool interface*

Before we get into the AOP solution for database connection pooling, let's understand the problem and its traditional solution. In this section, we briefly examine a database connection pool interface and its usage.

First, let's look at the DBConnectionPool interface, in listing 7.3. Later, in listing 7.6, we will look at a simple implementation of this interface.

Listing 7.3   DBConnectionPool.java

```java
import java.sql.*;

public interface DBConnectionPool {
    public Connection getConnection(String url, String userName,
                                    String password)
        throws SQLException;

    public boolean putConnection(Connection connection);

    public void registerConnection(Connection connection,
            String url, String userName, String password);
}
```

The method getConnection() tries to get a database connection matching the given description from the pool. If a matching connection is available, the pool should return it; otherwise, it should return null. The method putConnection() returns a connection once it is no longer needed. If the pool cannot accommodate the connection for some reason, it should return false. Note that some pool implementations may simply close the connection instead of returning false, requiring no further check or action by the pool user. The method registerConnection() stores the identifying properties of the new connection so that they can be used later in the implementation of getConnection() to retrieve the connection. This is needed because after the creation of a connection, there is no other way for the pool to know the connection's URL, username, and password.

In a conventional implementation of database connection pooling, you would have to change each creation and destruction method of the connection object to use the pooling interface in listing 7.3. The following code snippet is an example of the changes that would be necessary in each method, which will help you to understand the alternative solution provided by AspectJ in the next section.

```
// connPool object of type DBConnectionPool is constructed elsewhere
Connection connection
    = connPool.getConnection(url, user, password);        Requesting a pooled
if (connection == null) {                                 connection
    connection
        = DriverManager.getConnection(url, user, password);   Creating a new
    connPool.registerConnection(connection, url, user, password);  connection
}
                                                          Registering the connection
...
// use connection object     <--- Using the connection
...

if (connPool.putConnection(connection) == false) {       Returning the
    connection.close();                                   connection
}
```

This interaction follows the snippet we discussed in section 7.1.1. There is, however, a step that we need to perform that is unique to database connection pooling. Whenever we create a new connection, we must register it with the pool, since the `Connection` class does not have an API to query for its URL, username, and password. The pool associates the information with the connection object so that it can return a correct matching connection the next time someone requests a connection.

7.3.2 *AspectJ-based database connection pooling*

Let's now design an aspect to implement modular database connection pooling. We approach the solution by mapping each element from the pooling template in listing 7.2 to an element appropriate for database connection pooling. Table 7.1 shows the mapping of template elements to the actual entities needed for connection pooling.

Table 7.1 **The mapping of elements in the template to specific elements for database connection pooling**

Template Element	Mapped Element
Resource	The `java.sql.Connection` class
Resource pool	Any suitable resource pool implementation (in our case, an implementation of the `DBConnectionPool` interface)
Resource description	A combination of the database URL, username, and password

In table 7.2, we map the join points used by the template solution to specific join points in database connection pooling.

Table 7.2   The mapping of join points in the template to specific join points for database connection pooling. These join points will be advised to introduce the connection pooling.

Template Join Point	Mapped Join Point
Resource creation	The call to the `DriverManager.getConnection()` methods. The argument's database URL, username, and password form the resource description context.
Resource destruction	The call to the `Connection.close()` method. The pointcut collects the connection object on which the method is called as the context.

Now that we have a mapping from template elements to the concrete elements, we are ready to implement a database connection pooling aspect. Listing 7.4 shows the `DBConnectionPoolingAspect` that uses the mappings from tables 7.1 and 7.2.

Listing 7.4   DBConnectionPoolingAspect.java

```
import java.sql.*;
                                                        Resource
                                                        pool
public aspect DBConnectionPoolingAspect {           ➊ creation
    DBConnectionPool _connPool = new SimpleDBConnectionPool();

    pointcut connectionCreation(String url, String username,
                            String password)       Connection creation  ➋
        : call(public static Connection              pointcut
            DriverManager.getConnection(String, String, String))
          && args(url, username, password);

    pointcut connectionRelease(Connection connection)    ➌ Connection
        : call(public void Connection.close())             destruction
          && target(connection);                           pointcut

    Connection around(String url, String userName, String password)
        throws SQLException
        : connectionCreation(url, userName, password) {  Advice to resource  ➍
        Connection connection                            creation join points
            = _connPool.getConnection(url, userName, password);
        if (connection == null) {
            connection = proceed(url, userName, password);
            _connPool.registerConnection(connection, url,
                                    userName, password);
        }
        return connection;
    }

    void around(Connection connection)       ➎ Advice to resource
        : connectionRelease(connection) {        destruction join points
```

```
            if (!_connPool.putConnection(connection)) {
                proceed(connection);
            }
        }
    }
```

❶ Since there will be only one instance of this aspect in a virtual machine, there will be only one instance of the resource pool created. We use a simple implementation of the DBConnectionPool interface—SimpleDBConnectionPool—that we will examine later in listing 7.6. If you have a different implementation of DBConnectionPool, all you need to do is change the aspect to instantiate the new implementation.

❷ This pointcut captures calls to the DriverManager.getConnection(String, String, String) method. The args() pointcut designator collects all the arguments to the method call. A more complete solution will also capture other DriverManager.getConnection() methods that take different arguments.

❸ This pointcut captures calls to the Connection.close() method. The target object, the connection itself, is collected as context.

❹ The around advice allows us to bypass the original execution path that creates a connection. This advice first attempts to obtain a connection from the pool object. If a matching connection can be obtained, the advice simply returns it and bypasses the original execution path. Otherwise, it calls proceed() to take the normal execution path that would create a new resource. Since the resource description (URL, username, and password) is available only at the time of creation, the advice must store the information that associates the description with the connection object in the resource pool. The aspect performs this task by calling the DBConnectionPool.registerConnection() method after it has created a new resource using proceed(). Note that registerConnection() needs to be called only for newly created connections and not connections obtained from the pool. The advice finally returns the connection obtained.

❺ Just like earlier advice, the around advice allows us to bypass the original execution path that closes the connection. This advice calls putConnection() to return the connection object to the pool. If the pool rejects the resource by returning false, the advice simply calls proceed(), thus causing the connection to close.

NOTE   One implication of our solution is that if a JDBC 2.0 driver supporting resource pooling is used, our solution will override the default resource pooling that it performs. However, if we introduced a scheme of periodically visiting each connection in the pool and closing the idle connections, then the driver-supported resource pooling would kick in as a secondary pooling.

7.3.3 *Implementing the connection pool*

Next let's look at the classes that implement the database connection pool. Note that the connection pool interface and its implementation are required even in the conventional solution. The purpose of our implementation is to see the result of an AspectJ-based solution. Since the pool needs a way to identify a resource request, and the Connection class does not have an API to access the information needed to identify the connection, we will first create a class to capture this information. The DBConnectionDescription class in listing 7.5 simply consolidates connection properties: URL, username, and password.

> **Listing 7.5   DBConnectionDescription.java**

```java
public class DBConnectionDescription {
    private String _url;
    private String _userName;
    private String _password;

    public DBConnectionDescription(String url, String userName,
                                   String password) {
        _url = url;
        _userName = userName;
        _password = password;
    }

    public int hashCode() {
        return _url.hashCode();
    }

    public boolean equals(Object obj) {
        if (this == obj) {
            return true;
        }

        if (!obj.getClass().equals(getClass())) {
            return false;
        }

        DBConnectionDescription desc = (DBConnectionDescription)obj;
        return (_url == null ?
                    desc._url == null :
                    _url.equals(desc._url))
            && (_userName == null ?
                    desc._userName == null :
                    _userName.equals(desc._userName))
            && (_password == null ?
                    desc._password == null :
                    _password.equals(desc._password));
    }
}
```

DBConnectionDescription contains hashCode() and equals() methods to ensure that we can use it correctly inside a map and compare it for equivalence.

The SimpleDBConnectionPool implementation is quite simple. A more complex resource pool would consider several other factors, such as the maximum number of resources to be pooled, the specified time that a resource should sit idle in a pool before it is released, and perhaps even user equivalency that would allow a resource created by one user to be used by another user with equivalent access. Listing 7.6 shows an implementation of the DBConnectionPool interface.

Listing 7.6 SimpleDBConnectionPool.java

```java
import java.sql.*;
import java.util.*;

public class SimpleDBConnectionPool implements DBConnectionPool {
    List _pooledConnections = new ArrayList();        // Holding pooled
                                                       // connections

    Map _connectionDescriptionMap = new HashMap();    // Mapping the description
                                                       // to connections
    synchronized
    public Connection getConnection(String url, String userName,
                                     String password)
        throws SQLException {
        DBConnectionDescription desc
            = new DBConnectionDescription(url, userName, password);
        List connectionsList = getConnections(desc);  // Finding
        if (connectionsList == null) {                 // candidate
            return null;                               // resources
        }

        for (int size = _pooledConnections.size(), i = 0; i < size; ++i) {
            Connection connection = (Connection)_pooledConnections.get(i);
            if (connectionsList.contains(connection)) {
                _pooledConnections.remove(connection);
                if (!connection.isClosed()) {
                    return connection;                 // Checking
                }                                      // against
            }                                          // pooled
        }                                              // resources
        return null;
    }

    synchronized
    public boolean putConnection(Connection connection) {
        _pooledConnections.add(connection);           // Adding to pooled
        return true;                                   // resources
    }
```

```
    synchronized
    public void registerConnection(Connection connection,
                                   String url, String userName,
                                   String password) {
        DBConnectionDescription desc
            = new DBConnectionDescription(url, userName, password);
        List connectionsList = getConnections(desc);
        if (connectionsList == null) {
            connectionsList = new ArrayList();
            _connectionDescriptionMap.put(desc, connectionsList);
        }                                      Adding description and
        connectionsList.add(connection);         connection to the map
    }

    private List getConnections(DBConnectionDescription desc) {
        return (List)_connectionDescriptionMap.get(desc);
    }
}
```

Since the implementation of the pool is not the core part of this chapter, we will not spend too much time on the details of it. The `_connectionDescriptionMap` member keeps track of the mapping between the connection object and its description (URL, username, and password). The `getConnection()` method looks for a pooled connection. The private method `getConnections()` returns a list of pooled resources with the matching description. If the returned list is not empty, `getConnection()` removes a connection object from the list and returns the removed connection to the caller. The `putConnection()` method returns the given resource to the available resource pool. The `registerConnection()` method establishes a mapping between the given connection object and its properties.

7.3.4 *Testing our solution*

Finally, let's write a test program to illustrate the AspectJ pooling solution. Our test program first creates two connections for two sets of user/password combinations. We release each connection after using it. On the next requests to those connections, we expect to get a pooled connection instead of creating a new one. Listing 7.7 shows the Test class that sets up this scenario.

Listing 7.7   Test.java

```
import java.sql.*;

public class Test {
    public static void main(String[] args) throws Exception {
```

```
        Class.forName("sun.jdbc.odbc.JdbcOdbcDriver");
        printTable("jdbc:odbc:stock", "price",        Interacting
                   "user1", "password1");             with user1

        printTable("jdbc:odbc:stock", "price",        Interacting
                   "user2", "password2");             with user2

        printTable("jdbc:odbc:stock", "price",        Repeating the
                   "user1", "password1");             first interaction

        printTable("jdbc:odbc:stock", "price",        Repeating the
                   "user2", "password2");             second interaction
    }

    static void printTable(String url, String table,
                           String user, String password)
        throws SQLException {
        Connection connection                Creating a connection
            = DriverManager.getConnection(url, user, password);
        Statement stmt = connection.createStatement();
        ResultSet rs = stmt.executeQuery("select * from " + table);

        ResultSetMetaData rsmd = rs.getMetaData();
        int numCols = rsmd.getColumnCount();            Using the
                                                        connection
        while (rs.next()) {
            for (int i = 1; i < numCols+1; ++i) {
                System.out.print(rs.getString(i) + "\t");
            }
            System.out.println();
        }
        rs.close();
        connection.close();    ←── Closing the connection
    }
}
```

The Test class examines the behavior of the connection pooling aspect when the pool has a matching connection and when it does not. For simplicity, the only interaction with the database is to iterate over the rows and print their content.

Adding a logging aspect
How do we know our solution works? Let's write a simple logging aspect to understand the behavior of the pooling aspect. The DBConnectionPoolLoggingAspect aspect in listing 7.8 logs the operations of DBConnectionPool and prints the relevant context. Notice, by the way, the easy and noninvasive logging implementation.

Listing 7.8 DBConnectionPoolLoggingAspect.java

```
import java.sql.*;                                    Precedence to
                                                      make pooling
public aspect DBConnectionPoolLoggingAspect {         happen before
    declare precedence: *, DBConnectionPoolLoggingAspect;  ◁─┘ logging

    after(String url, String userName, String password)
        returning(Connection connection)
        : call(Connection DBConnectionPool.getConnection(..))
          && args(url, userName, password) {
        System.out.println("For [" + url + "," + userName
                        + "," + password + "]"
                        + "\n\tGot from pool: " + connection);
    }
                                            Logging resource retrieval

    after(String url, String userName, String password)
        returning(Connection connection)
        : call(Connection DriverManager.getConnection(..))
          && args(url, userName, password) {
        System.out.println("For [" + url + "," + userName
                        + "," + password + "]"
                        + "\n\tCreated new : " + connection);
    }
                                            Logging resource creation

    before(Connection connection)
        : call(* DBConnectionPool.putConnection(Connection))
        && args(connection) {
        System.out.println("Putting in pool: " + connection + "\n");
    }
                                            Logging resource relinquishing

    before(Connection connection)
        : call(* Connection.close())
        && target(connection) {
        System.out.println("Closing: " + connection + "\n");
    }
                                            Logging resource destruction
}
```

The after advice to the DBConnectionPool.getConnection() method prints any attempt to get a connection from a database pool. We collect all the arguments as well as return the object to print the full information inside the advice body. Similarly, the after advice to DriverManager.getConnection() logs the creation of a new resource. The before advice to the DBConnectionPool.putConnection() method prints any attempt to put a connection into a database pool. We collect the connection argument to print the connection that was being returned. The before advice to Connection.close() prints the same information when a connection is closed.

You would not want to use this aspect in a production environment, since it logs the usernames and passwords. In that case, if you still want to log the operations, you could just change the advice to print only the desired information.

Running the test code

Running the code is simple. You will have to create the database tables with users and passwords as specified in the `Test.java` class. Detailed instructions for setting up the test database are provided in the source code distribution (downloadable at http://www.manning.com/laddad). Alternatively, you can modify `Test.java` itself to suit your existing test database. After the setup is complete, simply issue the command `java Test` to run the program. You should see output resembling the following:

```
> ajc *.java
> java Test
For [jdbc:odbc:stock,user1,password1]
        Got from pool: null
For [jdbc:odbc:stock,user1,password1]
        Created new : sun.jdbc.odbc.JdbcOdbcConnection@1cfb549
sunw    22
ibm     100
Putting in pool: sun.jdbc.odbc.JdbcOdbcConnection@1cfb549


For [jdbc:odbc:stock,user2,password2]
        Got from pool: null
For [jdbc:odbc:stock,user2,password2]
        Created new : sun.jdbc.odbc.JdbcOdbcConnection@422ede
sunw    22
ibm     100
Putting in pool: sun.jdbc.odbc.JdbcOdbcConnection@422ede


For [jdbc:odbc:stock,user1,password1]
        Got from pool: sun.jdbc.odbc.JdbcOdbcConnection@1cfb549
  sunw    22
ibm     100
Putting in pool: sun.jdbc.odbc.JdbcOdbcConnection@1cfb549


For [jdbc:odbc:stock,user2,password2]
        Got from pool: sun.jdbc.odbc.JdbcOdbcConnection@422ede
sunw    22
ibm     100
Putting in pool: sun.jdbc.odbc.JdbcOdbcConnection@422ede
```

❶ First interaction with user1

❷ First interaction with user2

❸ Second interaction with user1

❹ Second interaction with user2

❶ Since the pool is empty, a connection could not be obtained. Therefore, a new connection is created. When we are done with the connection, the advice puts it into the pool.

❷ The pool is not empty, but the only connection in the pool matches user1 and not user2. Therefore, the pool did not return any connection, and a new connection is created. When we are done with the connection, it too is returned to the pool.

❸ The pool had a matching connection for user1. The given URL and password matched as well. Thus, the pool returned the matching connection created in the first interaction. Note the IDs for the connection objects.

❹ Here too, the pool had a matching connection from the second interaction. Since the URL, username, and password matched, the pool returned the obtained connection object.

In the previous example, we do not see output corresponding to the before advice to the `Connection.close()` method in `DBConnectionPoolLoggingAspect`. This is because `DBConnectionPoolingAspect` intercepts all the calls to `Connection.close()` and puts the connection into the pool instead of closing it.

To better understand the interaction, play around with the `Test` class and try different combinations.

7.3.5 *Tweaking the solution*

It is likely that you will have to alter the solution to fit your specific needs. Here is some guidance to a few of the possible requirements.

The first tweak considers the requirement of selectively enabling database pooling, where instead of applying pooling to the whole system, we apply it only to a select list of clients. We can do so by modifying the resource creation and destruction pointcuts to specify selected clients, as shown in the following snippet:

```
pointcut selectedClients() : within(com.manning..*);

pointcut connectionCreation(String url, String username,
                            String password)
    : call(public static Connection
           DriverManager.getConnection(String, String, String))
          && args(url, username, password) && selectedClients();

pointcut connectionRelease(Connection connection)
    : call(public void Connection.close())
          && target(connection) && selectedClients();
```

In this code, we are defining `selectedClients()` to select all classes inside the `com.manning` package and its subpackages only. You can modify this pointcut to select any number of packages and classes by combining `within()` with `&&` and `||`. In addition, you can specify any other suitable selection criteria here. For example, you may want to enable resource pooling only for resources created within the control flow of a certain method or a set of methods.

The second tweak considers the requirement to turn off resource pooling completely. To achieve this, we must modify the creation and destruction point-cuts so that they do not match any join points, thus not allowing any of the advice to run. We use the "nullifying an advice" idiom (which we will formally introduce in chapter 8) to ensure that no join points match the selectedClients() pointcut, as follows:

```
pointcut selectedClients() : if(false);
```

Note, we could still specify other selection criteria and combine it with an if(false) pointcut. This can be especially useful when we are debugging and trying out what-if scenarios:

```
pointcut selectedClients() : within(com.manning..*) && if(false);
```

We can also use a variation of this to turn off other selection criteria, thus uncon-ditionally selecting all the clients by using if(true) and || as follows:

```
pointcut selectedClients() : within(com.manning..*) || if(true);
```

Now you can try out various combinations for enabling resource pooling to see the optimal combination for your system. The use of the "nullifying an advice" idiom also provides you with an opportunity to see the impact of resource pool-ing on your overall system performance.

7.4 *Example 2: thread pooling*

Thread pooling is often used for high-performance server-side applications. The thread resource is unusual in that the resource destruction point is not as obvious as that in the call to a method such as close(). Further, since the resource thread, by definition, is an active resource—it owns an execution flow of its own—putting it in a resource pool is a bit interesting.

Many application server providers internally recycle the threads to improve performance. However, other applications still require that each module that creates a new thread be modified to use the pool's API. In this section, we imple-ment a simple AspectJ-based solution that cures the problem of invasiveness associated with the conventional solution.

7.4.1 *The echo server*

First we will create a simple TCP/IP-based server—one that echoes back the request string and uses a new thread for serving each request. We will use this example to introduce thread pooling. Later we will write an aspect that recycles those threads using a thread pool.

EchoServer is a multithreaded application. It creates a server socket, waits on the socket for an incoming request, accepts a connection from a client, and spawns a new thread to interact with the client. Each spawned thread echoes back each line supplied by the client until the client chooses to terminate the interaction, at which time the spawned thread terminates as well. Listing 7.9 shows the EchoServer class.

Listing 7.9   EchoServer.java

```
import java.io.*;
import java.net.*;

public class EchoServer {
    public static void main(String[] args) throws Exception {
        if (args.length != 1) {
            System.out.println("Usage: java EchoServer <portNum>");
            System.exit(1);
        }

        int portNum = Integer.parseInt(args[0]);
        ServerSocket serverSocket = new ServerSocket(portNum);

        while(true) {
            Socket requestSocket = serverSocket.accept();
            Runnable worker = new EchoWorker(requestSocket);
            Thread serverThread = new Thread(worker);
            serverThread.start();
        }
    }
}
```

It is a common practice to utilize a separate class—often called the worker class—that encodes the thread's logic. You then supply an object of that class to a thread that calls the worker's run() method. The EchoServer class spawns a new thread with an object EchoWorker (shown in listing 7.10) as its worker object.

Listing 7.10   EchoWorker.java: the worker class

```java
import java.io.*;
import java.net.*;

class EchoWorker implements Runnable {
    private Socket _requestSocket;

    public EchoWorker(Socket requestSocket) throws IOException {
        _requestSocket = requestSocket;          ◁─┐ Initializes with the
    }                                                 socket to be served

    public void run() {                                        Initializes
        BufferedReader requestReader = null;                request and
        PrintWriter responseWriter = null;                   response
        try {                                                  streams
            requestReader
                = new BufferedReader(new InputStreamReader(
                    _requestSocket.getInputStream()));
            responseWriter
                = new PrintWriter(_requestSocket.getOutputStream());

            while(true) {
                String requestString = requestReader.readLine();
                if (requestString == null) {
                    break;
                }
                System.out.println("Got request: " + requestString);
                responseWriter.write(requestString + "\n");
                responseWriter.flush();                   Serves the
            }                                                 client
        } catch (IOException ex) {
        } finally {
            try {
                if(requestReader != null) {
                    requestReader.close();
                }                                      Cleans up
                if(responseWriter != null) {           all the
                    responseWriter.close();            resources
                }                                      used
                _requestSocket.close();
            } catch (IOException ex2) { }
        }
        System.out.println("Ending the session");
    }
}
```

EchoWorker performs its task in the run() method. It obtains the input and output streams from the socket supplied in the constructor; it then reads a line from the input and echoes it back by writing to the output.

7.4.2 Understanding the thread pool interface

Now that we have created the classes that demonstrate the thread usage, let's examine the thread pool interface. Later in this chapter, we will write an aspect that uses this interface to introduce thread pooling to the system. Listing 7.11 shows the ThreadPool interface that allows basic pooling operations.

> **Listing 7.11   The thread pool interface**
>
> ```
> public interface ThreadPool {
>     public boolean putThread(Thread thread);       ◁──❶  Putting the thread
>                                                           into the pool
>
>     public Thread getThread();    ◁──❷  Obtaining the
>                                          thread
>
>     public boolean wakeupThread(Thread thread);    ◁──❸  Waking up the
> }                                                        obtained thread
> ```

❶ The putThread() method puts the thread into the pool, gives the ownership of the thread to the pool, and puts the thread into the waiting state.

❷ The getThread() method, in contrast, gets an available thread, thus transferring ownership to the caller. The returned thread will be in a waiting state and the client should initialize its state, if necessary, before calling wakeupThread().

❸ The wakeupThread() method activates a thread obtained from the pool. If the thread could not be woken up, presumably because it was not waiting, then the method returns false.

7.4.3 AspectJ-based thread pooling

Before we build the pooling aspect, we need to create a class that allows us to use the same pooled thread to perform different work. We need this class because the Thread class can only set its worker object during the thread's construction, and we must have a way to change a pooled thread's worker object each time we obtain it from the pool. DelegatingThread is simply a thread that delegates its run() method to its delegatee object. By setting a different delegatee object, we can make a thread perform different tasks. Listing 7.12 shows the implementation for the DelegatingThread class.

Listing 7.12   DelegatingThread.java

```java
public class DelegatingThread extends Thread {
    private Runnable _delegatee;

    public void setDelegatee(Runnable delegatee) {
        _delegatee = delegatee;
    }

    public void run() {
        _delegatee.run();
    }
}
```

Now that we have our basic classes and interfaces, let's build our thread pooling aspect. As with the database connection pooling example in section 7.3, we will first map each element from the resource pooling template (listing 7.2) to specific elements needed for thread pooling. Table 7.3 shows the mapping of template elements to the actual entities needed for thread pooling.

Table 7.3   The mapping of elements in the template to specific elements for thread pooling

Template Element	Mapped Element
Resource	The `java.lang.Thread` class.
Resource pool	Any suitable resource pool implementation (in our case, an implementation of the `ThreadPool` interface).
Resource description	None considered here; all threads are treated alike.

In table 7.4, we map the join points used by the template solution to specific join points in thread pooling.

Table 7.4   The mapping of join points in the template to specific join points for thread pooling. These join points will be advised to introduce the thread pooling.

Template Join Point	Mapped Join Point
Resource creation	The call to `Thread`'s constructor and the `Thread.start()` method.
Resource destruction	The completion of the `Thread.run()` or `Runnable.run()` method. The target socket object forms the context collected.

Let's use this mapping to write `ThreadPoolingAspect` (listing 7.13), which will introduce thread pooling to a system.

Listing 7.13   ThreadPoolingAspect.java

```java
public aspect ThreadPoolingAspect {
    ThreadPool _pool = new SimpleThreadPool();        ◄─❶ Creating the
                                                            thread pool
    pointcut threadCreation(Runnable worker)
        : call(Thread.new(Runnable)) && args(worker);   Defining the    ❷
                                                          pointcuts
    pointcut session(DelegatingThread thread)
        : execution(void DelegatingThread.run()) && this(thread);

    pointcut threadStart(DelegatingThread thread)
        : call(void Thread.start()) && target(thread);

    Thread around(Runnable worker) : threadCreation(worker) {
        DelegatingThread availableThread
            = (DelegatingThread)_pool.getThread();          Advising
        if (availableThread == null) {                      thread
            availableThread = new DelegatingThread();       creations
        }                                                   ❸
        availableThread.setDelegatee(worker);  ◄─┐
        return availableThread;                  ❹ Changing the
    }                                              delegatee

    void around(DelegatingThread thread) : session(thread) {
        while (true) {                                      Advising
            proceed(thread);                                the thread
            _pool.putThread(thread);                        session
        }
    }                                                       ❺

    void around(Thread thread) : threadStart(thread) {
        if (!_pool.wakeupThread(thread)) {           Advising
            proceed(thread);                         the thread
        }                                            start
    }                                                ❻
}
```

❶ This code initializes the thread pool object. Here we use a simple implementation of the ThreadPool interface—SimpleThreadPool—that we will examine in listing 7.14.

❷ The aspect needs to capture three join points: thread creation, thread service session, and thread start. The pointcut threadCreation() captures the calls to the Thread's constructor that takes a Runnable argument. It collects the argument as context. Similarly, the session() pointcut captures the executions of the run() method in the DelegatingThread class. The pointcut threadStart() captures calls to the Thread.start() method, and collects the thread object that is to be started as the context.

3 When a client needs to start a task in a different thread, the around advice to the threadCreation() pointcut first attempts to get a thread from the pool. If it cannot get a pooled thread, it creates a new DelegatingThread object. In either case, it sets the thread's target Runnable with the Runnable object that was the constructor argument collected as context by the threadCreation() pointcut. It returns to the caller the thread initialized with the given Runnable object. Note that the caller will always get an object of type DelegatingThread. This is fine since the client was expecting a Thread object to be constructed by a constructor and DelegatingThread *is* a Thread. The client would typically call the start() method on the obtained thread to start the thread.

4 The _delegatee object of a thread obtained from the pool is changed to the worker context collected by the threadCreation() pointcut. This enables the pool to perform the new work requested by the clients.

5 The around advice to the session() pointcut puts the captured method, DelegatingThread.run(), in an infinite loop with the while(true) statement, which ensures that the caller thread never dies. (This is because a thread, once dead, cannot be resurrected, and we need to keep all pooled threads alive to hand over to the requesting clients.) The proceed() statement causes the captured method to execute, which, in turn, executes the run() method of the collected thread's delegatee. After each execution, the thread is put into the thread pool object by the ThreadPool.putThread() method, which will cause that thread to go into a waiting state until it is woken up again by another thread. Note that even though we have an infinite while loop inside the advice, the captured thread's run() method will execute only once before ThreadPool.putThread() is called to put the thread into the pool until it is needed by another thread. Once the thread is woken up, it will execute the captured thread's run() method one more time, and the cycle continues.

6 The around advice to the threadStart() pointcut attempts to wake up the thread. If this thread was obtained from the pool, it will be woken up. If this was a newly created thread, wakeupThread() will return false. In that case, proceed() will call the original start() method to start the new thread. In either case, the thread will execute the delegated run() method once before the thread is put into the waiting state by the advice to the session() pointcut.

NOTE   One implication of our solution is that it will pool all threads created in the system—not just for the server. This may or may not be desirable. We discuss ways to handle this situation later in this section.

7.4.4 *Implementing the thread pool*

Next let's look at the class that implements the thread pool interface. Listing 7.14 shows the `SimpleThreadPool` interface that we used in our thread pooling aspect.

Listing 7.14   SimpleThreadPool.java

```java
import java.util.*;

public class SimpleThreadPool implements ThreadPool {
    List _waitingThreads = new ArrayList();

    public boolean putThread(Thread thread) {
        assert Thread.currentThread() == thread;
        synchronized(thread) {
            synchronized (this) {
                _waitingThreads.add(thread);
            }

            try {
                thread.wait();
            } catch(InterruptedException ex) {
            }
        }
        return true;
    }

    synchronized public Thread getThread() {
        if (!_waitingThreads.isEmpty()) {
            Thread availableThread
                = (Thread)_waitingThreads.remove(0);
            return availableThread;
        }
        return null;
    }

    public boolean wakeupThread(Thread thread) {
        if (thread.isAlive()) {
            synchronized(thread) {
                thread.notify();
                return true;
            }
        }
        return false;
    }
}
```

❶ Putting the thread into the pool

❷ Obtaining the thread

❸ Waking up the obtained thread

❶ The `putThread()` method requires that the caller thread be the same thread it is attempting to pool. This requirement is enforced using an `assert` statement[1] (provided you have enabled the assertions, of course). It adds the thread to the list of waiting threads, where it will wait until notified by the `wakeupThread()` method, which is typically called after someone obtains it from the pool using `getThread()`.

❷ The `getThread()` method provides a thread to the caller by returning an available thread from the pool. The thread still continues to be in a waiting state until it is woken up. The client will change the thread's state to that needed by the task it is about to perform—much like initializing a newly created thread before waking it up.

❸ The `wakeupThread()` method wakes up the thread. Once woken up, the thread starts performing its given task.

7.4.5 Testing our solution

Now that we have the implementation, it is time to test our thread pooling using the AspectJ-based solution. Let's first write a test client to exercise the pooling functionality, as shown in listing 7.15.

Listing 7.15   EchoClient.java

```java
import java.io.*;
import java.net.*;

public class EchoClient {
    public static void main(String[] args) throws Exception {
        if (args.length != 2) {
            System.out.println(
                "Usage: java EchoClient <server> <portNum>");
            System.exit(1);
        }
        String serverName = args[0];
        int portNum = Integer.parseInt(args[1]);
        setup(serverName, portNum);
    }

    private static void setup(String serverName, int portNum)
        throws IOException {
        Socket requestSocket
            = new Socket(InetAddress.getByName(serverName),
                         portNum);
```

---

[1] The new functionality of `assert` allows you to programmatically express contracts. At runtime, you can selectively enable or disable assertion for a class, package, and package trees. See http://java.sun.com/j2se/1.4/docs/guide/lang/assert.html for more details.

```
BufferedReader consoleReader
    = new BufferedReader(new InputStreamReader(System.in));

BufferedReader responseReader = new BufferedReader(
    new InputStreamReader(requestSocket.getInputStream()));
PrintWriter requestWriter
    = new PrintWriter(requestSocket.getOutputStream());

while(true) {
    String requestString = consoleReader.readLine();
    if (requestString.equals("quit")) {
        break;
    }
    requestWriter.println(requestString);
    requestWriter.flush();
    System.out.println("Response: "
                        + responseReader.readLine());
}
requestWriter.close();
responseReader.close();
requestSocket.close();
    }
}
```

The class `EchoClient` accepts two arguments to the program: the server name and the server port number. After parsing the arguments, it invokes the `setup()` method that performs the real work. The `setup()` method connects to the server by creating a client socket. The method then simply reads the user input from the console, writes it to an output stream of the client socket, reads from the input stream of the client socket, and writes the text.

Adding a logging aspect

To observe the behavior of the `EchoClient` test program, let's write a simple logging aspect, shown in listing 7.16, just as we did for the database connection-pooling example.

Listing 7.16 Logging the pool operations: `ThreadPoolLoggingAspect`

```
public aspect ThreadPoolLoggingAspect {
    after() returning(Thread thread)
        : execution(Thread ThreadPool.getThread(..)) {
        System.out.println("Got from pool: " + thread);
    }

    before(Thread thread)
        : execution(boolean ThreadPool.putThread(Thread))
```

```
        && args(thread) {
        System.out.println("Putting in pool: " + thread + "\n");
    }

    before(Thread thread)
        : execution(boolean ThreadPool.wakeupThread(Thread))
        && args(thread) {
        System.out.println("Waking up: " + thread);
    }
}
```

The after advice to the `ThreadPool.getThread()` method prints the return object—the thread obtained from the pool. Similarly, the before advice to `ThreadPool.putThread()` and `ThreadPool.wakeupThread()` prints the thread that is returned to the pool and the thread being woken up.

Running the test code

To run the test program, follow these steps:

1   Compile the code. Since we are using the assertion facility, you need to pass the `-source 1.4` flag to the compiler invocation:

```
> ajc -source 1.4 *.java
```

2   In a command shell, start the server by issuing the following command. You should start the server on port 10000. If that port is unavailable, try another port. The `-ea` option to JVM ensures that assertions are enabled:

```
> java -ea EchoServer 10000
```

3   In another command shell, start a client by issuing the following command. The client host should be the same as the server host:

```
> java -ea EchoClient localhost 10000
```

4   Type a few strings for the server to echo in the client shell. Quit the shell by typing `quit`.

```
First string
Second String
quit
```

5   Start another client by following step 2. Enter a few strings and quit.

6   Observe the output in the server window. You should see something like this:

```
Got from pool: null
Waking up: Thread[Thread-1,5,main]
```
❶

```
Got request: First string
Got request: Second string
Ending the session
Putting in pool: Thread[Thread-1,5,main]

Got from pool: Thread[Thread-1,5,main]
Waking up: Thread[Thread-1,5,main]
Got request: Third string
Got request: Fourth string
Ending the session
Putting in pool: Thread[Thread-1,5,main]
```

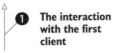
The interaction with the first client

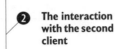
The interaction with the second client

1 The server could not obtain a thread from the thread pool; therefore, a new thread [Thread-1,5,main] was created. Upon ending the first session, [Thread-1,5,main] is returned to the thread pool.

2 This time, the server could obtain a thread from the pool—[Thread-1,5,main], which was placed there by an earlier client. No new thread was created! Once this session is over, the thread is returned to the pool.

Try variations, such as simultaneously starting more than one client and quitting them in and out of order.

7.4.6 *Tweaking the solution*

The solution we've presented here applies resource pooling to all threads in the system using the `Thread(Runnable)` constructor. In most cases, since the AspectJ-based solution offers pooling for free, this can be considered an added bonus. In other cases, however, you may want a more controlled usage of pooling. This section looks at some of those.

One of the most common requirements of thread pooling is to apply it selectively based on the client. The solution in section 7.3.5, which uses the `selectedClients()` pointcut for database connection pooling, applies equally well here. Just as in the database connection example, you can specify any criteria you need in a new pointcut and combine it using `&&` with the `threadCreation()`, `session()`, and `threadStart()` pointcuts to restrict the aspect's scope.

It is sometimes desirable to restrict pooling to certain kinds of jobs. In our example, for instance, we may want to restrict it to threads used for the echo service. It is easy to modify the aspect to do this. Simply modify the `threadCreation()` pointcut as follows. In this case, we are restricting the thread pooling to threads delegating their work to a `Runnable` type of `EchoWorker`:

```
pointcut threadCreation(Runnable worker)
    : call(Thread.new(Runnable)) && args(worker)
        && args(EchoWorker);
```

When you become more familiar with AspectJ, you can add many other tweaks to optimally configure the AspectJ-based pooling solution to fit your system's needs.

7.5 *Extending pooling concepts to caching*

Caching is often confused with pooling, partially because of the apparent similarity between their implementations. However, the difference between the two is simple: with pooling, there is only one exclusive owner of the pooled object at any given time, whereas with caching, multiple users could use a cached object. The exclusive ownership in pooling also necessitates the explicit transfer of the ownership between the users and the pool. By addressing these differences, we can extend the AspectJ implementation of pooling for caching purposes. In this section, we examine XSLT stylesheet caching as an example.

First let's create a simple Test program, as shown in listing 7.17, that illustrates a scenario where the use of caching can boost system performance by reusing the stylesheet transformer. This program will also be used to show the effect of the caching aspect that we will develop later.

Listing 7.17   Test.java: reusing the stylesheet transformer

```java
import java.io.*;

import javax.xml.transform.*;
import javax.xml.transform.stream.*;

public class Test {
    public static void main(String[] args) throws Exception {
        printTableRaw("input1.xml");
        printTablePretty("input1.xml");
        printTableRaw("input2.xml");
        printTablePretty("input2.xml");
    }

    private static void printTableRaw(String xmlFile)
        throws TransformerConfigurationException, TransformerException {
        TransformerFactory tFactory = TransformerFactory.newInstance();
        Transformer transformer
            = tFactory.newTransformer(
                new StreamSource(new File("tableRaw.xsl")));

        // Use the transformer
    }

    private static void printTablePretty(String xmlFile)
        throws TransformerConfigurationException, TransformerException {
```

```
    TransformerFactory tFactory = TransformerFactory.newInstance();
    Transformer transformer
        = tFactory.newTransformer(
            new StreamSource(new File("tablePretty.xsl")));
    // Use the transformer
    }
}
```

In listing 7.17, the `printTableRaw()` and `printTablePretty()` methods take an argument for the XML file to be transformed. Each method creates an XSLT transformer object that can be used later to transform the input XML file for, say, the purpose of printing or creating HTML documents. Note that both methods create a fresh `Transformer` object each time they are invoked—that is the caching opportunity we will explore later. The code for `printTableRaw()` and `printTablePretty()` is very similar, and in a real application they would be refactored to share the common code. However, we leave them as is to mimic the situation in which the only logic shared between such methods is the creation of the transformer.

Also consider a simple logging aspect that monitors the creation of new `Transformer` objects. The aspect in listing 7.18 prints the transformer obtained by invoking the `TransformerFactory.newTransformer()` method in the `Test` class.

Listing 7.18   LogTransformerCreation.java: monitors the creation of `Transformer` objects

```
import javax.xml.transform.*;

public aspect LogTransformerCreation {
    declare precedence: LogTransformerCreation, *;

    after(Source source) returning (Transformer transformer)
        : call(* TransformerFactory.newTransformer(..))
        && args(source) {
        System.out.println("Obtained transformer for:\n\t"
                            + source.getSystemId() + "\n\t"
                            + transformer);
    }
}
```

We assume the existence of input1.xml, input2.xml, tableRaw.xsl, and tablePretty.xsl. You can use any valid XML and XSLT files in place of these. You can also find example files in the downloadable source code. When we compile these files and run the program, we see that a new `Transformer` is instantiated every time:

```
> ajc Test.java LogTransformerCreation.java
> java Test
Obtained transformer for:
        file:///F:/stylesheets/tableRaw.xsl
        org.apache.xalan.transformer.TransformerImpl@fc9944
Obtained transformer for:
        file:///F:/stylesheets/tablePretty.xsl
        org.apache.xalan.transformer.TransformerImpl@a8c488
Obtained transformer for:
        file:///F:/stylesheets/tableRaw.xsl
        org.apache.xalan.transformer.TransformerImpl@76cbf7
Obtained transformer for:
        file:///F:/stylesheets/tablePretty.xsl
        org.apache.xalan.transformer.TransformerImpl@cec0c5
```

This output shows that each invocation of a method resulted in creating a brand-new `Transformer` object even for the same-source stylesheet file. In the next section, you will see how you can use a caching aspect to avoid creating a new `Transformer` object if the stylesheet is the same.

7.5.1 *AspectJ-based caching: the first version*

Now let's introduce caching using AspectJ. We would like to cache the `Transformer` instances for each source stylesheet file, and create the `Transformer` for `tableRaw.xsl` and `tablePretty.xsl` only once. The subsequent transformations should just reuse those instances. Extending the pooling concept, we need to surround the `Transformer` creation with an around advice. The advice should first check whether the cache already has a matching `Transformer`; if it exists, the advice should return it. Otherwise, the around advice should proceed with creating a new instance and add it to the cache before returning. We encode this logic into an aspect, as shown in listing 7.19.

Listing 7.19 TransformerCacheAspect.java: the caching aspect for `Transformer` instances

```
import java.util.*;

import javax.xml.transform.*;

public aspect TransformerCacheAspect {
    Map _cache = new Hashtable();          <─❶ The cache map

    pointcut transformerCreation(Source source)
        : call(* TransformerFactory.newTransformer(..))
          && args(source);
```

❷ The transformer creation pointcut

```
Transformer around(Source source)
    throws TransformerConfigurationException
    : transformerCreation(source) {
    Transformer transformer
        = (Transformer)_cache.get(source.getSystemId());
    if (transformer == null) {
        transformer = proceed(source);
        _cache.put(source.getSystemId(), transformer);
    }
    return transformer;
}
}
```

❸
**The
caching
advice**

❶ We keep the cache in a map with the stylesheet's system identifier as the key and the `Transformer` instance as the value.

❷ The `transformerCreation()` pointcut captures the call join points to `Transformer-Factory.newTransformer()`, which creates a new `Transformer` instance. We also capture the argument to the method calls in order to use it for cache identification.

❸ The around advice first queries the cache for a matching `Transformer`. If no match is found, it uses `proceed()` to carry out the original operation, which is the creation of a new `Transformer` that it then puts in the cache. Finally, it returns either the `Transformer` object obtained from the cache or the newly created one.

When we compile the source along with the aspect and run the program, we see the following output:

```
> ajc Test.java LogTransformerCreation.java TransformerCacheAspect.java
> java Test
Obtained transformer for:
        file:///F:/stylesheets/tableRaw.xsl
        org.apache.xalan.transformer.TransformerImpl@1b26af3
Obtained transformer for:
        file:///F:/stylesheets/tablePretty.xsl
        org.apache.xalan.transformer.TransformerImpl@1feca64
Obtained transformer for:
        file:///F:/stylesheets/tableRaw.xsl
        org.apache.xalan.transformer.TransformerImpl@1b26af3
Obtained transformer for:
        file:///F:/stylesheets/tablePretty.xsl
        org.apache.xalan.transformer.TransformerImpl@1feca64
```

Observe that the last two requests resulted in obtaining the same `Transformer` objects they obtained before. We now have implemented the caching of the `Transformer` objects simply by adding an aspect and without touching any of the original modules.

7.5.2 *AspectJ-based caching: the second version*

The previous solution has one problem when used in programs that obtain `Trans-former` objects in multiple threads. This is due to the limitation of the `Transformer` object that allows only one thread to use it at a time. This may not be a problem if your program only needs to access the `Transformer` objects from one thread at a time. To address the other cases, we need to modify our solution. There are a few ways to fix the problem. One is to cache templates instead of the `Transformer`, since the `Templates` class allows multiple threads to create `Transformers` based on it. This implementation change is also simple, requiring only that we modify the around advice in `TransformerCacheAspect` in the following way:

```
Transformer around(Source source, TransformerFactory tFactory)
    throws TransformerConfigurationException
    : transformerCreation(source) && target(tFactory) {
    Templates templates = (Templates)_cache.get(source.getSystemId());
    if (templates == null) {
        templates = tFactory.newTemplates(source);
        _cache.put(source.getSystemId(), templates);
    }
    return templates.newTransformer();
}
```

With this around advice, although we will be creating a new `Transformer` for each request, creating them from a template is a lot cheaper than creating them from a source stylesheet, since the direct creation of the `Transformer` object requires loading and parsing the stylesheet file. To observe the effect of our changes, let's modify the logging aspect from listing 7.18 by adding an advice to it, as shown in listing 7.20.

> **Listing 7.20 LogTransformerCreation.java: modified to monitor `Template` creation**

```
import javax.xml.transform.*;

public aspect LogTransformerCreation {
    declare precedence: LogTransformerCreation, *;

    after(Source source) returning (Transformer transformer)
        : call(* TransformerFactory.newTransformer(..))
        && args(source) {
        System.out.println("Obtained transformer for:\n\t"
                            + source.getSystemId() + "\n\t"
                            + transformer);
    }

    after(Source source) returning (Templates templates)
        : call(* TransformerFactory.newTemplates(..))
```

```
            && args(source) {
            System.out.println("Obtained template for:\n\t"
                                + source.getSystemId() + "\n\t"
                                + templates);
        }
    }
```

Now when we compile and run the program, we see the following output:

```
> ajc Test.java LogTransformerCreation.java TransformerCacheAspect.java
> java Test
Obtained template for:
        file:///F:/stylesheets/tableRaw.xsl
        org.apache.xalan.templates.StylesheetRoot@1b16e52
Obtained transformer for:
        file:///F:/stylesheets/tableRaw.xsl
        org.apache.xalan.transformer.TransformerImpl@8b819f
Obtained template for:
        file:///F:/stylesheets/tablePretty.xsl
        org.apache.xalan.templates.StylesheetRoot@998b08
Obtained transformer for:
        file:///F:/stylesheets/tablePretty.xsl
        org.apache.xalan.transformer.TransformerImpl@76cbf7
Obtained transformer for:
        file:///F:/stylesheets/tableRaw.xsl
        org.apache.xalan.transformer.TransformerImpl@3bb2b8
Obtained transformer for:
        file:///F:/stylesheets/tablePretty.xsl
        org.apache.xalan.transformer.TransformerImpl@152544e
```

While the test program made four creation requests, it resulted in the creation of only two template objects: one for each stylesheet.

From these two versions of the caching program, you can see that the modularity of the AspectJ-based caching solution not only helps implement the solution in a noninvasive manner, but also localizes the changes during the evolution.

7.5.3 *Ideas for further improvements*

We conclude our discussion of AspectJ-based caching with some ideas for improving the solution further. Each of these improvements requires changes only to the aspect:

- We have not considered the validness of the cached object. If the stylesheet file has been modified since the last time the template was added to the cache, you need to invalidate the cache and re-create the Template object. You can achieve this objective by keeping additional data in the cache corresponding to the modification time of the file. During cache retrieval, if the cache timestamp doesn't match the last modified time of the stylesheet file, you must proceed with the logic of creating a new `Transformer` and updating the cache.

- In our examples, we never removed any `Transformer`s from the cache, thus letting it grow unbounded. This may eventually lead to the VM running out of memory. You can fix this problem by adding a `SoftReference`-wrapped `Transformer` object. Before running out of memory, the VM will garbage-collect these `SoftReferences` instead of issuing the devastating `OutOfMemory-Error`. Instead of waiting for the low memory condition to trigger the cache cleanup, you could also actively monitor the cache to remove, say, the least recently used `Transformer`.[2] You could, of course, still use the `SoftReferences` to augment the monitoring logic, especially since monitoring parameters such as frequency of cleanup and the cache size are hard to determine and if chosen incorrectly will lead to out-of-memory errors.

7.6 *Summary*

Performance optimization is often a secondary consideration, not because it is unimportant, but because placing a primary consideration on it causes the design and implementation to carry baggage with a questionable value. However, adding performance improvements such as pooling and caching as an afterthought requires potentially massive changes to design and implementation. There is usually no satisfactory resolution to this dilemma—using conventional solutions, that is. An AOP-based solution resolves a good part of this dilemma by offering a way to introduce performance optimization when you need it without requiring any system-wide changes.

After reading this chapter, you know how AspectJ provides an easy, plug-and-play pooling and caching solution. By simply introducing a few prewritten aspects to the system, you ensure that your applications benefit from performance improvement, while the main logic of the application is completely oblivious to the fact that pooling or caching is taking place. Modifications to the pooling and caching policy are easy to implement and require only localized changes. Unlike conventional solutions, minimum change is required if you

---

[2] You can easily implement such functionality using `LinkedHashMap` instead of `Hashtable` in listing 7.19. For details, see http://developer.java.sun.com/developer/JDCTechTips/2002/tt0709.html and http://javaalmanac.com/egs/java.util/coll_Cache.html.

replace the underlying API for the pool or cache with a new one. The impact of the differences in APIs is limited to the aspects. In other words, the aspect absorbs the API differences. The aspect-oriented solution takes pooling and caching to a completely new level.

In your progression to adopt AspectJ, pooling and caching are similar to the logging and policy enforcement implementations in that they do not require you to commit to the use of AspectJ in your deployed system. You can remove pooling and caching aspects from the final system and lose only the performance gains, without any changes to core system functionality. With such an approach, you can initially use AspectJ to determine the modules needing pooling and caching, and then, if you do not want AspectJ in the final system, simply remove the aspects from the system. You can then implement pooling by modifying the modules that need pooling in a conventional manner.

Part 3

Advanced applications of AspectJ

Now that we have looked into simple applications of AspectJ, it is time to understand how AspectJ is useful in modularizing complex crosscutting concerns. In part 3, we utilize the advanced constructs.

Unlike the aspects in the second part of this book, you must continue to use these aspects in the deployed system to gain any benefit. We often refer to the aspects in part 3 as *deployment* or *production* aspects.

Chapter 8 introduces a few AspectJ design patterns and idioms that we will use in the remaining chapters. In chapters 9, 10, 11, and 12, we deal with crosscutting concerns such as thread safety, authentication and authorization, transaction management, and business rules. Using and extending the examples we provide, you will be well on your way to creating an EJB-lite, make-your-own server. Chapter 13 concludes this book with a discussion on incorporating AspectJ into your organization.

Design patterns
and idioms

8

Along with the various idioms, this chapter covers

- Worker object creation pattern
- Wormhole pattern
- Exception introduction pattern
- Participant pattern

245

Design patterns and idioms define solutions to recurring design issues, and we use them to avoid reinventing the wheel for often-encountered problems. Familiarity with these patterns and idioms often leads to a quick and proven solution; no wonder several books and articles are devoted to design patterns in every major technology. Consider, for instance, a situation where you are faced with the task of providing a mechanism for creating a coherent set of related objects without specifying the concrete classes. Instead of attempting ad hoc approaches, you can use the factory pattern to reach a solution. In a similar way, when you need to define a large set of related constants, using the idiom of putting them in an interface leads you to a quick answer and lets you understand all the implications.

The difference between design patterns and idioms involves the scope at which they solve problems and their language specificity. From the scope point of view, idioms are just smaller patterns. From the language point of view, idioms apply to a specific language whereas the design patterns apply to multiple languages using the same methodology. Only a few languages currently support AOP. Therefore, at this point, the differences between patterns and idioms from the AOP perspective are mostly based on their scope and complexity. Some years from now, when we may have a significant number of languages supporting the AOP paradigm, we will be able to make a better differentiation. The patterns we examine in this chapter are so powerful that any emerging languages will likely support them, thus making them language-independent.

The object-oriented programming community names these design patterns and idioms to simplify the communication of design concepts. Naming the pattern (*factory*, *visitor*, and *decorator* are examples) conveys the intent and decisions succinctly and accurately without providing all the details. For instance, as soon as I tell you "The `javax.jms.Session` interface is a factory for message producers and consumers," you immediately know what kind of methods to expect in the interface. You also know that most likely the direct creation of message producers and consumers (without using the factory) won't be allowed.

Whether we call a recurring usage arrangement a design pattern or an idiom, it serves the same purpose of providing a template we can use to solve certain design problems. Our goal in this chapter is to present patterns and idioms that will guide you when you start applying AspectJ to your own problems. We also hope that they will help you start thinking about problems in more abstract terms. Although this book covers problems from many domains, you will no doubt encounter new problems as you begin using AspectJ in your projects. When that happens, you will find that a combination of these design patterns and idioms will lead you to a solution more quickly.

In this chapter, we examine four design patterns and four idioms. Once you understand them well, they will come handy for a variety of problems. You must understand these patterns and idioms before you continue to part 3 of this book.

NOTE   You can also apply AspectJ to implement existing object-oriented design patterns such as factory and visitor. Such usage results in a clean and reusable implementation of those patterns. For more details on this usage of AspectJ, please refer to http://www.cs.ubc.ca/~jan/AODPs and the "Resources" section at the back of this book.

8.1 *The worker object creation pattern*

Suppose you need to route each direct call to a specific set of methods through a worker object in a crosscutting manner. A *worker object* is an instance of a class that encapsulates a method (called a *worker method*) so that the method can be treated like an object. The worker object can then be passed around, stored, and invoked. In Java, the common way to realize a worker class is to create a class that implements `Runnable`, with the `run()` method calling the worker method. When you execute such an object, it in turn executes the worker method. The *worker object creation pattern* offers a way to capture operations with a pointcut and automatically generate worker objects that encapsulate those operations. You can then pass these objects to the appropriate methods to be executed. When you use this pattern, you ensure a consistent behavior in your system—and you also save a ton of code.

I first discovered this pattern while adding thread safety to a Swing-based project, where a network reader thread was performing some UI updates. To comply with Swing's single-thread rule,[1] the network reader thread could not directly call the UI update methods. Quite early on, I decided to use an aspect that would advise the join points performing the UI updates to route the calls through `Event-Queue.invokeLater()`. However, in the first solution, I used one hand-coded worker class to individually route *each* update method. These classes were similar to those in listings 6.8 and 6.9, which provide worker classes to remove table rows and set the value of a table cell. The thread-safety aspect advised each method to

---

[1] If calls that access or modify any state of Swing components are made from a thread other than the event-dispatching thread, they must be wrapped in `Runnable` classes and routed through either the `EventQueue.invokeLater()` or `invokeAndWait()` method, which will then execute them in the event-dispatching thread through their `run()` methods. We will deal with this specific problem in chapter 9.

pass an instance of the corresponding worker class to the event queue instead of directly invoking the method. While AspectJ clearly helped to avoid polluting the core code with the logic that complied with the Swing rules, writing the boilerplate classes for each kind of update was boring, to say the least. Feeling that something was amiss, I experimented and created a single aspect that advised all the update methods with an around advice that invoked `proceed()` in an unconventional manner (as I will describe shortly). The result was that all the hand-coded classes were replaced with a single aspect consisting of only a few lines.

Soon, I was encountering problems of authorization and transaction management and found that using the same scheme provided an elegant solution. Then I realized that I could use this approach to execute certain time-consuming operations in a separate thread and thus improve the responsiveness of the UI application. So what I had on my hands was a scheme that solved a recurring set of problems—in other words, a pattern. Discovering this pattern was one of my "Aha!" moments. (In part 3 of this book, you will see in detail how you can use the same pattern to modularize crosscutting concerns.)

8.1.1 *The current solution*

If you were to solve the problem of creating worker objects without using the pattern, you would have to address two chief tasks for each method involved:

1   Implement a class that will route the method and create an object of that class.

2   Use that object instead of the method that was originally called.

Depending on the situation, you may use either named or anonymous classes. In either case, you implement an interface such as `Runnable` that contains a `run()` method for calling the operation. If you use named classes, you must add a constructor to accept all the arguments that will be passed to the operation. If you use anonymous classes, you don't (and can't) write a constructor. Instead, you create the class locally and pass the variables from the outer context (where the class is implemented) as arguments to the method called in the `run()` method. You should mark each local variable passed as final to comply with Java's requirement on local classes.

NOTE   Although our discussion uses the `Runnable` interface with a `run()` method for illustration purposes, any interface with one method that executes the operation will work equally well. The authorization example in chapter 10 uses various interfaces.

With either style, you need to replace the normal method call with the creation of a worker object (step 1) and invoke the object (step 2). The sheer amount of code makes implementation a daunting task; it also increases the risk of missing certain changes, which may result in undesired system behavior. For example, if you do not reroute certain calls to Swing components that originate in threads other than the event-dispatching thread, you may observe hard-to-explain UI anomalies or even crashes.

As you will see in the next section, the worker object creation pattern encapsulates these steps into just one aspect for all such methods, eliminating the need to create multiple worker classes.

8.1.2 *An overview of the worker object creation pattern*

In this pattern, you use the aspect to automatically create objects of anonymous classes (which are the worker objects). You write a pointcut capturing all the join points that need routing through the worker objects, and then you write advice that simply executes the join point inside the `run()` method in the body of the anonymous worker class.

Normally, when `proceed()` is called directly from within around advice, it executes the captured join point. In this case, if you call it from around advice that is inside a `run()` method of an anonymous class that is implementing `Runnable`, you get a worker object. Calling the `run()` method of such an object—perhaps at a later time or even in another thread—will execute the captured join point.

8.1.3 *The pattern template*

Let's write a pattern template that you can use to easily create your own implementation. First we must write a pointcut capturing the needed join points. We can use a named or anonymous pointcut for this purpose; we don't need to capture any context in this pointcut as far as the pattern is concerned. Next, we advise this pointcut with an around advice, as shown in the following snippet. In the around advice body, we create a worker object using an anonymous class. To do this, instead of calling the specific method in `run()`, we call `proceed()`. We then use this worker object as needed:

```
void around() : <pointcut> {
    Runnable worker = new Runnable () {
        public void run() {
            proceed();
        }
    }
    ... send the worker object to  some queue for execution,
```

```
        ... or pass it to another subsystem for execution,
        ... or simply call run() directly
    }
```

Let's use a simple example to illustrate the worker object creation pattern. We've decided that cache pre-fetching and saving a backup copy of a project are expensive operations and can be better executed in a separate thread. (Later, in chapter 9, we expand this example to demonstrate how we can avoid locking the GUI when calling a time-consuming task.)

Let's set up the example with the following three classes, and then we will apply the pattern to it. The class CachePreFetcher (listing 8.1) contains one method that simulates the fetching operation by printing a message. Similarly, the ProjectSaver class (listing 8.2) contains a single method that simulates backing up a project by printing a message.

Listing 8.1   CachePreFetcher.java

```java
public class CachePreFetcher {
    static void fetch() {
        System.out.println("Fetching in thread "
                        + Thread.currentThread());
    }
}
```

Listing 8.2   ProjectSaver.java

```java
public class ProjectSaver {
    static void backupSave() {
        System.out.println("Saving backup copy in thread "
                        + Thread.currentThread());
    }
}
```

Now we write a simple Test class (listing 8.3) to exercise the functionality. Later we will use the same class to see the effect of the aspect we will introduce in the system.

Listing 8.3   Test.java: exercising the simulated expensive operations

```java
public class Test {
    public static void main(String[] args) {
        CachePreFetcher.fetch();
        ProjectSaver.backupSave();
    }
}
```

When we compile these classes and run the test program, we get following output:

```
> ajc CachePreFetcher.java ProjectSaver.java Test.java
> java Test
Fetching in thread Thread[main,5,main]
Saving backup copy in thread Thread[main,5,main]
```

The output shows that both methods are executed by the main thread itself. Consequently, the main thread will be blocked for the period of time that the method is running.

Now let's write a simple reusable aspect that executes all join points defined by the pointcut `asyncOperations()` in a separate thread. The abstract aspect `AsynchronousExecutionAspect` (listing 8.4) contains an abstract pointcut that will be defined in the concrete aspect. It also contains an advice to the pointcut.

Listing 8.4   AsynchronousExecutionAspect.java

```
public abstract aspect AsynchronousExecutionAspect {
    public abstract pointcut asyncOperations();

    void around() : asyncOperations() {
        Runnable worker = new Runnable() {
            public void run() {
                proceed();
            }
        };
        Thread asyncExecutionThread = new Thread(worker);
        asyncExecutionThread.start();
    }
}
```

In the aspect in listing 8.4, the advice body creates an object of an anonymous class that implements the `Runnable` interface. In the `run()` method, it simply calls `proceed()` to execute the captured join point. Since `worker` performs the operation captured by the advised join point, it is the worker object here. It then creates a new thread using that object and starts the thread. The effect of this advice is that instead of directly invoking the join point, the aspect routes the join point execution in a new thread.

Next, we create a subaspect that defines the pointcut needed. In this case, we define that cache pre-fetching and backups should be performed in a separate thread. The `SystemAsynchronousExecutionAspect` aspect in listing 8.5 enables asynchronous execution of the `CachePreFetcher.fetch()` and `ProjectSaver.backupSave()` methods.

Listing 8.5   SystemAsynchronousExecutionAspect.java

```
public aspect SystemAsynchronousExecutionAspect
    extends AsynchronousExecutionAspect{
    public pointcut asyncOperations()
        : call(* CachePreFetcher.fetch())
        || call(* ProjectSaver.backupSave())
        /* || ... */;
}
```

Now when we compile all the classes and aspects created so far and run the test program, we get this output:

```
> ajc CachePreFetcher.java ProjectSaver.java Test.java
    AsynchronousExecutionAspect.java
    SystemAsynchronousExecutionAspect.java
> java Test
Fetching in thread Thread[Thread-1,5,main]
Saving backup copy in thread Thread[Thread-2,5,main]
```

As you can see, by introducing a simple aspect to the system, we ensured that each operation ran in a new thread instead of the main thread.

Getting the return value

Some of the routed calls could be returning a value to the caller. In that case, `proceed()` returns the value of the method when the operation has completed. We can keep this value in the worker object as well as return it from the around advice. Of course, for the value to make sense, the caller must wait until the execution of the worker object finishes. In our earlier example, since the caller thread returns immediately and the operation may execute later, the value returned to the caller thread will not be the return value of the operation.

To facilitate managing the return value in a generic fashion, let's write a simple abstract class, `RunnableWithReturn`, that implements `Runnable`. The `run()` method in classes implementing `RunnableWithReturn` must set the `_returnValue` member to the return value of the `proceed()` statement, which is the return value of the executed join point. Listing 8.6 shows the `RunnableWithReturn` abstract class.

Listing 8.6   RunnableWithReturn.java

```
package pattern.worker;

public abstract class RunnableWithReturn implements Runnable {
    protected Object _returnValue;
```

```
        public Object getReturnValue() {
        return _returnValue;
    }
}
```

Instead of using `Runnable`, we use the class shown in listing 8.6 as the base class for an anonymous class inside the advice, as we've done in the code snippet that follows. We also set `_returnValue` to the value returned by `proceed()`. After the worker object is executed, we simply return the object obtained by invoking `worker.getReturnValue()`:

```
Object around() : <pointcut> {
    RunnableWithReturn worker = new RunnableWithReturn() {
        public void run() {
            _returnValue = proceed();
        }
    }
    ... use the worker object
    return worker.getReturnValue();
}
```

Note that you do not need to worry about the type of the object returned from `proceed()`. For example, if the captured method returns a `float`, the AspectJ compiler will take care of it by creating a wrapper object to be returned by `proceed()` and unwrapping it when you assign the advice's return value to a `float` variable.

Let's look at a simple example using this mechanism. We will implement an aspect that uses a worker class for a synchronous call to a method that returns a value. First, we create a reusable aspect that routes all the calls specified by `sync-Operation()` synchronously through a new worker object that we create named `worker`. We use a simple mechanism that directly calls the `run()` method on the worker object. Typically, you would pass the worker object to an execution thread and wait for the execution of the worker; for instance, you would pass it to `Event-Queue.invokeAndWait()` when using Swing. We will log a message when we are about to execute the worker object. Listing 8.7 shows the implementation of the `SynchronousExecutionAspect` abstract aspect.

Listing 8.7   SynchronousExecutionAspect.java

```
import pattern.worker.*;

public abstract aspect SynchronousExecutionAspect {
    public abstract pointcut syncOperations();
```

```
        Object around() : syncOperations() {
            RunnableWithReturn worker = new RunnableWithReturn() {
                public void run() {
                    _returnValue = proceed();
                }};
            System.out.println("About to run " + worker);
            worker.run();
            return worker.getReturnValue();
        }
    }
```

NOTE   While executing the worker object by invoking it immediately after its creation seems wasteful, it does help in certain situations since it provides the worker object as context. You will see how to use immediate invocation in chapter 11 when we implement transaction management using AspectJ.

At this point, let's write a subaspect, `SystemSynchronousExecutionAspect.java` (listing 8.8), that will route the calls to `Math.max()` and to all methods of the `Vector` class through automatically created worker objects. The reason for choosing these methods is to illustrate that the aspect handles returning a primitive type, returning `void`, and returning an object just as well. The around advice does all the hard work of wrapping the primitive return values before they are returned from the advice and then unwrapping and casting the objects correctly after they are returned from the advice.

Listing 8.8   SystemSynchronousExecutionAspect.java

```
import java.util.Vector;

public aspect SystemSynchronousExecutionAspect
    extends SynchronousExecutionAspect{
    public pointcut syncOperations()
        : (call(* Math.max(..))
        || call(* Vector.*(..))
        /* || ... */);

}
```

Finally, let's write a simple test program (listing 8.9). It prints the result of each operation as it executes.

Listing 8.9   TestSynchronous.java

```java
import java.util.Vector;

public class TestSynchronous {
    public static void main(String[] args) {
        int intMax = Math.max(1, 2);
        System.out.println("intMax = " + intMax);
        double doubleMax = Math.max(3.0, 4.0);
        System.out.println("doubleMax = " + doubleMax);

        Vector v = new Vector();
        v.add(0, "AspectJ");
        Object str = v.get(0);
        System.out.println("str = " + str);
    }
}
```

First we compile the program without aspects and see the output:

```
> ajc TestSynchronous.java
> java TestSynchronous
intMax = 2
doubleMax = 4.0
str = Aspectj
```

Now when we compile the program with the aspects and run the program, we see output similar to this:

```
> ajc TestSynchronous.java SynchronousExecutionAspect.java
    SystemSynchronousExecutionAspect.java
    pattern\worker\RunnableWithReturn.java
> java TestSynchronous
About to run SynchronousExecutionAspect$1@affc70
intMax = 2
About to run SynchronousExecutionAspect$1@1e63e3d
doubleMax = 4.0
About to run SynchronousExecutionAspect$1@1b90b39
About to run SynchronousExecutionAspect$1@18fe7c3
str = AspectJ
```

As illustrated by the output, the resulting program's behavior is unchanged from the original program that did not include any aspects. We now have a mechanism for routing the direct calls through worker objects that requires writing only a few lines of code. You can extend this mechanism to storing other context information as well, as you'll see in chapter 11.

Managing the context collected by the pointcut

Although the pattern itself doesn't need to collect any context at the pointcut, you may want to collect some if you need to reuse the pointcut for other purposes. If you do so, just pass the unaltered context to `proceed()`, as shown here:

```
void around([context]) : <pointcut> {
    Runnable worker = new Runnable () {
        public void run() {
            proceed([context]);
        }
    }
    ... use the worker object
}
```

Now by passing the captured context, you can reuse the defined pointcuts for other purposes.

8.1.4 A summary of the worker object creation pattern

The worker object creation pattern offers a new opportunity to deal with otherwise complex problems. You can use this pattern in a variety of situations: from implementing thread safety in Swing applications and improving responsiveness of GUI applications to performing authorization and transaction management. Initially, I was fascinated by the amount of time I saved by not having to write as much code. Later, I felt that the pattern's real value lies in the sheer elegance and consistency it brings to the solution. I am sure your experience will be similar.

8.2 The wormhole pattern

The *wormhole pattern* makes context information from a caller available to a callee—without having to pass the information as a set of parameters to each method in the control flow. For example, consider an authorization system, where many methods need to know who invoked them in order to determine if the caller should be allowed to execute the operation. The wormhole allows the methods to access the caller object and its context to obtain this information.

By creating a direct route between two levels in the call stack, you create a wormhole and avoid linearly traveling through each layer. This saves you from having to modify the call chain when you want to pass additional context information, and it prevents API pollution.

8.2.1 *The current solution*

If you don't use AspectJ, there are two ways to pass the caller's context in a multi-threaded environment: you can pass additional parameters containing context or you can use thread-specific storage to set and access the context information. In either case, multiple modules are involved in the logic that is passing the context. The first way of passing a parameter causes API pollution—every method in the execution stack must have extra parameters to pass on the context collected. The second way requires the caller to create a `ThreadLocal` variable to store the context information and set its context. While the second approach avoids API pollution, it entails changes in both caller and callee implementation and requires an understanding of how the context is stored.

8.2.2 *An overview of the wormhole pattern*

The basic idea behind the wormhole pattern, shown in figure 8.1, is to specify two pointcuts: one for the caller and the other for the callee, with the former collecting the context to be transferred through the wormhole. Then you specify the wormhole at the places of execution of the callee's join points in the control flow of a caller's join points.

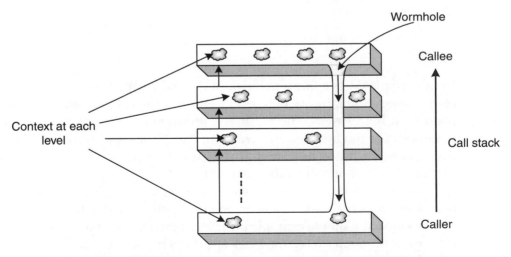

Figure 8.1 The wormhole pattern. Each horizontal bar shows a level in the call. The wormhole makes the object in the caller plane available to the methods in the called plane without passing the object through the call stack.

In figure 8.1, each level in the call stack is depicted as a plane in the space. To transfer context from one plane to another, you would normally have to pass it on to the next plane until it reached the desired location. The wormhole pattern provides a path that cuts directly through the planes, which avoids having the context trickle through the levels from caller to callee.

8.2.3 *The pattern template*

Let's create a template for the pattern that will allow you to "plug" the pattern into your system by simply replacing the entities in the template with concrete ones in your system:

```
public aspect WormholeAspect {
    pointcut callerSpace(<caller context>)
        : <caller pointcut>;

    pointcut calleeSpace(<callee context>)
        : <callee pointcut>;

    pointcut wormhole(<caller context>, <callee context>)
        : cflow(callerSpace(<caller context>))
          && calleeSpace(<callee context>);

    // advices to wormhole
    around(<caller context>, <callee context>)
        : wormhole(<caller context>, <callee context>) {
        ... advice body
    }
}
```

In this template we define a pointcut in the caller's space that collects the associated context. Similarly, we define a pointcut in the callee's space. The collected context in both cases could be an execution and target object as well as any parameters to the methods involved. We then create a wormhole through these two spaces with a pointcut that defines the join points captured by the `calleeSpace()` pointcut in the control flow of the join points captured by the `callerSpace()` pointcut. Since we have the context available for both of these join points, we can write advice to the `wormhole()` pointcut using this information.

Let's look at a simple example using this pattern; for more complex and complete examples, refer to chapters 11 and 12. The aspect in listing 8.10 creates a wormhole between a transaction initiator such as an ATM, teller, or Internet bank and the actual account operations.

Listing 8.10 AccountTransactionAspect.java

```
public aspect AccountTransactionAspect {
    pointcut transactionSystemUsage(TransactionSystem ts)
        : execution(* TransactionSystem.*(..))
        && this(ts);                          Using transaction   ❶
                                              system operations

    pointcut accountTransactions(Account account, float amount)  ❷
        : this(account) && args(amount)        Using
        && (execution(public * Account.credit(float))   account
        || execution(public * Account.debit(float)));   operations

    pointcut wormhole(TransactionSystem ts,             ❸
                    Account account, float amount)
        : cflow(transactionSystemUsage(ts))    Creating a
        && accountTransactions(account, amount);   wormhole
                                              through ❶ and ❷

    before(TransactionSystem ts,
        Account account, float amount) returning
        : wormhole(ts, account, amount) {

        ... log the operation along with information about
        ... transaction system, perform authorization, etc.
                                              Using the        ❹
    }                                         wormholed context
}
```

❶ The `transactionSystemUsage()` pointcut captures all execution join points in a `TransactionSystem` object. It collects the object itself as the context.

❷ The `accountTransactions()` pointcut captures execution of `credit()` and `debit()` methods in the `Account` class. It collects the account and the amount involved as the context.

❸ The `wormhole()` pointcut creates a wormhole between the transaction system operations and the account operation by capturing all join points that match `accountTransactions()` that occur in the control flow of `transactionSystemUsage()`. The pointcut also makes available the context captured by the constituent pointcuts.

❹ The advice on the `wormhole()` pointcut can now use the context. The advice knows not only the account and the amount but also the transaction system responsible for causing the account activity.

If this information is logged, perhaps to a database, it can be used to generate monthly statements showing ATMs accessed by customer for each transaction.

NOTE	Although this implementation of the wormhole pattern collects some explicit context in form of the caller object and the method arguments, the implicit context associated with the caller's *type* is important information in and of itself. For example, in a banking system, activities performed in crediting an account may depend on which *kind* of system invoked them. If a debit action is initiated through a check clearance system, you may fire overdraft protection logic. However, if the same action were invoked through an ATM machine, you would limit the withdrawal amount—it doesn't matter which specific ATM machine initiated the transaction; it's enough that *an* ATM machine did it. Using a wormhole pattern in these cases helps avoid passing an extra parameter to the account operations in order to indicate the type of transaction system. This not only avoids API pollution, but also offers nonintrusive changes if a new kind of caller is added to the system. In this banking example, you can implement additional rules when a new kind of account access system is added, such as Internet banking, without making any system-wide changes.

8.2.4 *A summary of the wormhole pattern*

You use the wormhole pattern to avoid modifying multiple modules for passing the caller's context. This pattern allows you to transfer context without requiring changes to any of the core modules. With the knowledge available at the callee's join point execution, you can easily implement this kind of functionality, which would otherwise be quite complex.

Perhaps your next assignment will apply this pattern to real space travel!

8.3 *The exception introduction pattern*

When using aspects to introduce crosscutting concerns into a system, I have often found it necessary to throw a checked exception that was not originally part of the join point's list of declared exceptions. On each occasion, I had to make a few choices in handling the specific exception for the crosscutting concern, and I needed a pattern to deal with all these situations in a consistent way. For that reason, I created the *exception introduction pattern* to address concern-specific checked exceptions in a systematic manner. In this book, you will see examples of this pattern in chapters 10 and 11.

AspectJ does not allow an advice to declare that it may throw a checked exception (an exception that extends `Exception` directly or indirectly instead of

RuntimeException) unless its advised join points have declared that they may throw the same exception. However, on many occasions, the weaving of concerns into a system requires that an aspect deal with new checked exceptions. For example, your aspects may use commonly available libraries and services to implement the underlying mechanism, such as JDBC for database access or JAAS for authentication; the exceptions they throw are usually checked exceptions. Because the advice cannot declare that it may be throwing these exceptions, you need another way of dealing with them.

Further, certain kinds of crosscutting concerns, such as error recovery and transaction management, require that aspects capture exceptions of *all* types thrown by the join points under consideration and perform logic in the catch blocks. However, what should the aspect do with the exception after performing its concern-specific logic in the catch block? This is an especially complex problem when aspects are reusable and do not know about business-specific exceptions.

NOTE　AspectJ's restriction that prevents an advice from declaring that it may throw additional checked exceptions is neither an oversight nor a shortcoming. If this restriction did not exist, it would mean potential system-wide changes. Consider, for example, adding a database persistence layer using AspectJ. If AspectJ allowed advice to add a new checked exception, such as SQLException, to the list of declared exceptions for an advised method, the callers of the methods, who never expected the called method to throw SQLException, would now have to deal with it. They could either catch the exception or declare that they will also throw SQLException. With the later choice, the second-level caller would also have to make a similar choice, and so on. In a way, this "limitation" is similar to Java's restriction of not allowing overridden methods in a derived class to declare that they will throw any new checked exception.

In this section, we explain the exception introduction pattern that deals with the problems associated with the introduction of concern-specific exceptions via AspectJ. The pattern can also be used to handle business-specific exceptions that are caught in reusable, generic aspects.

8.3.1　*The current solution*

Sometimes when you add an aspect that implements some crosscutting logic into a system, the advice in the aspect needs to catch a checked exception thrown by the execution of the underlying logic. Dealing with the caught exception after executing the logic often poses unclear choices. Let's set up an example to help us understand the problem and its current solution.

Consider `BusinessClass`, in listing 8.11, a generic representation of any business entity that implements core concerns. It contains a few business methods, one of which will throw a checked `BusinessException`.

Listing 8.11   BusinessClass.java

```java
public class BusinessClass {
    void businessMethod1() {
        // business logic...
    }

    void businessMethod2() throws BusinessException {
        // business logic...
        throw new BusinessException();
    }
}
```

Listing 8.12 shows the implementation of `BusinessException` that extends `Exception`.

Listing 8.12   BusinessException.java

```java
public class BusinessException extends Exception {
}
```

Now let's write an aspect that will introduce a crosscutting concern (such as authentication) to `BusinessClass`. As a part of the concern implementation, the before advice to the `operations()` pointcut calls a method `concernLogic()`, which throws a checked exception. As a first implementation, we let the exception thrown by `concernLogic()` propagate to callers and we declare that the advice may throw `ConcernCheckedException`. Listing 8.13 shows the abstract `ConcernAspect`.

Listing 8.13   ConcernAspect.java

```java
public abstract aspect ConcernAspect {
    abstract pointcut operations();

    before() throws ConcernCheckedException : operations() {
        concernLogic();
    }
```

```
    void concernLogic() throws ConcernCheckedException {
        throw new ConcernCheckedException(); // simulating failure
    }
}
```

Because the advice in the aspect in listing 8.13 declares that it will throw ConcernCheckedException and because the advised methods (defined by the concrete aspect BusinessConcernAspect in listing 8.15) do not declare that they may throw that exception, we will get compiler errors. Note that if the advice did not declare that it would throw the exception, we would still get compiler errors. ConcernCheckedException, in listing 8.14, is the concern-specific checked exception that is caught and thrown by the advice.

Listing 8.14   ConcernCheckedException.java

```
public class ConcernCheckedException extends Exception {
}
```

To enable concern weaving in the core implementation, let's write a subaspect, BusinessConcernAspect (listing 8.15), that extends ConcernAspect and provides a definition for the abstract pointcut in the base aspect.

Listing 8.15   BusinessConcernAspect.java

```
public aspect BusinessConcernAspect extends ConcernAspect {
    pointcut operations() : call(* BusinessClass.business*());
}
```

Finally, consider a simple test class (listing 8.16) that calls both methods on BusinessClass. We put the second method in a try/catch block to capture the checked exception that may be thrown so that we can suitably respond to the failure.

Listing 8.16   TestException.java

```
public class TestException {
    public static void main(String[] args) {
        BusinessClass bc = new BusinessClass();
        bc.businessMethod1();
        try {
            bc.businessMethod2();
        } catch (BusinessException ex) {
```

```
            // Do something...
            // Log it, execute recovery mechanism, etc.
            System.out.println("Caught:" + ex);
        }
    }
}
```

When we compile these classes and the aspect, we get this output:

```
> ajc *.java
F:\aspectj-book\ch08\section8.3.1\TestException.java:6
   can't throw checked exception 'ConcernCheckedException' at this
   join point 'method-call(void BusinessClass.businessMethod1())'
F:\aspectj-book\ch08\section8.3.1\ConcernAspect.java:6
   can't throw checked exception 'ConcernCheckedException' at this
   join point 'method-call(void BusinessClass.businessMethod1())'
F:\aspectj-book\ch08\section8.3.1\TestException.java:8
   can't throw checked exception 'ConcernCheckedException' at this
   join point 'method-call(void BusinessClass.businessMethod2())'
F:\aspectj-book\ch08\section8.3.1\ConcernAspect.java:6
   can't throw checked exception 'ConcernCheckedException' at this
   join point 'method-call(void BusinessClass.businessMethod2())'

4 errors
```

The execution resulted in exceptions that indicate that it is an error to throw the checked exception ConcernCheckedException from the advice on any business method. In the case of businessMethod1(), throwing any checked exception from it is an error, whereas in the case of businessMethod2(), throwing any checked exception other than BusinessException is an error.

The most common way to deal with the situation is to simply log the caught exception and continue. We can modify the advice in ConcernAspect (listing 8.13) in the following way to catch the exception:

```
before() : operations() {
    try {
        concernLogic(); // throws ConcernCheckedException
    } catch (ConcernCheckedException ex) {
        // log the exception
    }
}
```

In this snippet, the advice no longer declares that it will throw ConcernChecked-Exception since the advice consumes the exception thrown by concernLogic(). This is often undesirable since the higher-level caller may need to be aware of the failure condition so that it can make an informed choice in dealing with it. A much better approach is to propagate the caught exception directly to the callers after wrapping it in an exception. In the next section, we will examine a pattern that shows how to achieve this desirable behavior in a systematic fashion.

8.3.2 *An overview of the exception introduction pattern*

The exception introduction pattern simply suggests that you catch the original checked exception, perform any logic, and throw a new runtime exception that wraps the checked exception. We need to create a concern-specific runtime exception that can set the checked exception as its cause (by either passing the caught exception to the new exception's constructor or by using the initCause() method). For example, when you are implementing a persistence aspect using JDBC, you may throw a PersistenceRuntimeException that wraps the original checked SQLException.

While throwing a runtime exception propagates the exception to higher-level caller, there will be a problem because the callers, unaware of the aspects present in the system, aren't prepared to catch the unchecked exception. Later, we will deal with this situation, which builds on top of the base exception introduction pattern and restores the original checked exception thrown.

8.3.3 *The pattern template*

Let's develop a template for the exception introduction pattern to achieve the goal of propagating the thrown exception to the caller of the advised methods and preserving the exception type so that the callers can see the original exception.

Propagating the concern-specific exception

The template will catch the concern-specific ConcernCheckedException, wrap it in a ConcernRuntimeException, and throw the runtime exception. We will develop our template using the generic entities that we used in section 8.3.1. (When using this pattern, you would replace the generic entities with specific entities.) Listing 8.17 shows the modified version of ConcernAspect that uses the exception introduction pattern.

Listing 8.17 ConcernAspect.java: modified to use the exception introduction pattern

```
public abstract aspect ConcernAspect {
    abstract pointcut operations();

    before() : operations() {
        try {
```

```
        concernLogic();
    } catch (ConcernCheckedException ex) {
        throw new ConcernRuntimeException(ex);
    }
}

void concernLogic() throws ConcernCheckedException {
    throw new ConcernCheckedException(); // simulating failure
}
}
```

The aspect in listing 8.17 uses `ConcernRuntimeException`, which is implemented in listing 8.18. The constructor of this exception takes the originally thrown exception as a parameter that indicates the cause of the exception.

Listing 8.18   ConcernRuntimeException.java

```
public class ConcernRuntimeException extends RuntimeException {
    public ConcernRuntimeException(Throwable cause) {
        super(cause);
    }
}
```

The before advice in `ConcernAspect` simply catches any concern-specific checked exception, wraps it in a concern-specific unchecked exception, and throws it. Wrapping the original exception as the thrown exception's cause provides access to the original exception, if a caller needs it. Now when we compile the classes along with `ConcernAspect` in listing 8.17, we get a successful compilation:

```
> ajc *.java
> java TestException
Exception in thread "main" ConcernRuntimeException:
➡ ConcernCheckedException
... more stack trace
```

As the output shows, a `ConcernRuntimeException` that wraps a `ConcernChecked-Exception` is thrown.

You may be wondering why we chose a concern-specific runtime exception as opposed to a generic runtime exception. If we were to use a generic runtime exception (such as the `RuntimeException` class itself), we'd have to consider at least two issues:

- The exception call stack would be harder to understand since exceptions thrown by all such aspects would result in same exception type.

- More seriously, if the exception were generic, a caller would have difficulty distinguishing between various concern-specific exceptions. The exception handler would capture all the exceptions, which could potentially be thrown by other aspects using the same exception-handling policy. The handler would then need to examine the cause of the original exception to determine if the exception were of any interest. Further, if two concerns generated the same type of exception, it would be impossible to decipher which concern led to the failure.

Another question you may have is, why not simply soften the exception thrown by `concernLogic()`? Using `declare soft` may suffice in demoting the checked concern-specific exceptions to unchecked ones. However, you'd have the same problems you'd have with using the generic runtime exception. After all, softening is equivalent to using `SoftException` as a generic runtime exception.

Propagating the business-specific exception

While so far we have applied the exception introduction pattern only to concern-specific checked exceptions, it can be used in dealing with business-specific checked exceptions as well. On occasion, the advice in a generic aspect needs to catch all exceptions. The problem is that the aspect cannot rethrow the business-specific checked exceptions because it does not know about them and hence cannot declare that its advice should throw them. Once an exception is caught, we have to deal with it somehow. Besides the obviously poor choice of doing nothing, we can choose to throw a runtime exception modeled after the exception introduction pattern.

Let's see how we can apply the pattern to business-specific exceptions by modifying the `ConcernAspect` to catch all the exceptions that are thrown by methods that its pointcut captures. First, we write around advice that proceeds with the captured operation in a try/catch block. When the catch block is executed, it performs concern-specific error-handling logic and throws a new `ConcernRuntime-Exception`, wrapping the caught exception. Listing 8.19 shows the aspect implementation after we've made the modifications.

Listing 8.19 ConcernAspect.java: with advice that catches all exceptions

```
public abstract aspect ConcernAspect {
    abstract pointcut operations();

    Object around() : operations()  {
        try {
            return proceed();
```

```
        } catch (Throwable ex) {
            // do something
            throw new ConcernRuntimeException(ex);
        }
    }
}
```

When we compile the aspect in listing 8.19 with the rest of classes and run the Test class, we get the following output:

```
> ajc *.java
> java TestException
Exception in thread "main" ConcernRuntimeException: BusinessException
... more stack trace
```

As you can see, a runtime exception wrapping the original business-specific checked exception is now propagated to the caller.

Preserving the exception specification requirement

While we achieved a successful compilation and propagation of an exception, the output is bound to baffle TestException class developers; they expect the catch block for businessMethod2() to execute, but that didn't happen here. The reason is that the around advice in ConcernAspect is catching the BusinessException (along with any other exception) and throwing it after wrapping in a ConcernRuntime-Exception. This also violates the requirement of the businessMethod2() method to throw a business-specific exception instead of concern-specific one. This problem is not created by applying the basic pattern, but is the inherent issue associated with the aspect's need to summarily capture exceptions—the business exception and everything else—to perform its logic.

Note that we did not have the same problem with the aspect in listing 8.17; there we only caught the ConcernCheckedException, letting the business-specific exception automatically propagate.

So we now have to deal with the challenge of preserving the exception specification requirement on the methods that are affected by concern implementation, while letting the aspect perform its logic by capturing all types of exceptions. In this section, we add another aspect to the system that will augment the exception introduction pattern by restoring the originally thrown checked exception. Note that this aspect is specific to your system and not reusable. Listing 8.20 shows the implementation of the aspect that restores BusinessException when it is caught by the ConcernRuntimeException thrown by ConcernAspect.

Listing 8.20   PreserveBusinessException.java

```
public aspect PreserveBusinessException {
    declare precedence: PreserveBusinessException, BusinessConcernAspect;

    after() throwing(ConcernRuntimeException ex)
        throws BusinessException
        : call(* *.*(..) throws BusinessException) {
        Throwable cause = ex.getCause();
        if (cause instanceof BusinessException) {
            throw (BusinessException)cause;
        }
        throw ex;
    }
}
```

The advice will be invoked after `ConcernRuntimeException` is thrown by any method that declares that it may throw a business-specific exception. The advice declares that it also may throw the business exception. In the body of the advice, we check whether the cause for the runtime exception that has been caught is the business exception we are trying to preserve. If it is, we throw the cause exception after casting it to the `BusinessException` type.

Now when we run the program, we get the following output, just as expected:

```
> ajc *.java
> java TestException
Caught: BusinessException
```

Problem solved. Now the callers get the exception they are prepared for and won't need to modify their exception-processing logic.

8.3.4   *A summary of the exception introduction pattern*

You often have to deal with concern-specific exceptions when implementing crosscutting concerns. We've presented a pattern that addresses this need in a simple and systematic way using concern-specific runtime exceptions in place of checked exceptions. The pattern also deals with the problem that arises when you must implement a crosscutting concern to summarily catch all types of exceptions, including business exceptions. I encourage you to experiment with the basic pattern as well as the variations in order to understand the interaction.

8.4 *The participant pattern*

Many operations in a system share common characteristics, ranging from simple transactional properties, to expected duration of method calls, to IO-access properties, to remote access properties. Since these operations are spread over many modules, augmenting or altering their behavior is a crosscutting concern. The participant pattern provides a way to modularize such characteristics-based crosscutting concerns using AspectJ. The pattern helps to capture join points based on their characteristics when the name-based pointcuts just aren't enough.

Capturing operations with common characteristics across a system is essential in ensuring consistent system behavior. For example, you may want to surround all slow operations in the system with a wait cursor. The common AspectJ approach for accomplishing this is to define pointcuts based on the method signature. For example, a method throwing an IOException is potentially performing some IO operation. This information, in conjunction with the hypothesis that IO operations are slow to execute, allows us to identify and capture a few slow methods. Similarly, we can consider all methods whose name starts with set as potentially state-atering operations. However, we often cannot capture all the join points sharing similar characteristics just by looking at the method signatures. For example, while we did characterize all IO operations as potentially slow, how do we capture other operations that are slow simply because they perform complex computations?

Many crosscutting concerns, such as transaction management and authentication, tend to consist of operations that cannot be captured by property-based pointcuts. Developers usually assign the name of a method based on the core operation carried by it, so the method's name does not reflect the peripheral characteristics of a method. For example, we know that methods setting a state typically start with set. However, the method name does not reflect the peripheral characteristics of the method, such as speed or its need to execute in a transaction context. This makes it hard to capture methods that have those auxiliary characteristics.

Consider a transaction management problem: The methods that need to be in a transaction are likely to be named after the business logic they perform, such as processOrder(). The names in this case give no indication that the methods need transaction management support. Therefore, property-based pointcuts using wildcards cannot identify the join points in these methods.

To capture such join points, you need the collaboration of the implementing classes. One possibility is to supplement the implementation with metadata indicating the characteristics that are not derivable from the signature patterns of the implementation.

NOTE	JSR 175 proposes a way to add metadata in Java. While it is not clear if this will mean a language extension, special JavaDoc tags, or some other form, the presence of metadata specifying the characteristics of the methods will help immensely in capturing crosscutting concerns for characteristics that cannot be ascertained by the signature. For example, you could use metadata to specify that a method needs a long execution time. With JSR 175, AspectJ would also need to be augmented to allow defining pointcuts based on the method's metadata. Until such a facility is available, though, we will have to rely on other techniques.

The participant pattern helps capture the methods based on their characteristics. Keep in mind, though, that the participant pattern (or a variation of it) does require modifications to the core implementation, and there is the possibility that you may not identify all of the operations that need changes. For this reason, you should use the regular name- and property-based pointcuts to the fullest extent possible.

8.4.1 *Current solutions*

In this section, we look at characteristics-based crosscutting using AspectJ. First we look at a simple technique that allows you to advise join points that share certain characteristics. However, because it makes tracking changes in the implementation difficult, we then improve the solution to make it easier to maintain.

Take one

Let's write an aspect, DesiredCharacteristicsAspect (listing 8.21), that advises all the join points that share certain characteristics.

Listing 8.21 DesiredCharacteristicsAspect.java: the first version

```
public aspect DesiredCharacteristicsAspect {
    Object around() : call(* MyClass1.desiredCharacteristicMethod1())
        || call(* MyClass1.desiredCharacteristicMethod2())
        || call(* MyClass2.desiredCharacteristicMethod1())
        || call(* MyClass2.desiredCharacteristicMethod2())
        /* || ... */ {

        // advice code

    }
}
```

The aspect simply includes a list in the pointcut of all the methods that have the characteristics. The problem with this approach is that the aspect is explicitly aware of all the classes and methods in the list. If a new class is added to the system containing a method with the same characteristics, it will not be advised until it is added to the pointcut. Similarly, if a method that is originally part of the list changes its implementation so that it no longer bears the characteristics, it will continue to be advised until the aspect is changed to remove the method from the pointcut definition. Both the classes and aspects need to be explicitly aware of the existence of each other to remain coordinated.

Take two

Another fundamental problem is that characteristics such as expected execution time are implementation-dependent and may change often between implementation versions. Therefore, let's see if we can tie the pointcut definitions to the classes themselves.

Recall that a class can include pointcuts (but not advice). Since classes know about characteristics of the methods contained in them, they are qualified to specify pointcuts identifying certain characteristics. One way you can perform characteristics-based crosscutting is by requiring classes to encode a pointcut that captures join points with specific characteristics. Listing 8.22 shows how MyClass1 includes a pointcut to capture all its methods that have the desired characteristics. Similarly, MyClass2 (listing 8.23) includes a pointcut that captures its methods with the desired characteristics.

Listing 8.22   MyClass1.java

```
public class MyClass1 {

    // MyClass1's implementation

    public pointcut desiredCharacteristicJoinPoints() :
        call(* MyClass1.desiredCharacteristicMethod1())
        || call(* MyClass1.desiredCharacteristicMethod2())
        /* || ... */;
}
```

Listing 8.23   MyClass2.java

```
public class MyClass2 {

    // MyClass2's implementation

    public pointcut desiredCharacteristicJoinPoints() :
```

```
        call(* MyClass2.desiredCharacteristicMethod1())
        || call(* MyClass2.desiredCharacteristicMethod2())
        /* || ... */;
}
```

Now we can write an aspect to advise both desiredCharacteristicJoinPoints()
pointcuts defined in MyClass1 and MyClass2. Listing 8.24 shows the second version of DesiredCharacteristicsAspect, which advises pointcuts specified in
MyClass1 and MyClass2.

Listing 8.24   DesiredCharacteristicsAspect.java: the second version

```
public aspect DesiredCharacteristicsAspect {
    Object around() : MyClass1.desiredCharacteristicJoinPoints()
        || MyClass2.desiredCharacteristicJoinPoints() {
        // advice code
    }
}
```

The version in listing 8.24 is better than the earlier solution. Instead of being
aware of classes and methods, the aspect is now aware of only the classes
because it uses the pointcuts defined in them to capture the methods. Nevertheless, the need to be explicitly aware of all the classes doesn't make it an
optimal solution. If a new class is added to the system, the aspect will not
advise the new class until you add it to the aspect. Note also that in the
advice, it is illegal to specify a pointcut such as *.desiredCharacteristicJoin-
Points(). We must explicitly enumerate all the pointcuts we want to advise
from each class.

8.4.2 *An overview of the participant pattern*

The participant pattern builds on the idea of classes that contain a pointcut
denoting certain characteristics. Instead of including a pointcut definition
directly inside each class and using those pointcuts in an aspect that provides the
advice, the classes themselves define a subaspect that extends the advising aspect
and provides the pointcut definition. In a way, this pattern reverses the roles—
instead of making aspects aware of classes and methods, we now make the classes
aware of the aspects.

Let's examine the structural overview of the pattern:

1 We first must write an abstract aspect that contains abstract pointcut(s) denoting join points with the desired characteristics. These pointcuts form a kind of "aspectual interface." The aspect also advises each pointcut (or combination of them) with the required behavior. We will think of this as an *inviting* aspect—it invites others to participate in the advice it offers. Such an offer is strictly an invitation or opt-in only.

2 Each class that wants to participate in such a behavior includes a concrete subaspect extending the abstract invitation aspect. Each of these subaspects simply provides the implementation of the abstract pointcut for the enclosing class. Note that the concrete subaspects do not actually have to be nested aspects of the class—they could be peer aspects, for example. This way, each class that wants to participate in the collaboration needs to do so explicitly—hence the name of the pattern.

8.4.3 *The pattern template*

In this section, we develop a template for the pattern, and you will be able to implement characteristics-based crosscutting in your system by creating concrete implementations based on this template. Listing 8.25 shows the abstract aspect that contains the core logic for implementing the concern; however, it defers the definition of the desiredCharacteristicJoinPoints() pointcut to subaspects.

Listing 8.25   AbstractDesiredCharacteristicAspect.java: the base

```
abstract aspect AbstractDesiredCharacteristicAspect {
    public abstract pointcut desiredCharacteristicJoinPoints();

    // Example uses around(), but before() and after() work as well
    Object  around() : desiredCharacteristicJoinPoints() {
        // advice code
    }
}
```

The required crosscutting behavior is in the around advice to the abstract pointcut. Listing 8.26 contains a version of MyClass1 that includes a nested subaspect of AbstractDesiredCharacteristicAspect; the subaspect defines the abstract pointcut of the base aspect.

Listing 8.26 MyClass1.java: participating in the collaboration

```
public class MyClass1 {

    // MyClass1's implementation

    public static aspect DesiredCharacteristicParticipant
        extends AbstractDesiredCharacteristicAspect {
        public pointcut desiredCharacteristicJoinPoints() :
            call(* MyClass1.desiredCharacteristicMethod1())
            || call(* MyClass1.desiredCharacteristicMethod2())
            /* || ... */;
    }
}
```

In listing 8.26, the nested subaspect declares that the `MyClass1.desired-CharacteristicMethod1()` and `MyClass1.desiredCharacteristicMethod2()` methods have the desired characteristics to participate in the functionality offered by the base `AbstractDesiredCharacteristicAspect`. The effect of this aspect is that the advice to `desiredCharacteristicJoinPoints()` in the base aspect is applied to the specified methods. `MyClass2` in listing 8.27 participates in the collaboration in the same way.

Listing 8.27 MyClass2.java: participating in the collaboration

```
public class MyClass2 {

    // MyClass2's implementation

    public static aspect DesiredCharacteristicParticipant
        extends AbstractDesiredCharacteristicAspect {
        public pointcut desiredCharacteristicJoinPoints() :
            call(* MyClass2.desiredCharacteristicMethod1())
            || call(* MyClass2.desiredCharacteristicMethod2())
            /* || ... */;
    }
}
```

There can be many more participants in addition to `MyClass1` and `MyClass2` in the system. Each of the participating nested subaspects provide a definition to capture the join points in their enclosing class, thus applying the functionality of the base aspect to those join points. Figure 8.2 depicts the structure.

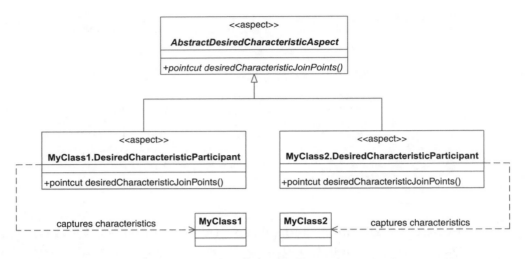

Figure 8.2   A typical structure using the participant pattern. For each class, a nested subaspect exists to make the class participate in the collaboration offered by the base aspect.

With the participant pattern, the collaborating classes explicitly participate in the implementation of the crosscutting concerns by extending an inviting abstract aspect and providing the definition for its abstract pointcut. Note that although we show a one-class/one-participant kind of collaboration, the participant pattern does not require it. It is possible, for example, to have one participant per class hierarchy or package. However, in such cases, because the aspect is not nested in the class with the characteristics-bearing methods, you must remember to modify the pointcut in the participant aspect when the list of methods matching the desired characteristics changes. Additionally, if a signature pattern exists, the participating aspect may also use property-based pointcuts to capture the methods that have the required characteristics.

8.4.4   A summary of the participant pattern

The participant pattern lets you implement characteristic-based crosscutting by embedding the knowledge of such characteristics where it belongs—in the classes. Only classes have the potential of knowing such information, so the pattern makes tracking changes in the class a local affair. While the pattern requires explicit participation by classes in the aspect collaboration, their knowledge of the aspect is limited to defining the implementation of the abstract aspect.

The biggest consequence of using this pattern, unlike with most other patterns and usages, is that the collaboration flow is reversed. In the participant pattern, the aspect makes the class participate in the aspect collaboration, while in other cases, aspects affect classes without their knowledge.

8.5 *Idioms*

As we discussed earlier, idioms are really smaller, simpler design patterns. They allow you to apply a solution to a specific problem, much in the same way you use a design pattern. You can also think of idioms as "programming tips" providing solutions that fit more naturally into the target programming language. In this section, we introduce a few of those idioms. You will see how we use them in real examples throughout the rest of this book. Understanding these idioms up front will allow you to focus more on the core logic of your solution rather than on its intricacies.

8.5.1 *Avoiding infinite recursion*

This is actually an "anti-idiom" in that you should avoid getting into these situations. Infinite recursion caused by advice to a join point in the aspect itself is probably the most common problem faced by beginners using AspectJ. Fortunately, the problem is simple to understand and the solution is easy to implement.

Consider the `TestRecursion` class in listing 8.28, which prints a message in the `main()` method. Also consider a tracing aspect (listing 8.29) that advises calls to all the methods in any class to print the join point's information.

Listing 8.28   TestRecursion.java

```java
public class TestRecursion {
    public static void main(String[] args) {
        System.out.println("Hello");
    }
}
```

Listing 8.29   Tracing.java

```java
public aspect Tracing {
    before() : call(* *.*(..)) {
        System.out.println("Calling: " + thisJoinPointStaticPart);
    }
}
```

The tracing aspect is a simple aspect that contains a before advice and prints `thisJoinPointStaticPart` in the advice body. When we compile and run the test program, we get the following output:

```
> ajc TestRecursion.java Tracing.java
> java TestRecursion
Exception in thread "main" java.lang.StackOverflowError
        at org.aspectj.runtime.reflect.StringMaker.
          makeTypeName(StringMaker.java:99)
        at org.aspectj.runtime.reflect.StringMaker.
          makeTypeName(StringMaker.java:108)
        at org.aspectj.runtime.
          reflect.StringMaker.addTypeNames(StringMaker.java:118)
        at org.aspectj.runtime.reflect.StringMaker.
          addSignature(StringMaker.java:134)
        at org.aspectj.runtime.reflect.MethodSignatureImpl.
          toString(MethodSignatureImpl.java:61)
        at org.aspectj.runtime.reflect.JoinpointImpl$StaticPartImpl.
          toString(JoinpointImpl.java:51)
        at org.aspectj.runtime.reflect.JoinpointImpl$StaticPartImpl.
          toString(JoinpointImpl.java:56)
        at java.lang.String.valueOf(String.java:2173)
        at java.lang.StringBuffer.append(StringBuffer.java:369)
        at Tracing.before0$ajc(Test.java:9)
        ...
```

What gives? The problem is that the call to `System.out.println()` in the advice itself is being advised. Therefore, the advice gets invoked recursively, eventually leading to a stack overflow.

The idiom to avoid such undesirable behavior is to prevent tracing the join points in the aspect itself by adding the within pointcut, as follows:

```
public aspect Tracing {
    before() : call(* *.*(..)) && !within(Tracing) {
        System.out.println("Calling: " + thisJoinPointStaticPart);
    }
}
```

Now when we compile and run the program, we get this output:

```
> ajc TestRecursion.java Tracing.java
> java TestRecursion
Calling: call(void java.io.PrintStream.println(String))
Hello
```

In general, you should be careful when you define a pointcut that captures a wide range of join points, such as the call to all methods in the system. You usually want to exclude join points in the aspect itself. This simple idiom will save you quite a bit of frustration, especially if you are just starting to learn AspectJ. If you are a seasoned AspectJ developer, you probably know this so well that you may have just skipped over this section!

8.5.2 *Nullifying advice*

When using AspectJ on projects, I often try removing advice for what-if scenarios and isolating advice to see the effect of other advice when multiple advices apply to a join point. This idiom presents a simple way to abrogate certain advice in the system. There are a few ways to achieve this goal, and they carry certain implications. In this section, we will also show you how to (and how not to) nullify advice.

Consider the following snippet from an aspect:

```
pointcut operation(): <pointcut-definition>;

before() : operation() {
    ...
}
```

Now if we need to turn off the advice, we simply combine the pointcut with an if(false), as shown here:

```
before() : operation() && if(false) {
    ...
}
```

This pointcut will not match any join point, given that it is impossible to evaluate an if(false) to true. The result, therefore, is the logical removal of the advice from the system.

A common mistake that is made when trying to achieve the same result with around advice is to use the if(false) construct to surround the code inside the advice body, as shown in the following snippet:

```
void around() : operation() {
    if(false) {
        ...
        proceed();
        ...
    }
}
```

While the use of the if(false) construct works well for commenting out a block of code in Java methods, it doesn't behave as expected for around advice that calls proceed() in its body. In this case, if(false) in the advice body results in bypassing the captured join point. The reason is that unless the around advice calls proceed(), the captured join point will not be executed at all. Now the advice is doing exactly the opposite of what we expected; we wanted the advice to leave the program flow unaltered as if the advice did not exist—and instead it eliminated the captured join point's execution.

There are other ways to nullify advice. All the techniques revolve around modifying the pointcut definition so it doesn't match any other join point. For example, we could combine the pointcut with the negated version of it, as follows:

```
before() : operation() && !operation() {
    ...
}
```

While this code performs as expected, the suggested technique of `if(false)` is decisively simple and clearly catches the eye. In this code snippet, readers will need to think for a while to decipher the pointcut definition to realize that the `&& !operation()` is meant to nullify the advice. For pointcut definitions containing a complex combination of multiple other pointcuts, this becomes needlessly complicated.

So, instead of analyzing the scenario in each case and trying out a different style for various kinds of advice, simply follow the suggested idiom of combining `if(false)` with the pointcut itself.

Now you know precisely how to nullify advice. Equally important, you also know how *not* to do it. Using an idiom not only saves you effort, but also lets you mechanically perform simple tasks and avoid potential traps.

8.5.3 *Providing empty pointcut definitions*

Sometimes you need to supply a pointcut definition that matches no join point in the system. You need to do this, for example, when you create concrete subaspects that must define each abstract pointcut in the base aspect but you do not have any matching join points for some of the abstract pointcuts. Using this technique is equivalent to a concrete class providing a blank implementation for certain abstract methods in the base class. Listing 8.30 shows a reusable aspect that contains two abstract pointcuts: one to capture normal operations and the other to capture critical operations so that the advice can log exceptions thrown by those join points.

Listing 8.30   AbstractErrorReportingAspect.java

```
public abstract aspect AbstractErrorReportingAspect {
    public abstract pointcut normalOperations();

    public abstract pointcut criticalOperations();

    after() throwing : normalOperations() || criticalOperations() {
        ... log the error
    }

    after() throwing : criticalOperations() {
```

```
        ... code to handle critical errors
        ... page, email, call, contact by all available means
    }
}
```

Any aspect that is implementing `AbstractErrorReportingAspect` must provide the definition for both the `normalOperations()` and `criticalOperations()` point-cuts. The problem occurs when your system does not have any join points that match such a pointcut, since you still need to define each abstract pointcut in the concrete subaspects. While you may apply a variation of the idiom in section 8.5.2 and use the `if(false)` pointcut as the pointcut definition, the scheme does not work with around advice due to the mismatch of the advice's return type and the join points' return type. The solution is to use a special form of named pointcut that omits the colon (`:`) and the pointcut definition following it. This pointcut will capture no join point, and that is exactly what we need. Listing 8.31 illustrates this idiom.

Listing 8.31   SystemErrorReportingAspect.java

```
public aspect SystemErrorReportingAspect
    extends AbstractErrorReportingAspect {
    public pointcut normalOperations();

    public pointcut criticalOperations() : call(* com..System.*(..));
}
```

In this case, `SystemErrorReportingAspect` does not have any operations that can be categorized as normal operations and therefore does not have to capture any join points with the `normalOperations()` pointcut. However, to make `System-ErrorReportingAspect` a concrete aspect, we must supply a definition for each pointcut. We use the special form of poincut syntax to get the effect of not capturing any join points for normal operations.

8.5.4 *Providing a default interface implementation*

AspectJ's introduction mechanism allows you to introduce members not only to classes but also to interfaces. This means you now can introduce data as well as methods. By using this mechanism to provide a default interface implementation, you can avoid writing code in many classes and make changes easy to implement.

Plain Java does not allow interfaces to contain implementation code; only classes are allowed to implement the methods. On a few occasions, it would be useful to have some default implementation in the interfaces as well. Without AspectJ, the usual strategy is to create a default implementation of the interface and let the classes that would normally implement the interface actually extend this default implementation class instead. This works fine as long as the implementing classes need to extend this class alone. If there are two such default implementation classes, this solution starts to break down. It also breaks down if you want to extend some other class and implement an interface using its default implementation class. You can make the task somewhat easier with the delegation pattern (which delegates each method to an instance of the default implementation class). Nevertheless, you do end up with several one-line methods, which causes code scattering—one of the symptoms of a crosscutting concern.

Consider the simple interface in listing 8.32, which models entities that can have a name. We will use this interface to show how AspectJ can simplify the job of providing the default implementation for an interface.

Listing 8.32   Nameable.java: an interface for entities with a name

```java
public interface Nameable {
    public void setName(String name);
    public String getName();
}
```

Now with pure Java, we have to implement the two methods in each class that implements this interface, as in listing 8.33.

Listing 8.33   Entity.java: implementing the `Nameable` interface in a conventional way

```java
public class Entity implements Nameable {
    private String _name;

    public void setName(String name) {
        _name = name;
    }

    public String getName() {
        return _name;
    }
}
```

For a complex implementation, we can use a delegate object to perform the actual work. In any case, we must add some nearly identical code in all implementing classes.

With this idiom, we create an aspect that introduces the default implementation of the methods to the interface. Listing 8.34 shows the implementation of the methods in the `Nameable` interface.

Listing 8.34   Nameable.java: with the default implementation

```
public interface Nameable {
    public void setName(String name);
    public String getName();

    static aspect Impl {
        private String Nameable._name;

        public void Nameable.setName(String name) {
            _name = name;
        }

        public String Nameable.getName() {
            return _name;
        }
    }
}
```

Now the classes implementing the `Nameable` interface no longer have to contain these methods. Listing 8.35 shows the new version of `Entity` that works with the `Nameable` interface in listing 8.34.

Listing 8.35   Entity.java: implementing the Nameable interface the AspectJ way

```
public class Entity implements Nameable {
}
```

Using pure Java, we could achieve a similar effect by creating a class, say, `Default-Nameable`, that provides the default implementation, and then making `Entity` extend that class. However, this approach works only when we are implementing a single interface. Consider another interface, `Identifiable`, in listing 8.36.

Listing 8.36   Identifiable.java: without any default implementation

```
public interface Identifiable {
    public void setId(String id);
    public String getId();
}
```

Now if `Entity` were to implement both `Nameable` and `Identifiable` without using AspectJ, we would have to implement one of the interfaces and extend the other's default implementation. When we use the default interface idiom, all we need to do is declare that the `Entity` class implements both the interfaces, and we are done. As you can see in listing 8.37, the nested aspect inside `Identifiable` is similar to the one in `Nameable`.

Listing 8.37   Identifiable.java: with default implementation

```
public interface Identifiable {
    public void setId(String id);
    public String getId();

    static aspect Impl {
        private String Identifiable._id;

        public void Identifiable.setId(String id) {
            _id = id;
        }

        public String Identifiable.getId() {
            return _id;
        }
    }
}
```

Now the `Entity` class simply implements both interfaces, as shown in listing 8.38. The effect is the same as extending the default implementation for both (if multiple inheritance were allowed in Java).

Listing 8.38   Entity.java: implementing `Nameable` and `Identifiable` the AspectJ way

```
public class Entity implements Nameable, Identifiable {
}
```

While the classes that implement these interfaces no longer have to implement their methods, in some cases it is necessary to add some customization to the methods. When such methods are directly implemented in classes, they override the default implementation introduced by the aspect, just as you would expect.

Another variation that you may use is to provide only a partial default implementation for an interface. For example, consider situations where the default implementation needs information from the concrete classes or you want to force the implementing class's developers to think about the right semantics on a certain method. In those cases, this idiom lets you implement as many methods as appropriate in the interface, and lets the concrete classes implement the rest.

This idiom not only saves you from writing code, it also facilitates making changes. If you need to modify the default implementation, all you need to do is change the `Impl` nested aspects

8.6 *Summary*

The existence of design patterns and idioms—knowledge in a condensed form—reflects the maturity of programming methodologies and languages. The patterns and idioms we introduced in this chapter are merely the beginning; both AOP and AspectJ are new, and there are a lot more patterns waiting to be discovered.

When you encounter problems, knowing how to apply and reuse patterns will help you solve them efficiently. Instead of thinking about each problem afresh, you can determine whether one of the patterns will fit your problem.

Once you get a good grasp of using patterns, you will see how combining them can be even more effective in tackling complex problems. In the transaction management system in chapter 11, for example, we use all four patterns—worker object creation, wormhole, exception introduction, and participant—as well as a few of the idioms.

Experiment with these patterns, gain an understanding of them, and think about places that you may be able to apply them. Such investment will pay off later when you introduce aspects into a real system. Once you know these patterns, instead of being surprised by the problem posed, you will probably respond by saying, "Yes, I can use the <name-the-pattern> pattern."

9

Implementing thread safety

This chapter covers AspectJ solutions for

- Ensuring Swing's thread-safety rule
- Improving responsiveness of UI applications
- Implementing a reusable read-write lock pattern

Thread safety requires maintaining correct system behavior when multiple threads are accessing the system state. Analyzing, implementing, testing, and debugging this classic concern is difficult—especially since the code tends to be widely spread throughout the system. Failing to maintain a high degree of diligence in modifying any part can result in problems as simple as visual anomalies or in outright failures, such as compromised data integrity and deadlocks. AspectJ can help you modularize the implementation of this concern and thus simplify it.

Some patterns are designed to facilitate the task of ensuring thread safety. Instead of analyzing an ad hoc implementation, you start with proven ways to address thread-safety problems. A pattern, for example, would specify when and how to obtain locks on an object in order to avoid deadlocks, provide maximum concurrency, and minimize overhead. Of course, each pattern suits a particular kind of problem, and you must analyze your problem to choose the right pattern.

In this chapter, we examine AspectJ-based solutions to thread-safety problems. We examine how AspectJ can modularize the implementation of two patterns: a Swing-related pattern that involves routing all requests to protected objects through a predefined thread and the read-write lock pattern.

9.1 *Swing's single-thread rule*

Swing, currently the most popular Java GUI library, uses one of the simple thread-safety patterns that requires accessing all the Swing components only through the event-dispatching thread. By limiting the access to only one preassigned thread, the pattern moves the issue of thread-safe access away from the components. When another thread needs to access a Swing component, it must request the event-dispatching thread to carry out the operation on its behalf instead of doing so itself.

In chapter 6, we developed an AspectJ-based solution for catching the violations of Swing's single-thread rule and logging the context under which they occurred. Once you understand the violations by using the aspects, you can use conventional solutions to fix them. However, fixing the violations in a conventional way can be a daunting task that requires significant modifications in multiple modules. In the first part of this chapter, we develop a way to fix the problem automatically. We examine an AspectJ-based solution that enables you to introduce thread safety simply by adding a couple of aspects to your system; no modifications to the core system are required. (This solution also provides a useful example of the worker object creation pattern presented in chapter 8. In fact, I discovered that pattern while trying to solve this very problem in an application I was working on.) Later in the chapter, we explore other ways you can use this pattern, such as executing time-consuming tasks in separate threads to improve the responsiveness of the user interface.

To better understand the problem and the solutions, let's go over the thread-safety issues in Swing. If you are already familiar with the problem and solution using `EventQueue.invokeLater()` and `EventQueue.invokeAndWait()`, you can skip through the next few sections and go directly to section 9.4, which introduces an AspectJ-based solution.

9.1.1 *The rule*

Swing's single-thread rule states, "Once a Swing component has been realized, all code that might affect or depend on the state of that component should be executed in the event-dispatching thread" (see http://java.sun.com/docs/books/tutorial/uiswing/overview/threads.html). The term *realized* in this context refers to making a component visible. Once a component is visible, the event-dispatching thread (sometimes called the AWT thread) is the only thread that can safely access or update the state of the realized component. The rule exempts certain methods, allowing them to be safely called from any thread. The important ones are `repaint()`, `revalidate()`, and listener management methods.

For the benefit of UI component developers, Swing decided to take the route of permitting only single-thread access in order to reduce the burden of ensuring thread safety individually.

9.1.2 *The problem*

In simple applications that do not use any user-created threads, single-thread access is usually not a big concern. Since the components are updated in response to user actions, which are called in the event-dispatching thread, the single-thread rule is automatically observed. For example, you don't have to worry about this rule when you are deleting a row in `JTable` in direct response to a user pressing a button.

In complex applications that need access to UI components from a nonevent-dispatching thread, however, the single-threaded restriction becomes a problem. A typical example is a thread performing network or I/O-intensive operations or database-related activities. In such cases, these nonevent threads may need to update the UI. For example, consider a situation where you need to update the UI based on information from a server (a table's contents in a database, for instance). You make a request to the server, wait for a response, and then update the UI based on that response. You most definitely don't want the event-dispatching thread to be blocked on the response, since doing so locks your whole GUI until the server responds. A simple solution is to let some other thread wait for the server to respond and update the UI with the response obtained. Bingo! You just encountered Swing's single-thread rule problem. You are not supposed to update any UI component in a nonevent-dispatching thread. If the thread waiting for the server to respond updates the component while the AWT thread is repainting the UI component, it may result in UI anomalies or even worse—a crash. The same kind of problem would occur if you used a callback mechanism using RMI. In that case, the callbacks would be invoked in RMI threads, and updating the state of Swing components from the thread would lead to a violation of the thread-safety rule. As with most multithreading-related problems, these problems are hard to reproduce and therefore hard to fix. Murphy's law seems to work well with the single-thread rule: If you violate the single-thread rule, the problems always seem to occur during the customer demo of your product!

9.1.3 *The solution*

To ensure safe access from a nonevent-dispatching thread, Swing allows a thread to request that the event-dispatching thread carry out the operation on its behalf. With this mechanism, the caller thread makes the request, while the event-dispatching thread carries out the actual operation when processing the request. By requiring that the component's state be accessed and manipulated only from a preassigned thread, and by providing a mechanism for passing the request to the preassigned thread, Swing removes the burden of dealing with thread-safety issues from the Swing component's developers.

Threads can pass requests to perform operations to an event-dispatching thread through the use of `EventQueue.invokeLater()` or `EventQueue.invokeAnd-Wait()`. (You will see the difference between both shortly.) With either, you pass a `Runnable` object, and the `run()` method within it performs the intended operation. Such a solution requires writing a class extending `Runnable` for each method that needs to be called from a nonAWT thread and using those classes instead of direct calls. This has two problems:

- Writing a class for each method is cumbersome.
- You must ensure that the class, in combination with `EventQueue`, replaces any call from the nonAWT thread.

The first limitation is an easier one to deal with—you could create a library of such classes and use it for any of your projects. The second one is, however, not trivial. It is not always easy to statically determine if the method call is being made from a nonAWT thread. Missing a few such calls can lead to unexplainable UI problems. Dynamically determining the callers' thread ensures correct behavior if employed consistently, but those checks and the routing logic result in hard-to-read code.

9.2 A test problem

Let's examine a test program (listing 9.1) that exhibits the multithread access problem. We will use a test program that is similar to the one shown in chapter 6 (listing 6.7) and add a few more calls to illustrate specific issues. Later we will use the same program to show how the conventional solution as well as the AspectJ solution works.

> **Listing 9.1 A test program showing incorrect usage of the UI update call**

```java
import java.awt.*;
import javax.swing.*;
import javax.swing.table.*;

public class Test {
    public static void main(String[] args) {
        JFrame appFrame = new JFrame();
        appFrame.setDefaultCloseOperation(JFrame.EXIT_ON_CLOSE);

        DefaultTableModel tableModel = new DefaultTableModel(4,2);
        JTable table = new JTable(tableModel);

        appFrame.getContentPane().add(table);

        appFrame.pack();
        appFrame.setVisible(true);

        String value = "[0,0]";

        tableModel.setValueAt(value, 0, 0);      ◄━❶ Updating
                                                       the UI
        JOptionPane.showMessageDialog(appFrame,
                                "Press OK to continue");

        int rowCount = tableModel.getRowCount();
        System.out.println("Row count = " + rowCount);

        Color gridColor = table.getGridColor();
        System.out.println("Grid color = " + gridColor);
    }
}
```

❷ Requesting user input

❸ Accessing the return value

The last four UI accesses in this program are made from the main thread. To correct this situation, we need to route such calls through the event-dispatching thread. Although we are making these calls in the main thread itself, in real situations such calls will typically occur from some other user thread. For example, it could be a user thread performing some complex task or a callback from an RMI thread.

❶ The call to set the value of a cell will ultimately result in updating the table component. This call can typically be invoked asynchronously—the caller does not have to wait until the execution is carried out, since showing the new values won't occur until the AWT thread repaints the table. Such asynchronous calls are also called nonblocking operations.

❷ The call to show a message must be made synchronously—the caller must wait until the call has completed the execution, which means after the user has seen and dismissed the message. Such operations are also called blocking operations.

❸ These calls also must wait before returning to the caller—for the return value of `getRowCount()` and `getGridColor()` to make any sense, the call must execute first.

Let's write a simple aspect to monitor UI access calls and the thread executing them (listing 9.2).

Listing 9.2   LogUIActivitiesAspect.java

```
import java.awt.EventQueue;

public aspect LogUIActivitiesAspect {
    pointcut uiActivities()
        : call(* javax..*+.*(..));

    before() : uiActivities() {
        System.out.println("Executing:\n\t"
                            + thisJoinPointStaticPart.getSignature()
                            + "\n\t"
                            + Thread.currentThread() + "\n");
    }
}
```

In the logging aspect, we simply log all the calls to any method in any class in the `javax` package and any of its subpackages. The before advice prints the method signature and the caller thread using `Thread.currentThread()`.

When we compile[1] and run the `Test` class with the logging aspect, we get output similar to the following:

---

[1] You need to use the `-1.4` flag to the ajc compiler to get the `setVisible()` calls logged. This is a result of the interaction between the byte code produced by pre-1.4 compilers and the AspectJ weaver.

```
> ajc -1.4 *.java
> java Test
Executing:
        void javax.swing.JFrame.setDefaultCloseOperation(int)
        Thread[main,5,main]

Executing:
        Container javax.swing.JFrame.getContentPane()
        Thread[main,5,main]

Executing:
        void javax.swing.JFrame.pack()
        Thread[main,5,main]

Executing:
        void javax.swing.JFrame.setVisible(boolean)
        Thread[main,5,main]

Executing:
        void javax.swing.table.DefaultTableModel.setValueAt(Object,
➡       int, int)
        Thread[main,5,main]

Executing:
        void javax.swing.JOptionPane.showMessageDialog(Component,
➡       Object)
        Thread[main,5,main]

Executing:
        int javax.swing.table.DefaultTableModel.getRowCount()
        Thread[main,5,main]

Row count = 4
Executing:
        Color javax.swing.JTable.getGridColor()
        Thread[main,5,main]

Grid color = javax.swing.plaf.ColorUIResource[r=153,g=153,b=153]
```

The output shows that all the calls are made in the main thread. The calls made in the main thread after the call to setVisible() are in violation of the single-thread rule. The correct usage requires them to be executed only in the event-dispatching thread.

Now that we have a simple illustrative program showing the problem, let's see how to solve it using the conventional solution.

9.3 *Solution: the conventional way*

Before we discuss the AspectJ solution, let's look at an implementation of a conventional solution; this will help you to see the complexity of such a solution and how thread safety is a crosscutting concern. You will also understand the behavior expected from an AspectJ-based solution; ultimately, we want both solutions to be behaviorally identical.

While this section may seem rather long, and you may be eager to see the AspectJ-based solution, be patient and work along with me. This provides the background you need to create the AspectJ-based solution, and unless you are already intimately familiar with the conventional solution, you will need a firm grasp of these concepts. You'll also probably gain a greater appreciation for the AspectJ-based solution.

In our implementation (listing 9.3), we wrap each method call made after realizing the frame in anonymous `Runnable` classes, also known as routing classes. The class's `run()` method simply calls the intended operation. Although we used anonymous classes here, you could very well use named classes similar to the ones we developed in listings 6.8 and 6.9 when we were illustrating policy enforcement. We then call either `EventQueue.invokeLater()` or `EventQueue.invokeAndWait()` and pass an instance of the routing class. For calls that can be performed in a nonblocking manner, we use `invokeLater()`, whereas for calls that must block the caller, we use `invokeAndWait()`.

Listing 9.3 Test.java: the conventional implementation

```java
import java.awt.*;
import javax.swing.*;
import javax.swing.table.*;

public class Test {
    public static void main(String[] args) {
        final JFrame appFrame = new JFrame();
        appFrame.setDefaultCloseOperation(JFrame.EXIT_ON_CLOSE);

        final DefaultTableModel tableModel = new DefaultTableModel(4,2);
        final JTable table = new JTable(tableModel);

        appFrame.getContentPane().add(table);

        appFrame.pack();
        appFrame.setVisible(true);          ◄─❶  The trigger point for
        final String value = "[0,0]";            the single-thread rule
        EventQueue.invokeLater(new Runnable() {      ❷
```

```
    public void run() {
        tableModel.setValueAt(value, 0, 0);        ❷ Asynchronous
    }                                                  routing
});

try {
    EventQueue.invokeAndWait(new Runnable() {
        public void run() {
            JOptionPane.
                showMessageDialog(appFrame,
                                  "Press OK to continue");
        }
    });                                          Synchronous
} catch (Exception ex) {                         routing to
    // ignore...                                 get user  ❸
}                                                input

final int[] rowCountValueArray = new int[1];
try {
    EventQueue.invokeAndWait(new Runnable() {
        public void run() {
            rowCountValueArray[0] = tableModel.getRowCount();
        }
    });
} catch (Exception ex) {                         Synchronous
    // ignore...                                 routing to get
}                                                the primitive  ❹
int rowCount = rowCountValueArray[0];            return value

System.out.println("Row count = " + rowCount);

final Color[] gridColorValueArray = new Color[1];
try {
    EventQueue.invokeAndWait(new Runnable() {
        public void run() {
            gridColorValueArray[0] = table.getGridColor();
        }
    });
} catch (Exception ex) {                         Synchronous
    // ignore...                                 routing to get
}                                                the object's  ❺
Color gridColor = gridColorValueArray[0];        return value

System.out.println("Grid color = " + gridColor);
    }
}
```

In listing 9.3, we routed all the calls that access or update the UI components'
state by posting a request in EventQueue. Let's look at the code in more detail:

❶ This is the point where the UI is realized—the frame is shown on the screen. It is okay to call UI methods in a nonevent-dispatching thread before this point. Since the AWT thread is not accessing the components, the main thread is the only thread updating the UI component's state.

Once the UI is on the screen, the AWT thread will read and update the state. For example, it may invoke an operation to get the row count of table widget to paint the table components. Because the AWT thread is accessing the state and because Swing classes do not provide any exclusive access protection, we must request that the event-dispatching thread perform the operation on behalf of the calling thread. With this policy, we ensure that the event-dispatching thread is the only thread managing UI components.

❷ The call to set the value of a particular cell in the table can be made asynchronously since there is no inherent requirement to wait for completion of this operation. We first wrap our request in an anonymous class implementing `Runnable`. In the `run()` method, we simply carry out the original operation. Note that we marked several local variables (such as `tableModel`) as `final`. This is necessary because Java enforces that the variables accessed in local classes be declared `final`.

Since synchronous execution is not a requirement, we use `EventQueue.invokeLater()` to send our request to perform these operations. This results in the request being added to the event-dispatch queue. The event-dispatching thread will eventually pick the request object and call its `run()` method, thus carrying out the operation.

❸ The call to `JOptionPane.showMessageDialog()` has an inherent requirement to be executed synchronously with the caller—the caller must not proceed with the next operation until the call is executed. Consider a scenario where your program flow depends on the user's input, such as clicking on a Yes or No button in a message dialog box. This means you must show the dialog box, wait for the user response, and only then proceed further based on the input. Even in cases where the dialog box serves a notification purpose, as in our case, you still need to show the dialog box and proceed only after the user has seen and dismissed it.

To fulfill the blocking requirement on the operation, we use `EventQueue.invokeAndWait()` to send our request. The request is added to the event-dispatch queue, and the caller will be blocked pending the execution of the request object. Eventually the event-dispatching thread will pick up the request, execute it, and unblock the caller. In our case, the execution in the `main()` method will be blocked until the message box is shown to the user and the user clicks the OK button or closes the message box.

❹ When a return value is expected from a method call, the operation must run synchronously with the caller. The next operation may depend on the return value, so there is no point in proceeding without obtaining the return value by executing the operation.

Just as in the earlier call, we use `invokeAndWait()` to synchronously request that the event-dispatching thread execute the operation and block the caller until it is finished. We now focus on how to communicate the return value from the worker object to the caller. Since the variables accessed from local classes must be `final`, we cannot just assign the result of `getRowCount()` to the `rowCount` variable.[2] We need to go through the hoops of creating an integer array of length one, marking it final, assigning the element in it to the return value of `getRowCount()`, and finally assigning that element to `rowCount`. So much for getting a return value!

If we used named classes, we still would have to consider the return value, typically by adding an additional member to the class to store the return value.

⑤ The call to `getGridColor()` has an identical issue, except that the return value in this case is not a primitive.

We have not handled the exceptions in this example, in order to limit further complexity in the already complex code. In most implementations, you will need to deal with exceptions in a certain way. Toward the end of the chapter, we show how you can deal with exceptions with our AspectJ-based solution (where both the base solution as well as the exception-handling task are vastly simpler).

Another point to note is that we could have simply called all the methods after the frame was realized in a single worker object. It certainly would have worked here. Nevertheless, to mimic the real programming problem where a different individual or a group of calls may be made from different parts of a program, we deal with each operation independently. Further, this grouping of methods requires altering the exception-handling policy; you now need to address exceptions thrown by any of the called methods together instead of dealing with them separately.

When we compile the previous class along with the logging aspect and run it, we get the following output:

```
> ajc -1.4 *.java
> java Test
```

---

[2] You cannot use a blank final variable (the final variable that does not have an assigned value) for this purpose to defer the assignment to an inner class's method. The Java Language Specification (section 8.1.2) requires that "Any local variable, formal method parameter or exception handler parameter used but not declared in an inner class must be declared final, and must be definitely assigned before the body of the inner class."

```
Executing:
        void javax.swing.JFrame.setDefaultCloseOperation(int)
        Thread[main,5,main]

Executing:
        Container javax.swing.JFrame.getContentPane()
        Thread[main,5,main]

Executing:
        void javax.swing.JFrame.pack()
        Thread[main,5,main]

Executing:
        void javax.swing.JFrame.setVisible(boolean)
        Thread[main,5,main]

Executing:
        void javax.swing.table.DefaultTableModel.setValueAt(Object,
        int, int)
        Thread[AWT-EventQueue-0,6,main]

Executing:
        void javax.swing.JOptionPane.showMessageDialog(Component,
        Object)
        Thread[AWT-EventQueue-0,6,main]

Executing:
        int javax.swing.table.DefaultTableModel.getRowCount()
        Thread[AWT-EventQueue-0,6,main]

Row count = 4
Executing:
        Color javax.swing.JTable.getGridColor()
        Thread[AWT-EventQueue-0,6,main]

Grid color = javax.swing.plaf.ColorUIResource[r=153,g=153,b=153]
```

As you can see, our hard work has paid off. All the calls made after making the frame visible are indeed called in the event-dispatching thread (note the thread ID printed in the log). We no longer violate Swing's single-thread rule. However, the complexity of the program is overwhelming.

9.4 *Solution: the AspectJ way*

To summarize the conventional solution that ensures adherence to Swing's single-thread rule, we need two kinds of modifications:

1   Implement execution classes that encapsulate the UI operations and create worker objects from those classes rather than making the direct calls.

2 Pass the worker object to `EventQueue.invokeLater()` or `EventQueue.invoke-AndWait()`. When we must have access to the return values of invoked synchronous operations, we also need a mechanism for transferring the return value from the `run()` method to the caller of `EventQueue.invoke-AndWait()`.

In this section, we create a basic AspectJ-based solution that avoids violating the single-thread rule. We will then improve upon this solution in a later section.

The key element of our solution is to use the worker object creation pattern explained in chapter 8. We capture calls to all the required methods, use the pattern to create a new `Runnable` object, and hand over the object to the event queue for execution. Before releasing the object to the queue, we also check whether the caller thread is already the event-dispatching thread; in that case, we let the original method execute directly.

With the AspectJ-based solution, we will implement Swing's single-thread rule without making any change to the `Test` class in listing 9.1. This aspect will automatically route any method call that accesses or modifies a Swing component's state through the event-dispatching thread.

In this section, we implement multiple versions of the solution, with each new solution building on the prior version. Note that each version of the solution uses the original `Test` program from listing 9.1 and also uses the `LogUIActivities-Aspect` from listing 9.2 to log the execution of the UI operations.

Each version consists of an abstract aspect that is implemented in a concrete aspect. While we could have implemented just one concrete aspect in each case, this refactoring offers flexibility that can be quite important when you use the solutions in your system. For instance, you can include the abstract aspect in your system unaltered and then write a simple subaspect, similar to the ones we show, to handle your system-specific requirements. In section 9.5 we will examine the kinds of customization you may need. Besides making the final solution easy to understand, this step-by-step approach will suggest a typical way you might want to develop an AspectJ-based solution to tackle new problems—start simple and handle more issues as you progress.

9.4.1 *The first version*

In the first version of our solution, we route all the calls through `EventQueue.invokeAndWait()`. With this arrangement, the caller will be blocked until the event-dispatching thread executes the operation. In practice, blocking the caller is often undesirable and should be limited to situations that warrant its usage.

The implementation, however, does provide a simple solution to ensure compliance with Swing's single-thread rule. Later we will improve on this solution. Note that we use the `RunnableWithReturn` class developed in chapter 8 in our solution. Listing 9.4 shows the base abstract aspect that routes all join points captured by the `uiMethodCalls()` pointcut synchronously.

Listing 9.4   The base swing thread-safety aspect: First version

```
import java.awt.*;
import java.util.*;
import javax.swing.*;

import  pattern.worker.*;

public abstract aspect SwingThreadSafetyAspect {
    abstract pointcut uiMethodCalls();        ◀──❶  Pointcut capturing
                                                     UI method calls
    pointcut threadSafeCalls()
        : call(void JComponent.revalidate())       ❷
        || call(void JComponent.repaint(..))       Pointcut
        || call(void add*Listener(EventListener))  capturing
        || call(void remove*Listener(EventListener)); exempted calls

    pointcut excludedJoinpoints()               ❸  Pointcut
        : threadSafeCalls()                         capturing all
        || within(SwingThreadSafetyAspect)          excluded join
        || if(EventQueue.isDispatchThread());       points

    pointcut routedMethods()                    ❹  Methods that
        : uiMethodCalls() && !excludedJoinpoints();  need routing

    Object around() : routedMethods() {
        RunnableWithReturn worker = new RunnableWithReturn() {
            public void run() {
                _returnValue = proceed();
            }};
                                                    ❺
        try {                                       Advice
            EventQueue.invokeAndWait(worker);       routing
        } catch (Exception ex) {                    the calls
            // ... log exception
            return null;
        }
        return worker.getReturnValue();
    }
}
```

This abstract aspect provides the basic functionality of routing all the required calls through EventQueue.invokeAndWait() using the worker object creation pattern. Let's study the implementation in detail:

❶ The aspect declares one pointcut, uiMethodCalls(), as an abstract pointcut. The concrete subaspects must provide a definition for this pointcut that captures all the calls accessing or affecting the Swing components.

❷ The threadSafeCalls() pointcut lists the calls to all the methods exempted from the single-thread rule—calls to JComponent.repaint(), JComponent.revalidate(), and methods for adding and removing listeners.

❸ For the excludedJoinpoints() pointcut, we combine the threadSafeCalls() pointcut with the pointcut capturing all the join points in the aspect itself and those executed in the event-dispatching thread. The latter is achieved by using if(EventQueue.isDispatchThread()). The EventQueue.isDispatchThread() method returns true only if the current execution thread is the event-dispatching thread.

❹ We combine the uiMethodCalls() pointcut with the negation of excludedJoinpoints() to capture the join points that need routing of the calls through the event-dispatching thread.

❺ In the advice body, we call EventQueue.invokeAndWait() with an anonymous class extending the RunnableWithReturn class. In the run() method, we simply call proceed() to carry out the original operation. The task that this anonymous class performs is similar to the tasks of the classes in listings 6.8 and 6.9 in chapter 6. The invokeAndWait() method makes the request and is blocked until the event-dispatching thread executes the run() method. The event-dispatching thread eventually calls the run() method, resulting in the invocation of the original call, and then unblocks the caller thread. The advice itself assigns the return value of the proceed() statement to the _returnValue member of the worker object. It later obtains this return value by calling the getReturnValue() method on the worker object. This return value management is a result of directly applying the worker object creation pattern discussed in chapter 8.

The invokeAndWait() method can throw InterruptedException and InvocationTargetException. For now, we will ignore the exceptions and revisit this issue toward the end of this chapter.

Now that we have the base aspect taking care of all the details, let's create a subaspect that extends it. The DefaultSwingThreadSafetyAspect subaspect defines the uiMethodCalls() pointcut, which collects all methods in Swing components. It captures calls to all methods in all of JComponent's direct or indirect subclasses; it also captures calls to all methods in all model classes and their subclasses. Notice that the pointcut definition is identical to that defined in listing 6.10 (which we developed while creating the policy-enforcement aspect). Listing 9.5 shows the `DefaultSwingThreadSafetyAspect` implementation.

Listing 9.5 The subaspect

```
public aspect DefaultSwingThreadSafetyAspect
    extends SwingThreadSafetyAspect {
    pointcut viewMethodCalls()                        Calls to UI
        : call(* javax..JComponent+.*(..));           component methods

    pointcut modelMethodCalls()                       Calls to UI
        : call(* javax..*Model+.*(..))                model
        || call(* javax.swing.text.Document+.*(..));  methods

    pointcut uiMethodCalls()                          Calls to UI
        : viewMethodCalls() || modelMethodCalls();    methods
}
```

The subaspect in listing 9.5 is all you need to ensure adherence to Swing's single-thread rule as long as all your UI components are based on Swing's components and models. If you have additional custom components that do not use any of the standard Swing models as a base class, all you need to do is write a subaspect similar to the one in listing 9.5 with a defined pointcut corresponding to all the update methods in your classes. You may want to consider writing the subaspect as a nested subaspect of the classes, which makes it easy to modify the nested aspect when the implementation of the enclosing class changes. For details of the participant pattern, see chapter 8.

Seeing is believing. To see that the calls are indeed routed as intended, we need an additional logging aspect that prints a log message before executing any UI operation in the control flow of `RunnableWithReturn.run()`. Listing 9.6 shows `LogRoutingDetailsAspect`, which implements such logging.

Listing 9.6 LogRoutingDetailsAspect.java

```
import  pattern.worker.*;

public aspect LogRoutingDetailsAspect {
    pointcut syncRoutingExecution()
        : cflow(execution(* RunnableWithReturn.run()));

    before() : LogUIActivitiesAspect.uiActivities()
```

```
            && syncRoutingExecution() {
            System.out.println("Executing operation synchronously");
    }
}
```

Since advice in all three aspects—DefaultSwingThreadSafetyAspect, LogRouting-
DetailsAspect, and LogUIActivitiesAspect—share common join points, we
need to control their precedence. We would like the advice in DefaultSwingThread-
SafetyAspect to apply first so that the routing takes place prior to any logging.
We also would like LogRoutingDetailsAspect's advice to apply before that of
LogUIActivitiesAspect so that we can see how the calls will be routed before they
are executed. PrecedenceControlAspect (listing 9.7) enforces the required prece-
dence control.

Listing 9.7   PrecedenceControlAspect.java

```
public aspect PrecedenceControlAspect {
    declare precedence:
        DefaultSwingThreadSafetyAspect,
        LogRoutingDetailsAspect,
        LogUIActivitiesAspect;
}
```

The aspect in listing 9.7 declares that DefaultSwingThreadSafetyAspect has the
highest precedence and that LogUIActivitiesAspect has the lowest precedence.
Refer to chapter 4, section 4.2, for more details on aspect-precedence control.

   Let's continue to use the test program from listing 9.1. When we compile all
the classes and aspects, and run the test program, we get output similar to this:

```
> ajc -1.4 *.java pattern\worker\*.java
> java Test
Executing:
        void javax.swing.JFrame.setDefaultCloseOperation(int)
        Thread[main,5,main]

Executing:
        Container javax.swing.JFrame.getContentPane()
        Thread[main,5,main]

Executing:
        void javax.swing.JFrame.pack()
        Thread[main,5,main]
```

```
Executing:
        void javax.swing.JFrame.setVisible(boolean)
        Thread[main,5,main]

Executing operation synchronously
Executing:
        void javax.swing.table.DefaultTableModel.setValueAt(Object,
    ➡ int, int)
        Thread[AWT-EventQueue-0,6,main]

Executing operation synchronously
Executing:
        void javax.swing.JOptionPane.showMessageDialog(Component,
    ➡ Object)
        Thread[AWT-EventQueue-0,6,main]

Executing operation synchronously
Executing:
        int javax.swing.table.DefaultTableModel.getRowCount()
        Thread[AWT-EventQueue-0,6,main]

Row count = 4
Executing operation synchronously
Executing:
        Color javax.swing.JTable.getGridColor()
        Thread[AWT-EventQueue-0,6,main]

Grid color = javax.swing.plaf.ColorUIResource[r=153,g=153,b=153]
```

We can see from the output that all UI operations are indeed executed in the event-dispatching thread. Further, all calls are executed in the control flow of RunnableWithReturn.run() synchronously with the caller. The return values printed are correct too—for both primitive and object return types.

This first version of the solution enabled us to adhere to the Swing's single-thread rule, and we did not have to touch any of the core classes. Further, the use of a worker object creation pattern helped us save the ton of code it would have taken to create a class to encapsulate each individual operation.

Our solution, however, has the shortcoming of routing all the calls through EventQueue.invokeAndWait(), causing the caller to be blocked until the AWT thread picks up the request and executes it. In the next section, we address this shortcoming.

9.4.2 *The second version*

The central idea behind the second version is to detect the need to route a method synchronously or asynchronously based on its return type. If the method is returning a non-void type, we must execute the method synchronously. To obtain the return value of such an operation, we need to execute the operation and not merely put it into the event-processing queue. For these calls, we must use `EventQueue.invokeAndWait()`, and we will use `ReturnWithRunnable` as the base class for the execution class, just as we did in the first version. For the other operations, we assume that it is fine to invoke those operations asynchronously. For those calls, we use `EventQueue.invokeLater()`, and we will use `Runnable` as the base interface for the execution class.

Listing 9.8 shows the second version of the `SwingThreadSafetyAspect` base aspect, which routes methods synchronously or asynchronously based on the return type of the method.

Listing 9.8   The base swing thread-safety aspect: second version

```
import java.awt.*;
import java.util.*;
import javax.swing.*;

import pattern.worker.*;

public abstract aspect SwingThreadSafetyAspect {
    abstract pointcut uiMethodCalls();

    pointcut threadSafeCalls()
        : call(void JComponent.revalidate())
        || call(void JComponent.repaint(..))
        || call(void add*Listener(EventListener))
        || call(void remove*Listener(EventListener));

    pointcut excludedJoinpoints()
        : threadSafeCalls()
        || within(SwingThreadSafetyAspect)
        || if(EventQueue.isDispatchThread());

    pointcut routedMethods()
        : uiMethodCalls() && !excludedJoinpoints();
    pointcut voidReturnValueCalls()
        : call(void *.*(..));

    Object around()
        : routedMethods() && !voidReturnValueCalls() {
        RunnableWithReturn worker = new RunnableWithReturn() {
            public void run() {
                _returnValue = proceed();
            }};

        try {
```

❶ Unchanged portion from listing 9.4

❷ Captures methods returning void

❸

```
            EventQueue.invokeAndWait(worker);       △ ❸ Synchronously
        } catch (Exception ex) {                          routes all
            // ... log exception                          routed
            return null;                                  methods with
        }                                                 the non-void
        return worker.getReturnValue();                   return type
    }

    void around()
        : routedMethods() && voidReturnValueCalls() {
        Runnable worker = new Runnable() {          ❹ Asynchronously
            public void run() {                         executes the
                proceed();                              other routed
            }};                                         methods

        EventQueue.invokeLater(worker);
    }
}
```

❶ The `uiMethodCalls()`, `threadSafeCalls()`, `excludedJoinpoints()`, and `routed-Methods()` pointcuts remain unchanged from those in listing 9.4.

❷ We define the `voidReturnValueCalls()` pointcut to capture all the methods that do not return a value.

❸ We modify the advice that causes synchronous execution in the first version. We want it to apply only to the join points that return a value, so we combine `routedMethods()` with the negation of the `voidReturnValueCalls()` pointcut. Except for this change, the body of the advice remains unchanged from the first version.

❹ We add new advice to cause asynchronous execution of calls that do not return a value. We identify the join points needing this advice by combining the `routedMethods()` pointcut with the `voidReturnValueCalls()` pointcut. The advice body is similar to the synchronous routing advice shown in the previous code section. We use `Runnable` instead of `RunnableWithReturn` to implement the execution class, because we no longer need to consider the return value. To cause asynchronous execution, we use `EventQueue.invokeLater()` instead of `EventQueue.invokeAndWait()`. Since `EventQueue.invokeLater()` does not throw any checked exception, we do not need the exception-handling logic in this advice.

The subaspect in listing 9.5 (which simply provides the definition for a pointcut corresponding to all UI operations) continues to work fine with this aspect.

Before we check how our solution works, let's include additional advice in the `LogRoutingDetailsAspect` aspect (listing 9.9) to differentiate between synchronously and asynchronously invoked calls.

Listing 9.9 LogRoutingDetailsAspect

```
import pattern.worker.*;

public aspect LogRoutingDetailsAspect {
    pointcut syncRoutingExecution()
        : cflow(execution(* RunnableWithReturn.run()));

    before() : LogUIActivitiesAspect.uiActivities()
        && syncRoutingExecution() {
        System.out.println("Executing operation synchronously");
    }

    pointcut asyncRoutingExecution()
        : cflow(execution(* Runnable.run()))
        && !syncRoutingExecution();

    before() : LogUIActivitiesAspect.uiActivities()
        && asyncRoutingExecution() {
        System.out.println("Executing operation asynchronously");
    }
}
```

This addition to the aspect simply logs any calls in the `uiActivities()` pointcut that are carried out in the `Runnable.run()` method's control flow but that are not in the `RunnableWithReturn.run()` method's control flow.

Let's see how our solution fares. When we compile all the classes and aspects and run the test program, we get output similar to this:

```
> ajc -1.4 *.java pattern\worker\*.java
> java Test
Executing:
        void javax.swing.JFrame.setDefaultCloseOperation(int)
        Thread[main,5,main]

Executing:
        Container javax.swing.JFrame.getContentPane()
        Thread[main,5,main]

Executing:
        void javax.swing.JFrame.pack()
        Thread[main,5,main]

Executing:
        void javax.swing.JFrame.setVisible(boolean)
        Thread[main,5,main]
```

```
Executing operation asynchronously
Executing:
        void javax.swing.table.DefaultTableModel.setValueAt(Object,
        ➥ int, int)
        Thread[AWT-EventQueue-0,6,main]

Executing operation asynchronously
Executing:
        void javax.swing.JOptionPane.showMessageDialog(Component,
        ➥ Object)
        Thread[AWT-EventQueue-0,6,main]

Executing operation synchronously
Executing:
        int javax.swing.table.DefaultTableModel.getRowCount()
        Thread[AWT-EventQueue-0,6,main]

Row count = 4
Executing operation synchronously
Executing:
        Color javax.swing.JTable.getGridColor()
        Thread[AWT-EventQueue-0,6,main]

Grid color = javax.swing.plaf.ColorUIResource[r=153,g=153,b=153]
```

The output shows that the call to setValueAt(), which was invoked synchronously using the earlier version of the solution, is now being invoked asynchronously. This is what we expected, since it does not return any value. However, note how JOptionPane.showMessageDialog() is also invoked asynchronously. This is not the correct behavior; it needs to wait until the user has dismissed the message dialog box before continuing. This is because JOptionPane.showMessageDialog() declares that it will return void, and therefore our aspect routed it asynchronously. If we had invoked other JOptionPane methods—such as showConfirmDialog(), which returns a non-void return type—we would get synchronous execution without needing any further modifications. If you ran the program yourself, you would see that getRowCount() and getGridColor() are executed even before you close the message dialog box.

As you can see, our modified solution, taking its cue from the return value type, addresses most needs but behaves incorrectly in certain cases. Let's fix that.

9.4.3 *The third version*

The idea behind the third version is to let subaspects have explicit control over methods that require synchronous routing. We will capture such methods in a pointcut irrespective of their return value type. This way, methods such as JOptionPane.showMessageDialog() that return void can still be routed synchronously. Listing 9.10 shows an aspect that explicitly specifies the methods that must be routed synchronously.

Listing 9.10   The base swing thread-safety aspect: third version

```
import java.awt.*;
import java.util.*;
import javax.swing.*;

import pattern.worker.*;

public abstract aspect SwingThreadSafetyAspect {
    abstract pointcut uiMethodCalls();

    abstract pointcut uiSyncMethodCalls();          ◁──❶ Captures methods needing
                                                          synchronous execution
    pointcut threadSafeCalls()
        : call(void JComponent.revalidate())
        || call(void JComponent.repaint(..))
        || call(void add*Listener(EventListener))
        || call(void remove*Listener(EventListener));

    pointcut excludedJoinpoints()
        : threadSafeCalls()                         ❷ Unchanged
        || within(SwingThreadSafetyAspect)            code from
        || if(EventQueue.isDispatchThread());         listings 9.4
                                                      and 9.8
    pointcut routedMethods()
        : uiMethodCalls() && !excludedJoinpoints();

    pointcut voidReturnValueCalls()
        : call(void *.*(..));
    void around()
        : routedMethods() && voidReturnValueCalls()
          && !uiSyncMethodCalls() {                 ◁──❸ Ensures no
        Runnable worker = new Runnable() {               asynchronous execution
            public void run() {                          of methods needing
                proceed();                               synchronous execution
            }};

        EventQueue.invokeLater(worker);
    }

    Object around()
        : routedMethods()
        && (!voidReturnValueCalls() || uiSyncMethodCalls()) {    ❹
        RunnableWithReturn worker = new RunnableWithReturn() {
            public void run() {
                _returnValue = proceed();
            }};
```

```
        try {
            EventQueue.invokeAndWait(worker);
        } catch (Exception ex) {
            // ... log exception
            return null;
        }
        return worker.getReturnValue();
    }
}
```

Ensures ❹
synchronous
execution of
methods
needing
synchronous
execution

❶ We add a new abstract pointcut, `uiSyncMethodCalls()`, to let subaspects define methods that they wish to route synchronously.

❷ The various pointcuts remain unchanged from the aspect in our first version (which we also carried through to the second version).

❸ We must ensure that all methods captured by the `uiSyncMethodCalls()` pointcut—even those with the void return type—are not advised to execute asynchronously. We do this by combining the negated `uiSyncMethodCalls()` pointcut with the `routedMethod()` and `voidReturnValueCalls()` pointcuts. The advice body itself is unchanged from listing 9.8.

❹ We use the `uiSyncMethodCalls()` pointcut to apply synchronous routing advice to the join points that are captured by the pointcut. This ensures synchronous routing of methods returning a non-void return value by advising the `!voidReturnValueCalls()` pointcut in addition to the `uiSyncMethodCalls()` pointcut.

We need to modify the subaspect to add a definition for `uiSyncMethodCalls()`. Listing 9.11 shows a modified version of `DefaultSwingThreadSafetyAspect` that explicitly specifies the methods needing synchronous routing.

Listing 9.11 A subaspect that lists synchronous execution join points explicitly

```
public aspect DefaultSwingThreadSafetyAspect
    extends SwingThreadSafetyAspect {
    pointcut viewMethodCalls()
        : call(* javax..JComponent+.*(..));

    pointcut modelMethodCalls()
        : call(* javax..*Model+.*(..))
        || call(* javax.swing.text.Document+.*(..));

    pointcut uiMethodCalls()
        : viewMethodCalls() || modelMethodCalls();

    pointcut uiSyncMethodCalls() :
        call(* javax..JOptionPane+.*(..))
        /* || ... */;
}
```

The aspect in listing 9.11 simply defines uiSyncMethodCalls() to capture all the calls to any method in JOptionPane or its subclasses. You can modify the point-cut definition to add other join points that you wish to run synchronously with the caller.

When we run the test program, we see that the message dialog box appears before getRowCount() and getGridColor() are invoked:

```
> ajc -1.4 *.java pattern\worker\*.java
> java Test
Executing:
        void javax.swing.JFrame.setDefaultCloseOperation(int)
        Thread[main,5,main]

Executing:
        Container javax.swing.JFrame.getContentPane()
        Thread[main,5,main]

Executing:
        void javax.swing.JFrame.pack()
        Thread[main,5,main]

Executing:
        void javax.swing.JFrame.setVisible(boolean)
        Thread[main,5,main]

Executing operation asynchronously
Executing:
        void javax.swing.table.DefaultTableModel.setValueAt(Object,
        int, int)
        Thread[AWT-EventQueue-0,6,main]

Executing operation synchronously
Executing:
        void javax.swing.JOptionPane.showMessageDialog(Component,
        Object)
        Thread[AWT-EventQueue-0,6,main]

Executing operation synchronously
Executing:
        int javax.swing.table.DefaultTableModel.getRowCount()
        Thread[AWT-EventQueue-0,6,main]

Row count = 4
Executing operation synchronously
Executing:
        Color javax.swing.JTable.getGridColor()
        Thread[AWT-EventQueue-0,6,main]

Grid color = javax.swing.plaf.ColorUIResource[r=153,g=153,b=153]
```

The output is nearly identical to that for the conventional solution. The only difference is the additional log statement for monitoring synchronous versus asynchronous execution.

We now have a complete solution that implements Swing's single-thread rule without requiring any modification to the core classes. If you have adopted AspectJ fully, you can actually use AspectJ to fix the problems instead of only detecting the problems (as suggested in chapter 6). The result is guaranteed compliance with the threading rule without the need to make system-wide modifications.

9.5 *Improving the solution*

In this section, we discuss a few enhancements to our previous solution, such as handling exceptions and optimizing the solution using system-specific knowledge.

9.5.1 *Dealing with exceptions*

Exception handling poses an interesting challenge when the exceptions are thrown by asynchronously routed calls. For example, if you route a call asynchronously using `EventQueue.invokeLater()`, since the caller isn't going to wait for the execution to be complete, it does not have access to the exceptions thrown. Further, exceptions are thrown in the control flow of the AWT thread and not the caller thread. A reasonable strategy to deal with these exceptions is to set a listener that will be notified if the operation fails. Let's look at the modification we need to make in the first around advice of the final version of the `SwingThreadSafety-Aspect` aspect. All we need to do is surround the `proceed()` statement with a try/catch block, as shown in the following snippet. In the catch block, you can perform any operations you need to do in order to match your exception-handling policy (such as logging it or passing it to an exception listener object). You may also rethrow the exception after wrapping the caught exception in a `RuntimeException`. See chapter 8 for more details on dealing with exceptions in these cases:

```
void around()
    : routedMethods() && voidReturnValueCalls()
    && !uiSyncMethodCalls() {
    Runnable worker = new Runnable() {
        public void run() {
            try {
                proceed();
            } catch (Exception ex) {
                ... deal with exception
                ... call exception listener, log it, etc.
                ... and then optionally rethrow it after wrapping
            }
        }
```

```
        }};
    EventQueue.invokeLater(worker);
}
```

Notice how easy it was to modify our exception-handling strategy. If you were not using AspectJ and you employed anonymous classes, you would have to modify every instance in which calls are routed asynchronously. If you used named classes to carry out the operations, you would have to modify each of those classes. With such widespread modifications, ensuring consistent implementation becomes a daunting task. Using the conventional solution, it is possible to get the expected behavior the first time—with a lot of labor and diligence. However, ensuring continual adherence to the policy becomes challenging. With AspectJ, making changes in the exception-handling strategy becomes quite easy. For example, if you decide to log an exception in addition to passing it to an exception listener, all you need to change is the aspect itself and nothing else. This is the power of AOP and AspectJ—not only do you save a huge amount of code in the core implementation, you make it easy to implement additional system-wide concerns.

For synchronous invocation, you can use the exception introduction pattern presented in chapter 8. With this pattern, you throw a concern-specific runtime exception, then write another aspect to unwrap it and throw the exception originally thrown by the operation. This way, the clients need not be aware of the routing and issues related to it.

The use of AspectJ to implement Swing's single-thread rule not only modularizes and simplifies the implementation, it also makes it easy to implement an exception-handling strategy that is itself modularized.

9.5.2 Avoiding the overhead

In our solution so far, we captured all the calls to the UI methods. This is somewhat inefficient because before every call, the aspect would perform an `Event-Queue.isDispatchThread()` call in the pointcut. Usually the overhead is not high enough to warrant any modifications. However, if overhead is a problem for your system, you can use the typical technique of limiting join points captured by a pointcut to a certain package. For example, when the code updated by a non-AWT thread is limited to certain classes and/or packages, you may limit automatic routing to only those modules. You can do this easily with pointcuts that include `within()` and `withincode()`, as described in chapter 3.

Instead of using `DefaultSwingThreadSafetyAspect`, we can use our own aspect to limit the applicability of the routing advice, as shown here:

```
public aspect LimitedSwingThreadSafetyAspect
    extends SwingThreadSafetyAspect {
    pointcut viewMethodCalls()
        : call(* javax..JComponent+.*(..));

    pointcut modelMethodCalls()
        : call(* javax..*Model+.*(..))
        || call(* javax.swing.text.Document+.*(..));

    pointcut uiMethodCalls()
        : (viewMethodCalls() || modelMethodCalls())
          && within(com.manning.network..*);

    pointcut uiSyncMethodCalls() :
        call(* javax..JOptionPane+.*(..))
        && within(com.manning.network..*);
}
```

In this aspect, we restrict the application of `SwingThreadSafetyAspect` to calls made from `com.manning.network` and all its direct and indirect subpackages.

If you use this kind of optimization, I strongly recommend that you also use the policy-enforcement aspect developed in chapter 6, section 6.6, which detects the violations of Swing's single-thread rule during the development and testing phases. This way, wrong assumptions, if any, will be caught early on.

9.6 *Improving the responsiveness of UI applications*

While we have focused on the use of the worker object creation pattern to ensure thread safety, a small variation of the same theme can be used to improve the responsiveness of UI applications. For example, a common need in UI applications is to avoid locking the GUI when performing a time-consuming task. Let's say that you want to implement a time-consuming task, such as sending an email. You do not want to lock up the UI while the email is being sent. Let's consider the example class in listing 9.12.

Listing 9.12   TestResponsiveness.java

```
import java.awt.*;
import java.awt.event.*;
import javax.swing.*;

public class TestResponsiveness {
    public static void main(String[] args) {
        JFrame appFrame = new JFrame();
        appFrame.setDefaultCloseOperation(JFrame.EXIT_ON_CLOSE);
```

```
        JButton sendEmailButton = new JButton("Send Emails");
        sendEmailButton.addActionListener(new ActionListener() {
            public void actionPerformed(ActionEvent e) {
                sendEmails();
            }
        });
        appFrame.getContentPane().add(sendEmailButton);

        appFrame.pack();
        appFrame.setVisible(true);
    }

    private static void sendEmails() {
        try {
            // simulate long execution...
            Thread.sleep(20000);
        } catch (InterruptedException ex) {
        }
    }
}
```

Compile and run this program and click on the Send Emails button. The whole GUI will be locked for about 20 seconds. The reason is that sendEmails() is executed in the event-dispatching thread, preventing it from refreshing the GUI. Locking up the GUI in this way is undesirable, and yet it is seen quite frequently. The reason, I suspect, is the invasiveness associated with implementing a solution that performs operations in the background. The result is that asynchronous executions are often implemented only for really time-consuming operations, and other not-so-time-consuming operations are allowed to execute directly in the caller thread.

Implementing asynchronous execution of a thread is a simple task when you are using AspectJ. All you need to do is use the reusable aspect shown in listing 9.13 and provide concrete subaspects of it. We first introduced this aspect in chapter 8, listing 8.4, when we used it to demonstrate the worker object creation pattern. Let's enhance it to show how we can avoid locking the GUI by asynchronously routing calls to time-consuming methods from the event-dispatching thread itself. The reusable implementation in listing 9.13 enables the subaspect to improve responsiveness by simply providing the definition for a pointcut.

Listing 9.13   AsynchronousExecutionAspect.java

```
import java.awt.EventQueue;

public abstract aspect AsynchronousExecutionAspect {
    public abstract pointcut asyncOperations();
```

```
    void around() : asyncOperations()
        && if(EventQueue.isDispatchThread()) {
        Runnable worker = new Runnable() {
            public void run() {
                proceed();
            }
        };
        Thread asyncExecutionThread = new Thread(worker);
        asyncExecutionThread.start();
    }
}
```

The aspect in listing 9.13 dispatches the operation to a new thread if the requester thread is the event-dispatching thread. You can modify this base aspect to augment additional functionality, such as indicating the progress of an executing operation by displaying a progress bar.

We can enable asynchronous execution of the `sendEmails()` operation by providing a concrete subaspect (listing 9.14).

Listing 9.14   TestAsynchronousExecutionAspect.java

```
public aspect TestAsynchronousExecutionAspect
    extends AsynchronousExecutionAspect {
    public pointcut asyncOperations()
        : call(void sendEmails());
}
```

While the simple implementation in listing 9.14 utilizes a new thread for each new request, you could modify it to use a prestarted background worker thread and push background jobs into it. You could also combine thread-pooling techniques from chapter 7. Whichever strategy you use, you can be sure that the modifications are limited only to the aspect. This approach allows you to "pay as you go." Rather than deciding up front whether to use a dedicated thread and thread pooling, you can initially think only about the problem at hand—running a task asynchronously. All you need to be concerned about is that this task requires you to have a *separate* thread executing the job—whether that thread is a dedicated thread or is obtained from a thread pool is not the concern of the moment. If you don't use AspectJ, you either have to make these decisions up front or risk embracing invasive changes later on (the architect's dilemma once again). With AOP, you can implement exactly what you need at the time, with the assurance that it will not force you to add a system-wide change later. With the ease of implementing these background tasks, you can improve the user experience by creating a program that is perceived as fast and responsive.

9.7 *Modularizing the read-write lock pattern*

As a sample of modularizing classic thread-safety patterns using AspectJ, let's look at the read-write lock pattern. This pattern offers maximal liveliness while ensuring the integrity of objects in situations where you expect there will be a lot of reader threads for an object but only a few writer threads that can modify it. The fundamental idea is that any number of readers could be simultaneously reading the state of the object as long as there is no thread modifying the state at the same time. See the references listed in the "Resources" section at the end of the book to learn more about the read-write lock pattern.

Implementing this pattern in the conventional way requires adding certain code to each method that reads or modifies the state of an object. In this section, we modularize the pattern using AspectJ. We introduce a reusable aspect that enables you to implement this pattern with your classes just by adding a simple subaspect.

We base our conventional and AspectJ solutions on the concurrency utility library by Doug Lea available at http://gee.cs.oswego.edu/dl/classes/EDU/oswego/cs/dl/util/concurrent/intro.html. This library provides high-level thread concurrency support and is being considered for inclusion in a future version of Java under JSR 166.

9.7.1 *Implementation: the conventional way*

Consider the banking-related classes introduced in chapter 2. In this section, you will learn about the read-write lock pattern by implementing it with the Account class[3] from listing 2.5 that models accounts in a banking system.

The read-write lock pattern uses a pair of locks: the reader lock and the writer lock. Multiple readers can simultaneously acquire the reader lock as long as the writer lock isn't acquired. Only one writer, on the other hand, can acquire the write lock, and it can be acquired only when no reader locks are in force. Implementing the pattern with the Account class requires that each method that per-

---

[3] The read-write lock pattern is more appropriate where the protected operations are computationally expensive. Our Account class's operation is too simple for this. A more suitable candidate would perform, say, JDBC operations or business-rule evaluations. However, using the Account class illustrates the core concepts without worrying about the details.

forms a read-only operation acquire the read lock, whereas the methods that affect the state of the class must acquire the write lock. Once the operation is over, it must release the lock that it acquired. Listing 9.15 shows the Account class with the necessary modifications.

Listing 9.15   Account.java: with the read-write lock pattern implemented

```
import EDU.oswego.cs.dl.util.concurrent.*;

public abstract class Account {
    private float _balance;
    private int _accountNumber;

    private ReadWriteLock _lock                                    Creating the
        = new ReentrantWriterPreferenceReadWriteLock();           read-write lock

    public Account(int accountNumber) {
        _accountNumber = accountNumber;
    }

    public void credit(float amount) {
        try {
            _lock.writeLock().acquire();                    Acquiring the
            setBalance(getBalance() + amount);              write lock
        } catch (InterruptedException ex) {
            throw new RuntimeException(ex);
        } finally {
            _lock.writeLock().release();              Releasing the
        }                                             write lock
    }

    public void debit(float amount)
        throws InsufficientBalanceException {
        try {
            _lock.writeLock().acquire();              Acquiring the
            float balance = getBalance();             write lock
            if (balance < amount) {
                throw new InsufficientBalanceException(
                    "Total balance not sufficient");
            } else {
                setBalance(balance - amount);
            }
        } catch (InterruptedException ex) {
            throw new RuntimeException(ex);
        } finally {
            _lock.writeLock().release();              Releasing the
        }                                             write lock
    }
```

```
    public float getBalance() {
        try {
            _lock.readLock().acquire();          ◁─┐ Acquiring the
            return _balance;                         │ read lock
        } catch (InterruptedException ex) {
            throw new RuntimeException(ex);
        } finally {
            _lock.readLock().release();          ◁─┐ Releasing the
        }                                            │ read lock
    }

    public void setBalance(float balance) {
        try {
            _lock.writeLock().acquire();         ◁─┐ Acquiring the
            _balance = balance;                      │ write lock
        } catch (InterruptedException ex) {
            throw new RuntimeException(ex);
        } finally {
            _lock.writeLock().release();         ◁─┐ Releasing the
        }                                            │ write lock
    }
}
```

We add a lock object of type `ReentrantWriterPreferenceReadWriteLock` in the `ReadWriteLock` implementation that allows the same thread to acquire a lock in a reentrant manner; that way, a thread can acquire a lock even if it is already in possession of it. The `acquire()` method on the locks throws `InterruptedException`. We simply rethrow it by wrapping it in a `RuntimeException` and thus avoid having to change each method to declare it will throw `InterruptedException`. The use of try/finally ensures the locks' release even when the core operation aborts due to an exception.

Clearly, the necessary code is invasive even for a class as simple as `Account`. You must modify each class that needs this pattern in a similar manner. Any missed method will result in potentially fatal program behavior. Further, you must make sure that the method that acquires a read lock releases only the read lock and not a write lock, and vice versa.

9.7.2 *Implementation: the AspectJ way*

The core concept behind the AspectJ-based solution is to create an aspect that encapsulates the pattern. This way, we can avoid the need to modify each class. Further, because the pattern is reusable, we would like the aspect to be reusable as well.

To achieve our goal, let's write a base aspect that captures the read-write lock pattern. To enable synchronization in this aspect, let's write a concrete aspect to extend it that provides the definition for two pointcuts: one to capture the execution of read methods and the other to capture the execution of write methods. Listing 9.16 shows the implementation of the thread-safety pattern in an abstract aspect.

Listing 9.16   ReadWriteLockSynchronizationAspect.java

```
import EDU.oswego.cs.dl.util.concurrent.*;

public abstract aspect ReadWriteLockSynchronizationAspect
    perthis(readOperations() || writeOperations()) {          ❶ Aspect association

    public abstract pointcut readOperations();         ❷ Read operations

    public abstract pointcut writeOperations();         ❸ Write operations

    private ReadWriteLock _lock                                    ❹ Lock
        = new ReentrantWriterPreferenceReadWriteLock();              object

    before() : readOperations() {
        _lock.readLock().acquire();
    }                                          ❺ Read
                                                   operation
    after() : readOperations() {                   management
        _lock.readLock().release();
    }

    before() : writeOperations() {
        _lock.writeLock().acquire();
    }                                          ❻ Write
                                                   operation
    after() : writeOperations() {                  management
        _lock.writeLock().release();
    }

    static aspect SoftenInterruptedException {
        declare soft : InterruptedException :          ❼ Softening of
            call(void Sync.acquire());                    InterruptedException
    }
}
```

❶ Using the perthis() association specification, we associate an aspect instance with each worker object that matches the read or write methods defined in the concrete aspects. (See chapter 4, section 4.3.2, to learn more about aspect association.) A new aspect instance will be created for each object for which a captured method is executed. Association lets us introduce the lock object to each synchronized class without knowing about the specific type of the object.[4]

❷ The abstract `readOperations()` pointcut requires the concrete subaspects to define it to capture all methods that do not modify the state of the object.

❸ Similarly, the abstract `writeOperations()` pointcut captures methods that modify the state of the objects.

❹ The `_lock` member serves as the synchronization support for the read-write lock pattern. Since the aspect is associated with the objects of the matched join points, the `_lock` member is in turn associated with the instances of the objects.

❺ The before and after advice to the `readOperations()` pointcut acquires and releases the read lock, respectively.

❻ Similarly, the before and after advice to the `writeOperations()` pointcut acquires and releases the write lock, respectively.

❼ The softening of the exception converts the `InterruptedException` thrown by `acquire()` method calls, thus eliminating the need to alter the APIs for the captured operations. You may want to use the exception introduction pattern introduced in chapter 8, section 8.3, to handle the exception correctly at a higher level in the call stack.

To enable the read-write lock pattern for the `Account` class, you can write a subaspect providing the definition for abstract pointcuts. Note that you do not need to write one aspect per class. It is okay, for example, to write an aspect capturing methods for all classes in a package. Listing 9.17 shows a subaspect that extends `ReadWriteLockSynchronizationAspect` to enable safe concurrent access to the `Account` class.

Listing 9.17   BankingSynchronizationAspect.java

```
aspect BankingSynchronizationAspect
    extends ReadWriteLockSynchronizationAspect {
    public pointcut readOperations()
```

---

[4] An alternative would have been to use a member introduction mechanism to introduce a lock object in each participating class. However, with this technique, keeping the base aspect reusable requires jumping through a couple of hoops. First, you need to write an interface and introduce the lock object to it. Then each subaspect must use `declare parents` to make all the participating classes implement the interface. There is no programmatic way to communicate the need for `declare parents`. Instead, we use `perthis()` association with abstract pointcuts; in this way the compiler will force each subaspect to provide a definition for each abstract pointcut that is in the base aspect before it can declare itself as a concrete aspect. Such is the power of using an aspect association technique for creating reusable aspects. See section 4.3.5 for more details on the two approaches.

```
        : execution(* Account.get*(..))
        || execution(* Account.toString(..));

    public pointcut writeOperations()
        : execution(* Account.*(..))
        && !readOperations();
}
```

The `BankingSynchronizationAspect` aspect provides definitions for both the abstract pointcuts, `readOperations()` and `writeOperations()`, in the base aspect. It defines the execution of any methods whose name starts with `get` (as well as any method with the name `toString()`) as *read* operations. Notice the way that the `writeOperations()` pointcut is defined to specify all the operations except those captured by the `readOperations()` pointcut. This is a defensive approach; it is better to err on the side of safety by declaring that all the methods that are not performing read-only operations are state-altering methods.

Now the synchronization concern of the `Account` class has been taken care of by simply writing an aspect consisting of a handful of lines. If you wanted to provide thread-safe access to other classes, you could simply modify pointcuts in this aspect or write new concrete aspects for those classes. You could also use the participant pattern, described in chapter 8, to let classes have closer control over the methods that participate in the synchronization aspect.

We now have a reusable implementation for a reusable pattern. You can make the `ReadWriteLockSynchronizationAspect` a part of your library of aspects and avoid reinventing the wheel each time. By doing so, you will be assured that the pattern is being implemented correctly and consistently.

9.8 *Summary*

Ensuring thread safety is inherently complex. The conventional solutions make it even more complex by requiring system-wide invasive changes. The conceptual reusability of the few thread-safety patterns is lost in the conventional implementations. AOP/AspectJ fills this gap between the concepts and the implementation by modularizing the pattern into reusable aspects.

Swing's single-thread rule is simple for component developers, but often requires system-wide changes for developers who are implementing it in multi-threaded UI applications. The solution we've presented eliminates the need for invasive changes while ensuring a consistent behavior. By employing reusable aspects, you make adhering to Swing's thread-safety rule as easy as extending that aspect and providing a few definitions. With AspectJ, you have a simple model for thread safety that does not burden application developers with its complex usage.

Similarly, by introducing a reusable aspect encapsulating the read-write lock pattern, implementing this feature of thread safety is as easy as adding a few simple aspects. You no longer have to hit the books every time you need to understand exactly how the pattern is supposed to work. Instead, you just need to know which methods access the state in a read-only manner and which ones alter the state. The ideas presented in these examples can be extended to offer interesting solutions to otherwise laborious work. For example, you can extend aspects from the Swing UI solution in section 9.4 to provide thread-safe access to your own classes. You can then require that only a preassigned thread be able to access objects of those classes and that other threads route the calls through the preassigned thread using an aspect.

The power of AspectJ and the worker object creation pattern should be clear to you now. In the following chapters, we will use this pattern to solve complex crosscutting concerns using AspectJ.

Authentication and authorization

An important consideration for modern software systems, security consists of many components, including authentication, authorization, auditing, protection against web site attacks, and cryptography. In this chapter, we focus on two of these: authentication and authorization. Together these security components manage system access by evaluating users' identities and credentials.

This chapter introduces an AspectJ-based solution using the Java Authentication and Authorization Service (JAAS), one of the newest ways to implement authentication and authorization in Java applications. You'll see how AspectJ-based solutions work in cooperation—and not in competition—with existing technologies. Using AspectJ helps you to modularize your implementation, which leads to better response to requirement changes, while at the same time greatly reducing the amount of code you have to write.

To get a clear understanding of the core problem and how you'd use JAAS to address it, we also examine the conventional solution for implementing authentication and authorization. Developing the conventional solution serves two purposes: it introduces the basic mechanism offered by JAAS and it demonstrates its shortcomings. Later when we present the AspectJ-based solution, this knowledge will come in handy.

10.1 Problem overview

Authentication is a process that verifies that you are who you say you are. *Authorization*, on the other hand, is a process that establishes whether an authenticated user has sufficient permissions to access certain resources. Both components are so closely related that it is difficult to talk about one without the other—authorization cannot be accomplished without first performing authentication, and authentication alone is rarely sufficient to determine access to resources.

Since authentication and authorization are so important—and continue to become even more so given our highly connected world—we must learn to deal with the various ways of implementing such control. Modern APIs like JAAS (which is now a standard part of J2SE 1.4) abstract the underlying mechanisms and allow you to separate the access control configuration from the code. The application-level developer doesn't have to be aware of the underlying mechanism and won't need to make any invasive changes when it changes. In parallel to these APIs, efforts such as the Security Assertion Markup Language (SAML) and the Extensible Access Control Markup Language (XACML) aim to standardize the configuration specification language. The overall goal of these APIs and standardization efforts is to reduce complexity and provide agile implementations.

Conventional programming methods, even when using APIs such as JAAS, require you to modify multiple modules individually to equip them with authentication and authorization code. For instance, to implement access control in a banking system, you must add calls to JAAS methods to all the business methods. As the business logic is spread over multiple modules, so too is the implementation of the access control logic.

Unlike the bare OOP solution, an EJB framework handles authorization in a much more modular way, separating the security attributes in the deployment descriptor. As we mentioned in chapter 1, the very existence of EJB is proof that we need to modularize such concerns. When EJB or a similar framework is not a choice, as in a UI program, the solution often lacks the desired modularization. With AspectJ, you now have a much better solution for all such situations.

NOTE   Even with the EJB framework, you may face situations that need a custom solution for authentication and authorization. Consider, for example, data-driven authorization where the authorization check not only considers the identity of the user and the functionality being accessed, but also the data involved. Current EJB frameworks do not offer a good solution to these problems that demand flexibility.

10.2 A simple banking example

To illustrate the problem and provide a test bed, let's write a simple banking system. We'll examine only the parts of the system that illustrate issues involved in conventional and AspectJ-based solutions to authentication and authorization implementation. The banking example here differs from the one in chapter 2 in a few ways: We refactor the classes to create interfaces, we put all the classes and interfaces in the `banking` package, and we introduce a new class. We will continue to build on this system in the next two chapters.

Listing 10.1 shows the `Account` interface. (As you can see, we have omitted some of the methods that you would expect to see in an `Account` interface.) Later we'll create a simple implementation of this interface. The exception `Insufficient-BalanceException` that we'll use to identify an insufficient balance is implemented in listing 10.2.

Listing 10.1   Account.java

```
package banking;

public interface Account {
    public int getAccountNumber();
```

```
    public void credit(float amount);

    public void debit(float amount)
        throws InsufficientBalanceException;

    public float getBalance();
}
```

Listing 10.2   InsufficientBalanceException.java

```
package banking;

public class InsufficientBalanceException extends Exception {
    public InsufficientBalanceException(String message) {
        super(message);
    }
}
```

Now, let's look at a simple, bare-bones implementation of the `Account` interface. Later, we'll pose the problem of authorizing all of its methods, using both conventional and AspectJ-based solutions. Listing 10.3 shows a simple implementation of the `Account` interface that models a banking account.

Listing 10.3   AccountSimpleImpl.java

```
package banking;

public class AccountSimpleImpl implements Account {
    private int _accountNumber;
    private float _balance;

    public AccountSimpleImpl(int accountNumber) {
        _accountNumber = accountNumber;
    }

    public int getAccountNumber() {
        return _accountNumber;
    }

    public void credit(float amount) {
        _balance = _balance + amount;
    }

    public void debit(float amount)
        throws InsufficientBalanceException {
        if (_balance < amount) {
            throw new InsufficientBalanceException(
                "Total balance not sufficient");
```

```
        } else {
            _balance = _balance - amount;
        }
    }

    public float getBalance() {
        return _balance;
    }
}
```

The code for `AccountSimpleImpl` is straightforward. To examine how our solution works across multiple modules and with nested methods that need authorization, let's introduce another class, `InterAccountTransferSystem` (listing 10.4), which simply contains one method for transferring funds from one account to another.

Listing 10.4   InterAccountTransferSystem.java

```
package banking;

public class InterAccountTransferSystem {
    public static void transfer(Account from, Account to,
                                float amount)
        throws InsufficientBalanceException {
        to.credit(amount);
        from.debit(amount);
    }
}
```

Finally, to test our solution we'll write a simple `Test` class. In the sections that follow, we will use this class as a basis for adding authentication and authorization in the conventional way; later in the chapter, we will use the class to test the AspectJ-based solution. Listing 10.5 shows the implementation of the `Test` class.

Listing 10.5   Test.java: version with no authentication or authorization

```
package banking;

public class Test {
    public static void main(String[] args) throws Exception {
        Account account1 = new AccountSimpleImpl(1);
        Account account2 = new AccountSimpleImpl(2);

        account1.credit(300);
        account1.debit(200);
```

```
            InterAccountTransferSystem.transfer(account1, account2, 100);
            InterAccountTransferSystem.transfer(account1, account2, 100);
        }
    }
```

Because of the way the operations are arranged, the last operation should throw an `InsufficientBalanceException`. We will ensure that our solutions satisfy the requirement of throwing this exception (as opposed to some other type of exception or no exception at all) when the business logic detects insufficient funds in the debiting account.

Next, let's implement a basic logging aspect (listing 10.6) to help us understand the activities taking place.

Listing 10.6   AuthLogging.java: logging banking operations

```
package banking;

import org.aspectj.lang.*;

import logging.*;

public aspect AuthLogging extends IndentedLogging {
    declare precedence: AuthLogging, *;

    public pointcut accountActivities()
        : execution(public * Account.*(..))
        || execution(public * InterAccountTransferSystem.*(..));

    public pointcut loggedOperations()
        : accountActivities();

    before() : loggedOperations() {
        Signature sig = thisJoinPointStaticPart.getSignature();
        System.out.println("<" + sig.getName() + ">");
    }
}
```

The base aspect, `IndentedLogging`, was discussed in section 5.5.2. It provides the support for indenting the log statements according to their call depth. We need to define the `loggedOperation()` pointcut that was declared in the base `IndentedLogging` aspect. Later, we will add authentication and authorization logging to it as we develop the solution. We won't log more details about the activities (such as account number and amount involved), since the correctness of the core implementation is not the focus of this chapter.

When we compile the basic banking application and the logging aspect, and then run the test program, we see output similar to this:

```
> ajc banking\*.java logging\*.java
> java banking.Test
<credit>
<debit>
<transfer>
    <credit>
    <debit>
<transfer>
    <credit>
    <debit>
Exception in thread "main" banking.InsufficientBalanceException:
    Total balance not sufficient
...more call stack
```

The output shows the interaction when no authentication or authorization is in place. This interaction log will serve as the basis for comparison when we add authentication and authorization.

Coverage of the JAAS mechanism is brief since our purpose is to demonstrate the AOP solution. We encourage you to read a good JAAS book or tutorial so that you will understand the more complex issues that we do not deal with here; then you can extend the AspectJ-based solution to them as well. Please note that although we use a JAAS-based example to explain the AspectJ-based solution, you can also use the solution as a template for other kinds of access control systems.

10.3 *Authentication: the conventional way*

In this section, we add authentication functionality to our basic banking system. We employ the upfront login approach—asking for the username and password at the beginning of the program. Because of its complexity, we won't look at an example of just-in-time authentication (in which authentication does not occur until the user accesses the system functionality that requires user identity verification) in this section, since the point we are demonstrating is basically the same.

10.3.1 *Implementing the solution*

The authentication functionality in JAAS consists of the following:

- A `LoginContext` object
- Callback handlers that present the login challenge to the user
- A login configuration file that enables you to modify the configuration without changing the source code

The callback handler provides a mechanism for acquiring authentication information. It asks users to provide their name and password either on the console, in a login dialog box, or through some other means. In our case, we use a simple `TextCallbackHandler` that is part of Sun's JRE 1.4 distribution. If you are using another JRE, this class may not be available, and you will have to either find an equivalent or write one of your own. `TextCallbackHandler`, when invoked, simply asks for the username and password and supplies the information to the authentication system invoking it. Since the username and password are visible to the user, you are unlikely to use this callback handler in a real system, but it serves as a simple, illustrative mechanism for our purposes.

NOTE   We use the term *user* to mean anyone and anything accessing the system. It includes human as well as nonhuman users—people and other parts of the system. For example, in a business-to-business transaction, a machine is likely to represent the identity of a business accessing the service.

The login configuration file sets up the class that is used as the authentication module. We use a very simple authentication module, `sample.module.SampleLogin-Module`, provided as a part of the JAAS tutorial (see http://java.sun.com/j2se/1.4/docs/guide/security/jaas/tutorials/GeneralAcnAndAzn.html). The classes from the `sample` package we use are described in the tutorial. Employing this simple scheme allows us to focus on using AOP instead of the details of JAAS. The following login configuration file (sample_jaas.config) associates the `Sample` configuration with the `sample.module.SampleLoginModule` class:

```
Sample {
    sample.module.SampleLoginModule required debug=true;
};
```

The `LoginContext` object needs two parameters: a configuration name and a callback handler. The configuration name (`Sample`), in conjunction with the configuration file, determines the login module used by the system.

Let's change the `Test` class to implement authentication with JAAS in the conventional way, as shown in listing 10.7.

> **Listing 10.7   Test.java: with authentication functionality**

```
package banking;

import javax.security.auth.login.LoginContext;

import com.sun.security.auth.callback.TextCallbackHandler;
```

```
public class Test {
    public static void main(String[] args) throws Exception {
        LoginContext lc
            = new LoginContext("Sample",
                                    new TextCallbackHandler());
        lc.login();

        Account account1 = new AccountSimpleImpl(1);
        Account account2 = new AccountSimpleImpl(2);

        account1.credit(300);
        account1.debit(200);

        InterAccountTransferSystem.transfer(account1, account2, 100);
        InterAccountTransferSystem.transfer(account1, account2, 100);
    }
}
```

We enable authentication in our banking system by performing login before executing any core code. First, we create a LoginContext object, supplying it with the name of the configuration we wish to use and the callback handler that will request the username and password. Next, we invoke the login() method on the LoginContext object. If the username and password pass the authentication test, the method simply returns normally. If, however, the username and password fail to match, it throws a checked exception of type Login-Exception. Once the authentication is passed successfully, we continue with the main program functionality.

Since we have chosen to implement upfront login authentication, this arrangement will satisfy that requirement. If, however, you want just-in-time authentication, you will need to add similar authentication coding in every such operation. Just-in-time authentication is useful when the system contains several parts that do not require authenticating the user. Pre-authenticating users may be less than desirable in such cases.

10.3.2 *Testing the solution*

To examine the interaction, let's improve the logging aspect for capturing the authentication join points. We will change the pointcuts to log the login join points, as shown in listing 10.8. In the section that follows, we will use the same logging aspect when we test our AspectJ-based solution.

Listing 10.8 AuthLogging.java: with authentication logging implemented

```
package banking;

import org.aspectj.lang.*;

import javax.security.auth.Subject;
import javax.security.auth.login.LoginContext;

import logging.*;

public aspect AuthLogging extends IndentedLogging {
    declare precedence: AuthLogging, *;

    public pointcut accountActivities()
        : execution(public * Account.*(..))
        || execution(public * InterAccountTransferSystem.*(..));

    public pointcut authenticationActivities()
        : call(* LoginContext.login(..));

    public pointcut loggedOperations()
        : accountActivities()
        || authenticationActivities();

    before() : loggedOperations() {
        Signature sig = thisJoinPointStaticPart.getSignature();
        System.out.println("<" + sig.getName() + ">");
    }
}
```

When we run the program, it asks for a username and password. If the user can be authenticated, it proceeds with the remaining part of the program. Otherwise, it throws a LoginException:

```
> ajc banking\*.java logging\*.java
  sample\module\*.java sample\principal\*.java
> java -Djava.security.auth.login.config=sample_jaas.config
  banking.Test
<login>
user name: testUser
password: testPassword
            [SampleLoginModule] user entered user name: testUser
            [SampleLoginModule] user entered password: testPassword
            [SampleLoginModule] authentication succeeded
            [SampleLoginModule] added SamplePrincipal to Subject
<credit>
<debit>
<transfer>
```

```
        <credit>
        <debit>
<transfer>
        <credit>
        <debit>
Exception in thread "main" banking.InsufficientBalanceException:
➡   Total balance not sufficient
... the rest of call stack
```

With the exception of presenting the user with a login challenge, there is no difference in interaction compared with the base system. We now have a banking system that allows access only to authenticated users.

10.4 Authentication: the AspectJ way

At this point, you should have a good understanding of how to use JAAS for authentication. However, you'll recall that when we used it in the conventional solution, we were forced to make changes to the core system in order to add the authentication. Additionally, if we had implemented just-in-time authentication in the conventional solution, it would have forced us to change multiple modules, causing code scattering. The AspectJ-based solution will improve the modularity of the solution and avoid code scattering. Let's take a look.

10.4.1 Developing the solution

In this section, we will create a base aspect that we can use to authenticate any system and a subaspect of it that will enable the banking system's authentication mechanism. To enable authentication in your system, all you need to do is extend the base aspect and provide a list of operations that need authentication in the pointcut. Listing 10.9 shows the base aspect that modularizes the authentication functionality.

Listing 10.9   AbstractAuthAspect.java: the base authentication aspect

```
package auth;

import javax.security.auth.Subject;
import javax.security.auth.login.*;

import com.sun.security.auth.callback.TextCallbackHandler;

public abstract aspect AbstractAuthAspect {
    private Subject _authenticatedSubject;        ❶ Authenticated subject

    public abstract pointcut authOperations();    ◀❷ Pointcut for operations
                                                     needing authentication
```

```
before() : authOperations() {
    if(_authenticatedSubject != null) {
        return;
    }

    try {
        authenticate();
    } catch (LoginException ex) {
        throw new AuthenticationException(ex);
    }
}

private void authenticate() throws LoginException {
    LoginContext lc = new LoginContext("Sample",
                            new TextCallbackHandler());
    lc.login();
    _authenticatedSubject = lc.getSubject();
}

public static class AuthenticationException
    extends RuntimeException {
    public AuthenticationException(Exception cause) {
        super(cause);
    }
}
}
```

❸ Authentication advice

❹ Authentication logic

❺ Authentication exception

❶ The aspect stores the authenticated subject in an instance variable. By storing the authenticated subject and checking for it prior to invoking the login logic, we avoid asking for a login every time a method that needs authentication is called. After a successful login operation, we can obtain this member from the LoginContext object.

In our implementation, we will use the whole process as the login scope. Once a user is logged in, he will never have to log in again during the lifetime of the program. Depending on your system's specific requirements, you may want to move this member to an appropriate place. For example, if you are writing a servlet, you may want to keep this member in the session object. We also assume that a user, once logged in, never logs out. If this is not true in your system, you need to set this member to null when the current user logs out.

❷ The abstract pointcut is meant to be defined in subaspects capturing all the operations needing authentication.

❸ The before advice to the authOperations() pointcut ensures that our code performs authentication logic only if this is the first time during the program's lifetime that a method that needs authentication is being executed. If it is the first time, _authenticatedSubject will be null, and the authenticate() method will be invoked to perform the core authentication logic. When subsequent join points that need authentication are executed, because the _authenticatedSubject is already not null the login process won't be carried out.

Since the LoginException is a checked exception, the before advice cannot throw it. Throwing such exceptions would result in compiler errors. We could have simply softened this exception using the declare soft construct. However, following the exception introduction pattern discussed in chapter 8, we instead define a concern-specific runtime exception that identifies the cause of the exception, should a caller wish to handle the exception.

❹ The core authentication operation is performed in this method. If the login fails, it throws a LoginException that aborts the program. If the login succeeds, it obtains the subject from the login context and sets it to the instance variable _authenticatedSubject.

❺ AuthenticationException is simply a RuntimeException that wraps the original exception.

Adding authentication functionality to banking is a now a simple matter of writing an aspect, as shown in listing 10.10, that extends AbstractAuthAspect and defines the authOperations() pointcut. In our example, we define the pointcut to capture calls to all methods in the Account and InterAccountTransferSystem classes.

Listing 10.10   BankingAuthAspect.java: authenticating banking operations

```
package banking;

import auth.AbstractAuthAspect;

public aspect BankingAuthAspect extends AbstractAuthAspect {
    public pointcut authOperations()
        : execution(public * banking.Account.*(..))
        || execution(public * banking.InterAccountTransferSystem.*(..));
}
```

Although we have used just-in-time authentication in this example, you can easily implement up-front authentication by simply adding a pointcut corresponding to the method that represents "up-front" for you, such as the main() method in the console application or the frame initialization in a UI application. For example, defining the authOperations() pointcut as follows will perform authentication as soon as the main() method begins to execute:

```
public pointcut authOperations()
    : execution(void banking.Test.main(String[]));
```

With such a pointcut, the authentication advice will kick in as soon as the program starts entering the `main()` method. Further, when you choose up-front authentication, you can write an additional advice that tests for authentication status before executing a method that needs authenticated access. This advice could simply throw a runtime exception, because accessing this method without prior authentication is a violation.

10.4.2 Testing the solution

We now have the system equipped with authentication. When we compile the new aspects with the classes and interfaces in section 10.2, along with the logging aspect in listing 10.8, and run the test program, it prompts for a username and password, as in the conventional solution developed earlier:

```
> ajc banking\*.java auth\*.java logging\*.java
➥ sample\module\*.java sample\principal\*.java
> java -Djava.security.auth.login.config=sample_jaas.config
➥ banking.Test
<credit>
    <login>
user name: testUser
password: testPassword
                [SampleLoginModule] user entered user name: testUser
                [SampleLoginModule] user entered password: testPassword
                [SampleLoginModule] authentication succeeded
                [SampleLoginModule] added SamplePrincipal to Subject
<debit>
<transfer>
    <credit>
    <debit>
<transfer>
    <credit>
    <debit>
Exception in thread "main" banking.InsufficientBalanceException:
➥ Total balance not sufficient
... the rest of call stack
```

As expected, this output is identical to that shown in section 10.3. We now have a system with authentication modularized in one reusable abstract aspect and one system-specific concrete aspect.

10.5 Authorization: the conventional way

The authorization process determines whether the user has sufficient credentials to access certain functions within the system. Let's consider a banking system where the authorization rule specifies that only users with managerial credentials may waive certain fees. We need to perform the following operations:

1. Authentication is a prerequisite to authorization; unless we are certain that users are who they claim to be, there is no point in checking their credentials. Therefore, we first need to verify that users have been authenticated, and if they have not, we need to do so.

2. Then we need to retrieve users' credentials. You can do this in various ways depending on the authorization scheme you use. For example, the authorization system could check a policy file to extract the credentials associated with the authorized person.

3. Last, we need to verify whether those credentials are sufficient to access the fee-waiving operation. For example, if a person has only the teller credential and not the managerial credential, fee-waiving operations won't be available to that user.

10.5.1 *Understanding JAAS-based authorization*

While the exact way you use JAAS will depend on your system's access control requirements, a typical way to use it to perform authorization requires that you follow these steps:

1. *Perform authentication*—The system first needs to authenticate the user using a login or any suitable mechanism. Then it must obtain a verified subject from the authentication subsystem. The `Subject` class encapsulates information about a single entity, such as its identification and credentials. All subsequent operations that require authorization must check that this subject has sufficient credentials to access the operations.

2. *Create an action object*—JAAS requires that each method that needs an authorization check be encapsulated in an *action object*. This object must implement either `PrivilegedAction` or `PrivilegedExceptionAction`. Both interfaces contain just one method: `run()`. The only difference is that the `run()` method has no exception declaration in the former interface, whereas in the latter, it declares that it may throw an exception of type `Exception`. In either case, the `run()` method needs to execute the intended operation.

3. *Execute the action object*—The action object we just created needs to be executed on behalf of the authenticated subject using static methods in

the `Subject` class: `Subject.doAsPrivileged(Subject, PrivilegedAction, AccessControlContext)` or `Subject.doAsPrivileged(Subject, PrivilegedExceptionAction, AccessControlContext)`. In cases where `doAsPrivileged()` is called with a `PrivilegedExceptionAction` parameter, if the `run()` method throws a checked exception, it will wrap it inside `PrivilegedActionException` before throwing it.

4 *Check access*—The methods that need to ensure authorized access must check the subject's credentials by calling the `AccessController.checkPermission()` method and passing it a permission object that contains the required permissions. If the user doesn't have sufficient permissions, this method throws an unchecked `AccessControlException` exception.

5 *Create a system-level access control policy*—At the system level, you write a policy file that grants to a set of subjects permissions to certain operations. The `AccessController.checkPermission()` method indirectly uses this policy file to grant access only to those operations that are allowed by the accessing subject's credentials and permissions.

10.5.2 *Developing the solution*

Now that we've looked at the changes needed in the system to implement authorization, let's look at the modifications we need to make in the banking example. In listing 10.11, we define a simple permission class, `BankingPermission`. The `name` string passed in its constructor defines the permissions. We will later map these strings in a security policy file to allow only certain users to access certain functionality.

Listing 10.11 BankingPermission.java: permission class for banking system authorization

```
package banking;

import java.security.*;

public final class BankingPermission extends BasicPermission {
    public BankingPermission(String name) {
        super(name);
    }

    public BankingPermission(String name, String actions) {
        super(name, actions);
    }
}
```

The class `BankingPermission` defines two constructors to match those in the base `BasicPermission` class. The `actions` parameter in the second constructor is unused and exists only to instantiate the permission object from a policy file. To learn more, refer to the JDK documentation.

Now let's modify the `AccountSimpleImpl` class to check permission in each of its public methods. Each change is simply a call to `AccessController.check-Permission()` with a `BankingPermission` object as an argument. Each `Banking-Permission` needs a name argument to specify the kind of permission sought. We employ a simple scheme that uses the method name itself as the permission string. Listing 10.12 shows the implementation of `AccountSimpleImpl` where each method checks the permission before executing its core logic.

Listing 10.12 AccountSimpleImpl.java: the conventional way

```java
package banking;

import java.security.AccessController;

public class AccountSimpleImpl implements Account {
    private int _accountNumber;
    private float _balance;

    public AccountSimpleImpl(int accountNumber) {
        _accountNumber = accountNumber;
    }

    public int getAccountNumber() {
        AccessController.checkPermission(
            new BankingPermission("getAccountNumber"));

        ...

    }

    public void credit(float amount) {
        AccessController.checkPermission(
            new BankingPermission("credit"));

        ...

    }

    public void debit(float amount)
        throws InsufficientBalanceException {
        AccessController.checkPermission(
            new BankingPermission("debit"));

        ...

    }
```

```
    public float getBalance() {
        AccessController.checkPermission(
            new BankingPermission("getBalance"));

        ...

    }

    ... implementation for private methods ...
}
```

We now have an `Account` implementation that performs access checks for each public operation. We must make similar changes to `InterAccountTransferSystem` (we'll omit that discussion here for brevity's sake). Next, let's look at the changes needed in our test program (listing 10.13) that invokes these operations.

Listing 10.13   Test.java: the conventional way

```java
package banking;

import java.security.*;
import javax.security.auth.Subject;
import javax.security.auth.login.LoginContext;

import com.sun.security.auth.callback.TextCallbackHandler;

public class Test {
    public static void main(String[] args) throws Exception {
        LoginContext lc
            = new LoginContext("Sample",
                                new TextCallbackHandler());
        lc.login();

        final Account account1 = new AccountSimpleImpl(1);
        final Account account2 = new AccountSimpleImpl(2);

        Subject authenticatedSubject = lc.getSubject();

        Subject
            .doAsPrivileged(authenticatedSubject,
                new PrivilegedAction() {
                    public Object run() {
                        account1.credit(300);
                        return null;
                    }}, null);
        try {
            Subject
                .doAsPrivileged(authenticatedSubject,
                    new PrivilegedExceptionAction() {
```

```
                        public Object run() throws Exception {
                            account1.debit(200);
                            return null;
                        }}, null);
            } catch (PrivilegedActionException ex) {
                Throwable cause = ex.getCause();
                if (cause instanceof InsufficientBalanceException) {
                    throw (InsufficientBalanceException)ex.getCause();
                }
            }

            try {
                    Subject
                    .doAsPrivileged(authenticatedSubject,
                        new PrivilegedExceptionAction() {
                            public Object run() throws Exception {
                                InterAccountTransferSystem
                                    .transfer(account1, account2,
                                              100);
                                return null;
                            }}, null);
            } catch (PrivilegedActionException ex) {
                Throwable cause = ex.getCause();
                if (cause instanceof InsufficientBalanceException) {
                    throw (InsufficientBalanceException)ex.getCause();
                }
            }

            try {
                Subject
                    .doAsPrivileged(authenticatedSubject,
                        new PrivilegedExceptionAction() {
                            public Object run() throws Exception {
                                InterAccountTransferSystem
                                    .transfer(account1, account2,
                                                100);
                                return null;
                            }}, null);
            } catch (PrivilegedActionException ex) {
                Throwable cause = ex.getCause();
                if (cause instanceof InsufficientBalanceException) {
                    throw (InsufficientBalanceException)ex.getCause();
                }
            }
        }
    }
```

Clearly, we've had to use too much code. For each operation needing access control, we create an anonymous class extending either `PrivilegedExceptionAction` or `PrivilegedAction`, based on whether the operation can throw a checked exception. The `run()` method of each anonymous class simply calls the operation under consideration.

We put the calls to the methods that are routed through a `PrivilegedException-Action` object in a try/catch block. In the catch block, we check to see if the cause for the exception is an `InsufficientBalanceException`. If so, we throw that exception because the caller of the business method would expect it to be `Insufficient-BalanceException` and not `PrivilegedExceptionAction`. Please refer to the JDK documentation for `PrivilegedExceptionAction` for more details on how the checked exceptions are handled differently than the runtime exceptions.

While we use anonymous classes here, we could have used named classes as well. Each named class would require a constructor taking all the parameters of the method. It would then store those parameters as instance variables. Later, while implementing the `run()` method, it would pass the stored instance variables to the method.

We could have also combined all the operations into one action by creating a single `PrivilegedExceptionAction` and routing all the actions through it. However, we did not do so in order to better mimic the real system, where not all the operations that need authorization will be in one or two places. Further, combining several methods into one action requires that you consider exception-handling carefully. By routing the methods individually through the `PrivilegedException-Action` class, you can handle an exception thrown by each method separately and make the appropriate decisions. With the combined method, you will need to handle the exceptions thrown by a set of methods together. While such an arrangement may not always be a problem, you need to consider it anyway.

10.5.3 *Testing the solution*

Let's see if the solution works. To do so, we add authorization logging to the `AuthLogging` aspect, as shown in listing 10.14.

> **Listing 10.14 AuthLogging.java: adding authorization logging**

```
package banking;

import org.aspectj.lang.*;

import javax.security.auth.Subject;
import javax.security.auth.login.LoginContext;

import logging.*;

public aspect AuthLogging extends IndentedLogging {
```

```
        declare precedence: AuthLogging, *;

        public pointcut accountActivities()
            : call(void Account.credit(..))
            || call(void Account.debit(..))
            || call(* Account.getBalance(..))
            || call(void InterAccountTransferSystem.transfer(..));

        public pointcut authenticationActivities()
            : call(* LoginContext.login(..));

        public pointcut authorizationActivities()
            : call(* Subject.doAsPrivileged(..));

        public pointcut loggedOperations()
            : accountActivities()
            || authenticationActivities()
            || authorizationActivities();

        before() : loggedOperations() {
            Signature sig = thisJoinPointStaticPart.getSignature();
            System.out.println("<" + sig.getName() + ">");
        }
    }
```

The aspect in listing 10.14 modified the one in listing 10.8 to add a new point-cut, authorizationActivities(), and include that pointcut in the loggedOperation() pointcut.

In the BankingPermission class (listing 10.11), the constructor took an argument name that was a string defining the permissions for the system. We said that we would later map name to a security policy file to allow only certain users to access certain functionality. Let's define that security policy file now. We want to permit testUser to be able to carry out all the operations in the banking system. Listing 10.15 shows the policy file that grants testUser the permissions to access all the operations (credit, debit, getBalance, and transfer).

Listing 10.15   security.policy: the policy file for authorization

```
grant Principal sample.principal.SamplePrincipal "testUser" {
    permission banking.BankingPermission "credit";
    permission banking.BankingPermission "debit";
    permission banking.BankingPermission "getBalance";
    permission banking.BankingPermission "transfer";
};
```

When we compile and run the test program, it not only asks for a name and password, but also executes all the operations that have been authorized through `Subject.doAsPrivileged()`:

```
> ajc banking\*.java logging\*.java
    sample\module\*.java sample\principal\*.java
> java -Djava.security.auth.login.config=sample_jaas.config
    -Djava.security.policy=security.policy banking.Test
<login>
user name: testUser
password: testPassword
                   [SampleLoginModule] user entered user name: testUser
                   [SampleLoginModule] user entered password: testPassword
                   [SampleLoginModule] authentication succeeded
                   [SampleLoginModule] added SamplePrincipal to Subject
<doAsPrivileged>
    <credit>
<doAsPrivileged>
    <debit>
<doAsPrivileged>
    <transfer>
        <credit>
        <debit>
<doAsPrivileged>
    <transfer>
        <credit>
        <debit>
Exception in thread "main" banking.InsufficientBalanceException:
    Total balance not sufficient
... the rest of call stack
```

The output shows that each method that needs authorization is called in the context of the `doAsPrivileged()` method. We will compare this output to one using AspectJ-based authorization in section 10.6; we expect them to be identical.

If you want to learn more about JAAS, modify the security policy file to see the effect of different permissions. This will allow you to see how JAAS prevents certain users from accessing a set of operations while allowing others to access those operations.

Now extend this problem to a real system and try to answer the following question: Which operations in your system need to be authenticated/authorized? The answer will not be easy to come by. You will have to examine all the modules and create a list of operations that perform access control checks. This task is laborious and error-prone.

10.5.4 *Issues with the conventional solution*

Let's summarize the problems posed by the conventional object-oriented solution:

- *Scattering of decisions*—The decision for operations to be checked against permissions is scattered throughout the system, and therefore any modifications to it will cause invasive changes.

- *Difficulty of determining access-controlled operations*—Consider the same problem of deciding if an operation needs to perform authorization checks from the business component developer's point of view. Since deciding whether an operation needs authorization depends on the system using the components, it is even harder to identify these operations in components than in system-specific classes.

- *The need to write a class for each access-controlled operation*—For each simple operation, you must write a named or anonymous class carrying out the desired operation.

- *Incoherent system behavior*—The implementation for authorizing a method is separated into two parts: the *callee* and the *caller*. The callee side uses `AccessController.checkPermission()` to check the permissions (as in listing 10.12), whereas the caller side uses `Subject.doAsPrivileged()` to execute the operation on a subject's behalf. Failure to check permissions on the callee side may allow unauthorized subjects to access your system. On the caller side, if you forget to use `Subject.doAsPrivileged()`, your operation will fail even if the user accessing the operation has the proper set of permissions. If you don't find and fix the problem during a code review or a testing phase, it will pop up after the deployment, potentially causing a major loss of business functionality.

- *Difficult evolution*—Any change in authorization operations means making changes in every place the call is made. Any such change will require that the entire test be run through again, increasing the cost of the change.

This list demonstrates the sheer amount of code you will need to write. However, the amount of code is not the biggest problem. Just examine the tangling of the authorization code—it simply overwhelms the core logic. The conventional methods force you to stuff the system-level authorization concern into every part of the system. A utility wrapper can reduce the amount of code, but the fundamental problem of tangling remains unsolved.

10.6 Authorization: the AspectJ way

In extending the AspectJ solution to address authorization, we use the worker object creation pattern described in chapter 8. As with authentication, AspectJ enables you to add authorization to the system without changing the core implementation. In this section, we develop a reusable aspect that enables you to add authorization to your system by simply writing a few lines for a subaspect.

10.6.1 Developing the solution

To recap, using JAAS to implement authorization involves routing the authorized call through a class that implements either `PrivilegedExceptionAction` or `PrivilegedAction`, depending on whether the operation throws checked exceptions. As you saw in section 10.5, the conventional solution requires the coding of both classes implementing `PrivilegedAction` and their invocations. The worker object creation pattern takes the pain out of this process. Without this pattern, we would have to implement classes for each operation that needs authorization. We could still use AspectJ to provide around advice to intercept each of the operations *separately* and to create and execute the corresponding, hand-written action objects through `Subject.doAsPrivileged(Subject, PrivilegedAction, AccessControl-Context)`, or `Subject.doAsPrivileged(Subject, PrivilegedExceptionAction, Access-ControlContext)`. Now, with the use of a worker object creation pattern, instead of writing a class for each operation that needs authorization, we simply write an aspect that advises all corresponding join points of such operations to auto-create worker classes and execute them through `Subject.doAsPrivileged()`.

The result is a real savings in the amount of code we have to write, since the concern is modularized within just one aspect. Listing 10.16 shows the base aspect that implements the authorization concern in addition to authentication.

Listing 10.16   AbstractAuthAspect.java: adding authorization capabilities

```java
package auth;

import org.aspectj.lang.JoinPoint;

import java.security.*;
import javax.security.auth.Subject;
import javax.security.auth.login.*;

import com.sun.security.auth.callback.TextCallbackHandler;

public abstract aspect AbstractAuthAspect {
```

```
private Subject _authenticatedSubject;

public abstract pointcut authOperations();        ◁─❶ Pointcut for
                                                      operations
                                                      that need
before() : authOperations() {                         authorization
    if(_authenticatedSubject != null) {
        return;
    }

    try {
        authenticate();
    } catch (LoginException ex) {
        throw new AuthenticationException(ex);          Method that
    }                                                   obtains the
}                                                       needed
                                                        permissions
public abstract Permission getPermission(
            JoinPoint.StaticPart joinPointStaticPart);─❷

Object around()
    : authOperations() && !cflowbelow(authOperations()) {  ❸
    try {                                              Around advice
        return Subject                                 that creates and
            .doAsPrivileged(_authenticatedSubject,     executes the
                new PrivilegedExceptionAction() {      worker object
                    public Object run() throws Exception {
                        return proceed();
                    }}, null);
    } catch (PrivilegedActionException ex) {
        throw new AuthorizationException(ex.getException());
    }
}

before() : authOperations() {
    AccessController.checkPermission(              ❹ Permissions
        getPermission(thisJoinPointStaticPart));      checking
}

private void authenticate() throws LoginException {
    LoginContext lc = new LoginContext("Sample",
                                    new TextCallbackHandler());
    lc.login();
    _authenticatedSubject = lc.getSubject();
}

public static class AuthenticationException
    extends RuntimeException {
    public AuthenticationException(Exception cause) {
        super(cause);
    }
}
```

```
public static class AuthorizationException
    extends RuntimeException {
    public AuthorizationException(Exception cause) {
        super(cause);
    }
}
```

⑤ Authorization exception

This aspect routes every call that needs authorization through an anonymous class implementing the `PrivilegedExceptionAction` interface. By inserting `proceed()` in the implemented `run()` method, we take care of wrapping all operations that require any type and number of arguments, as well as any type of return value. This pattern saves us from writing a class for each operation that needs authorization.

Let's examine the aspect in more detail:

❶ The `authOperations()` abstract pointcut is identical to the one in the authentication solution we presented earlier. When we define the pointcut in the subaspect, we will list all the operations that need authentication, which are the same as the ones that need authorization. Later, toward the end of chapter, we show you a simple modification you can use if you have to separate the list for operations that need authentication from those that need authorization.

❷ This abstract method allows the subaspects to define the permission needed for the captured operation. It passes the static information about the captured join point to the `getPermission()` method in case the permission depends on a class and method for the operation.

❸ This around advice first creates a worker object for the captured operation and then executes it using `Subject.doAsPrivileged()` on behalf of the authenticated subject. By using the `&&` operator to combine the `authOperations()` pointcut with `!cflowbelow(authOperations())`, we ensure that the worker object is created only for the top-level operations that need authorization. Note that we do not need to separately route an operation if it is already in the control flow of another routed operation.

❹ This before advice determines whether the caller of the method has sufficient permissions. Note we did not put the logic to check permissions in the preceding around advice. This is because we first need to create the worker object and pass it to `Subject.doAsPrivileged()`; only then can we check for the permissions called by the worker object.

❺ `AuthorizationException` is simply a `RuntimeException` that wraps the original exception.

Notice how the two before advice and an around advice to the `authOperations()` pointcut are lexically arranged. (Please refer to section 4.2.4 for more information about how lexical ordering of advice in an aspect affects their precedence.) This arrangement is critical for the correct functioning of this aspect. With this arrangement the advice is executed as follows:

1 The first before advice is executed prior to executing the join point. This advice performs the authentication, if needed, and obtains an authenticated subject after authenticating.

2 The around advice is executed next. It creates a wrapper worker object and invokes it using `Subject.doAsPrivileged()`. This results in calling the original captured join point when the advice body encounters `proceed()`.

3 The second before advice is executed just prior to proceeding with the execution of the captured join point. Essentially, think of the before advice as being called right before the `proceed()` method in the around advice. This advice uses `AccessController.checkPermission()` to check the permission needed.

In summary, by controlling the precedence, we ensure that authentication occurs before authorization; we verify the identity of the subject before we check the permissions for that subject.

To enable authorization in our banking system, we must modify `Banking-AuthAspect` to implement the abstract `getPermission()` method. This is all we have to change in order to enable authorization—the reusable base aspect takes care of all the complexities. Listing 10.17 shows `BankingAuthAspect`, which enables authorization in our example banking system.

Listing 10.17 BankingAuthAspect.java: adding authorization capabilities

```java
package banking;

import org.aspectj.lang.JoinPoint;

import java.security.Permission;

import auth.AbstractAuthAspect;

public aspect BankingAuthAspect extends AbstractAuthAspect {
    public pointcut authOperations()
        : execution(public * banking.Account.*(..))
        || execution(public * banking.InterAccountTransferSystem.*(..));
```

```
    public Permission getPermission(
        JoinPoint.StaticPart joinPointStaticPart) {
        return new BankingPermission(
            joinPointStaticPart.getSignature().getName());
    }
}
```

In this concrete aspect, we add a definition for the `getPermission()` method. In our implementation, we return a new `BankingPermission` class with the name of the method obtained from the join point's static information as the permission identification string. This permission scheme is identical to the one we used for the conventional solution in listing 10.15.

10.6.2 *Testing the solution*

When we compile all the classes and aspects and run the test program, we see output similar to the following:

```
> ajc banking\*.java auth\*.java logging\*.java
    sample\module\*.java sample\principal\*.java
> java -Djava.security.auth.login.config=sample_jaas.config
    -Djava.security.policy=security.policy banking.Test
<credit>
    <login>
user name: testUser
password: testPassword
                [SampleLoginModule] user entered user name: testUser
                [SampleLoginModule] user entered password: testPassword
                [SampleLoginModule] authentication succeeded
                [SampleLoginModule] added SamplePrincipal to Subject
    <doAsPrivileged>
<debit>
    <doAsPrivileged>
<transfer>
    <doAsPrivileged>
        <credit>
        <debit>
<transfer>
    <doAsPrivileged>
        <credit>
        <debit>
Exception in thread "main"
    auth.AbstractAuthAspect$AuthorizationException:
    banking.InsufficientBalanceException: Total balance not sufficient
```

Note that the output is nearly identical to that in section 10.5.4. However, there are a few differences. The first difference is that the login occurs in a different place due to the just-in-time policy. Second, the log for each operation occurs before the log for the `doPrivileged()` method that routed the operation. This is because the logging aspect has a higher precedence, and its before advice is applied before the around advice in `AbstractAuthAspect`. Refer to chapter 4, section 4.2, for details on aspect precedence rules. Also note that the type of exception thrown by the last `transfer()` call is not the expected `Insufficient-BalanceException`. This behavior is due to the fact that any exception thrown by the `PrivilegedExceptionAction.run()` method is wrapped in an `Authorization-Exception`. Since we cannot throw a checked exception of a type other than that declared by the method itself, we wrap the exception in a runtime exception `AbstractAuthAspect.AuthorizationException`.

We can remedy the situation by simply adding one more aspect, modeled after the exception introduction pattern in chapter 8, to the system. This aspect's job is to catch the `AbstractAuthAspect.AuthorizationException` thrown by any method that could throw an `InsufficientBalanceException` and check the cause of the thrown exception. If the cause's type is `InsufficientBalanceException`, it then throws the cause exception instead of `AuthorizationException`. Listing 10.18 shows the implementation of this logic in an aspect.

Listing 10.18 PreserveCheckedException.java: aspect preserving checked exceptions

```
package banking;

import auth.AbstractAuthAspect;

public aspect PreserveCheckedException {
    after() throwing(AbstractAuthAspect.AuthorizationException ex)
        throws InsufficientBalanceException
        : call(* banking..*.*(..)
               throws InsufficientBalanceException) {
        Throwable cause = ex.getCause();
        if (cause instanceof InsufficientBalanceException) {
            throw (InsufficientBalanceException)cause;
        }
        throw ex;
    }
}
```

In this case, the only exception that we need to preserve is `InsufficientBalance-Exception`. Now when we compile all the classes and aspects, we see that the checked exception is preserved:

```
> ajc banking\*.java auth\*.java logging\*.java
     sample\module\*.java sample\principal\*.java
> java -Djava.security.auth.login.config=sample_jaas.config
     -Djava.security.policy=security.policy banking.Test
<credit>
    <login>
user name: testUser
password: testPassword
                [SampleLoginModule] user entered user name: testUser
                [SampleLoginModule] user entered password: testPassword
                [SampleLoginModule] authentication succeeded
                [SampleLoginModule] added SamplePrincipal to Subject
    <doAsPrivileged>
<debit>
    <doAsPrivileged>
<transfer>
    <doAsPrivileged>
        <credit>
        <debit>
<transfer>
    <doAsPrivileged>
        <credit>
        <debit>
Exception in thread "main" banking.InsufficientBalanceException:
Total balance not sufficient
... the rest of call stack
```

We now have an aspect-oriented solution to authentication and authorization for the banking system. The most beneficial characteristics of this solution are:

- You can add functionality without touching even a single core source file.

- The specifications are captured in a single aspect.

- The base aspect that implements most of the functionality is reusable.

You now should be able to write a simple subaspect of this reusable aspect to get a comprehensive access-controlled system.

Now that we have a modularized implementation of authorization concerns, we can quickly react to any changes in the authorization requirements. For example, consider data-driven authorization in a banking system where the credentials needed for performing the fee-waiving operations depend on the amount involved. We can implement this requirement easily by capturing the join points corresponding to the fee-waiving operations and collecting the waived amount as a context. We then advise such join points to check the credentials based on the amount. Consider another requirement: providing the opportunity for re-login with a different identity upon determining that the credentials with the current identity are not sufficient to perform an operation. We can easily implement this functionality by modifying the authorization advice to present the user with a login opportunity upon authorization failure. In a nutshell, the ease of implementation brought forth by AspectJ-based authorization makes it practical to implement useful variations of the core functionality.

10.7 Fine-tuning the solution

In this section, we examine a few finer points that you may want to consider when customizing the access control solution for your system.

10.7.1 Using multiple subaspects

In most common situations, the list of operations that need authentication and authorization is a system-wide consideration, similar to the solution in this chapter. However, suppose each subsystem must control its list of operations. In this case, you need multiple subaspects, one for each subsystem, each specifying operations in the associated subsystem. For example, the following aspect extends `AbstractAuthAspect` to authenticate all the public operations in the `com.mycompany.secretprocessing` package:

```
public aspect SecretProcessingAuthenticationAspect {
    extends AbstractAuthAspect {
    public pointcut authOperations() :
        execution(public * com.mycompany.secretprocessing.*(..));
}
```

Using this scheme, you can include multiple subaspects in a system, each specifying a list of join points needing authentication and authorization. Then the advice in the base aspect applies to join points captured by the pointcut in each subaspect. This is similar to the participant pattern, in which each class controls the subaspect that defines the pointcuts for the class. However, in this case the subaspect defines the pointcuts for a subsystem, which results in greater flexibility and ease of maintenance for the owners of the subsystem.

Remember that if you use multiple subaspects, the system will create an instance of each of the concrete subaspects that share the common base aspect. If you store the authenticated subject as an instance variable of the base aspect, as we did in the solution in this chapter, the user will be forced to log in multiple times—upon reaching the first join point captured by the pointcut in each concrete subaspect. You will need to store the authenticated subject in a different way. For instance, if your authentication has program scope, you may want to keep the authenticated subject as a static variable inside the `AbstractAuthAspect`.

10.7.2 *Separating authentication and authorization*

In the chapter's solution, we used a single pointcut to capture both authorization and authentication join points. While this scheme is fine in most cases, there are situations when you need to separate these join points. For example, consider a requirement for up-front login. You need the method corresponding to the main entry in the program to be authenticated but not necessarily authorized. Satisfying such a requirement is quite simple. First you need two pointcuts: one for authentication and another for authorization. Then you must modify the aspect we developed to separate out the authentication advice to apply to the authentication pointcut, and you will have to modify the authorization advice in a similar way.

What happens if your authorization join point is encountered prior to an authentication one? The solution depends on your system's requirements. One solution is to fall back to just-in-time authentication, thus performing authentication prior to the execution of the first method that needs to check authorization (if the user was never authenticated). The easiest way to achieve this would be to include an authorization pointcut in an authentication pointcut as well:

```
pointcut authenticatedOperations()
    : primaryAuthenticatedOperations() || authorizedOperations();
```

The other possibility is to simply throw an exception if an authorization join point is reached before the user is authenticated. Checking to see if the _authenticatedSubject is null in the authorization advice may be the easiest option. Both the choices can be implemented easily, and the choice you make depends on your system requirements.

10.8 *Summary*

The JAAS API provides a standard way to introduce authentication and authorization into your system without requiring application developers to know the complex implementation details. The conventional JAAS-based solution suffers from code bloat and poses the problem of having no single place to list or enforce authentication and authorization decisions. On a large system, this makes it almost impossible to figure out which operations are being authorized. Further, it separates the implementation on the caller side from the callee side. Failing to add an authentication check on the caller side leads to making resources unavailable to otherwise qualified users. Failing to add an authorization check on the callee side, on the other hand, results in potential unauthorized access to the operations, compromising the system's integrity.

The beauty of an AspectJ solution for authentication and authorization lies in modularizing the access control implementation into a few modules, separate from the core system logic. You still use JAAS to perform the core part of authentication and authorization, but you no longer need to have calls to its API all over the system. By simply including a few aspects and specifying operations that require access control, you complete the implementation. If you have to add or remove operations under access control, you just change the list of operations needing such control—no change is required to the core parts of the system. AOP and AspectJ make authentication and authorization not only easy to implement but also easy to evolve.

By combining such aspects along with those in the rest of the book, you could create an EJB-lite framework and benefit from improved control over the services you need.

Transaction management

This chapter covers
- Conventional transaction management
- AspectJ-based transaction management using JDBC
- AspectJ-based transaction management using JTA

Consider the shopping cart example from chapter 5. When we add an item to the cart, we remove it from inventory. What would happen if the second operation failed? The system would be in an inconsistent state, with the same item counted as being in the shopping cart and as part of inventory.

To prevent this undesirable situation, we can execute both operations within a *transaction*. A transaction defines an atomic unit of work that ensures the system remains in a consistent state before and after its execution. Atomicity, consistency, isolation, and durability (ACID) are considered the four properties of a transaction. In this chapter, we focus on the first property—atomicity—because it is the most important and the hardest to achieve. Atomicity ensures that either all the operations within a transaction succeed as a single unit, or if one of the constituent operations fails, the system aborts the whole sequence of updates and rolls back any prior updates. If you want to read more on this topic, you can go to almost any JDBC or J2EE book (although the concept isn't limited to these areas).

Transaction management is a crosscutting concern (by now, you probably saw it coming!). The operations under transaction control span multiple modules. Even in the simple case of the shopping cart example in chapter 5, the concern is spread across three classes: ShoppingCart, Inventory, and ShoppingCartOperator. In a real system, such operations touch many more classes and packages. The non-AOP solution causes the transaction management implementation to be integrated into all those modules, creating the usual set of problems associated with a lack of modularization of crosscutting concerns.

The EJB application framework offers an elaborate and elegant system for transaction management. Transaction support for bean operations is expressed in a declarative form, in the deployment descriptor, separate from the core operation. This arrangement is similar in spirit to AOP—separation of crosscutting concerns. But in many cases, you do not have the advantage of this built-in support. Using AspectJ in this situation extends the spirit of declarative transaction management to all your transaction management needs.

In this chapter, we develop an aspect-oriented solution for transaction management in a simple JDBC-based system. This first version provides the essential concepts, and we will refine it as we go. We use just the basic commit and rollback functionality available with JDBC connections instead of using Java Transaction API (JTA) and transaction-aware connection objects. The JTA makes it possible to manage transactions that span multiple resources. Once you are familiar with the basic idea behind modularizing transaction management using AspectJ for a simple JDBC-based system, we briefly look at a template for a JTA-based transaction management system using AspectJ.

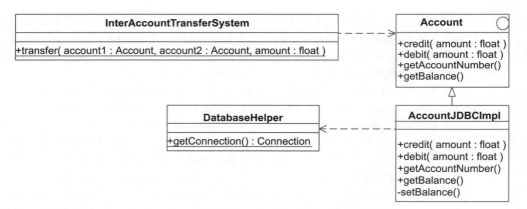

Figure 11.1   An overview of our banking example. The DatabaseHelper class is a result of refactoring to avoid duplicated code for creating a connection.

11.1 *Example: a banking system with persistence*

To illustrate the problem of transaction management and AspectJ-based solutions, let's develop a part of a banking system that must use transaction management. First, we will create the system without transaction management so that we can see which actions need to be within a transaction. We will also develop a logging aspect that allows us to observe the activities taking place.

11.1.1 *Implementing the core concern*

In this section, we modify the banking system example introduced in chapter 10 to use JDBC for database persistence. Figure 11.1 shows our example system.

The `AccountJDBCImpl` class is a concrete implementation of the `Account` interface from listing 10.1. Besides implementing all the methods specified in the interface, it contains a private method for setting balances. The `InterAccount-TransferSystem` class, from listing 10.4, contains a single method for transferring an amount from one account to the other.

Before we look at the JDBC implementation of this interface, let's build the helper class (listing 11.1) for creating database connections that we will use in our implementation.

> **Listing 11.1   DatabaseHelper.java**

```
package banking;

import java.sql.*;
```

```
public class DatabaseHelper {
    static {
        try {
            Class.forName("sun.jdbc.odbc.JdbcOdbcDriver");
        } catch (Exception ex) {
            // ignore...
        }
    }

    public static Connection getConnection() throws SQLException {
        String url = "jdbc:odbc:bank";
        String user = "user1";
        String password = "password1";
        Connection connection
            = DriverManager.getConnection(url, user, password);
        connection.setAutoCommit(true);
        return connection;
    }
}
```

The `DatabaseHelper` class contains a single method, `getConnection()`, that returns a connection to the database. The auto-commit mode will be switched on for the connection, which means we won't have to programmatically commit the updates to the database—each one will be committed automatically. However, enabling the auto-commit mode also means we won't be able to make multiple updates within a transaction; if one of the updates in an operation fails, all the updates that succeeded prior to the failure will still be committed. Note that we enable auto-commit mode only to keep the base solution simple, since it does not involve transaction management.

Let's write a simple JDBC implementation of the `Account` interface.[1] The class in listing 11.2 directly manipulates the database.

Listing 11.2   AccountJDBCImpl.java

```
package banking;

import java.sql.*;

public class AccountJDBCImpl implements Account {
    private int _accountNumber;
```

---

[1] The downloadable source code provides detailed information on setting up the database tables and changes needed to make this program work with various databases.

```
public AccountJDBCImpl(int accountNumber) {
    _accountNumber = accountNumber;
}

public int getAccountNumber() {
    return _accountNumber;
}

public void credit(float amount) {
    float updatedBalance = getBalance() + amount;
    setBalance(updatedBalance);
}

public void debit(float amount)
    throws InsufficientBalanceException {
    float balance = getBalance();
    if (balance < amount) {
        throw new InsufficientBalanceException(
            "Total balance not sufficient");
    } else {
        float updatedBalance = balance - amount;
        setBalance(updatedBalance);
    }
}

public float getBalance() {
    Connection conn = DatabaseHelper.getConnection();
    Statement stmt = conn.createStatement();

    ResultSet rs
        = stmt.executeQuery("select balance from accounts "
                            + "where accountNumber = "
                            + _accountNumber);
    rs.next();
    float balance = rs.getFloat(1);
    stmt.close();
    conn.close();
    return balance;
}

private void setBalance(float balance) throws SQLException {
    Connection conn = DatabaseHelper.getConnection();
    Statement stmt = conn.createStatement();
    stmt.executeUpdate("update accounts set balance = "
                        + balance +
                        " where accountNumber = "
                        + _accountNumber);
    stmt.close();
    conn.close();
}
```

```
private static aspect SoftenSQLException {
    declare soft : SQLException
        : execution(* Account.*(..))
        && within(AccountJDBCImpl);
}
}
```

Each method creates a new database connection. While this behavior has performance implications, it is a correct implementation from each method's limited perspective.

NOTE   We use the nested `SoftenSQLException` aspect to soften the `SQLException` thrown by the `Account` class's business methods. Because a `SQLException` that may be thrown by the JDBC operations does not make sense from the business method's point of view, and because throwing such an exception requires that the base `Account`'s methods must declare it, we use this aspect to soften any `SQLException` thrown. Notice the definition of the pointcut used in `declare soft`: By using only `Account.*(..)` instead of `AccountJDBCImpl.*(..)`, we soften the exception only if it is thrown by business methods declared in the `Account` interface. This means, for example, that the aspect will not soften a `SQLException` thrown by the `setBalance()` method, which will force the methods that call `setBalance()` to deal with the exception. The code `&& within(AccountJDBCImpl)` ensures that the exception is softened only when it is thrown by the methods of `AccountJDBCImpl`, and not by methods in any other potential implementations of the `Account` interface. When we limit the exception softening in this way, the compiler still forces the callers of methods in other implementations of the `Account` interface to either handle the exception or declare that they will throw it. For more details of exception softening, see section 4.4 in chapter 4.

A superior alternative to exception softening would have been to use the exception introduction pattern discussed in chapter 8. The use of the pattern would enable an easier retrieval of `SQLException` by a caller at a higher level. However, we chose the exception-softening approach for simplicity, since we want to focus on the core concepts of this chapter.

So far we have worked with methods like `credit()` that contain simple transactions. Methods like these do not need to be concerned with updates to the database that occur in other methods. However, we must also handle nested transactions, in which the updates issued to the database from within the method have to be coordinated with database updates from other methods. Before we delve into the implementation of transaction management, we will use InterAccountTransferSystem (from listing 10.4) to help us understand nested transactions. The InterAccountTransferSystem class consists of just one method that allows us to transfer money from one account to another. We call this a *nested transaction* because transactional integrity requires that both the individual operations invoked—credit() and debit()—succeed or the changes to the database are rolled back. For example, when the credit() method is called directly, it commits its changes before returning. Yet the same method called from InterAccountTransferSystem.transfer() must *not* commit the changes in the credit() method, but rather wait for successful completion of the debit() method that follows. Because the transactions taking place inside the credit() and debit() methods are nested inside the transaction of the InterAccountTransferSystem.transfer() method, they are called nested transactions.

11.1.2 Setting up the test scenario

To test the solution, let's use the simple Test class in listing 11.3, which is nearly identical to one developed in chapter 10 (listing 10.5) except that we instantiate AccountJDBCImpl instead of AccountSimpleImpl. We will use the same scenario throughout this chapter.

Listing 11.3 Test.java: a test scenario for the transaction integrity problem

```java
package banking;

public class Test {
    public static void main(String[] args) throws Exception {
        Account account1 = new AccountJDBCImpl(1);
        Account account2 = new AccountJDBCImpl(2);

        account1.credit(300);        ◁┘ First transaction
        account1.debit(200);         ◁── Second transaction                    Nested
                                                                               transaction
        InterAccountTransferSystem.transfer(account1, account2, 100);  ◁┘
        InterAccountTransferSystem.transfer(account1, account2, 100);  ◁┐
    }                                          Transaction that           │
}                                              should be aborted ─────────┘
```

The first two methods, credit() and debit(), trigger database updates. The first transfer() method performs the operation with the nested transaction requirements. Assuming that both accounts start with a zero balance, the last transfer operation in the test program will throw an exception.

Let's write a logging aspect, shown in listing 11.4, so we can see if the example works as expected.

Listing 11.4   The logging aspect

```java
package banking;

import java.sql.*;
import org.aspectj.lang.*;
import logging.*;

public aspect TransactionLogging extends IndentedLogging {
    declare precedence: TransactionLogging, *;

    public pointcut accountActivities()
        : call(void Account.credit(..))
        || call(void Account.debit(..))
        || call(void InterAccountTransferSystem.transfer(..));

    public pointcut connectionActivities(Connection conn)
        : (call(* Connection.commit(..))
           || call(* Connection.rollback(..)))
        && target(conn);

    public pointcut updateActivities(Statement stmt)
        : call(* Statement.executeUpdate(..))
        && target(stmt);

    public pointcut loggedOperations()
        : accountActivities()
        || connectionActivities(Connection)
        || updateActivities(Statement);

    before() : accountActivities() {
        Signature sig = thisJoinPointStaticPart.getSignature();
        System.out.println("[" + sig.getName() + "]");
    }

    before(Connection conn) : connectionActivities(conn) {
        Signature sig = thisJoinPointStaticPart.getSignature();
        System.out.println("[" + sig.getName() + "] " + conn);
    }

    before(Statement stmt) throws SQLException
        : updateActivities(stmt) {
        Signature sig = thisJoinPointStaticPart.getSignature();
        System.out.println("[" + sig.getName()
                                + "] " + stmt.getConnection());
    }
}
```

The aspect in listing 11.4 logs account activities, such as credits and debits; connection activities, such as committing and rolling back; and database update activities. We extend the `IndentedLogging` aspect (from chapter 5) to give an indentation effect to the log output; this makes for a more readable log. The base aspect `IndentedLogging` contains an abstract pointcut, `loggedOperations()`, and the subaspect will provide a definition for it. We define the `loggedOperations()` pointcut to capture all the join points captured by the `accountActivities()`, `connectionActivities()`, and `updateActivities()` pointcuts.

When we compile all the classes and aspects (including the log aspects) and run the program, we see output similar to this:

```
> ajc banking\*.java logging\*.java
> java banking.Test
[credit]
    [executeUpdate] sun.jdbc.odbc.JdbcOdbcConnection@117a8bd
[debit]
    [executeUpdate] sun.jdbc.odbc.JdbcOdbcConnection@867e89
[transfer]
    [credit]
        [executeUpdate] sun.jdbc.odbc.JdbcOdbcConnection@e86da0
    [debit]
        [executeUpdate] sun.jdbc.odbc.JdbcOdbcConnection@291aff
[transfer]
    [credit]
        [executeUpdate] sun.jdbc.odbc.JdbcOdbcConnection@13582d
    [debit]
Exception in thread "main" banking.InsufficientBalanceException:
 Total balance not sufficient
...more call stack
```

Now that we have our basic banking example, let's apply transaction management to it. First, we will examine the conventional approach, and then we will explain the AspectJ solutions.

11.2 *The conventional solution*

In this section, we take a brief look at conventional ways to implement transaction management for our previous example. This discussion will not only give you a better grasp of the problem but will also help you understand the AspectJ-based solution described in the next section. In the end, both the conventional and the AspectJ-based system must have identical behavior.

Let's see what we need to do to implement transaction management in the banking example we created in section 11.1. From the perspective of transaction integrity, the `transfer()` method should ensure that both the `credit()` and `debit()` methods complete successfully before committing the changes. If one database update fails, the transaction manager must roll back all the updates that have already occurred. However, this is not happening in our example. The `DatabaseHelper.getConnection()` method creates a new connection for each database operation and enables the auto-commit mode of each connection; the result is that each operation gets committed immediately. This means that if the second update fails, the result of the first update is still in effect.

Fixing this problem will require us to:

1   Switch off the auto-commit mode.
2   Use the same connection object for all the database updates.
3   Commit the pending updates once all the operations succeed; otherwise, if any of the operations fail, we must roll back all the updates.

Satisfying the first requirement is a simple matter of modifying the `Database-Helper` class to not switch on the auto-commit mode. For the remaining two requirements, as you'll see in the following section, there are a couple of ways you can implement them.

11.2.1 *Using the same connection object*

The two general ways to manage simple transactions using conventional techniques are:

- Passing an extra argument to each method that corresponds to the connection object
- Using thread-specific storage

We will examine each of these solutions briefly.

Passing the connection object around

The `transfer()` method calls two methods within its body. Both methods must complete for the transaction to be successful. Let's take another look at the `transfer()` method in the `InterAccountTransferSystem` class from listing 10.4:

```
public static void transfer(Account from, Account to,
                            float amount)
    throws InsufficientBalanceException {
    to.credit(amount);
    from.debit(amount);
}
```

We need to ensure that both the `credit()` and `debit()` methods use the same connection object. We also need to ensure that we commit the connection only after the successful completion of all the suboperations. To achieve this goal, we make the following modifications:

1   Create a new connection object in the `transfer()` method. (Be sure to modify `DatabaseHelper` to switch off the auto-commit mode for the connection).

2   Pass the connection object as an additional argument to both `credit()` and `debit()`.

3   Modify both methods to use this connection object instead of creating a new one.

4   Remove commit operations performed inside any suboperations.

5   Commit the connection object after successful completion of all updates; otherwise, roll back the connection.

6   Close the connection.

The following snippet shows the resulting `transfer()` method's implementation. Note that we assume that we soften the `SQLExceptions` thrown by `commit()`, `rollback()`, and `close()`:

```
public static void transfer(Account from, Account to,
                            float amount)
    throws InsufficientBalanceException {
    Connection conn = DatabaseHelper.getConnection();
    conn.setAutoCommit(false);

    try {
        to.credit(amount, conn);
        from.debit(amount, conn);
        conn.commit();
    } catch (Exception ex) {
        conn.rollback();
        // log exception etc.
    } finally {
        conn.close();
    }
}
```

We will need to modify the implementation of `credit()` and `debit()` as well to use the supplied connection object instead of creating a new one.

The problem with the scheme of passing the connection object is its sheer invasiveness. Even in the simple case of the `transfer()` method, you must modify three methods to support transaction management.

Using thread-specific storage

An alternative to passing around the connection object as an extra argument is to use thread-specific storage, which is provided by `ThreadLocal`.[2] We have to modify `DatabaseHelper` in two ways. First, add a `static final ThreadLocal` member that wraps a connection object. Second, modify `DatabaseHelper.getConnection()` to attempt to first obtain a connection object from this thread-local member. If `getConnection()` succeeds, it returns the thread-specific connection instead of creating a new one. Otherwise, it creates a new connection and sets it into the thread-local member. Of course, for this solution to work, it is necessary that every module use `DatabaseHelper` to obtain a database connection.

This solution is well modularized in one class and one method, and if propagating the connection was the sole issue, we would not need an AspectJ-based solution. Ultimately, our goal is to modularize the concern's implementation—whether we use AspectJ is a secondary consideration. However, as you will see in section 11.2.2, we should also be concerned with performing commits only in the top-level operation, which is the method that initiates all the database updates.

11.2.2 Committing at the top level only

So far, we have dealt with the issue of using the same connection object for all the database updates inside a transaction. We now have to ensure that within nested transactions, only the top-level operations perform a commit.

Think about the requirement of committing connections only after the successful completion of all the database updates that are in methods called by the "top-level" method. The fundamental problem here is that "top-level" is a perspective-dependent concept. A method by itself does not have a property of top-levelness. For instance, both `credit()` and `debit()` can be considered top-level methods when they are called by themselves. Their success does not depend on the success of any other method. But `debit()` is also called by `InterAccountTransferSystem`, and in a transfer of funds, it cannot succeed unless `credit()` succeeds as well. Thus, `credit()` and `debit()` are both nested inside `InterAccountTransferSystem` and are dependent on each other. This means that determining who should be responsible for committing the transaction becomes a complex decision.

One solution is to use an extra argument or thread-local variable indicating the call depth. You increment the call depth as you enter a method and decrement before exiting each method. At the end of each method with the transaction

---

[2] The `ThreadLocal` class supports storing thread-specific data. For details, refer to the J2SE API documentation.

requirement, you can check if the call depth is zero (indicating the top-level method) and only then proceed with the commit. The result is an implementation that requires you to modify every method dealing with database updates—a cumbersome and error-prone process.

In summary, conventional solutions have two disadvantages:

1   The scattering of transaction management code in multiple methods in multiple modules, making a large part of the system explicitly aware of transaction management issues

2   The tangling of business logic, such as transferring amounts, with implementation issues related purely to transaction management

11.3 *Developing a simple AspectJ-based solution*

Now that we have looked at conventional solutions and their inherent limitations, we are ready to examine aspect-oriented solutions to the same problem. In this section, we examine an AspectJ-based way of introducing transaction management in the banking example.

11.3.1 *Implementing the JDBC transaction aspect*

Before delving into the implementation details, let's first look at the requirements of the AspectJ solution at a higher level:

1   All the updates in an operation with a transaction requirement must use a single connection object that contains the transaction state. This implies that while in the control flow of a method that needs transaction management, once a connection is created, all the subsequent updates in that control flow must use the same connection object. In other words, the connection object forms the context for the operations.

2   All the updates must be committed when the top-level operation completes successfully. If any update fails or if any business methods throw an exception, all the updates on the connection objects must be rolled back.

3   A non-core requirement is to create a reusable solution. Because you will likely need transaction management for JDBC-based systems in multiple projects, developing a reusable solution saves the subsequent development cost.

We can transform the above requirements into an aspect as follows:

1   To make the implementation reusable, we create an abstract aspect that implements the bulk of the logic. Any subsystem that needs to introduce transaction management simply has to write a subaspect that provides a definition for all abstract pointcuts in the aspect.

2   To let the subaspects define the operations that need transaction management, we include an abstract pointcut for which a concrete subaspect must provide a definition.

3   To capture the top-level operation, we define a pointcut that captures operations not already in the control flow of another transacted operation.

4   To check the success of all operations in a transaction, we need a means of communicating the failure of an operation and a way to check for such failures. We define the success criterion as the execution of all the operations without any exceptions being thrown. We can detect the failure condition by providing an around advice to the top-level operation that proceeds with the captured operation in a try/catch block; the execution of the catch block indicates a failure.

5   To ensure the use of the same connection object for all the updates in a transaction, we advise the join point that creates the connection in the control-flow transaction. The first time a connection is needed in a transaction, we proceed with the captured operation, obtain the connection, and store it in an instance variable inside the aspect. Then for all subsequent attempts to obtain a connection object, the advice simply returns the stored connection, bypassing the captured operation. We also associate the aspect with the control flow of the top-level operations. Since the aspect stores the connection object used for all updates, the aspect instance also serves as the transaction context that exists for the duration of the transaction.

6   To accommodate the various connection-creation methods, such as using a helper class or resource pooling, we define an abstract pointcut corresponding to the creation of the connection. All concrete subaspects will need to define this pointcut appropriately.

Figure 11.2 illustrates how we put all these fragments into an aspect. The figure shows that the `JDBCTransactionAspect` base aspect contains two abstract pointcuts—`transactedOperation()` and `obtainConnection()`—and a concrete pointcut, `topLevelTransactedOperation()`. The `JDBCTransactionAspect` is associated with the `topLevelTransactedOperation()` pointcut using `percflow` association specification.

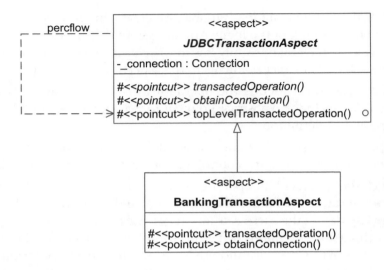

Figure 11.2
The transaction management aspects for the banking example. The base abstract aspect is a reusable aspect. For your system, you need to write a subaspect similar to `BankingTransaction-Aspect`.

The subaspect `BankingTransactionAspect` contains two concrete pointcuts that provide definitions for the abstract pointcuts in the base aspect. Listing 11.5 shows the `JDBCTransactionAspect` that follows this structure.

Listing 11.5   JDBCTransactionAspect.java

```
package transaction.jdbc;

import java.sql.*;

public abstract aspect JDBCTransactionAspect
    percflow(topLevelTransactedOperation()) {

    private Connection _connection;

    protected abstract pointcut transactedOperation();

    protected abstract pointcut obtainConnection();

    protected pointcut topLevelTransactedOperation()
        : transactedOperation()
        && !cflowbelow(transactedOperation());

    Object around() : topLevelTransactedOperation() {
        Object operationResult;
        try {
            operationResult = proceed();
            if (_connection != null) {
                _connection.commit();
```

❶ Association with top-level transaction control flow

❷ Abstract pointcuts

❸ Top-level transaction

❹

```
            }
        } catch (Exception ex) {
            if (_connection != null) {
                _connection.rollback();
            }
            throw new TransactionException(ex);
        } finally {
            if (_connection != null) {
                _connection.close();
            }
        }
        return operationResult;
    }
```

4 **Transaction management advice**

```
    Connection around() throws SQLException
        : obtainConnection() && cflow(transactedOperation()) {
        if (_connection == null) {
            _connection = proceed();
            _connection.setAutoCommit(false);
        }
        return _connection;
    }
```

5 **Pointcut capturing connection creation**

```
    public static class TransactionException
        extends RuntimeException {
        public TransactionException(Exception cause) {
            super(cause);
        }
    }
```

6 **Exception indicating a failed transaction**

```
    private static aspect SoftenSQLException {
        declare soft : java.sql.SQLException
        : (call(void Connection.rollback())
            || call(void Connection.close()))
        && within(JDBCTransactionAspect);
    }
```

7 **Softening of connection method calls**

```
    pointcut illegalConnectionManagement()
        : (call(void Connection.close())
            || call(void Connection.commit())
            || call(void Connection.rollback())
            || call(void Connection.setAutoCommit(boolean)))
        && !within(JDBCTransactionAspect);

    void around() : illegalConnectionManagement() {
        // Don't call proceed(); we want to bypass
        // illegal connection management here
    }
}
```

8 **Handling of illegal connection management**

Let's get into the implementation details:

❶ The aspect is associated with each top-level transaction's control flow. This association forces the creation of a new instance of the subaspect for each invocation of the operation specified by the `topLevelTransactedOperation()` pointcut; this instance maintains the state of the transaction.

❷ All the concrete subaspects of `JDBCTransactionAspect` must implement the abstract pointcuts `transactedOperation()` and `obtainConnection()`. The `transactedOperation()` definition should declare the execution of transactional operations. The `obtainConnection()` definition should capture join points that obtain the connections.

❸ The `topLevelTransactedOperation()` pointcut is defined to be the top-level operation needing transaction support by using the abstract `transactedOperation()` pointcut. This pointcut needs to be advised to perform the transaction management.

The top-level pointcut is the one with which a new instance of the aspect is associated. As soon as a join point matching this top-level transaction pointcut is about to execute, a new instance of the concrete subaspect is created.

❹ The around advice to `topLevelTransactedOperation()` puts the captured operation in a try/catch block. In the try block, it simply calls `proceed()` to carry on the captured operation. If an operation throws an exception during the execution of the captured join point, the execution will reach the catch block that calls `rollback()` on the connection object. The `finally` block closes the connection. The protection of `if(_connection != null)` handles the cases where the business logic did not need any updates/queries and therefore did not create a connection object.

❺ One of the core requirements for JDBC-based transaction management is that the same connection must be used for all the updates so that we can commit all the updates at once by invoking `commit()` on that object. The around advice checks the `connection` instance to see if it is `null`. If it is, that means that this is the first time it is needed during the execution of the top-level operation. The advice will then proceed to obtain a new connection, switch off its auto-commit mode, and assign the result to the `_connection` instance member. For subsequent requests to `_connection`, it simply returns the `_connection` object that was stored earlier instead of creating a new connection.

❻ We declare `TransactionException` as a runtime exception. Throwing this exception indicates to the caller that the transaction has failed. The nested exception indicates the cause that led to the failure.

❼ The softening declaration avoids the need for a try/catch block around the `rollback()` and `close()` calls made in this advice.

❽ Since our solution requires that only the aspect should invoke the transaction management calls on connection objects, we use an around advice to bypass any such call made from outside the aspect. For our test scenario, this results in bypassing `Connection.setAutoCommit()` called in the `DatabaseHelper` class and `Connection.close()` called in the `AccountJDBCImpl` class. We discuss this solution and an improvement using policy enforcement approach in section 11.3.2.

You can now enable transaction functionality in your JDBC-based database system by writing a subaspect. All the subaspect needs to do is provide a definition for two pointcuts: `transactedOperation()` (to capture operations that need transaction support) and `obtainConnection()` (to capture join points that create connection objects).

11.3.2 *Handling legacy system issues*

The solution we just described expects that only the aspect will perform any actions on the connection object, such as committing, changing auto-commit mode, or closing the connection. However, this expectation is not a given. You have two choices here: either advise all join points that perform the specified actions on a connection object to bypass their execution, or include policy enforcement to cause a compile-time error on all such operations. You may choose either of the ways based on your comfort level with AspectJ.

For either approach, we must define a pointcut that captures all connection-management join points. If we add the following pointcut to `JDBCTransaction-Aspect`, it does just that:

```
pointcut illegalConnectionManagement()
    : (call(void Connection.close())
        || call(void Connection.commit())
        || call(void Connection.rollback())
        || call(void Connection.setAutoCommit(boolean)))
    && !within(JDBCTransactionAspect);
```

If you choose to bypass the execution of the join points, you can use empty around advice in this way:

```
void around() : illegalConnectionManagement() {
    // Don't call proceed(); we want to bypass
    // illegal connection management here
}
```

This advice protects us from committing or closing a connection in the transactional method itself. This way, the methods no longer manage the connection object. Without such advice, the connection could be committed right in the middle of an operation. This advice is especially useful for legacy systems that are unaware that a transaction management aspect is present in the system.

If you would rather use the policy-enforcement approach, you have to declare an error for the join points, as follows:

```
declare error : illegalConnectionManagement()
    : "Do not call close(), commit(), rollback(), or setAutoCommit()
➡ on Connection objects from here";
```

Now the classes will not compile unless the developer removes all the calls to the methods specified by the pointcut. You no longer need the around advice, because the enforcement will ensure that the system does not contain such a join point.

A combination of both approaches is also possible. In this case, you keep the around advice and demote `declare error` to `declare warning`. This way, developers won't have to modify the system immediately, but you will still eliminate connection-management calls.

11.3.3 *Enabling transaction management for the banking system*

Now that we have the base aspect that provides most of the functionality, let's write a concrete subaspect that enables transaction management for the banking system. All we need to do is to write an aspect extending the `JDBCTransaction-Aspect` and define the two abstract pointcuts, as shown in listing 11.6.

> **Listing 11.6 BankingTransactionAspect.java**

```
package banking;

import java.sql.Connection;

import transaction.jdbc.JDBCTransactionAspect;

public aspect BankingTransactionAspect
    extends JDBCTransactionAspect {
    protected pointcut transactedOperation()
        : execution(* AccountJDBCImpl.debit(..))
        || execution(* AccountJDBCImpl.credit(..))
        || execution(* InterAccountTransferSystem.transfer(..));

    protected pointcut obtainConnection()
        : call(Connection DatabaseHelper.getConnection(..));
}
```

The `BankingTransactionAspect` simply defines the first pointcut that captures the execution of all the methods needing transaction support. The second pointcut defines all calls to methods that are used for obtaining database connections.

11.3.4 *Testing the solution*

At this point, we have implemented transaction management for the banking system. To better understand the solution, let's improve the logging aspect (listing 11.7) by adding a pointcut that captures the aspect-creation join points, which will allow us to observe the creation of new aspects associated with the control flow of the top-level operations. The changes from listing 11.4 are indicated in bold.

Listing 11.7 TransactionLogging.java: an improved version

```java
package banking;

import java.sql.*;
import org.aspectj.lang.*;
import logging.*;

import transaction.jdbc.*;

public aspect TransactionLogging extends IndentedLogging {
    declare precedence: TransactionLogging, *;

    public pointcut accountActivities()
        : call(void Account.credit(..))
        || call(void Account.debit(..))
        || call(void InterAccountTransferSystem.transfer(..));

    public pointcut connectionActivities(Connection conn)
        : (call(* Connection.commit(..))
            || call(* Connection.rollback(..)))
        && target(conn);

    public pointcut updateActivities(Statement stmt)
        : call(* Statement.executeUpdate(..))
        && target(stmt);

    public pointcut aspectInstantiation()
        : execution(JDBCTransactionAspect+.new(..));

    public pointcut loggedOperations()
        : accountActivities()
        || connectionActivities(Connection)
        || updateActivities(Statement)
        || aspectInstantiation();

    before() : accountActivities() {
        Signature sig = thisJoinPointStaticPart.getSignature();
        System.out.println("[" + sig.getName() + "]");
    }
}
```

```
    before(Connection conn) : connectionActivities(conn) {
        Signature sig = thisJoinPointStaticPart.getSignature();
        System.out.println("[" + sig.getName() + "] " + conn);
    }

    before(Statement stmt) throws SQLException
        : updateActivities(stmt) {
        Signature sig = thisJoinPointStaticPart.getSignature();
        System.out.println("[" + sig.getName()
                + "] " + stmt.getConnection());
    }

    before() : aspectInstantiation() {
        Signature sig = thisJoinPointStaticPart.getSignature();
        System.out.println("[" + sig.getName() + "] "
                            + sig.getDeclaringType());
    }
}
```

When we compile all the classes and aspects and run the program, we see output
similar to the following:

```
> ajc banking\*.java logging\*.java transaction\jdbc\*.java
> java banking.Test
[credit]
    [<init>] class transaction.jdbc.JDBCTransactionAspect
    [<init>] class banking.BankingTransactionAspect
    [executeUpdate] sun.jdbc.odbc.JdbcOdbcConnection@fa3ac1
    [commit] sun.jdbc.odbc.JdbcOdbcConnection@fa3ac1
[debit]
    [<init>] class transaction.jdbc.JDBCTransactionAspect
    [<init>] class banking.BankingTransactionAspect
    [executeUpdate] sun.jdbc.odbc.JdbcOdbcConnection@1833955
    [commit] sun.jdbc.odbc.JdbcOdbcConnection@1833955
[transfer]
    [<init>] class transaction.jdbc.JDBCTransactionAspect
    [<init>] class banking.BankingTransactionAspect
    [credit]
        [executeUpdate] sun.jdbc.odbc.JdbcOdbcConnection@21b6d
    [debit]
        [executeUpdate] sun.jdbc.odbc.JdbcOdbcConnection@21b6d
    [commit] sun.jdbc.odbc.JdbcOdbcConnection@21b6d
[transfer]
    [<init>] class transaction.jdbc.JDBCTransactionAspect
    [<init>] class banking.BankingTransactionAspect
    [credit]
        [executeUpdate] sun.jdbc.odbc.JdbcOdbcConnection@c9ba38
    [debit]
        [rollback] sun.jdbc.odbc.JdbcOdbcConnection@c9ba38
```

```
Exception in thread "main" transaction.jdbc.JDBCTransactionAspect
➥ $TransactionException: banking.InsufficientBalanceException:
➥ Total balance not sufficient
... the rest of call stack
```

Let's examine the output:

1   A new aspect instance is created at the beginning of each top-level operation as a result of associating the aspect with the control flow of each top-level operation.

2   The same connection object is used for all the operations inside each transaction. Specifically, both `credit()` and `debit()` operations called during the transfer of money from one account to the other use the same connection (`JdbcOdbcConnection@21b6d` and `JdbcOdbcConnection@c9ba38`).

3   The commit call is made only at the end of the transaction.

4   Even though `credit()` and `debit()` did call `commit()` on the connection object, our aspect bypassed it.

5   The connection is rolled back when the last transfer operation throws an exception.

Note the exception type, `JDBCTransactionAspect.TransactionException`, shown in the stack trace. It is wrapping the original `InsufficientBalanceException` exception. Because the `transfer()` method declares that it throws a checked `InsufficientBalanceException` exception, the caller of `transfer()` expects an `InsufficientBalanceException` and not a runtime exception. We can take care of this problem by adding an aspect (listing 11.8) that preserves the checked exception, based on the exception introduction pattern presented in chapter 8.

Listing 11.8   An aspect that preserves the checked exception

```
package banking;

import transaction.jdbc.JDBCTransactionAspect;

public aspect PreserveCheckedException {
    after() throwing(JDBCTransactionAspect.TransactionException ex)
        throws InsufficientBalanceException
        : call(* banking..*.*(..)
                    throws InsufficientBalanceException) {
        Throwable cause = ex.getCause();
        if (cause instanceof InsufficientBalanceException) {
            throw (InsufficientBalanceException)cause;
```

```
        } else {
            throw ex;
        }
    }
}
```

The aspect in listing 11.8 captures the methods throwing `InsufficientBalance-Exception` and advises them to check whether the cause of the exception is of the `InsufficientBalanceException` type; if so, it simply throws the cause instead of the caught exception. Now when we compile and run the test program after including this aspect, the last transaction log looks like this:

```
[transfer]
    [<init>] class transaction.jdbc.JDBCTransactionAspect
    [<init>] class banking.BankingTransactionAspect
    [credit]
        [executeUpdate] sun.jdbc.odbc.JdbcOdbcConnection@c9ba38
    [debit]
        [rollback] sun.jdbc.odbc.JdbcOdbcConnection@c9ba38
Exception in thread "main" banking.InsufficientBalanceException:
    Total balance not sufficient
... the rest of call stack
```

Now we have our first AspectJ-based solution for transaction management. This solution works fine if you have only one subaspect of `JDBCTransactionAspect`. However, if you need to use multiple subaspects to separately specify operations that require transaction support, you may have to enhance this solution, as we describe next.

11.4 *Improving the solution*

In many situations, operations that must be managed within one transaction may belong to different subsystems, and it may be desirable for each subsystem to have its own aspect for specifying the pointcuts for the operations that need transaction support. That way, any changes to a subsystem require changing only the associated subaspect. In this case, we need to ensure that the transaction management for one aspect does not conflict with that of the other. Let's use two of the patterns from chapter 8, the participant pattern and the worker object creation pattern, to create a solution that meets this requirement. In our realization of the participant pattern, we will create a participant subaspect for each subsystem. We will then use the worker object creation pattern to ensure that the solution works correctly in all cases. As we review the example in the next two sections, keep in mind that although the first pattern sets up the foundation for the solution, we need the second pattern to complete it.

11.4.1 *Using the participant pattern*

The first thing we want to do is create a separate participant subaspect to manage the transactions for each subsystem. We can use the participant pattern to do this, since it specifies that each of these subaspects will extend the same base abstract aspect that contains the transaction management logic. Therefore, the subaspects just need to define the pointcuts that specify the join points requiring transaction management in the subsystems they represent.

Let's set up an example so you can understand how this pattern is used. To keep it simple, we have chosen to nest two separate participant aspects inside the `AccountJDBCImpl` and `InterAccountTransferSystem` classes. Let's assume that these two classes are managed by two different developers and that they would like to specify the operations requiring transaction support independently. Both subaspects (listings 11.9 and 11.10) extend the abstract aspect from our first solution.

Listing 11.9   The participant aspect nested in the `AccountJDBCImpl` class

```
package banking;

import java.sql.*;
import transaction.jdbc.JDBCTransactionAspect;

public class AccountJDBCImpl implements Account {

    ... unchanged from listing 11.2

    public static aspect TransactionParticipantAspect
        extends JDBCTransactionAspect {
        protected pointcut transactedOperation()
            : execution(* AccountJDBCImpl.debit(..))
            || execution(* AccountJDBCImpl.credit(..));

        protected pointcut obtainConnection()
            : call(Connection DatabaseHelper
                .getConnection(..));
    }
}
```

Listing 11.10   The participant aspect nested in the `InterAccountTransferSystem` class

```
package banking;

import transaction.jdbc.JDBCTransactionAspect;

public class InterAccountTransferSystem {
    public static void transfer(Account from, Account to,
                                float amount)
```

```
                throws InsufficientBalanceException {
                to.credit(amount);
                from.debit(amount);
        }

        public static aspect TransactionParticipantAspect
            extends JDBCTransactionAspect {
            protected pointcut transactedOperation()
                : execution(* InterAccountTransferSystem.transfer(..));

            protected pointcut obtainConnection();
        }
    }
```

Note that the `AccountJDBCImpl.credit()` and `AccountJDBCImpl.debit()` methods will be called during the execution of `InterAccountTransferSystem.transfer()`. Although the former two methods will be captured by `AccountJDBCImpl.Transaction-ParticipantAspect`, the latter one will be captured by `InterAccountTransferSystem.TransactionParticipantAspect`.

In these listings, each class includes a nested concrete subaspect that extends `JDBCTransactionAspect` and defines the `transactedOperation()` pointcut to capture methods that need transaction support. Although `InterAccountTransferSystem` never obtains a connection itself, we still need to define the `obtainConnection()` pointcut. We use a special syntax that omits the : and the pointcut definition following it as described in chapter 3, section 3.1, to define the pointcut so that it matches no join point.

Although the use of this pattern helps us by encapsulating the transaction-management logic in the base aspect, there is a potential problem with it. At runtime, a separate aspect instance is created for each participant subaspect, and the connection object will not be shared across these instances. This is not a problem in many cases. However, the solution will not work if a join point captured by one subaspect falls in the control flow of a join point captured by another subaspect.

Let's examine the problem in the context of our example subaspects in listings 11.9 and 11.10. The base `JDBCTransactionAspect` is associated with the control flow of the join point captured by the `topLevelTransactedOperation()` pointcut. As soon as the first matching join point is encountered in a control flow, a new aspect instance is created automatically (as explained in chapter 4, section 4.3.3). With this arrangement, when `InterAccountTransferSystem.transfer()` is called, the system creates an instance of `InterAccountTransferSystem.`

TransactionParticipantAspect. Later, when credit() and debit() are called from InterAccountTransferSystem.transfer(), the system creates two more instances of AccountJDBCImpl.TransactionParticipantAspect, which are associated with each method's control flow. As a result, each of the aspect instances manages its associated control flow and commits its operations independently. Consider a partial output when we run the test program with the aspects in listings 11.9 and 11.10 (but without the BankingTransactionAspect in listing 10.6). For simplicity, we only show the log output for the last two transfer operations:

```
[transfer]
    [<init>] class transaction.jdbc.JDBCTransactionAspect
    [<init>] class banking.InterAccountTransferSystem$
        ➥   TransactionParticipantAspect
    [credit]
        [<init>] class transaction.jdbc.JDBCTransactionAspect
        [<init>] class banking.AccountJDBCImpl$
            ➥   TransactionParticipantAspect
        [executeUpdate] sun.jdbc.odbc.JdbcOdbcConnection@a1807c
        [commit] sun.jdbc.odbc.JdbcOdbcConnection@a1807c
    [debit]
        [<init>] class transaction.jdbc.JDBCTransactionAspect
        [<init>] class banking.AccountJDBCImpl$
            ➥   TransactionParticipantAspect
        [executeUpdate] sun.jdbc.odbc.JdbcOdbcConnection@1a679b7
        [commit] sun.jdbc.odbc.JdbcOdbcConnection@1a679b7
[transfer]
    [<init>] class transaction.jdbc.JDBCTransactionAspect
    [<init>] class banking.InterAccountTransferSystem$
        ➥   TransactionParticipantAspect
    [credit]
        [<init>] class transaction.jdbc.JDBCTransactionAspect
        [<init>] class banking.AccountJDBCImpl$
            ➥   TransactionParticipantAspect
        [executeUpdate] sun.jdbc.odbc.JdbcOdbcConnection@127734f
        [commit] sun.jdbc.odbc.JdbcOdbcConnection@127734f
    [debit]
        [<init>] class transaction.jdbc.JDBCTransactionAspect
        [<init>] class banking.AccountJDBCImpl$
            ➥   TransactionParticipantAspect
        [rollback] sun.jdbc.odbc.JdbcOdbcConnection@1546e25
Exception in thread "main" banking.InsufficientBalanceException:
➥  Total balance not sufficient
... the rest of call stack
```

Notice that a new connection object is created for both of the nested debit and credit operations that are called during the transfer transaction. The result is incorrect behavior in that if the second operation, debit(), fails, the first operation, `credit()`, will still succeed. In that case, the bank would have credited the amount to the receiving account while not debiting from the source account—a sure recipe for bankruptcy! In order to use the same connection object for all transactions, you would normally have to specify all the methods needing transaction management in a single aspect. In a large system, this pointcut definition may span over many classes and packages, making the use of only one aspect impractical. Obviously, something is still missing. In the next section, we add the worker object creation pattern to this example, which will correct the problem and provide us with a complete solution.

11.4.2 *Implementing the JDBC transaction aspect: the second version*

In order to use multiple subaspects to manage transactions, you must ensure that the same connection object is used to carry out all the updates in a transaction—even when different aspects capture different operations occurring in the transaction. In the solution in section 11.3, the aspect performed two roles: weaving the transaction commit and rollback calls, and storing the connection object so that all the operations in the transaction could refer to it. In the second version of the solution, we separate these two roles. We assign the aspect the responsibility to perform the commit and rollback only, and utilize a separate transaction context object to store the connection.

To implement this separation, first we use the default (instead of the `perc-flow`) association for the `JDBCTransactionAspect` aspect and remove the `_connection` instance member from it. The use of the default association results in the creation of at most *one* instance of each subaspect during the lifetime of a program's execution. Because the `_connection` instance is removed from the aspect, the aspect is a stateless aspect and the *instances* of aspects are no longer important to our solution. Next, we utilize the worker object creation pattern to automatically create the worker object for each new transaction, and assign to it the responsibility of storing the connection object. Thus, the worker object serves as the transaction context.

Following the pattern, we create a worker object for each top-level operation that needs transaction management, thus treating the top-level operation as a worker method. The worker object's `run()` method surrounds the worker method with the transaction-management logic. When the first method that needs transaction management executes, the connection object that gets created is stored inside the worker object. We use the context object to ensure that we do not create an additional connection object when we encounter a new join point while we are in the control flow of the run() method of the worker object. Let's modify the base aspect from our first solution to incorporate these modifications, as shown in listing 11.11.

Listing 11.11 JDBCTransactionAspect.java: the improved version

```
package transaction.jdbc;

import java.sql.*;

import pattern.worker.*;

public abstract aspect JDBCTransactionAspect {           ❶ Declaration of aspect
    protected abstract pointcut transactedOperation();
                                                          ❷ Abstract
                                                             pointcuts
    protected abstract pointcut obtainConnection();

    protected pointcut                                    ❸ Pointcut
        inTransactedOperation(TransactionContext context)    detecting
        : cflow(execution(* TransactionContext.run())        in-progress
            && this(context));                               transaction

    Object around() : transactedOperation()
        && !inTransactedOperation(TransactionContext) {
        TransactionContext transactionContext  Advice to the   ❹
            = new TransactionContext() {          top-level
                public void run() {                   method
                    try {
                        _returnValue = proceed();
                        if (_connection != null) {
                            _connection.commit();
                        }
                    } catch (Exception ex) {
                        if (_connection != null) {
                            _connection.rollback();
                        }
                        throw new TransactionException(ex);
                    } finally {
                        if (_connection != null) {
                            _connection.close();
                        }
                    }
                }
            }};                             Transaction context  ❺
                                            performing the
        transactionContext.run();           operation
        return transactionContext.getReturnValue();
    }
}
```

```
        Connection around(final TransactionContext context)
        throws SQLException
        : obtainConnection() && inTransactedOperation(context) {
        if (context._connection == null) {
            context._connection = proceed(context);
            context._connection.setAutoCommit(false);
        }
        return context._connection;
    }

    public static abstract class TransactionContext
        extends RunnableWithReturn {
        Connection _connection;
    }
```

Wormhole between ❻
context creation and
connection creation

❼ **TransactionContext**
class

```
    ... illegal connection management unchanged from the earlier version

    ... TransactionException class unchanged from the earlier version

    ... softening of connection methods unchanged from the earlier version

}
```

We implement a separate TransactionContext class that extends the Runnable-WithReturn class that was introduced along with the worker object creation pattern in chapter 8. All the concrete subclasses must provide implementations of the run() method. The run() method should execute the worker method and set the _returnValue member to the result of the operation.

A new context object is created for all operations that begin a transaction *unless* they are already in the control flow of the execution of a transaction context's run() method. This is the key point. No matter which aspect creates the transaction context, a new context will not be created for an operation that is already part of a transaction context. Because the transaction management is performed only through the context object and no new context is created for a nested transaction operation, we solve the problem we had in the earlier solution.

Let's now dive into the details of the implementation:

❶ There's nothing interesting here, except that we no longer associate the aspect with the per-control flow of any pointcut.

❷ This aspect has the same two abstract pointcuts as in the earlier implementation. Any aspect that wants to enable transaction management must provide a definition for both of these pointcuts.

❸ The inTransactedOperation() pointcut captures the control flow of the Transac-tionContext.run() method (explained later in ❼) and collects the object associated with the method. The collected object is passed through the call stack as explained in ❻.

❹ The advice to the `transactedOperation()` pointcut, which specifies join points that are not already in a transaction context execution, creates a new transaction context.

❺ The `run()` method implementation is identical to the around advice body in the earlier version of this solution. Note the call to `proceed()` from the `run()` method and the setting of `_returnValue` to the value returned by `proceed()`, as outlined by the worker object creation pattern.

❻ The advice for `obtainConnection()` needs the transaction object associated with the surrounding transaction so that it can access its `_connection` object. The `inTransactedOperation()` pointcut captures this context. This arrangement is a direct result of applying the wormhole pattern to create a direct path between the transaction object's `run()` method and any method that needs to obtain the connection.

❼ The `TransactionContext` abstract class extends the `RunnableWithReturn` class. It includes one instance member, `_connection`, to hold the transaction's connection object.

Now that we have this base aspect, we can use the participating aspects described in listings 11.9 and 11.10, since overlapping join points between the two aspects is no longer a problem.

11.4.3 *Testing the solution*

We are now ready to test our solution. The new solution's core theme is to use an automatically created transaction context class, so we need to understand the creation of the new context. Therefore, we add the logging of context-creation join points to our logging aspect, as shown in listing 11.12.

Listing 11.12   Adding context creation to logging

```
...

public aspect TransactionLogging extends IndentedLogging {
    declare precedence: TransactionLogging, *;

    ...

    public pointcut contextInstantiation()
        : execution(*.TransactionContext+.new(..));

    public pointcut loggedOperations()
        : accountActivities()
        || connectionActivities(Connection)
```

```
        || updateActivities(Statement)
        || aspectInstantiation()
        || contextInstantiation();

    ...

    before() : aspectInstantiation() || contextInstantiation() {
        Signature sig = thisJoinPointStaticPart.getSignature();
        System.out.println("[" + sig.getName() + "] "
                            + sig.getDeclaringType());
    }
}
```

When we compile all the classes and aspects together, including the nested aspects as shown in listings 11.9 and 11.10, and run the Test class, we get output similar to the following (make sure you do not include the BankingTransaction-Aspect from listing 10.6 during the compilation):

```
> ajc banking\*.java logging\*.java transaction\jdbc\*.java
> java banking.Test
[credit]
    [<init>] class transaction.jdbc.JDBCTransactionAspect
    [<init>] class banking.AccountJDBCImpl$
        ➥ TransactionParticipantAspect
    [<init>] class transaction.jdbc.JDBCTransactionAspect$
        ➥ TransactionContext
    [<init>] class transaction.jdbc.JDBCTransactionAspect$1
    [<init>] class transaction.jdbc.JDBCTransactionAspect
    [<init>] class banking.InterAccountTransferSystem$
        ➥ TransactionParticipantAspect
    [executeUpdate] sun.jdbc.odbc.JdbcOdbcConnection@e86da0
    [commit] sun.jdbc.odbc.JdbcOdbcConnection@e86da0
[debit]
    [<init>] class transaction.jdbc.JDBCTransactionAspect$
        ➥ TransactionContext
    [<init>] class transaction.jdbc.JDBCTransactionAspect$1
    [executeUpdate] sun.jdbc.odbc.JdbcOdbcConnection@a97b0b
    [commit] sun.jdbc.odbc.JdbcOdbcConnection@a97b0b
[transfer]
    [<init>] class transaction.jdbc.JDBCTransactionAspect$
        ➥ TransactionContext
    [<init>] class transaction.jdbc.JDBCTransactionAspect$1
    [credit]
        [executeUpdate] sun.jdbc.odbc.JdbcOdbcConnection@c9ba38
    [debit]
        [executeUpdate] sun.jdbc.odbc.JdbcOdbcConnection@c9ba38
    [commit] sun.jdbc.odbc.JdbcOdbcConnection@c9ba38
[transfer]
```

```
[<init>] class transaction.jdbc.JDBCTransactionAspect$
       ➥ TransactionContext
[<init>] class transaction.jdbc.JDBCTransactionAspect$1
[credit]
    [executeUpdate] sun.jdbc.odbc.JdbcOdbcConnection@c2a132
[debit]
    [rollback] sun.jdbc.odbc.JdbcOdbcConnection@c2a132
Exception in thread "main" banking.InsufficientBalanceException:
➥ Total balance not sufficient
```

The log output shows that we no longer create new aspects for each control flow. Instead, only one aspect is created for each participant and a new `Transaction-Context` object is created for each top-level operation's control flow. We now have a solution that allows us to use the participant pattern correctly with the transaction-management aspect. The participant pattern lets us separate the definition for transaction operations from various modules. Note how effectively we utilized all four patterns—worker object creation, wormhole, exception introduction, and participant—presented in chapter 8.

11.5 Using AspectJ with advanced transaction-management systems

In the previous sections, we dealt with transaction management for the systems that use the basic JDBC transaction support, and we demonstrated the basic concepts of using transaction management with AspectJ. In modern complex systems, however, the requirements tend to be more involved. In particular, it is often necessary to have distributed transaction management involving multiple resources spanning multiple databases. You may also have to update additional legacy databases or an Enterprise Resource Planning (ERP) database for each operation, and the transaction must ensure the correct functioning of updates to each database. In these cases, a transaction must span over multiple connection objects.

A transaction may also span over multiple kinds of resources. For example, you may have to update a database and send messages over a queue using JMS in the same transaction. In that case, both the database update and the message queue send must succeed in order to keep the system in a consistent state. These cases require the use of a Transaction Processing (TP) monitor to coordinate the transaction across multiple resources. Of course, for this scheme to work correctly, the resources (such as the database and JMS messaging middleware) must be capable of collaborating with a TP monitor. The use of an API like JTA allows you to work with the TP monitor without locking you into a particular implementation.

Even with JTA, the separation of the transaction concern from the core concern cannot be achieved when you are using a purely object-oriented approach. This is because the calls to the creation, commit, and rollback of transactions will span over all the modules that have operations requiring transaction management. JTA provides transparency with respect to the actual TP monitor implementation that is used, but it still requires the invocation of its API from multiple core modules.

In this section, we examine a template using AspectJ to modularize the crosscutting behavior for transaction management when we use JTA. Listing 11.13 shows an abstract base aspect that encapsulates all the JTA-based transactions. You will need to add one or more concrete subaspects, each defining the `transactedOperation()` pointcut.

Listing 11.13 JTATransactionAspect.java: the base aspect

```
package transaction.jta;

import javax.naming.*;
import javax.transaction.*;

import pattern.worker.*;

public abstract aspect JTATransactionAspect {
    protected abstract pointcut transactedOperation();

    protected pointcut
        inTransactedOperation(TransactionContext context)
        : cflow(execution(* TransactionContext.run())
                && this(context));

    Object around() : transactedOperation()
        && !inTransactedOperation(TransactionContext) {
        TransactionContext transactionContext
            = new TransactionContext() {
                public void run() {
                    UserTransaction ut = null;
                    try {
                        Context ctx = new InitialContext();
                        ut = (UserTransaction)
                            ctx.lookup("java:comp/ut");
                    } catch (NamingException ex) {
                        throw new TransactionException(ex);
                    }
                    try {
                        ut.begin();
                        _returnValue = proceed();
                        ut.commit();
```

```
                    } catch (Exception ex) {
                        ut.rollback();
                        throw new TransactionException(ex);
                    }
                }};

        transactionContext.run();
        return transactionContext.getReturnValue();
    }

    public static abstract class TransactionContext
        extends RunnableWithReturn {
    }

    public static class TransactionException
        extends RuntimeException {
        public TransactionException(Exception cause) {
            super(cause);
        }
    }

    private static aspect SoftenSystemException {
        declare soft : javax.transaction.SystemException
        : call(void UserTransaction.rollback())
        && within(JTATransactionAspect);
    }
}
```

This abstract aspect in listing 11.13 is similar to the one shown in listing 11.11. The differences include:

1   We use a `UserTransaction` object to provide transaction management; it supplies an API for committing and rolling back a transaction. We mark the start of a transaction using `UserTransaction.begin()`, commit the transaction using `UserTransaction.commit()`, and roll back using `User-Transaction.rollback()`.

2   We no longer have a pointcut and advice to ensure the use of the same connection object. With the use of JTA you no longer have to use only one resource (the database connection, for example) for the individual updates.

You might want to add a few policy-enforcement constructs in this aspect to ensure that, for example, the use of resources that are not JTA-friendly is prohibited. The details will depend on your system architecture.

11.6 *Summary*

Transaction management is a complex topic, although advances in transaction-processing monitors and standardization efforts have helped to simplify its implementation significantly. When a declarative mechanism such as the one used with EJB is not available, you need to deal with the issues arising from the lack of modularization of crosscutting concerns. The AspectJ-based solution presented in this chapter adds the missing link so that you can modularize the implementation of transaction management in a general-purpose way.

Although in this chapter we discussed transactions in the narrow sense of JDBC and JTA, the core concepts here are widely applicable. They can be used whenever you have to ensure atomicity of a complex operation. This will result in a modularized implementation of the atomicity concerns, and if your atomicity requirement should change, the modifications will be easy to implement. Using the worker object creation and participant patterns presented in this chapter should help you devise an AspectJ-based solution to a variety of problems you will encounter during your AspectJ journey.

12

Implementing business rules

This chapter covers

- Using AspectJ to modularize implementation of business rules
- Using plain Java with AspectJ to implement rules
- Using a rule engine with AspectJ

Business rule implementation is an essential part of any enterprise system; it applies to many facets of business behavior that support policy and strategy changes. Business rules range from the simple—such as sending email after users have completed their purchase on an e-commerce site—to the complex—such as suggesting additional items a user might want to purchase based on the user profile, recent purchases, and product availability. Business rules tend to change over time due to new policies, new business realities, and new laws and regulations.

Current mechanisms of implementing business rules require embedding the rule evaluation or calls to it right in core modules of the system, causing the implementation to be scattered over multiple modules. A change in the rule specification requires changes in all modules that are involved. These modifications are invasive and time-consuming. Further, because business rules (such as a discounting scheme) are a lot more volatile compared to core business logic (such as sales), mixing them together causes the core system to become just as volatile.

You can see how this can be a crosscutting concern. In this chapter, we explain how you can use AspectJ to modularize the solution for these concerns.

12.1 *Using business rules in enterprise applications*

For the purpose of this chapter, we make a distinction between core business logic and business rules so that we can understand their characteristics. We consider *core business logic* to be the implementation of basic business constraints, such as not being able to debit from a bank account when there is an insufficient balance. *Business rules*, on the other hand, model constraints due to forces such as business policies and regulations. For example, restricting the number of transactions per statement period and charging for extra transactions would normally be business rules. Although the distinction between the two is largely perspective-dependent, there is an understood boundary between the two for any given system. If, for example, charging for an extra transaction is fundamental to the business's operations, it may be treated as core business logic instead of a business rule. Core business logic tends to be more stable and inherently modular as opposed to business rules, which tend to change quickly and cross multiple modules.

In business-to-business (B2B) and business-to-consumer (B2C) applications, rules play an important role. With rapid changes in the business environment, the deployment of business rules separately from the business core logic provides the needed agility to respond to a changing environment. For example, business rules can implement cross-product promotions quite effectively. A shopping cart application can involve rules that offer product suggestions based on customers' shopping cart contents; it could also incorporate a more sophisticated system that is based on customers' purchasing history, their response to earlier product offers, their geographical location, current climatic conditions, the availability of to-be-suggested products, and even the profit margin of the promoted products. The result is an overall improvement in customer experience and increased revenue for the enterprise.

12.2 *An overview of business rule implementation*

In its simplest form, business rule implementation may involve code written in a general-purpose language such as Java. These implementations usually take the form of a series of if-then statements. Evaluating the business rules then requires that you evaluate all of these statements and take the associated action.

The most common way to implement business rules is to use a rule engine. Rule engines can significantly improve the process by separating the rule evaluations from rule invocations. Further, some engines allow a simpler way to express rules, using either a GUI or English-like language instead of expressing them using a programming language. This lets the nonprogrammer domain experts build the rules themselves.

Business rule implementation is common enough in enterprises that a Java Specification Request (JSR 94) for the Java Rule Engine API exists (currently in public review stage). This JSR is expected to come with a standard API to interact with rule engines. There are also several projects in development, such as RuleML and Simple Rule Markup Language (SRML), to formulate a common XML-based language for expressing rules. With these projects, we will have a common API to interact with the rule engine and a common language to express business rules, eliminating some barriers in effectively using rule engines.

In this chapter, we examine the use of AspectJ in modularizing business rule implementation. We first show you how to use plain Java for implementing rules, and we then use an engine to implement the same rules. In both cases, the use of AspectJ cleanly separates the rule implementation from the core business logic.

12.3 *Current mechanisms*

The integration of business logic and business rules varies a lot depending on the complexity of the rules. For simple rules, it is common to implement them along with the core business logic. However, this method results in several development and maintenance issues common with other crosscutting concerns.

Because the implementation of business rules is spread over as many modules as the core business logic, the core business logic is tangled with business rules, resulting in a hard-to-follow implementation. In addition, the same rules need to be embedded at many points—typically at all state-change points—in the business class, causing duplication of code.

Implementations of complex business rules often employ a set of modules called a *rule engine* for business rule evaluation that is separate from the core logic. In these cases, however, even if the implementation of the rule evaluation is separated, the core business logic must call the rule engine API from each module that may need the rules.

Whether you are using simple or complex rules, the fundamental problem is the same: the business rule implementation is scattered all over the core business modules. Since such scattering is a classic symptom of a crosscutting concern, you can employ AspectJ to modularize the concern.

12.4 *Introducing a solution using AspectJ*

Using AspectJ, you can cleanly separate the implementation of core business logic and the accompanying business rules. In this section, we focus on the abstract nature of the solution rather than the implementation details by creating a template solution. Later in the chapter, we develop example solutions based on this template. You can then take this template and apply it to your system to create your own solutions.

12.4.1 *The template*

The template solution for the implementation of business rules using AspectJ is more loosely defined than some of our previous template solutions, such as the one for resource pooling in chapter 7. The fundamental idea behind our solution is to identify join points that need business rule execution, capture them by defining the right set of pointcuts, and advise those join points to invoke the business rules.

Participating entities

The participating entities needed in a system that implements business rules are as follows:

- *Classes implementing the core business logic*—These classes are also clients for the business rule evaluator.
- *Classes, aspects, or a rule engine implementing business rules*—These entities take care of evaluating business rules that apply to the business objects. In

its simplest form, a class could be implementing the business rules. For complex rules, you could use a rule engine.

Participating join points

The participating join points for implementing business rules depend greatly on the business rules themselves. Typically, such join points capture important events in a business. For example, in an airline's booking system, a method that checks flight availability would be a join point where you could apply the rules to determine the extent to which a flight could be overbooked.

Because the evaluation of business rules often depends on the context of the join points (such as the state of the business object), the pointcuts must capture any such context. For instance, to determine flight availability, the methods need to know the flight being booked and the class (first class, business, or economy) for which a reservation is requested. You can then supply this information to the module that evaluates the rules to determine whether a booking should be allowed.

Concern weaving

After identifying join points in the system, we need to advise them to evaluate business rules. The advice body will either call a method in a business rule implementation, passing it the captured context, or run the business rule engine. If a rule engine is used, the advice body typically initializes it with the captured context of the join point before running the engine.

A template for the business rule aspect

Let's look at a template for an aspect that coordinates business rules. The template aspect contains a pointcut definition and advice to it. The pointcut captures all methods needed by the business rule invocation along with their context. If the business rules are implemented in the code, the advice to this pointcut invokes that implementation. If a rule engine is used, the advice initializes the rule engine with the context and runs the engine. Listing 12.1 shows our template.

Listing 12.1   A template for an aspect that coordinates business rule invocation

```
aspect BusinessRuleCoordinator {
    pointcut methodsNeedingBusinessRules(<context...>)
            : call(...) ...;

    before(<context...>) : methodsNeedingBusinessRules() {
       // Evaluate rules
       // Fire action for matching rules
```

```
        // If rule engine is used:
        // 1. Initialize rule engine with the context
        // 2. Run rule engine evaluation
    }
}
```

The `methodsNeedingBusinessRules()` pointcut captures all the join points where we need to evaluate business rules. This pointcut typically captures invocation of all important methods in the business logic. For each join point, the point-cut also collects the context that will be needed to evaluate the rules. The advice body to the `methodsNeedingBusinessRules()` pointcut may embed the rule evaluation logic directly in its body, in which case it fires actions for the matching rules. If a rule engine is used, the advice initializes the rule engine with the collected context and requests that the rule engine evaluate the rules. The rule engine, in turn, performs the actions associated with all rules that evaluate to `true`.

12.5 Example: the banking system

Now that we have a template, let's see how we can use it to create a real-life solution. First, we develop a simple banking system that implements the core business logic. We then create two aspects that implement business rules for minimum balance and overdraft protection, and show their effect through a test program.

12.5.1 Implementing the core business logic

Our banking system, shown in figure 12.1, is similar to one in chapter 10, except here we add a few new capabilities to help us illustrate business rule implementation. This system has the power to create new customers, add accounts to customers, mark certain accounts as overdraft accounts, and make transactions in the accounts. We've also included a facility mimicking a check clearance system.

The `Customer` class models a banking customer and is associated with a set of accounts that belong to a customer and a subset of those accounts marked as overdraft accounts. Overdraft accounts are designated to automatically transfer money to the checking account when a check clearance system detects an insufficient balance in that checking account. Listing 12.2 shows the implementation of the `Customer` class.

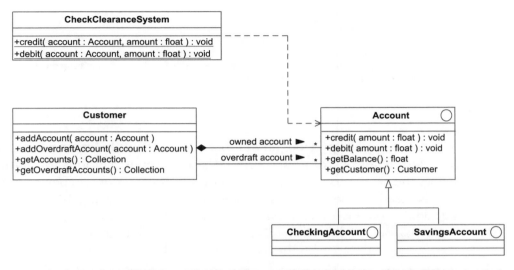

Figure 12.1 In our banking example, the customer owns a few accounts, some of which are marked as overdraft accounts. Checking and savings are two specific types of account; there could be many such specified accounts.

Listing 12.2 Customer.java: a banking customer

```
package banking;

import java.util.*;

public class Customer {
    private String _name;

    private Collection _accounts = new Vector();          ⟵ Owned accounts
    private Collection _overdraftAccounts = new Vector();  ⟵ Overdraft accounts

    public Customer(String name) {
        _name = name;
    }

    public String getName() {
        return _name;
    }

    public void addAccount(Account account) {
        _accounts.add(account);
    }

    public Collection getAccounts() {
        return _accounts;
    }
```

Owned account management

```
public void addOverdraftAccount(Account overdraftAccount) {
    _overdraftAccounts.add(overdraftAccount);
}                                                              Overdraft
                                                               account
public Collection getOverdraftAccounts() {                     management
    return _overdraftAccounts;
}
}
```

The Customer class provides an API that adds accounts belonging to a customer and designates overdraft accounts. It also contains methods for getting the name, the list of accounts, and the list of overdraft accounts. The Account interface is based on the one we introduced in chapter 10 (listing 10.1), except here we add the concept of an associated customer to this interface. We use Insufficient-BalanceException (from listing 10.2) without any modifications. Listing 12.3 shows the Account interface with the modifications indicated in bold.

Listing 12.3   Account.java: with customer information

```
package banking;

public interface Account {
    public int getAccountNumber();

    public void credit(float amount);

    public void debit(float amount)
        throws InsufficientBalanceException;

    public float getBalance();

    public Customer getCustomer();
}
```

We also introduce two tagging subinterfaces of Account—SavingsAccount and CheckingAccount—to designate the two types of accounts we will use. Listing 12.4 shows the code for the SavingsAccount interface. Similarly, listing 12.5 shows code for the CheckingAccount interface.

Listing 12.4   SavingsAccount.java

```
package banking;

public interface SavingsAccount extends Account {
}
```

Listing 12.5   CheckingAccount.java

```
package banking;

public interface CheckingAccount extends Account {
}
```

Now let's modify the AccountSimpleImpl implementation from chapter 10 (listing 10.3) so that it supports modeling the customer to whom an account belongs. The new implementation appears in listing 12.6; the changes are marked in bold.

Listing 12.6   AccountSimpleImpl.java: the base account implementation

```
package banking;

public abstract class AccountSimpleImpl implements Account {
    private int _accountNumber;
    private float _balance;
    private Customer _customer;

    public AccountSimpleImpl(int accountNumber, Customer customer) {
        _accountNumber = accountNumber;
        _customer = customer;
    }

    public int getAccountNumber() {
        return _accountNumber;
    }

    public void credit(float amount) {
        _balance = _balance + amount;
    }

    public void debit(float amount)
        throws InsufficientBalanceException {
        if (_balance < amount) {
            throw new InsufficientBalanceException(
                "Total balance not sufficient");
        } else {
            _balance = _balance - amount;
        }
    }

    public float getBalance() {
        return _balance;
    }
```

```
    public Customer getCustomer() {
        return _customer;
    }
}
```

We added an additional argument to the constructor of the `AccountSimpleImpl` class that denotes the customer to whom the account belongs; we store the argument in an instance variable. The class implements the `getCustomer()` method that is specified in the base interface that returns this stored instance. Note that we have marked this class as abstract to force developers to instantiate objects of its concrete subclasses according to the type of account.

The classes `SavingsAccountSimpleImpl` and `CheckingAccountSimpleImpl` extend the `AccountSimpleImpl` class and implement the tagging interfaces `SavingsAccount` and `CheckingAccount` to model savings and checking accounts, respectively. These classes, in listings 12.7 and 12.8, besides providing implementation for the `toString()` method, do not add any special behavior and as such serve as placeholders.

Listing 12.7   SavingsAccountSimpleImpl.java

```
package banking;

public class SavingsAccountSimpleImpl
    extends AccountSimpleImpl implements SavingsAccount {
    public SavingsAccountSimpleImpl(int accountNumber,
                                    Customer customer) {
        super(accountNumber, customer);
    }

    public String toString() {
        return "SavingsAccount(" + getAccountNumber() + ")";
    }
}
```

Listing 12.8   CheckingAccountSimpleImpl.java

```
package banking;

public class CheckingAccountSimpleImpl
    extends AccountSimpleImpl implements CheckingAccount {
    public CheckingAccountSimpleImpl(int accountNumber,
                                     Customer customer) {
        super(accountNumber, customer);
    }
```

```
    public String toString() {
        return "CheckingAccount(" + getAccountNumber() + ")";
    }
}
```

Both the SavingsAccountSimpleImpl and CheckingAccountSimpleImpl classes contain a constructor that simply calls the base class constructor.

Last, the CheckClearanceSystem class in listing 12.9 represents a check clearance system that is similar to other banking transaction systems, such as the ATM or teller systems. Its methods—debit() and credit()—simply delegate the operation to the account object supplied.

Listing 12.9   A class implementing the check clearance system

```
package banking;

public class CheckClearanceSystem {
    public static void debit(Account account, float amount)
        throws InsufficientBalanceException {
        account.debit(amount);
    }

    public static void credit(Account account, float amount) {
        account.credit(amount);
    }
}
```

We now have a simple banking system and are ready to demonstrate the implementation of rules using aspects.

12.5.2 *Implementing the first business rule*

The first rule we consider is a rather simple minimum balance rule. In natural language the rule reads:

> Do not allow the minimum balance to fall below a preset amount for savings accounts.

The aspect we will develop needs to implement this rule by advising the debit() method of SavingsAccount to check whether the transaction would reduce the balance so that it would be below the minimum balance; if it would, the advice needs to throw an exception.

Before we develop the concrete aspects, let's write an abstract aspect—Abstract-DebitRulesAspect—to allow the sharing of code, as shown in listing 12.10.

Listing 12.10   AbstractDebitRulesAspect.java: the base aspect

```
package rule.common;

import banking.*;

public abstract aspect AbstractDebitRulesAspect {          ❶ Introducing
    public float Account.getAvailableBalance() {              getAvailable-
        return getBalance();                                  Balance() in the
    }                                                         Account class

    public pointcut debitExecution(Account account,
                                   float withdrawalAmount)  ❷
        : execution(void Account.debit(float)                Capturing
                throws InsufficientBalanceException)          debit
        && this(account) && args(withdrawalAmount);          transactions
}
```

The abstract aspect AbstractDebitRulesAspect serves as the base aspect for all aspects that implement the business rules concerned with debit transactions. In a normal development cycle, you would create this aspect as a result of refactoring.

❶ Because we will be dealing with debit logic, we need to get the available balance for an account. The available balance may be different from the actual balance for certain kinds of accounts. The aspect introduces the getAvailableBalance() method in the Account interface that provides the default implementation for making the available balance the same as the actual balance. The concrete aspects introduce methods in appropriate subclasses to make the two balances different.

❷ The debitExecution() pointcut captures the execution of the debit() method in the Account interface. It collects the account object and the withdrawal amount as the context.

Now that we have our base aspect, let's extend it in a concrete aspect—Minimum-BalanceRuleAspect (listing 12.11)—that will implement the first business rule.

Listing 12.11   An aspect that implements the rule for enforcing a minimum balance

```
package rule.java;

import rule.common.*;
import banking.*;

public aspect MinimumBalanceRuleAspect
    extends AbstractDebitRulesAspect {
```

```
private static final float MINIMUM_BALANCE_REQD = 25;

public float SavingsAccount.getAvailableBalance() {
    return getBalance() - MINIMUM_BALANCE_REQD;
}

pointcut savingsDebitExecution(Account account,
                               float withdrawalAmount)
    : debitExecution(account, withdrawalAmount)
    && this(SavingsAccount);

before(Account account, float withdrawalAmount)
    throws InsufficientBalanceException
    : savingsDebitExecution(account, withdrawalAmount) {
    if (account.getAvailableBalance() < withdrawalAmount) {
        throw new InsufficientBalanceException(
            "Minimum balance condition not met");
    }
}
}
```

We introduce the getAvailableBalance() method in SavingsAccount, overriding the method introduced into the Account interface by the base aspect. This method reduces the available balance by MINIMUM_BALANCE_REQD. The savings-DebitExecution() pointcut captures the execution of debit transactions in the SavingsAccount interface. It uses the debitExecution() pointcut defined in the base aspect and restricts it with the this(SavingsAccount) pointcut. This restriction causes the pointcut to match only SavingsAccount transactions. The before advice to savingsDebitExecution() throws an InsufficientBalanceException exception if the *available* balance is less than the requested withdrawal amount.

12.5.3 *Implementing the second business rule*

The second business rule we consider is overdraft protection. In natural language the new rule reads:

> If a check could not be cleared and if there is a sufficient balance in an overdraft account, clear the check by transferring the required amount from that overdraft account to the checking account.

Note that the rule specifies that the application of the overdraft protection rule is only for transactions initiated by the check clearance system. Transactions initiated in other ways should not be affected by this rule. For example, if a customer attempts to withdraw an amount from an ATM that exceeds the balance, it will not trigger overdraft protection; instead, the ATM displays the message that the balance is not sufficient.

The aspect in listing 12.12 implements the overdraft protection rule by capturing the debit transaction on the checking account that was initiated by the check clearance system. The aspect captures the check clearance join point and performs the overdraft protection logic if the balance in the checking account is not sufficient.

Listing 12.12 An aspect that implements the overdraft protection rule

```java
package rule.java;

import java.util.*;

import banking.*;
import rule.common.*;

public aspect OverdraftProtectionRuleAspect
    extends AbstractDebitRulesAspect {

    pointcut checkClearanceTransaction()
        : execution(* CheckClearanceSystem.*(..));

    pointcut checkingDebitExecution(Account account,
                                    float withdrawalAmount)
        : debitExecution(account, withdrawalAmount)
        && this(CheckingAccount);

    before(Account account, float withdrawalAmount)
        throws InsufficientBalanceException
        : checkingDebitExecution(account, withdrawalAmount)
        && cflow(checkClearanceTransaction()) {
        if (account.getAvailableBalance() < withdrawalAmount) {
            performOverdraftProtection(account, withdrawalAmount);
        }
    }

    private void performOverdraftProtection(Account account,
                                            float withdrawalAmount)
        throws InsufficientBalanceException {
        float transferAmountNeeded
            = withdrawalAmount - account.getAvailableBalance();
        Customer customer = account.getCustomer();
        Collection overdraftAccounts
            = customer.getOverdraftAccounts();
        for (Iterator iter = overdraftAccounts.iterator();
```

❶ Pointcut for check clearance system transactions

❷ Pointcut for debit transaction in the checking account

❸ Overdraft protection advice

❹

```
        iter.hasNext();) {
    Account overdraftAccount = (Account)iter.next();
    if (overdraftAccount == account) {
        continue;
    }
    if (transferAmountNeeded <
        overdraftAccount.getAvailableBalance()) {
        overdraftAccount.debit(transferAmountNeeded);
        account.credit(transferAmountNeeded);
        return;
    }
}
throw new InsufficientBalanceException(
    "Insufficient funds in overdraft accounts");
    }
}
```

Overdraft protection logic ❹

Let's examine the implementation in more detail:

❶ The `checkClearanceTransaction()` pointcut captures the call to any method in the `CheckClearanceSystem` class. This pointcut excludes calls that are made to the account transaction from other systems, such as an ATM system.

❷ The `checkingDebitExecution()` pointcut restricts the `debitExecution()` pointcut to checking accounts only.

❸ The `before()` advice uses the `cflow()` pointcut to advise all `debitExecution()` methods that occurred in the control flow of the `checkClearanceTransaction()` pointcut. (This use of `cflow()` is modeled after the wormhole pattern that we studied in chapter 8.) This results in the advice being applied only to `debit()` methods executed during a check clearance process, thus ignoring transactions initiated from other systems. If the available balance is less than that withdrawal amount, the advice performs the overdraft protection logic by calling the `perform-OverdraftProtection()` method.

❹ The `performOverdraftProtection()` method performs the core logic of overdraft protection. If the account balance is not enough to cover the amount of the check, the method checks to see if one of the overdraft accounts has enough to cover it. If such an account is found, the advice transfers the required amount to the checking account. If no overdraft account has sufficient funds, we throw an `InsufficientBalanceException`. For simplicity, our overdraft protection does not consider partial withdrawals from multiple accounts to fulfill a request.

In a non-AOP solution, implementing the logic so that it checks for debit actions performed through the check clearance system is quite a task. There are multiple ways to achieve the goal, each with its own set of issues. One way would be to use additional APIs, such as `debit(float amount, boolean isCheckClearance-Transaction)`. The last parameter in the method call would indicate whether the caller of the method was the check clearance system.

NOTE   You could also detect the caller of the debit operation from the call stack. However, using the call stack in this way is unreliable due to compiler and VM optimizations, as we discussed in the context of logging in chapter 5, section 5.1.2.

We now have aspects that encode the evaluation of both banking rules without using a rule engine. If we need to modify the rules, we simply update these aspects. When we implement new business rules, we can just add additional aspects that extend the abstract aspect.

12.5.4 *Writing a test program*

Next, let's write a simple program that tests our solution (listing 12.13). Later in the chapter we will compile this program with and without the aspects and see how the behavior of the system changes.

Listing 12.13   The test program

```java
package banking;

import java.io.*;

public class Test {
    public static void main(String[] args) throws Exception {
        Customer customer1 = new Customer("Customer1");

        Account savingsAccount
            = new SavingsAccountSimpleImpl(1, customer1);
        Account checkingAccount
            = new CheckingAccountSimpleImpl(2, customer1);

        customer1.addAccount(savingsAccount);
        customer1.addAccount(checkingAccount);
        customer1.addOverdraftAccount(savingsAccount);

        savingsAccount.credit(1000);
        checkingAccount.credit(1000);

        savingsAccount.debit(500);
        savingsAccount.debit(480);
```

Initialization

Initial deposits

Savings account transactions

```
        checkingAccount.debit(500);        Checking
        checkingAccount.debit(480);        account
        checkingAccount.debit(100);        transactions

        CheckClearanceSystem.debit(checkingAccount, 400);    Check clearance
        CheckClearanceSystem.debit(checkingAccount, 600);    transactions
    }
}

aspect LogInsufficientBalanceException {
    pointcut methodCall() : call(void *.debit(..))
        && within(Test);

    void around() : methodCall() {              Insufficient
        try {                                   balance
            proceed();                          condition
        } catch(InsufficientBalanceException ex) {  log aspect
            System.out.println(ex);
        }
    }
}
```

The program in listing 12.13 tests each rule at least once. The `LogInsufficient-BalanceException` aspect allows us to write all exception-handling code in one place. Without it, we would have to write a try/catch block for each method that could throw `InsufficientBalanceException` in order to prevent the termination of the whole program when the exception is thrown. The advice in this aspect prints the caught exception. Note that we do not rethrow the caught exceptions and therefore the flow of the execution of the program is modified. In a non-test environment, ignoring the exception is seldom desirable. We use the `within()` pointcut to ensure that the advice applies only to calls originated from the `Test` class. Further, since this aspect only affects the `Test` class, we put the aspect inside Test.java.

Writing a logging aspect

Our logging aspect, shown in listing 12.14, logs every transaction in the account. As in previous chapters, we will indent the logging based on the nested call depth of the method that is being logged by extending the `IndentedLogging` aspect developed in chapter 5.

Listing 12.14 An aspect that logs account activities

```
package banking;

import logging.*;
```

```
public aspect LogAccountActivities extends IndentedLogging {
    declare precedence : LogAccountActivities, *;

    pointcut accountActivity(Account account, float amount)
        : ((execution(void Account.credit(float))
           || execution(void Account.debit(float)))
          && this(account)
          && args(amount))
        || (execution(void CheckClearanceSystem.*(Account, float))
           && args(account, amount));

    protected pointcut loggedOperations()
        : accountActivity(Account, float);

    void around(Account account, float amount)
        : accountActivity(account, amount) {
        try {
            System.out.println("[" +
                thisJoinPointStaticPart.getSignature().toShortString()
                + "] " + account + " " + amount);
            System.out.println("Before: " + account.getBalance());
            proceed(account, amount);
        } finally {
            System.out.println("After: " + account.getBalance());
        }
    }
}
```

The `accountActivity()` pointcut simply captures the `Account` interface's `debit()` and `credit()` methods as well as the `CheckClearanceSystem` class's methods that take `Account` and float arguments. The around advice prints the context information before and after the captured transactions.

Running the program

At this point, let's compile the code without including either a minimum balance or an overdraft protection aspect. We will, however, include the logging aspect so that we can understand the steps of the transaction. When we run the test program, we get this output:

```
> ajc banking\*.java logging\*.java
> java banking.Test
[AccountSimpleImpl.credit(..)] SavingsAccount(1) 1000.0
Before: 0.0
After: 1000.0
[AccountSimpleImpl.credit(..)] CheckingAccount(2) 1000.0
Before: 0.0
After: 1000.0
```

❶ Depositing into accounts

```
[AccountSimpleImpl.debit(..)] SavingsAccount(1) 500.0
Before: 1000.0
After: 500.0
[AccountSimpleImpl.debit(..)] SavingsAccount(1) 480.0
Before: 500.0
After: 20.0
[AccountSimpleImpl.debit(..)] CheckingAccount(2) 500.0
Before: 1000.0
After: 500.0
[AccountSimpleImpl.debit(..)] CheckingAccount(2) 480.0
Before: 500.0
After: 20.0
[AccountSimpleImpl.debit(..)] CheckingAccount(2) 100.0
Before: 20.0
After: 20.0
banking.InsufficientBalanceException: Total balance not sufficient
[CheckClearanceSystem.debit(..)] CheckingAccount(2) 400.0
Before: 20.0
    [AccountSimpleImpl.debit(..)] CheckingAccount(2) 400.0
    Before: 20.0
    After: 20.0
After: 20.0
banking.InsufficientBalanceException: Total balance not sufficient
[CheckClearanceSystem.debit(..)] CheckingAccount(2) 600.0
Before: 20.0
    [AccountSimpleImpl.debit(..)] CheckingAccount(2) 600.0
    Before: 20.0
    After: 20.0
After: 20.0
banking.InsufficientBalanceException: Total balance not sufficient
```

❷ Debiting from the savings account

❸ Debiting from the checking account directly

❹ Debiting from the checking account through the check clearance system

We see from the output that neither a minimum balance nor the overdraft protection rule is applied.

❶ $1000 is deposited to each account. Because both accounts started with a zero balance, they now each have $1000.

❷ The savings account is debited $500. This transaction is successful because the savings account has a $1000 balance. Now with $500 in the account, a debit request in the amount of $480 is made. This transaction also completes, leaving the savings account with a $20 balance.

❸ The request to debit $500 from the checking account is followed by a request to debit $480. Both transactions are successful because the account had $1000 initially. Now with a $20 balance in the checking account, a debit request in the amount of $100 is made. The withdrawal amount is less than the available balance, so we see that the transaction has thrown an InsufficientBalanceException.

❹ The check clearance system debits $400, followed by $600. Because the checking account had only $20 to begin with, both these operations result in throwing an InsufficientBalanceException.

Let's compile the banking classes with the aspects containing the business rules. We now expect both the minimum balance and overdraft protection rules to be applied:

```
> ajc banking\*.java logging\*.java rule\common\*.java rule\java\*.java
> java banking.Test
[AccountSimpleImpl.credit(..)] SavingsAccount(1) 1000.0
Before: 0.0                                                    ❶ Depositing
After: 1000.0                                                     into
[AccountSimpleImpl.credit(..)] CheckingAccount(2) 1000.0         accounts
Before: 0.0
After: 1000.0
[AccountSimpleImpl.debit(..)] SavingsAccount(1) 500.0
Before: 1000.0                                               Exercising the ❷
After: 500.0                                                 minimum
[AccountSimpleImpl.debit(..)] SavingsAccount(1) 480.0        balance rule
Before: 500.0                                                for the savings
After: 500.0                                                 account
banking.InsufficientBalanceException: Minimum balance condition not met
[AccountSimpleImpl.debit(..)] CheckingAccount(2) 500.0           Exercising
Before: 1000.0                                                ❸ the minimum
After: 500.0                                                    balance rule
[AccountSimpleImpl.debit(..)] CheckingAccount(2) 480.0          for the
Before: 500.0                                                   checking
After: 20.0                                                     account
[AccountSimpleImpl.debit(..)] CheckingAccount(2) 100.0
Before: 20.0
After: 20.0
banking.InsufficientBalanceException: Total balance not sufficient
[CheckClearanceSystem.debit(..)] CheckingAccount(2) 400.0
Before: 20.0
    [AccountSimpleImpl.debit(..)] CheckingAccount(2) 400.0
    Before: 20.0
        [AccountSimpleImpl.debit(..)] SavingsAccount(1) 380.0
        Before: 500.0
        After: 120.0
        [AccountSimpleImpl.credit(..)] CheckingAccount(2) 380.0
        Before: 20.0
        After: 400.0                                              ❹
    After: 0.0
After: 0.0                                                    Exercising
[CheckClearanceSystem.debit(..)] CheckingAccount(2) 600.0    the overdraft
Before: 0.0                                                  protection
    [AccountSimpleImpl.debit(..)] CheckingAccount(2) 600.0   rule
    Before: 0.0
    After: 0.0
After: 0.0
banking.InsufficientBalanceException: ➡
    Insufficient funds in overdraft accounts
```

❶ Each account receives a deposit of $1000.

❷ This block illustrates the effect of the minimum balance rule, which ensures that the savings accounts balance does not fall below $25. After a request to debit $500, the account has a $500 balance. The subsequent request to debit $480 would leave a balance of $20, which is less than the minimum balance requirement. We see that the rule that rejects the second debit request is applied.

❸ This block shows that the minimum balance requirement does not apply to the checking accounts. Therefore, the request to debit $480 that will result in leaving a $20 balance is fulfilled successfully.

❹ This block shows that the overdraft protection is not applied unless the debit request is made through the check clearance system. We see that debiting $100 from the checking account (which has a $20 balance) results in throwing an `InsufficientBalanceException`. With the checking account having a $20 balance and the savings account having $500, the check clearance system requests a $400 debit. We now see that the overdraft protection logic is performed. First, $380 is transferred from the savings account (which was designated to be the overdraft account). This leaves the checking account with $400—just enough to fulfill the debit requests. In the end, the checking account is left with a zero balance. We now observe another request to debit $600 coming in. The overdraft protection logic is applied; however, because the savings account also does not have enough money, it throws an exception.

Now we have a simple way to implement business rules for our banking system without touching any of the core classes. In the next section, we implement the same rules using a rule engine and aspects.

12.6 *Implementing business rules with a rule engine*

For complex business rules, a rule engine is often used to handle rule evaluation. Using a rule engine separates the rule evaluation concern from the core business logic. However, all core modules that need business rule support still have to embed code to populate the engine with business objects and invoke the rule evaluation. In this section, we examine a solution that allows the core modules to be completely oblivious to the business rule implementation; they no longer have to embed any business rule code. This creates an isolation layer between the rule engine and the business logic, allowing independent evolution of the two.

At a high level, the rule engine–based solution is similar to our earlier solution in section 12.5, except that here we employ a rule engine to carry out the rule evaluation.

12.6.1 *An overview of the rule engine*

Rule engines consist of two parts:

- A mechanism for expressing the rules and facts
- A fast implementation for evaluating the rules and taking appropriate action

Many of the rule engines are implementations of a well-known Rete algorithm.[1] Others use a backward-reasoning algorithm. Using these algorithms, the engines can evaluate the rules several times faster than the procedural evaluation of equivalent if-then statements.

Rules relate the facts pertaining to the current situation to corresponding actions. The set of facts is also called a *knowledge base,* or *working memory.* When it is run, the engine evaluates the rules based on the facts, and then triggers the actions associated with the rules that evaluate to `true`.

The languages that the engines use to express the rules and facts vary widely from LISP-like syntax to pseudo-English. They all, however, express the if-then rules in some engine-specific way. New languages on the horizon, such as RuleML, offer the possibility of a standard way to express rules independently of the rule engine.

Many rule engines are available, ranging from commercial offerings to free or open source projects. A few of them are implemented in Java. With these engines, Java objects are loaded into an engine's working memory as facts, and the engine can create facts based on those objects as well as invoke actions expressed in Java on those objects.

12.6.2 *Using a rule engine*

Implementing business rules using a rule engine involves the following steps:

1 *Expressing the rules*—Usually this step involves writing a separate file with rules written in a language understood by the engine. Some engines may also support programmatic construction of the rules.

2 *Expressing the facts*—These facts pertain to the state of the business objects under consideration. For example, in a banking application, facts would include accounts in a current transaction and the withdrawal amount.

3 *Evaluating the rules*—Once the engine is loaded with rules and facts, firing the engine causes the actual evaluation, which ultimately triggers the

---

[1] See http://herzberg.ca.sandia.gov/jess/docs/61/rete.html for a simple explanation of the Rete algorithm.

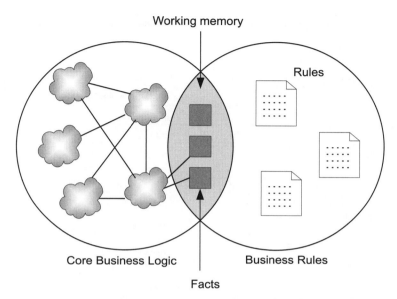

Figure 12.2 The rule engine collaborates with the core business logic through a shared knowledge base known as working memory. Business objects pertaining to current facts are put into the rule engine's working memory before the engine evaluates the rules.

actions associated with the rules that evaluated to true. During this evaluation process, the engine may ascertain other derived facts based on these basic facts and the rules, which help the engine decide what actions to take. For instance, when examining an account, the engine may determine that it would fall below the minimum balance if the requested amount of money were withdrawn; this potential violation of the minimum balance rule may lead to aborting the transaction.

Figure 12.2 shows the collaboration between business objects and the rule engine. While this figure shows the structural view of a system using a rule engine, figure 12.3 shows the behavioral view of these steps in a sequence diagram.

At the beginning of this section, we discussed the three steps involved in using a rule engine. In figure 12.3, the call to `initializeRules()` corresponds to the first step of expressing the rules. This step is needed only once to initialize the rule engine before it can be used. The next two steps are executed each time an operation is called by the core business logic execution. In step 2, expressing the facts, we store the facts into the rule engine's working memory (also referred

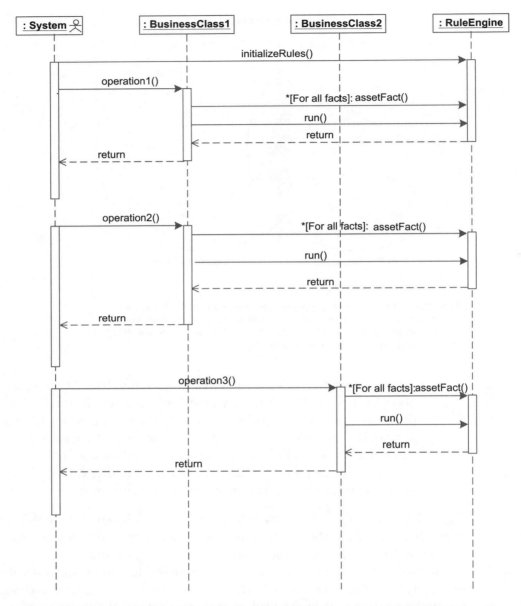

Figure 12.3 **The integration of business logic with business rules in a rule engine using current mechanisms. Whenever an operation is performed that may cause business rules to be fired, the operation must load the engine with the facts and ask it to perform the evaluation.**

to as asserting the facts) by calling the `assertFact()` method on the rule engine. Then we execute step 3, evaluating the rules, by calling the `run()` method on the rule engine.

A conventional implementation of this scheme would require us to add the code for executing steps 2 and 3 to each operation in the business classes that might need to use business rules. Additionally, any change in the business rule requirements, including the use of a different engine, will necessitate changing all the operations in the business classes. In the next section, we see how AspectJ can simplify this process.

12.6.3 *Modularizing with AspectJ*

Although a rule engine can help you separate the rule evaluation concern from the rule invocation, you still need to invoke the rule engine from each module in the system to which business rules may apply. The AspectJ-based solution we propose here separates the concern of invoking the rule engine from the core business logic. With this solution, the core business logic is unaware that the business rules are being applied and that a rule engine is part of the picture.

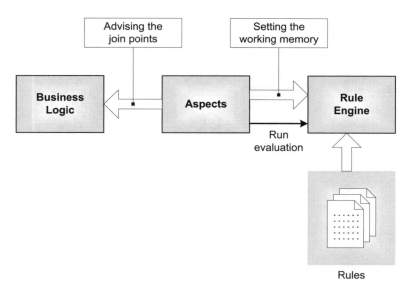

Figure 12.4   The collaboration between business logic, coordinating aspects, and the rule engine. The rule engine is set up with the rules. The aspect advises the important join points in the business logic to initialize the working memory of the rule engine and to request that rules be evaluated. The rule engine executes the actions corresponding to the matching rules.

Let's start by specifying a pointcut that captures all significant methods in the business classes. The advice to this pointcut populates the working memory of the rule engine with the context captured by the pointcut. With this approach, no change is required in the core business logic. Figure 12.4 shows the overall collaboration.

With the structure for AspectJ-based solution shown in figure 12.4, the coordinating aspects isolate the business logic from the rule engine. The aspects advise the join points to put the captured context into the working memory of the rule engine and then run the engine.

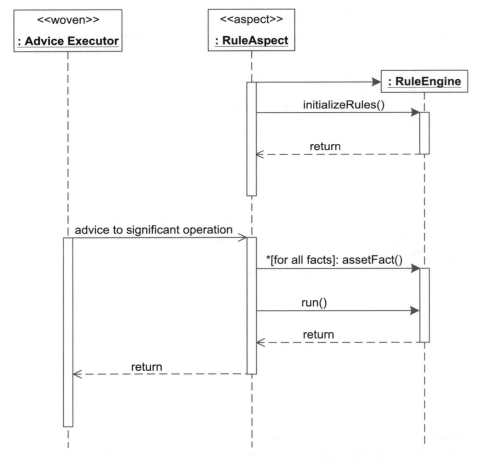

Figure 12.5 The integration of business logic with business rules using AspectJ. Advice Executor is a conceptual object created by the AspectJ compiler through the weaving process that automatically invokes advice associated with all significant operations in all business classes.

Figure 12.5 shows a sequence diagram for AspectJ-based business rule implementation.

With the AspectJ-based solution, you no longer have to embed the calls to the rule engine inside modules implementing business logic. All you need to do is write a rule aspect and embed the logic into its advice. With the rule aspect in the picture, any replacements of the rule engine or changes to its API (such as changing the Jess native API to the JSR 94 API) will impact only the rule aspect. In the next section, we examine an implementation of our banking system that uses a rule engine.

12.7 Example: a banking system with a rule engine

Earlier, we implemented and tested a solution for implementing rules using AspectJ. With that implementation, rules were expressed and evaluated using the Java language, and AspectJ performed the job of integrating the core logic with these business rules. In real life, business rules are complex enough to warrant the use of a specialized rule engine, and since the emphasis of this book is on real-world applications, we'll show you how to use AspectJ with a rule engine. Although in simple applications you could easily embed the rule engine directly into the core logic, on a large system with hundreds of classes, the AspectJ-based approach could be a real lifesaver.

We implement the same business rules that we used in the examples in section 12.5. The behavior of the programs we develop will be identical.

12.7.1 A brief overview of Jess (Java Expert System Shell)

Jess, an expert system shell, is a scripting language and a pure Java implementation of the Rete algorithm from Sandia National Laboratory.[2] With Jess, you can describe facts and rules in a LISP-like language. Each rule—using an if-then like construct—consists of two parts: rule evaluation and action. The rule evaluation part tests certain facts and invokes the corresponding actions if they evaluate to true. While we are using Jess as our rule engine, you should be able to extend the core idea to other expert systems, such as ILOG JRules and Blaze Advisor.

We chose Jess as the expert system to illustrate integrating AspectJ and a rule engine for the following reasons:

---

[2] For more information about Jess, please refer to Ernest Friedman-Hill, *Jess in Action* (Greenwich, CT: Manning Publications, 2003).

- *It's free*—Jess is available free for noncommercial use (you should, of course, check the license for yourself).
- *It's Java-based*—Jess supports easy interaction between the scripting language and Java objects.
- *It supports JSR 94*—Jess is part of the reference implementation for JSR 94, which you are likely to use if you integrate a rule engine with a Java system.

When you invoke Jess from a Java program, it stores Java objects containing the facts into the rule engine's working memory, also known as the knowledge base. It then runs the rule engine, which invokes the Jess script that evaluates the rules and the facts in the objects and acts on them. When a rule is evaluated to true, the rule engine invokes the action associated with that rule. As a part of that action, Jess can interact with other Java objects. It can, for example, set the state of an object, call a method, or throw an exception.

We won't go into more detail since an examination of Jess is beyond the scope of this book. You can access Jess and its documentation from http://herzberg.ca. sandia.gov/jess.

12.7.2 *Specifying rules*

With Jess, you specify the rules in a separate file, using the extension .clp, which means you can make changes in the rules without having to recompile Java or AspectJ source code. We provide only a cursory explanation of the code used to express the rules. In addition, our rule implementation leans toward simplicity rather than the efficiency of rule evaluation. If rule engine–based implementation is an important area for you, consult the Jess manual.

We have broken the business rule script into three listings in order to facilitate our discussion. Listing 12.15 shows the first portion of the script, in which we define the facts associated with the current environment.

Listing 12.15 Defining facts: debitRules.clp

```
(deftemplate account (slot availBalance) (slot type))

(defrule account-existance
    (test (neq (fetch current-account) nil))
    =>
    (bind ?account-object (fetch current-account))
    (bind ?account-avail (call ?account-object getAvailableBalance))
    (if (instanceof ?account-object banking.SavingsAccount) then
        (bind ?account-type savings)
    else (if (instanceof ?account-object banking.CheckingAccount) then
```

```
        (bind ?account-type checking)))
    (assert (account (type ?account-type)
            (availBalance ?account-avail)))
    (assert (transaction-amount (fetch transaction-amount)))
    (assert (isCheckClearance (fetch checkClearanceTransaction)))
)
```

Based on the existence of a nonnull account, we define a few derived facts—the account type, the available balance in the account, and the transaction amount. Note that each `bind` statement assigns a value to a variable and each `assert` statement defines a fact.

Next, based on the facts, we define the minimum balance rule (listing 12.16).

Listing 12.16   Defining the minimum balance rule: debitRules.clp (continued)

```
(defrule minimum-balance
    (account (availBalance ?account-avail) (type savings))
    (transaction-amount ?amount)
    (test (< ?account-avail ?amount))
    =>
    (throw (new banking.InsufficientBalanceException
        "Minimum balance condition not met"))
)
```

If the rule is fired, it throws an `InsufficientBalanceException` exception. This script ensures that the minimum balance rule applies only to savings accounts, as required by the rule. Therefore, when the rule encounters a checking account, the rule won't evaluate to true.

Last, we implement the overdraft protection rule (listing 12.17).

Listing 12.17   Defining the overdraft protection rule: debitRules.clp (continued)

```
(defrule overdraft-protection
    (account (availBalance ?account-avail) (type checking))
    (transaction-amount ?amount)
    (isCheckClearance TRUE)
    (test (< ?account-avail ?amount))
    =>
    (bind ?account-object (fetch current-account))
    (bind ?customer (call ?account-object getCustomer))
    (bind $?overdraft-accounts
        (call (call ?customer getOverdraftAccounts) toArray))
    (bind ?transfer-amount (- ?amount ?account-avail))
    (foreach ?overdraft-account $?overdraft-accounts
```

```
        (bind ?overdraft-avail
        (call ?overdraft-account getAvailableBalance))
        (if (< ?transfer-amount ?overdraft-avail) then
            (call ?overdraft-account debit ?transfer-amount)
            (call ?account-object credit ?transfer-amount)
            (return)
        )
    )
    (throw (new banking.InsufficientBalanceException
        "Insufficient funds in overdraft accounts"))
)
```

If a rule is fired, it will check to see if one of the overdraft accounts has a sufficient balance and will transfer the required amount from it. If no such account is found, it throws an `InsufficientBalanceException` exception. Similar to the minimum balance rule that applied only to savings accounts (listing 12.16), the overdraft protection rule applies only to checking accounts.

The debitRules.clp script encapsulates both the rules required by our banking system. The evaluation of rules depends on three facts: the `account` object, the debit amount, and a `boolean` indicating whether the operation was called from the check clearance system. In the next section, we develop an aspect that initializes a rule engine with rules in this script, stores the required facts, and invokes the rule engine.

12.7.3 *Understanding the rule invocation aspect*

We now need to integrate the core banking system with the rule engine using an aspect. Let's capture all the relevant join points and advise them to first store the associated Java objects in the rule engine and then run the engine. Unlike the implementation that uses Java alone (section 12.5), we do not have to restrict the join points based on account type and whether the operation was called from the check clearance system; the rule script embeds this knowledge. For example, we don't have to (and for best practices, should not) restrict the join points to check for a minimum balance only in the savings accounts. This way, the rule script does more work and has more flexibility to modify the rules. For instance, if we change the implementation to require a minimum balance on a checking account in the future, we will need to modify only the rules file and not the aspect.

Listing 12.18 shows the aspect that uses Jess to implement business rules for our banking system.

Listing 12.18 An aspect implementing rules using the Jess rule engine

```
package rule.jess;

import jess.*;

import banking.*;
import rule.common.*;

public aspect RuleEngineBasedDebitRulesAspect
    extends AbstractDebitRulesAspect {
    private static final float MINIMUM_BALANCE_REQD = 25;

    Rete _debitRete = new Rete();

    public RuleEngineBasedDebitRulesAspect() {
        try {
            _debitRete.executeCommand(
                        "(batch rule/jess/debitRules.clp)");
        } catch (JessException ex) {
            System.err.println(ex);
        }
    }

    public float SavingsAccount.getAvailableBalance() {
        return getBalance() - MINIMUM_BALANCE_REQD;
    }

    before(Account account, float withdrawalAmount)
        throws InsufficientBalanceException
        : debitExecution(account, withdrawalAmount) {
        invokeRules(account, withdrawalAmount, false);
    }

    pointcut checkClearanceTransaction()
        : execution(* CheckClearanceSystem.*(..));

    pointcut checkClearanceDebitExecution(Account account,
                                          float withdrawalAmount)
        : debitExecution(account, withdrawalAmount)
        && cflow(checkClearanceTransaction());

    before(Account account, float withdrawalAmount)
        throws InsufficientBalanceException
        : checkClearanceDebitExecution(account, withdrawalAmount) {
        invokeRules(account, withdrawalAmount, true);
    }

    private void invokeRules(Account account,
                             float withdrawalAmount,
                             boolean isCheckClearance)
```

❶ Initializing the engine

❷ Introducing getAvailableBalance()

❸ Advising the debit transaction

❹ Defining the check clearance transaction pointcut

Defining the check clearance transaction advice ❺

❻

```
throws InsufficientBalanceException {
try {
    _debitRete.store("checkClearanceTransaction",
                     new Value(isCheckClearance));
    _debitRete.store("current-account", account);
    _debitRete.store("transaction-amount",
                     new Value(withdrawalAmount,
                               RU.INTEGER));
    _debitRete.reset();
    _debitRete.run();
} catch (JessException ex) {
    Throwable originalException = ex.getNextException();
    if (originalException
        instanceof InsufficientBalanceException) {
        throw
            (InsufficientBalanceException)originalException;
    }
    System.err.println(ex);
}
}
}
}
```

Storing facts and running the engine

6

Let's examine the implementation:

1 We construct the rule engine object by passing the name of the batch file that contains the rules: debitRules.clp. The file is loaded and parsed only once.

2 We introduce getAvailableBalance() into SavingsAccount. It overrides the method in the base Account class to reduce the available balance by MINIMUM_BALANCE_REQD.

3 We advise debit transactions to simply call the invokeRules() method. Notice the last parameter in the call is set to false, indicating that this transaction is not originated by a check clearance system. Unlike the pointcut in MinimumBalance-RuleAspect in listing 12.11, this pointcut is not restricted to the savings account. Such details are left to the script describing the rules.

4 The checkClearanceDebitExecution() pointcut restricts the debitExecution() pointcut to capture only join points that occur in the control flow of a transaction initiated by the check clearance system.

5 The advice to checkClearanceDebitExecution() simply calls invokeRules() but with the last parameter set to true, indicating that this method has been called by a check clearance system.

6 The invokeRules() method is the core method that interacts with the engine. It takes three parameters—the account object, the amount, and a boolean to indicate whether the operation was invoked by the check clearance system—

corresponding to the three facts needed by our rule script. It first uses a series of `store()` methods on the engine object to store pertinent objects as facts in the engine's working memory. It then runs the engine by calling the `reset()` and `run()` methods. It also catches any exceptions thrown by engine operations. In our implementation, some rules throw exceptions in their action part. The Jess engine wraps any such exception in a `JessException` object. This method catches such an exception and checks if the original exception is `InsufficientBalance-Exception` and throws the original exception.

Running the program

To run the program, we simply issue the following commands:

```
> ajc banking\*.java logging\*.java rule\common\*.java rule\jess\*.java
> java banking.Test
```

Since our rule engine–based aspects are implementing the same rule as before, the output of the program is exactly the same as in section 12.5.4.

12.8 Summary

Business rules change constantly to respond to the changing nature of business. To remain competitive in the marketplace, you must have an agile scheme for implementing those rules. Rule engines serve as part of the solution by providing simple interfaces for expressing rules and a specialized engine that evaluates those rules. Rule engines also separate the core business logic from the rule evaluation logic. With a conventional use of a rule engine, code that invokes the rule engine's services is still tangled with the core logic. AspectJ provides the missing puzzle piece by separating the core logic from the invocation of the rule engine's services. The biggest benefit you get is that you maintain the stability of the core modules, while at the same time you are able to respond quickly to changes to the rules requirement. Another benefit is that the core system experts and the rule engine expert can work on their modules independently, thus improving the overall speed and quality of the system's implementation. Further, changes to the underlying rule engine itself do not require any changes to the core logic.

Unlike the aspects in the previous chapters, the business rule aspects are intimately aware of the core business logic. Here, the emphasis is not on reusability of aspects but on modularization of business rules. Despite the dependency of aspects on the core logic, the use of AspectJ still results in a more maintainable system by modularizing the concerns.

By reducing the cost and time to develop and modify the business rules and still maintaining the overall stability of the system, using AspectJ for business rule implementation becomes an attractive proposition. Your business can gain an edge by responding quickly to customer needs.

The next step

13

This chapter concludes the book by showing how to

- Approach new problems with AspectJ
- Apply AspectJ in development phases
- Evangelize AspectJ

As we come to the end of this book, let's consider some issues and practical solutions that will help your organization embrace AspectJ. Applying a new technology to your problems is not an easy task, especially if you haven't seen similar implementations that have been successful. In this chapter, we discuss how you can use an aspect-oriented approach to analyze new problems and design solutions. Each phase in the development cycle offers unique opportunities and challenges for AspectJ's application, and we make recommendations for each phase.

13.1 Applying AspectJ to new problems

Once you have committed to using AspectJ in your organization, you will need to decide whether it is appropriate for each target problem. You must consider an approach that will incorporate AspectJ while causing minimal destabilization of the overall system. Typically, you would want to apply AOP solutions to a restricted subsystem and then, once the solutions are proven, expand the use of AspectJ to the whole system. In this section, we examine the two phases of applying AspectJ to a problem: deciding to use it and then actually using it.

13.1.1 Talking the talk

How do you decide whether a concern is better addressed by AOP than the current method? In other words, how do you know if a concern is crosscutting? You can use the following as a guide:

- *Will the non-AOP alternative cause code scattering?* Code scattering is usually a sure sign of a crosscutting concern. If you have to copy and paste nearly identical code in multiple places or insert complementary blocks of code for a concern in several modules, AspectJ is a good choice. It will immediately yield a cleaner design and substantial code savings.

- *Will the non-AOP alternative cause code tangling?* Code tangling generally accompanies code scattering, but you might see code tangling by itself. For example, you may have just one database module that deals with the creation and release of database connections, but the module itself may contain resource pooling code tangled with the implementation of the persistence core concern. Using AspectJ in this case separates the two concepts, makes them less difficult to understand, and allows the easy evolution of both. It is much like refactoring code into private methods even when you know there is only one caller. (We discuss aspectual refactoring in more detail in section 13.2.2.) Over time, you will find more modules that call for the same separation of crosscutting concerns.

13.1.2 *Walking the walk*

Once you've determined that a certain functionality is a possible crosscutting concern, and you have decided to use AspectJ to implement it, you can use the following approach:

1 *Study the conventional solution first*—In this step, you sketch out, design, and even prototype the conventional solution. We followed this route in most chapters in parts 2 and 3. First, we studied the conventional solution and focused on repeated patterns of code. While illustrating the conventional solution helped you appreciate the AspectJ solution that followed, the main purpose was to help you understand the AspectJ design needed for a better solution. The idea is to first sketch the code tangling and code scattering, and then modularize it. Once you become reasonably experienced at this, you may reduce the emphasis on this step or even eliminate it.

2 *Limit the implementation*—By limiting the solution to only modules that currently need the functionality, you eliminate the impact—both positive and negative—on other modules. We discussed this approach in chapter 7 (resource pooling) and chapter 9 (thread safety in Swing applications). The goal is to leave as much of the system unaffected as possible and reduce the testing effort required. To do this, you can either use pointcuts such as `within()` to specify only join points in the modules you want to weave, or you can configure your build system to include only those modules.

3 *Let it loose*—Once you are comfortable with the solution and its impact, you should modify the pointcuts or build configurations that have been limiting the applicability. For example, instead of restricting resource pooling to only certain modules, you lift those restrictions to let it crosscut system wide. This way, if a new module joins the system, it starts benefiting from the aspects right away.

This systematic approach helps you tackle almost any problem with little risk. Experience will be your best guide in determining how much weight you should assign each step for your system.

13.2 *Employing AspectJ in development phases*

Each phase of a software project—design, implementation, testing, and maintenance—emphasizes certain activities. AOP methodology and the AspectJ language, therefore, play a different role in each of the phases. Further, if you are applying AspectJ-based implementation of crosscutting concerns in a legacy system, you will need to deal with issues that are specific to that system. Let's look at some typical ways AspectJ helps in each of these situations.

13.2.1 AspectJ in the design phase

If you consider AOP/AspectJ in the design phase, you will reap the maximum benefits the technology has to offer. From an architectural perspective, the main benefit AspectJ offers is that it helps you overcome the architect's dilemma discussed in chapter 1. Deferring the design and implementation of crosscutting concerns reduces the design cost, while AOP ensures a smooth integration of those concerns later.

Here is a typical way to use AOP/AspectJ in your design phase:

1 *Recognize crosscutting concerns*—This step is part of mapping requirements to modules. As a rule of thumb, consider concerns described with an adjective or adverb starting with "every," such as "every time" or "everywhere," as possible crosscutting concerns. Recognizing these concerns ahead of time lets you avoid the effort needed to modularize crosscutting concerns in the conventional fashion. Leaving such considerations to aspects results in improved design.

2 *Design core concerns first*—Apply standard conventional design techniques to the core concerns. The better you do this job, the easier it will be to apply crosscutting concerns, since it will simplify the specification of weaving rules. For the core parts of each concern, define interfaces with clear roles. A good interface helps clients access the functionality; an aspect module is simply one such client. For example, while the logging concern is crosscutting, a clean logging interface will make for better logging aspects.

3 *Design crosscutting concerns*—Address the prominent and immediate crosscutting concerns. It is also a good idea to sketch out the crosscutting concerns that you are aware of but do not need immediately. This approach helps you avoid overdesign, and since you will use AspectJ to implement the crosscutting concerns, deferring the decision will not lead to huge code changes.

13.2.2 AspectJ in the implementation phase

When you use AspectJ in the implementation phase, you should place additional emphasis on certain existing common practices, as well as follow a few new guidelines in order to make the process of implementing the core and crosscutting concerns as easy as possible. There are also several aspectual refactoring techniques that you can use.

Implementing core concerns

The decision to use AspectJ affects how you will implement the core concerns. Fortunately, if you are using AOP, much of the process and methodology is largely unchanged from OOP. Attention to a few practices, however, will make your job easier. You should follow these common principles regardless of whether you use AOP/AspectJ:

- *Write well-factored code*—Ideally, each operation implements a specific core functionality. Since in AspectJ most pointcut definitions specify join points for method invocations, methods can be considered as units of crosscutting granularity. Therefore, if each method maps to a specific functionality, you can capture join points at the right level of granularity in your aspects; this allows you to apply AspectJ consistently throughout your project.

- *Use consistent naming conventions*—Sticking to a consistent naming convention throughout your project will help you write pointcuts that use wildcards to capture join points. Using wildcards instead of fully specifying each join point not only makes writing aspects easier, but also ensures that the aspects automatically apply to any new modules that you add to the system later.

In addition to these common "good practices," here are some guidelines that are specific to AspectJ:

- *Separate the crosscutting concerns from the core modules in the initial phase*—When you come across a concern that affects multiple modules, apply the questions in section 13.1.1 to determine whether you should instead use aspects to implement the functionality. Then, if you find it is a crosscutting concern, do not implement it along with the core module; instead, plan to encapsulate it in separate aspects. You may decide to create those aspects immediately or wait until the functionality is really needed.

- *Watch out for any visible tangling and scattering*—Be on the lookout for code tangling and code scattering while implementing the core concerns; consider them a symptom of possible crosscutting concerns being implemented using OOP techniques that may actually be candidates for AOP. Initially, you will be looking for well-known crosscutting concerns, such as logging or resource pooling. Later on, with experience, you will be able to spot more subtle crosscutting concerns and modularize them.

Implementing crosscutting concerns

When you implement crosscutting concerns, you need to perform the following tasks. It is typical to iterate over them during the implementation phase:

- *Identify the join points*—In this step you identify the places in the code that need the crosscutting behavior. Then you need to decide the best way to express the pointcuts that capture the required join points: wildcard-based pointcuts, name-based pointcuts, control flow–based pointcuts, and so on.

- *Choose underlying technology*—To implement a crosscutting concern you often have to decide what the underlying implementation will be. For example, for a business rule concern, you have to choose whether to use the rule engine or the rule API used by the aspects. Your choice will be largely influenced by the overall system architecture and specific project requirements.

- *Design the aspects*—In this step you design the aspects themselves. You may want to consider using one or more of the patterns presented in chapter 8 (as well as any new patterns that you might have discovered) as a template. Pay particular attention to using consistent naming conventions for aspects; that will simplify the process of capturing join points inside the aspects. It will also help you when you want to specify aspect precedence. Finally, you also need to decide whether you can create reusable aspects so that you can leverage them the next time you deal with the same crosscutting concern.

Another issue to consider is how you can organize the aspects so that your build configurations are flexible and easy to work with. To use aspects in a plug-and-play manner, you need to separate them according to the functionality they implement (typically by adding them to separate packages). A proper separation of aspects will help you to more easily configure the build system to include or exclude certain aspects in your builds. In order to do this, pay attention to these two factors:

- *Deployment*—Certain aspects are most useful during the development phase, such as those that perform logging for debug/profiling purposes and policy enforcement. You will probably want to group these developmental aspects in a separate package so that you can easily add and remove them from your builds as you choose. That way, you can take advantage of those aspects during the development phase, while ensuring they don't affect the deployed system.

- *Correctness*—The most fundamental characteristic of any software system is its correctness—the other characteristics, such as efficiency, are secondary. For example, transaction management support is fundamental to the correctness of the system, whereas efficiency gained by resource pooling is not. Although you may choose to remove some aspects that you used in development from your deployed build system, you must ensure that the aspects that are necessary for correctness are always included in any build target.

Implementing aspectual refactoring

With recent interest in Extreme Programming, refactoring techniques are gaining well-deserved attention. With AspectJ, you get an added dimension when refactoring. Consider a check for a common pre- or post-condition for multiple operations in a class. With conventional refactoring, you would embed the checks in a method and call it from all the places requiring that check instead of repeating a block of code in all the places. With AspectJ, you can go one step further. Instead of calling the method performing the check from multiple places, you write an aspect to crosscut that check into all the required methods.

The differences between refactoring usage and normal usage of AspectJ include the following:

- Refactoring aspects are narrowly scoped to crosscut a class or two as opposed to potentially crosscutting the system.

- Since refactoring aspects are tightly bound to classes that they are refactoring, it is okay for these aspects to depend on implementation details. In fact, this kind of aspect *is* in part an implementation detail of a class.

13.2.3 AspectJ in the testing phase

AspectJ can help with various tasks during the testing phase. Here are a few possible scenarios that you may want to start with:

- *Creating test cases*—Because it can modify behavior without making invasive changes, AspectJ can help you create test programs. Occasionally, you need to access the private state of a class to create gray-box test cases. Using privileged aspects can help you achieve this without changing the class. This is perhaps one of the few legitimate uses of privileged aspects. There are other ways AspectJ can help with this testing task; see the "Resources" section at the end of the book for useful sites to get you started.

- *Implementing performance testing*—Many performance problems are uncovered only during close-to-real deployment. Such an environment is usually not available during development phases. By enabling performance-monitoring aspects during beta testing, you can perform dynamic profiling in a near-real environment. You then have the option to either continue using those aspects in the deployed system or take them out to avoid overhead.

- *Reporting errors*—During the testing phase, when you expect to uncover problems you can use aspects to collect a useful context, and not just exception call stacks. When it is time to ship the product, you can simply take out the context-collecting aspects. With an AspectJ-based approach, you have a flexible way to collect context and maintain better control over the inclusion or exclusion of the collection logic.

13.2.4 *AspectJ in the maintenance phase*

The maintenance phase consists primarily of two activities: adding implementation to satisfy new requirements and fixing bugs found in the deployed systems. AspectJ can handle the following tasks during the maintenance phase:

- *Creating protection walls*—A big challenge during the maintenance phase is making sure that new changes do not break other parts of the system. Policy-enforcement aspects ensure that the new features do not violate the policies, thus preventing the introduction of new bugs.

- *Implementing new features*—Just like during the implementation phase, AspectJ can implement new crosscutting concerns in a noninvasive manner. Using AspectJ helps minimize code changes to the core of the system for these concerns.

13.2.5 *AspectJ in legacy projects*

Legacy projects can be a challenge primarily for two reasons. First, the core code may lack the clean separation of functionality that allows you to use AspectJ's crosscutting constructs. Second, certain crosscutting concerns may already be implemented using conventional techniques. This may mean that you must first remove the concern from the core code and put it into aspects before improving its implementation. Through all these steps, you need to exercise care to avoid altering the core system behavior in an undesirable way. However, there are some ways to ease the process:

1 *Start out with no-commitment aspects*—Begin with simple aspects, such as policy enforcements and logging for debugging. These aspects enable you to introduce new behavior without requiring any modifications to the core modules. This way, you minimize the risk of inadvertently affecting the core system behavior. The application of aspects is limited to development, and you do not need a commitment to use AspectJ in deployment. This no-commitment, no-risk approach helps you use AspectJ almost immediately in almost any system.

2 *Refactor the code*—Any serious use of AspectJ requires that the core code within each module implement relatively clear responsibilities. Ensuring that this is the case and refactoring the code if necessary may require considerable effort. Fortunately, it will help your system regardless of whether you use AspectJ. Policy-enforcement aspects also help during refactoring to protect you against inadvertent violations.

3 *Refactor the crosscutting concern*—While refactoring the core concern, you will see code-tangling and code-scattering symptoms. Work your way through the modularization of a few prominent crosscutting concerns. A test suite will help during this step to ensure continual conformity to core system functionality.

13.3 *A word of warning*

Although AspectJ allows you to do wonders when used correctly, it can hurt you if you are not careful. If you encounter problems, they might be due to one of the following reasons:

- *Incorrect usage*—AOP and AspectJ are not meant to "patch" design and implementation flaws. For example, if someone forgot to initialize a variable before using it, you could advise its field-access join point to initialize it first. However, the right thing to do is modify the core module to initialize that variable! Similarly, do not use the privileged aspect just because you can then access the implementation details of a class.

- *Interaction of multiple aspects*—When multiple crosscutting concerns are implemented using separate aspects, they often affect the same join points in the system. For example, transaction management, authorization, and logging affect the same set of operations in the system. Understanding such interaction and coordinating it using aspect precedence requires you to consider global system requirements. The use of an IDE with AspectJ integration that shows the crosscutting view also helps identify multiple aspects affecting the same join points.

- *Newness of implementation*—AspectJ is a new language and a new implementation. It is remarkably stable, yet you will encounter problems once in a while that may necessitate a certain workaround. This situation, however, will improve with time as more and more people start using AspectJ.

13.4 Evangelizing AspectJ

Once you are convinced of AspectJ's power, the next step is to introduce it to your project or organization. This step may take a while and it requires persistence:

- *Use it for individual productivity*—It is best to avoid trying to convince your team or management of the virtues of AspectJ while you are still new to it. During the time you are learning it, your main purpose should be to improve individual productivity and gain confidence in AspectJ's application. Simple policy-enforcement and logging aspects that improve your productivity in your own development world are great ways to start. Policy enforcement will help you avoid getting into trenches in the first place; logging will help you find your way out if you still manage to get in. Performance profiling and studying the impact of resource pooling may be the next simple applications. With resource pooling, you may use an aspect to find where you need to introduce it, and then you may implement it using a conventional solution.

- *Convince management*—You must have the support and encouragement of management if you want your organization to fully embrace AOP and AspectJ. A good way to convince managers is to illustrate AspectJ's power in a before-and-after style by following these steps:

  1 Demonstrate good code before implementing functionality. Show how simple the code looks before adding a concern.

  2 Demonstrate bad code after implementing functionality without using AspectJ. Show how many lines of code you need to write and how invasive the changes are. Also, present a bug-fixing scenario that will necessitate changes to many modules.

  3 Demonstrate good code after implementing functionality in AspectJ. Show the cleanliness of the core and new functionality, the reduction in the number of lines of code, and the simplicity of fixing bugs.

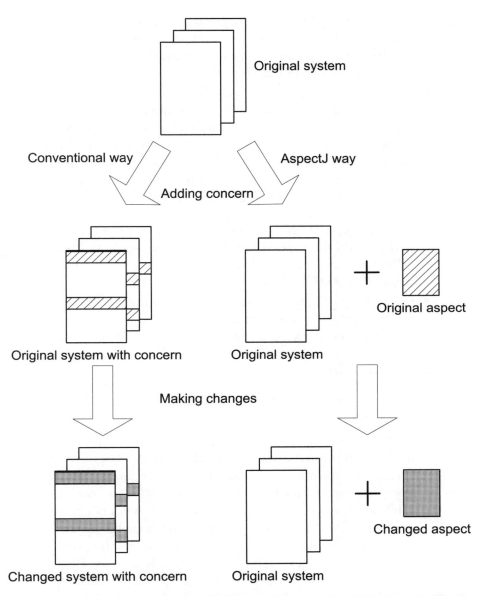

Figure 13.1 Here is a way to convince management and your team of the power of AOP and AspectJ. This figure shows that productivity can be improved during the development phase and that change management is easier after deployment when you use AspectJ.

Figure 13.1 illustrates the good-bad-good approach. The flow on the left side shows how a system changes when implementing a crosscutting concern using conventional techniques, whereas the right side shows how AOP achieves the same goal.

- *Convince your team*—Most software products are developed in a team. Therefore, it helps if all the team members are at least aware of AspectJ and its value. Showing how policy-enforcement aspects catch errors even before testing can be an effective eye-opener. The good-bad-good transformation also helps convince the team members of AspectJ's power.

- *Find a killer application*—You may come across a situation where your application needs to implement functionality, but it is postponed to a later release because it will require changing so many modules. Analyze the situation. If you find that you can use AspectJ to prevent such invasive changes and still add the needed functionality, you should try it out. The high visibility of the solution adds a "wow" factor and is a very effective way to bring in AspectJ for good.

- *Get training*—Grab any training opportunities you can—books, articles, seminars, formal classroom training, bringing in a mentor, and so forth. This book, of course, is meant to serve as one such training opportunity.

13.5 *Parting thoughts*

Here are some additional recommendations as you move forward on your path toward becoming an AOP and AspectJ expert:

- *Start simple*—AspectJ is a new language and has its own nuances that must be understood before you are comfortable with it. So, start simple. In particular, do not worry about reusable aspects in the beginning; adding these features later, even as an afterthought, is usually better than paying an upfront cost. While most aspects in this book are reusable, I did not design them that way in my first attempts. The typical process is to come up with the overall idea and design, implement a simple way that solves the problem at hand, and then see how to generalize it into reusable aspects. Remember your first encounter with OOP? You most likely did not create interfaces, function objects, and delegate objects right away. You probably used it only to encapsulate the implementation at first. The same applies to AOP adoption.

- *Join the community*—Learning from other people's experience can be quite useful. There are a couple of good mailing lists that you should consider joining—visit http://eclipse.org/aspectj and http://aosd.net. If you are having a problem, chances are someone has already faced the problem and perhaps solved it. I will be available on Author Online at http://www.manning.com/laddad to help you with your questions.

- *View AOP/AspectJ as augmenting technology*—Use the underlying conventional classes as much as possible. Throughout the book, we based our solutions on available technologies: logging toolkits for logging, rule engines for business rule implementation, JAAS for authentication and authorization, and so on. These technologies have been used by thousands of developers worldwide for several years, and such heavy usage results in mature solutions. When you use them, you can then use AspectJ to fill in the missing pieces of these technologies.

- *Experiment*—I learned most techniques through experimentation. Start with the examples in this book. Try them outside of real projects. You will get valuable insight into the AOP philosophy and its logistical issues. You will gradually become more comfortable with the new technology; then you can solve the more complex problems.

- *Develop a repertoire of reusable aspects*—When it comes to productivity, nothing beats reusing modules that have already been developed. Many crosscutting concerns apply not only to multiple modules, but also to multiple systems. As you gain more experience, start paying attention to reusable parts and create reusable libraries to benefit various projects. However, keep in mind that you should always start simple.

Aspect-oriented programming helps to bring order to the chaos introduced by crosscutting concerns. When you use it, the design is more clearly mapped to the implementation. However, AOP is not a silver bullet that will solve all your programming problems. Nevertheless, we have to make progress—one step at a time. I expect many more changes over the next decade in programming methodologies and languages in the direction that AOP started. These changes are what I love about this profession—there's always something new, and we're always in search of something newer!

The AspectJ compiler

A

This appendix covers
- Downloading and setting up the AspectJ compiler
- Compiling source files
- Building and using aspect libraries

The most fundamental tool for the AspectJ language is its compiler. For simple uses, the AspectJ compiler behaves like any Java compiler. However, it offers several more choices for enabling crosscutting implementation in AspectJ. In this appendix, we briefly examine the install and setup procedure for AspectJ version 1.1. We also examine compiler options and explain how you can use them to suit your needs.

A.1 Downloading and setting up

In this section, we provide installation instructions and show you how to set up your system to use AspectJ. We assume that you have already installed a compatible version of JDK. Depending on the version you downloaded, the details (such as filenames) may vary slightly:

1. *Download*—Download AspectJ tools, including the compiler, from http://eclipse.org/aspectj/.

2. *Install*—The downloaded JAR file is a self-executing installation file. You can execute it by issuing this command:

   ```
   > java -jar aspectj1.1.jar
   ```

   The installer will present a wizard asking you where you want to install AspectJ and where your current JDK installation is located. Simply follow the instructions. When the installation finishes, it will have extracted the necessary files as well as created batch files and shell scripts to match your environment.

3. *Modify the environment*—The installer outlines this step in the final screen. This step is not strictly necessary, but performing it will make working with the tools easier. It asks you to modify your CLASSPATH environment variable to include aspectjrt.jar. You may include aspectjtools.jar to ease work with Ant scripts. You should also modify your PATH environment variable to include AspectJ's bin directory.[1]

---

[1] If you want to change your environment on a Windows 2000 or Windows XP machine, right-click on My Computer, click Properties, and select the Advanced tab. Then, click the Environment Variables button. From there, you can edit or create system variables such as PATH and CLASSPATH. On UNIX and Linux systems, you may modify the login script file appropriate for your shell.

A.2 *An overview of the compiler*

The AspectJ compiler (ajc) is based on an open-source, industry-strength compiler created as a part of the Eclipse IDE. While it is one of the Eclipse technology projects, the AspectJ compiler is not tied to the Eclipse IDE in other ways—it works just as well with other IDEs, such as the NetBeans and the emacs JDEE, as well as command-line tools.

Given that AspectJ is a superset of Java, the AspectJ compiler is a superset of a Java compiler. Therefore, you can use ajc as a replacement for the Java compiler. The AspectJ compiler can accept input from source files and JAR files containing precompiled sources. The output produced by ajc can be classes or JAR files that are fully compliant with the Java byte-code specification. Therefore, you can use any compliant virtual machine to execute the program produced by ajc.

As you can with a Java compiler, you can pass certain options to ajc. Table A.1 summarizes the important options that are common between ajc and javac.[2]

Table A.1   Compiler options

Option	Arguments	Effect
-classpath	Directories and JAR files	Specifies where to find the user's class files.
-d	The directory	Specifies the output root directory for class files produced by the compiler.
-target	1.1 (the default) or 1.2	Specifies the format for the class files generated.
-source	1.3 or 1.4	Specifies the mode for compiling sources. Specifying 1.4 enables assertion functionality.
-deprecation	None	Warns about the use of deprecated types or members.
-g	[lines,vars,source] (the default) or none	Specifies the level of debugging information generated.

The AspectJ compiler also offers options available from the underlying Eclipse compiler. You can see the options available to ajc's invocation by issuing ajc without any argument. In the remainder of this appendix, we will examine the AspectJ-specific options.

---

[2] Throughout this appendix, we use the term *javac* to denote a Java compiler such as JDK javac, the Jikes compiler, and the Eclipse Java compiler.

A.3 *Compiling source files*

The simplest way to compile source files using ajc is to pass it the list of source files. This option is similar to using a Java compiler (such as javac) to compile Java sources. In this book, we have used this method to compile all our examples:

```
> ajc shopping\*.java tracing\TraceAspect.java
```

Note one important difference between javac and ajc. With javac, you can compile all source files together or each source file individually without any difference in the output. This is not the case with ajc; instead, you must pass all the input files together in one invocation. For example, the following two commands will *not* produce the same result as the earlier command:

```
> ajc shopping\*.java
> ajc tracing\TraceAspect.java
```

In this case, the apparent intention is to weave tracing into the shopping-related classes. However, `TraceAspect.java` is not included while compiling the shopping classes, so no such weaving will occur.

You can execute the classes produced by the compiler using any Java virtual machine. The following command executes the `Test` class compiled using ajc. You should have aspectjrt.jar in your classpath, as we discussed in A.1. If you don't, you will need to pass it explicitly to `java` using the `-classpath` option:

```
> java Test
```

A.4 *Compiling source directories*

You can specify the root directories of the source files you want to compile by passing the list of directories to the `-sourceroots` option. The AspectJ compiler will then compile all the source files under each specified directory and all their subdirectories. The following command will compile all the source files that have F:\aspectj-book\appendixA\sectionA.4\shopping or F:\aspectj-book\appendixA\sectionA.4\tracing as an ancestor directory:

```
> ajc -sourceroots F:\aspectj-book\appendixA\sectionA.4\shopping;
       F:\aspectj-book\appendixA\sectionA.4\tracing
```

The separator character between the multiple source directories specified must match the native path separator. On Windows systems, it is a semicolon (;), whereas on UNIX systems, it is a colon (:).

A.5 *Weaving into JAR files*

AspectJ can weave aspects into previously compiled source files (compiled with either javac or ajc) that are in a JAR. This enables you to apply crosscutting concerns without needing access to the source files. With this option, for example, you can weave aspects into third-party libraries.

The following command weaves the `TraceAspect` into all the class files in shopping.jar. The output of this command is the creation of class files, each with the tracing aspect woven in. The shopping.jar file itself remains unchanged:

```
> ajc -injars shopping.jar tracing\TraceAspect.java
```

You can use the `-outjar` option to create a JAR file instead of individual class files:

```
> ajc -injars shopping.jar tracing\TraceAspect.java
    -outjar tracedShopping.jar
```

The resulting tracedShopping.jar file will contain all the class files with the `Trace-Aspect` woven into them.

You may also use the `-sourceroots` option to specify the directories containing source files that you want to compile with the JAR files specified in `-injars`. If the directories specified in `-sourceroots` contain aspects, then those aspects will be woven into the JAR files. The following command compiles shopping.jar along with the sources in the tracing directory, weaving in any aspect from it:

```
> ajc -injars shopping.jar -sourceroots tracing
```

You may use the `-outjar` option in the previous command to produce a JAR file:

```
> ajc -injars shopping.jar -sourceroots tracing
    -outjar tracedShopping.jar
```

The input JAR files contain the class files that have been compiled with either javac or ajc. If the corresponding source files are pure Java, then you may simply use javac to compile those files. The possibility of using javac in the initial build simplifies the process of integrating AspectJ into an existing system. You can leave your build process unchanged until after you create the JAR files for pure Java source files, and then you can include an additional build step to weave the needed aspects into the JAR files. Figure A.1 depicts this process.

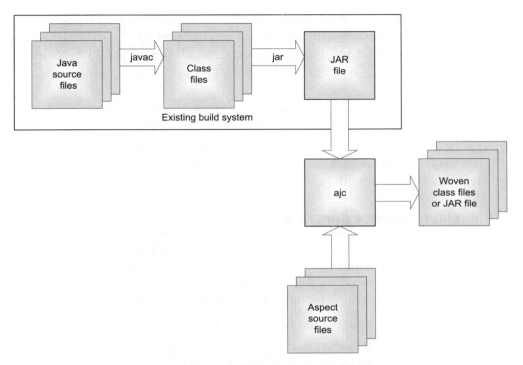

Figure A.1 Augmenting the existing build system to weave in the aspects

A.6 *Creating aspect libraries*

The AspectJ compiler allows you to create an aspect library in the form of a JAR file. This functionality is especially important if you have to provide reusable aspects for internal or external use without giving the source code. You can now distribute JAR files that contain the aspects as well as any supporting interfaces and classes. The following command creates an aspect library named tracing.jar by compiling all the sources under F:\aspectj-book\appendixA\sectionA.6\tracing:

```
> ajc -sourceroots F:\aspectj-book\appendixA\sectionA.6\tracing
    -outjar tracing.jar
```

AspectJ requires that an aspect can only weave an interface, class, or another aspect once. This means that the classes and aspects in the library JAR file must not have previously been woven during the creation of the library. If they have, when you try to build the final system incorporating the library, you will get compiler errors. You need to consider this issue only if some of the aspects are concrete aspects (only concrete aspects are woven). In other cases, you can use the -XnoWeave option to compile the sources but prevent the weaving. The following command specifies that the aspects and classes of the library should not be woven during the creation of the library:

```
> ajc -XnoWeave
    ➥ -sourceroots F:\aspectj-book\appendixA\sectionA.6\tracing
    ➥ -outjar tracing.jar
```

It is always safe to use the -XnoWeave option when you're creating an aspect library. By specifying no weaving during library creation, you postpone weaving until the final build.

A.7 *Using aspect libraries*

To use an aspect library, you specify the library JAR file using the -aspectpath option. The compiler then searches for all the aspects in each specified JAR file and weaves them into the specified code. The following command weaves the aspects that are inside tracing.jar into all the source files inside the shopping directory:

```
> ajc shopping\*.java -aspectpath tracing.jar
```

Since this command does not specify tracing.jar as one of the input files, no weaving will occur for the interfaces, classes, and aspects in tracing.jar. If the constituents of the library itself need to be woven, possibly by other aspects, you must specify the aspect library itself as input by using the -injars option. If a library contains support classes, specifying the library JAR file as an input will cause AspectJ to weave all the aspects specified in -aspectpath to those classes as well:

```
> ajc shopping\*.java -injars tracing.jar -aspectpath tracing.jar
```

This command will weave the aspects inside the tracing.jar file into all of the class files in the tracing.jar file and all the source files in the shopping directory. Figure A.2 shows how an aspect library is created and used.

A.8 *Utilizing incremental compilation mode*

Compiling all the files in a large project takes a lot of time. Because ajc needs to perform additional work compared to a pure Java compiler, it will take even longer. With plain Java, for most kinds of modification all you have to do is compile the modified source files. With AspectJ, however, you must recompile the whole system, which increases compilation time. The time it takes to recompile

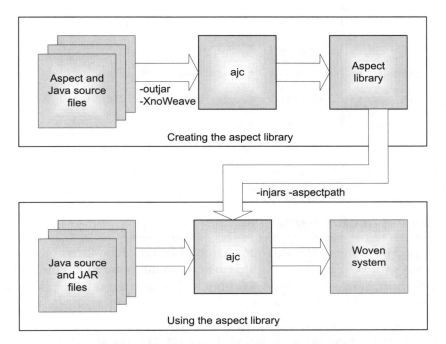

Figure A.2   The creation of an aspect library involves the use of the –outjar and –XnoWeave options. When you use the library, you need the –aspectpath and –injars options. The output of the system could be multiple class files or a JAR file, depending on how you use the –outjar option.

the source code can be an important issue during the development phase, when it is common to make a few modifications at a time and observe their effect.

To reduce the compilation time with each modification, the AspectJ compiler offers *incremental mode*. With this option, ajc keeps track of the files that need to be recompiled, thus avoiding the recompilation of *all* the classes for each modification.

When using incremental mode, ajc will first fully compile the files supplied and then wait for the user to press either Enter (to recompile), r (to rebuild), or q (to quit the process). The following command launches ajc in incremental mode. The compiler first compiles all the source files in the two directories: F:\aspectj-book\ appendixA\sectionA.8\shopping and F:\aspectj-book\appendixA\sectionA.8\tracing. Then it will monitor changes to those source files, compiling them as needed whenever the user presses Enter:

```
> ajc -incremental
   -sourceroots F:\aspectj-book\appendixA\sectionA.8\shopping;
            F:\aspectj-book\appendixA\sectionA.8\tracing
```

```
      press enter to recompile, r to rebuild, q to quit:

      press enter to recompile, r to rebuild, q to quit:

      press enter to recompile, r to rebuild, q to quit:
      r
      press enter to recompile, r to rebuild, q to quit:

      press enter to recompile, r to rebuild, q to quit:
  q
  >
```

Keep in mind that the `-incremental` option tracks changes only to source files, not binary JAR files. In addition, you must specify the `-sourceroots` option.

A.9 *Producing useful warnings*

The AspectJ compiler offers an option that when enabled warns you of potential problems with your code. The following command issues a warning when you misspell *TraceAspect* as *TaceAspect*. Without such warnings, tracking down a problem like this would be time-consuming:

```
> ajc -Xlint tracing\*.java -outjar tracing.jar
F:\aspectj-book\appendixA\sectionA.9\tracing\TraceAspect.java:10
➥ no match for this type name:
➥ TaceAspect [Xlint:invalidAbsoluteTypeName]

1 warning
```

> **TIP** The warnings offered by the `-Xlint` option are so useful that many developers make `-Xlint` the default option by modifying ajc.bat and the ajc shell script in AspectJ.

B
Understanding
Ant integration

This appendix covers

- Setting up Ant to work with AspectJ
- Compiling AspectJ sources with Ant
- Creating and using AspectJ libraries with Ant

Ant is an increasingly popular Java-based build system that uses XML-based build files to define rules. The core concepts in Ant include the project, the target, and the task. A *project* in a build file is the root element that nests all other elements. A *target* is a set of operations that need to be performed, whereas a *task* is the logic that needs to be executed to carry out an operation. A typical Ant build file contains such tasks as compiling the sources, running the system, and executing test suites. By specifying the commonly performed tasks in an Ant build file, you can simplify the build job. For more detailed information about Ant, please refer to the books listed in "Resources."

With Ant, a new functionality is supported by defining a new task. AspectJ bundles Ant tasks to enable you to compile source files using the AspectJ compiler (ajc). Most of the supported attributes in an AspectJ Ant task correspond directly to the options available to ajc (see appendix A). Once you understand each option's role, writing an Ant build file should be straightforward. Owing to the similarity between the AspectJ and Java compilers, for the most part an Ant build file is similar in structure to one using a `<javac>` Ant task. In this appendix, we examine ways you can use an AspectJ Ant task. For more details, refer to the documentation supplied with the AspectJ download.

Appendix A provides an overview of various compilation options that are available with ajc, and we provide examples of performing tasks, such as compiling source files and creating aspect libraries. In this appendix, we show you how to use Ant to perform the same tasks.

B.1 Compiling source files using an Ant task

In section A.3, you saw how to use ajc to compile specified source files. Here you'll learn how to carry out the same job using Ant targets. In the following build file, we assume that you have aspectjtools.jar and aspectjrt.jar (both available as a part of the AspectJ installation) in your classpath. (Later we will examine ways of handling situations when you do not want these JAR files in the classpath.)

Let's compile all the source files in a directory, using an Ant build file:

```
<project name="shopping-tracing" default="run">
    <taskdef
      resource=
        "org/aspectj/tools/ant/taskdefs/aspectjTaskdefs.properties">
    </taskdef>
```

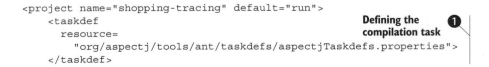

Defining the compilation task ❶

```
<target name="compile">
    <mkdir dir="dest"/>
    <iajc destdir="dest">
        <sourceroots>
            <pathelement location="shopping"/>
            <pathelement location="tracing"/>
        </sourceroots>
    </iajc>
</target>

<target name="run" depends="compile">
    <java classname="Test">
        <classpath>
            <pathelement location="dest"/>
            <pathelement path="${java.class.path}"/>
        </classpath>
    </java>
</target>
```

❷ Compiling sources

❸ Running the program

```
</project>
```

Here are the details:

❶ We make Aspect Ant tasks available by setting the value of the resource attribute to the org/aspectj/tools/ant/taskdefs/aspectjTaskdefs.properties file. This properties file, which is part of aspectjtools.jar, specifies the mapping of the Ant compile tasks to their corresponding classes. The resource file defines two tasks: ajc, which supports most options available in AspectJ 1.0, and iajc, which supports new options in AspectJ 1.1, including incremental compilation.

❷ We define the compile target by using the iajc task and specifying the sourceroots nested element. Here we specify two source directories: shopping and tracing.

❸ We define the run target using the java task element and specify Test as the class to execute.

To compile and run the program, issue the ant command by itself. Note that when you do not specify a target, Ant runs the default target—run in our case. Because that target depends on the compile target, it compiles the sources prior to running:

```
> ant
Buildfile: build.xml

compile:
    [mkdir] Created dir: F:\aspectj-book\appendixB\sectionB.1\dest

run:
    [java] Apr 10, 2003 12:09:35 AM Test main
    [java] INFO: Entering
```

```
    [java] Apr 10, 2003 12:09:35 AM Inventory addItem
    [java] INFO: Entering
    [java] Apr 10, 2003 12:09:35 AM Inventory addItem
    [java] INFO: Entering
    [java] Apr 10, 2003 12:09:35 AM Inventory addItem
    [java] INFO: Entering
    [java] Apr 10, 2003 12:09:35 AM ShoppingCartOperator
     ➡   addShoppingCartItem
    [java] INFO: Entering
    [java] Apr 10, 2003 12:09:35 AM Inventory removeItem
    [java] INFO: Entering
    [java] Apr 10, 2003 12:09:35 AM ShoppingCart addItem
    [java] INFO: Entering
    [java] Apr 10, 2003 12:09:35 AM ShoppingCartOperator
     ➡   addShoppingCartItem
    [java] INFO: Entering
    [java] Apr 10, 2003 12:09:35 AM Inventory removeItem
    [java] INFO: Entering
    [java] Apr 10, 2003 12:09:35 AM ShoppingCart addItem
    [java] INFO: Entering

BUILD SUCCESSFUL
Total time: 5 seconds
```

If you want to compile the source files without running the program, you can issue the following command:

```
> ant compile
Buildfile: build.xml

compile:
    [mkdir] Created dir: F:\aspectj-book\appendixB\sectionB.1\dest

BUILD SUCCESSFUL
Total time: 5 seconds
```

If you do not have aspectjtools.jar as a part of your CLASSPATH environment variable, in order to make the resource properties file available to the Ant build file, you must copy aspectjtools.jar to $(ANT_HOME)/lib. The other choice is to specify the classpath nested element for the taskdef element, as shown here:

```
<taskdef
  resource=
    "org/aspectj/tools/ant/taskdefs/aspectjTaskdefs.properties">
    <classpath>
        <pathelement
          location="${aspectj.dir}/lib/aspectjtools.jar"/>
    </classpath>
</taskdef>
```

You will then have to specify the value for aspectj.dir either directly inside the build file or by passing it to the Ant invocation:

```
> ant -Daspectj.dir=C:\aspectj1.1 compile
```

Now let's turn our attention to the situation when your classpath does not include aspectjrt.jar. In this case, you will have to specify it explicitly to the compile and run targets, as shown here:

```
<target name="compile">
    <mkdir dir="dest"/>
    <iajc destdir="dest">
        <sourceroots>
            <pathelement location="shopping"/>
            <pathelement location="tracing"/>
        </sourceroots>
        <classpath>
            <pathelement path="${java.class.path}"/>
            <pathelement location="${aspectj.dir}/lib/aspectjrt.jar"/>
        </classpath>
    </iajc>
</target>

<target name="run" depends="compile">
    <java classname="Test">
        <classpath>
            <pathelement location="dest"/>
            <pathelement path="${java.class.path}"/>
            <pathelement location="${aspectj.dir}/lib/aspectjrt.jar"/>
        </classpath>
    </java>
</target>
```

Just as in case of aspectjtools.jar, you must supply the value for aspectj.dir on the Ant command line, as follows:

```
> ant -Daspectj.dir=C:\aspectj1.1 compile
```

Now that you are familiar with compiling and running programs written in AspectJ, let's see how you can use the AspectJ Ant task for other jobs, such as creating and using libraries. We'll also look at setting the AspectJ Ant task to compile source files incrementally.

B.2 Weaving into JAR files using an Ant task

In section A.5, we studied the ajc command-line options for weaving aspects into a JAR file. In this section, we examine the Ant way of performing the same task.

The following Ant target weaves the aspects in the tracing directory into the shopping.jar file:

```
<target name="weave" depends="shopping-jar">
    <mkdir dir="dest"/>
    <iajc destdir="dest">
        <injars>
            <pathelement location="shopping.jar"/>
        </injars>
        <sourceroots>
            <pathelement location="tracing"/>
        </sourceroots>
    </iajc>
</target>
```

If the input JAR files contain pure Java sources, you could use the `javac` task to compile them instead of `iajc`. For example, the shopping.jar file could be produced through the following Ant targets:

```
<target name="compile-shopping">
    <mkdir dir="dest/shopping"/>
    <javac destdir="dest/shopping">
        <src>
            <pathelement location="shopping"/>
        </src>
    </javac>
</target>

<target name="shopping-jar" depends="compile-shopping">
    <jar destfile="shopping.jar"
         basedir="dest/shopping"/>
</target>
```

B.3 *Creating aspect libraries using an Ant task*

Let's turn our focus to creating aspect libraries using Ant, which is equivalent in functionality to the command-line way in section A.6. Using the `outjar` attribute and the `XnoWeave` attribute, you can create an aspect library, which can be later woven into the rest of the system. The following Ant target creates tracing.jar by compiling all the sources inside the tracing directory:

```
<target name="trace-lib">
    <iajc outjar="tracing.jar" XnoWeave="true">
        <sourceroots>
            <pathelement location="tracing"/>
        </sourceroots>
    </iajc>
</target>
```

Note that the XnoWeave attribute has the same function as the -XnoWeave option discussed in section A.6.

B.4 *Utilizing aspect libraries using an Ant task*

In section A.7, we explored command-line options for using an aspect library created by employing the technique described in section A.6 (or B.3). Performing the same task in Ant requires you to specify the corresponding JAR file for the aspect library in the aspectpath nested element in the iajc task. If you need to weave the aspects inside the library JAR file, specify them inside the injars element as well:

```
<target name="compile" depends="trace-lib">
    <mkdir dir="dest"/>
    <iajc destdir="dest">
        <sourceroots>
            <pathelement location="shopping"/>
        </sourceroots>
        <injars>
            <pathelement location="tracing.jar"/>
        </injars>
        <aspectpath>
            <pathelement location="tracing.jar"/>
        </aspectpath>
    </iajc>
</target>
```

You could weave the aspects in a library into a JAR file by specifying the target JAR file in the injars nested element:

```
<target name="compile" depends="trace-lib,shopping-jar">
    <mkdir dir="dest"/>
    <iajc destdir="dest">
        <injars>
            <pathelement location="shopping.jar"/>
            <pathelement location="tracing.jar"/>
        </injars>
        <aspectpath>
            <pathelement location="tracing.jar"/>
        </aspectpath>
    </iajc>
</target>
```

B.5 *Utilizing incremental compilation using an Ant task*

The AspectJ Ant task can be set to compile the source files incrementally, based on user input. Just like the -incremental option to ajc (discussed in section A.8), the incremental mode of the AspectJ Ant task tracks the files specified using the `sourceroots` element (or the `sourceRoots` or `sourceRootsList` attribute).

The following Ant task compiles the source files under the shopping and tracing directories in incremental mode:

```
<target name="inc-compile">
    <mkdir dir="dest"/>
    <iajc destdir="dest" incremental="true">
        <sourceroots>
            <pathelement location="shopping"/>
            <pathelement location="tracing"/>
        </sourceroots>
    </iajc>
</target>
```

Invoking the target results in a full initial compilation followed by a request for user input. The user must then press Enter (to recompile), r (to rebuild), or q (to quit the process):

```
> ant inc-compile
Buildfile: build.xml

inc-compile:
    [mkdir] Created dir: F:\aspectj-book\appendixB\sectionB.5\dest
     [iajc]  press enter to recompile, r to rebuild, q to quit:

     [iajc]  press enter to recompile, r to rebuild, q to quit:
r
     [iajc]  press enter to recompile, r to rebuild, q to quit:

     [iajc]  press enter to recompile, r to rebuild, q to quit:
q

BUILD SUCCESSFUL
Total time: 22 seconds
```

For large projects, you will notice a significantly reduced recompilation time compared to the initial compilation.

resources

Here we've compiled a listing of books, papers, and online resources related to AOP and AspectJ. In addition, we've listed sites where you can find the technologies used in our examples. We've also included URLs to useful mailing lists to which you can subscribe.

Recommended reading

Books

Beck, K. *Extreme Programming Explained: Embrace Change*. Reading, Mass.: Addison-Wesley, 2000.

Bloch, Joshua. *Effective Java Programming Language Guide*. Boston: Addison-Wesley Professional, 2001.

Czarnecki, Krzysztof, and Ulrich Eisenecker. *Generative Programming: Methods, Techniques, and Applications*. Reading, Mass.: Addison-Wesley, 2000.

Fowler, Martin. *Refactoring: Improving the Design of Existing Code*. Reading, Mass.: Addison-Wesley, 1999.

Friedman-Hill, Ernest. *Jess in Action*. Greenwich, Conn.: Manning Publications, 2003.

Gamma, Erich, Richard Helm, Ralph Johnson, and John Vlissides. *Design Patterns– Elements of Reusable Object-Oriented Software*. Reading, Mass.: Addison-Wesley, 1994.

Hatcher, Erik and Steve Loughran. *Java Development with Ant*. Greenwich, Conn.: Manning Publications, 2003.

Kiczales, Gregor, Jim Des Rivieres, and Daniel Bobrow. *The Art of the Metaobject Protocol*. Cambridge, Mass.: MIT Press, 1991.

Lea, Doug. *Concurrent Programming in Java: Design Principles and Patterns,* 2d ed. Reading, Mass.: Addison-Wesley, 1999.

Lieberherr, Karl J. *Adaptive Object-Oriented Software: The Demeter Method with Propagation Patterns*. Boston: PWS Publishing Co., 1996. Also available online at http://www.ccs.neu.edu/research/demeter/book/book-download.html.

Schmidt, Douglas C., Michael Stal, Hans Rohnert, and Frank Buschmann. *Pattern-Oriented Software Architecture: Patterns for Concurrent and Networked Objects*. New York: John Wiley & Sons, 2000.

Tate, Bruce. *Bitter Java*. Greenwich, Conn.: Manning Publications, 2002.

Tate, Bruce, Mike Clark, Bob Lee, and Patrick Linskey. *Bitter EJB*. Greenwich, Conn.: Manning Publications, 2003.

Journal articles

Aksit, M., B. Tekinerdogan, and L. Bergmans. "Achieving Adaptability through Separation and Composition of Concerns." In *Special Issues in Object-Oriented Programming*, M. Muhlhauser (ed.), dpunkt verlag, pp. 12–23, 1996.

Hannemann, Jan, and Gregor Kiczales. *Design Pattern Implementation in Java and AspectJ*. In *Proceedings of the 17th Annual ACM Conference on Object-Oriented Programming, Systems, Languages, and Applications (OOPSLA)*, pp. 161–73, November, 2002. Also available online at http://www.cs.ubc.ca/~gregor/hannemann-OOPSLA2002-aop-patterns.pdf.

Janzen, D., and K. De Volder. "Navigating and Querying Code without Getting Lost." In *Proceedings of the 2nd International Conference on Aspect-Oriented Software Development*, 2003: pp. 178–87.

Kiczales, Gregor, John Lamping, Anurag Mendhekar, Chris Maeda, Cristina Videira Lopes, Jean-Marc Loingtier, and John Irwin. "Aspect-Oriented Programming." In *Proceedings of European Conference on Object-Oriented Programming (ECOOP'97)*, June 1997. Available online at: ftp://ftp.ccs.neu.edu/pub/people/crista/publications/ecoop97/for-web.pdf.

Ossher, Harold, William Harrison, Frank Budinsky, and Ian Simmonds. "Subject-Oriented Programming: Supporting Decentralized Development of Objects." In *Proceedings of the 7th IBM Conference on Object-Oriented Technology*, July, 1994.

Parnas, David Longe. "On the Criteria to Be Used in Decomposing Systems into Modules." In *Communications of the ACM*, 15(12): 1053–58, December 1972.

Walker, Robert J., Elisa L.A. Baniassad, and Gail C. Murphy. "An Initial Assessment of Aspect-oriented Programming." In *Proceedings of the 21st International Conference on Software Engineering*, May, 1999.

Online resources

Kircher, Michael, Prashant Jain, and Angelo Corsaro. "XP + AOP = Better Software?" Available online at http://www.xp2003.org/xp2002/atti/Kircher-Jain-XPplusAOPBetterSoftware.pdf.

Laddad, Ramnivas. "I Want My AOP!, Part 1." In *JavaWorld*, January, 2002. Available online at http://www.javaworld.com/javaworld/jw-01-2002/jw-0118-aspect.html.

——— "I Want My AOP!, Part 2." In *JavaWorld*, March, 2002. Available online at http://www.javaworld.com/javaworld/jw-03-2002/jw-0301-aspect2.html.

——— "I Want My AOP!, Part 3." In *JavaWorld*, April, 2002. Available online at http://www.javaworld.com/javaworld/jw-04-2002/jw-0412-aspect3.html.

Lesiecki, Nicholas. "Test Flexibly with AspectJ and Mock Objects." IBM Developer Works, May 2002. Available online at http://www-106.ibm.com/developerworks/java/library/j-aspectj2/.

Monk, Simon, and Stephen Hall. "Virtual Mock Objects Using AspectJ with JUnit." Available online at http://www.xprogramming.com/xpmag/virtualMockObjects.htm.

Ossher, H., and P. Tarr. "Multi-Dimensional Separation of Concerns Using Hyperspaces." IBM Research Report 21452, April, 1999. Available online at http://www.research.ibm.com/hyperspace/Papers/tr21452.ps.

Sun Microsystems. "Threads and Swing." Available online at http://java.sun.com/docs/books/tutorial/uiswing/overview/threads.html.

Useful web sites

AOP and related methodology

Adaptive programming/Demeter: http://www.ccs.neu.edu/home/lieber/demeter.html

Aspect-oriented programming: http://aosd.net

Composition filters: http://trese.cs.utwente.nl/composition_filters

Hyper/J: http://www.research.ibm.com/hyperspace/HyperJ/HyperJ.htm

Intentional programming: http://intentsoft.com

Multi-dimensional separation of concerns: http://www.research.ibm.com/hyperspace

Subject-oriented programming: http://www.research.ibm.com/sop

Libraries and tools you need to complete examples in the book

JDK 1.4:   http://java.sun.com/j2se

AspectJ 1.1:   http://www.eclipse.org/aspectj

log4j 1.2:   http://jakarta.apache.org/log4j

J2EE SDK 1.3:   http://java.sun.com/j2ee

Doug Lea's Concurrency library: http://gee.cs.oswego.edu/dl/classes/EDU/oswego/cs/dl/util/
     concurrent/intro.html

Jess 6.1:   http://herzberg.ca.sandia.gov/jess/

Ant: http://ant.apache.org

Other AOP implementations

AspectC++:   http://www.aspectc.org

AspectWerkz: http://aspectwerkz.codehaus.org

DemeterJ: http://www.ccs.neu.edu/research/demeter/DemeterJava

Java Aspect Components (JAC):   http://jac.aopsys.com

JBoss/AOP: http://www.jboss.org/developers/projects/jboss/aop

JMangler: http://javalab.iai.uni-bonn.de/research/jmangler

Nanning Aspects: http://nanning.sourceforge.net

Pythius: http://sourceforge.net/projects/pythius

IDE integration of AspectJ

Eclipse/AspectJ integration: http://www.eclipse.org/ajdt

Emacs/AspectJ integration: http://aspectj4emacs.sourceforge.net

JBuilder/AspectJ integration: http://aspectj4jbuildr.sourceforge.net

NetBeans/AspectJ integration: http://aspectj4netbean.sourceforge.net

AOP/AspectJ tools and packages

Aspect-oriented design pattern implementations: http://www.cs.ubc.ca/~jan/AODPs

Aspect Mining Tool: http://www.cs.ubc.ca/~jan/amt

Concern Manipulation Environment (CME):   http://www.research.ibm.com/cme

Cricket Cage testing framework using AspectJ: http://cricketcage.sourceforge.net

Feature Exploration and Analysis Tool (FEAT):   http://www.cs.ubc.ca/labs/spl/projects/feat

Miscellaneous sites

Extensible Access Control Markup Language (XACML):   http://xml.coverpages.org/xacml.html

Jakarta Commons: http://jakarta.apache.org/commons

Java Rule Engine API (JSR 94):   http://jcp.org/aboutJava/communityprocess/review/jsr094

Rule Markup Language (RuleML):   http://www.dfki.uni-kl.de/ruleml

Security Assertion Markup Language (SAML):   http://xml.coverpages.org/saml.html

Simple Rule Markup Language (SRML):   http://xml.coverpages.org/srml.html

Mailing lists

AspectJ user mailing list: https://dev.eclipse.org/mailman/listinfo/aspectj-users

AOSD user mailing list: http://aosd.net/mailman/listinfo/discuss

index

Symbols

! operator 67
  example of 30, 107, 133–134,
    153, 160, 162, 187, 190,
    304, 321
#error, C/C++ 97
#warning, C/C++ 97
&& operator 67
  example of 93, 95, 162, 165,
    171, 222–223, 279
  misleading interpretation 98
* wildcard 67
  use in type signature
    pattern 159
+ wildcard 67
.. wildcard 67
  usage in constructor
    signature 70
  usage in method signature 70
  usage in type signature
    pattern 159
@deprecation
  policy enforcement, and 186
|| operator 67
  combining pointcuts, exam-
    ple of 199
  example of 158, 186–187,
    199, 223, 308

A

abstract aspects
  code reuse 58
  example of 57, 333, 402

restriction on declaration 57
reusability 298
Swing example 298
transaction management,
  example of 370
weaving 57
abstract pointcuts 56–57
  example of 125, 128, 171,
    251, 253, 299, 304, 319,
    333, 347, 370, 383, 388
  providing blank
    definition 280
  use in logging 171
access control
  factory pattern, and 188
  plain Java, limitations of 187
  using AspectJ 187
AccessControlContext
  authorization, use of 338
AccessControlException
  authorization, use of 338
AccessController
  authorization, use of 338
AccessController.check-
    Permission() 339
  authorization, use of 338
AccountJDBCImpl 358
ACID properties
  transaction 357
acquire()
  concurrency utility
    library 317
advice 81
  anatomy of 82
  aspect instance, accessing
    inside 124

body 83
categories 81
comparison with method 86–
  87
declaration 82
  context information,
    and 82
  exception declaration,
    and 83
declaring exception thrown,
    example of 377
definition of 35
exposed join point,
    restriction 82
inclusion in aspects 56
join point in aspect 277
methods, comparison 86
ordering 114
  lexical 119
  precedence, and 111
  single aspect 119
    example of 349
  unpredictability 115
passing context to 87
precedence 111
  authorization, example
    of 349
sequence diagram 81
use with pointcut 35
advice execution join points 50
  pointcut syntax 74
adviceexecution pointcut 74
after advice 83
  example of 53
  exceptional return, on 84
  successful return, on 84

variation 83
after returning advice 84
    context collection, example
        of 232
    efficiency consideration 98
    example of 93, 220
after throwing advice 84
    capturing exception, exam-
        ple of 269
    context collection, example
        of 269, 377
    use in exception logging 164
ajbrowser 60
    crosscutting view 60
    relation to IDE
        integration 60
ajc
    -1.4 flag, use of 291
    -aspectpath option 444
    -classpath option 440
    compiling source directories
        See -sourceroots option,
            ajc 441
    compiling source files 441
    creating aspect libraries
        See -outjar option, ajc 443
    creating JAR files
        See -outjars option, ajc 442
    -d option 440
    -deprecation option 440
    existing build system, incor-
        porating into 443
    -g option 440
    incremental compilation
        mode
        See -incremental option,
            ajc 444
    -injars option
        See -injars option, ajc 442
    javac, difference from 441
    -outjars option
        See -outjars option, ajc 442
    preventing weaving 444
    providing useful warnings
        See -Xlint option, ajc 446
    -source option 440
        example of 233
    -sourceroots option
        See -sourceroots option,
            ajc 441
    -target option 440

using aspect libraries
    See -aspectpath option,
        ajc 444
weaving into JAR file
    See -injars option, ajc 442
weaving, once-only
    restriction 443
-Xlint option
    See -Xlint option, ajc 446
-XnoWeave option 444
ajc ant task
    defining in build file 449
    iajc ant task, relation 449
ajc compiler
    iajc ant task, and 448
amount of code
    authorization example,
        conventional 345
anonymous pointcut 65
    using in a pointcut 66
    using in an advice 66
Ant
    AspectJ compilation task
        See iajc ant task 448
    AspectJ, using with 448
    build file 448
    build system
        policy enforcement 180
    overview 448
    projects 448
    targets 448
    tasks 448
ant command
    default settings 449
    specifying properties 451
anti-idiom
    infinite recursion 277
AOP
    anatomy of language 22
    benefits 27
        code reuse 28
        reduced cost 29
        time-to-market 29
    comparison with EJB 14, 31
    definition of 4
    development process
        See AOP development
            process 21
    difference from OOP 20
    effect on modularization 28
    effect on system evolution 28

history of 20
implementation of 20
in enterprise applications 31
inventors 20
learning curve 27, 31
mailing list, general
    discussion 436
methodology 21
myths 29
    fixing bad design 4, 29
    patching 30
    silver bullet 437
object encapsulation 30
obliviousness 20
OOP as the base 6
program flow 29
purpose 4
related methodologies 20
relation to AspectJ 20
relation to design pattern 30
relation to OOP 19, 30
relation to XP 28
separation of concerns 20
separation of
    responsibility 28
short overview 4
AOP development process
    aspects 21
    aspectual decomposition 21
    decomposing
        requirements 21
    implementing core
        concerns 21
    light-beam/prism analogy 22
AOP language
    base programming
        language 23
    implementation of
        concerns 23
    specification 23
    weaving rules
        specification 23
API, reflection
    See reflection API 101
application frameworks
    policy enforcement, and 181
architect's dilemma 5, 28
    AOP, and 5–6
    logging example 167
    opposing forces 5
    performance example 5, 241

resource pooling, and 207
thread pooling, example
    of 315
args pointcut 80
    context collection 87
        example of 233, 402, 408
    example of 80, 214, 220
    reflection, and 101
    type limiting, example of 234
around advice 85
    accommodating different
        return types 91–92, 253,
        254
    altering context 40
    bypassing join point, example
        of 209, 371, 373
    casting, example of 254
    detecting failure, use in 369
    example of 40, 82, 85, 214
    exception declaration 91–92
    failure handling example 90
    primitive return value 90
    proceed(), and 85
    returning Object, example
        of 253, 370
    returning value 89
        example of 228, 238
    throwing exception, example
        of 214, 238
    transaction management,
        example of 370
    try/catch block 267
    unwrapping, example of 254
    usage of 85
    using proceed() 40
    worker object creation pat-
        tern, and 249
    wrapping and unwrapping
        of 90
aspect libraries 321
    creating
        iajc ant task 452
        See outjar option, ajc 443
    using
        iajc ant task 453
        See -aspectpath option,
            ajc 444
aspect weaver 4
    See weaving 4, 24
AspectJ
    adoption 176, 426

policy enforcement,
    and 179
    See AspectJ adoption
applying to new
    problems 426
browser
    See ajbrowser 60
compiler 59
    byte-code conformance 59
    difference from Java
        compiler 98
    Eclipse, relation to 440
    Java byte-code specifica-
        tion, and 440
    Java compiler
        common compiler
            options 440
        similarity to 439
    overview 59, 440
    See ajc 440
    weaving 59
compiling sources 38
criteria for using 426
crosscutting classification 33
design patterns
    exception introduction pat-
        tern
        See exception introduction
            pattern 260–269
    participant pattern
        See participant
            pattern 270–277
    worker object creation pat-
        tern
        See worker object creation
            pattern 247–
            256
    wormhole pattern
        See wormhole
            pattern 256–260
design phase 428
development phases, use
    of 427
development process 427
    limiting impact 427
    restricting
        implementation 427
    using conventional
        solution 427
downloading 439

dynamic crosscutting
    See dynamic
        crosscutting 34
    evangelizing 434
    exposed join point 43
    implementation phase 428
    incorrect usage 433
    individual productivity,
        for 434
    installation
        JAR files 439
    installing 439
    internal details vs. language
        semantics 42
    internals 40
    Java, superset of 440
    join point model 43
    just-in-time weaving 60
    legacy project, and 432
    mailing list 436
    maintenance phase 432
    mapping of elements 41
    overview 33
    relation to Java 33
    running programs 38
    setting up 439
    simple program 37
    static crosscutting
        See static crosscutting 34
    testing phase 431
    word of warning 433
    XP, and 431
AspectJ-based authentication
    enabling access check 339
    just-in-time 333
AspectJ-based business rule
    implementation 394
    concern weaving 395
    isolation layer 411
    obliviousness 411
    participating entities 394
    participating join points 395
    template 394
AspectJ-based caching 237–241
AspectJ-based logging 156
    graphical illustration 157
    investment 176
    overview 146–154
    risk 176
AspectJ-based rule engine
    graphical illustration

behavioral 416
collaboration 415
AspectJ-based rule implementation
  aspect, banking example 421
  join point collection, when
    using rule engine 420
  join point, restricting 420
AspectJ-based transaction
  management 368–378
  defining operation 369
  JTA, using 388
  requirements, high-level 368
aspectjrt.jar
  AspectJ runtime library 439
  -classpath option, and 441
  iajc ant task 448
    specifying without modify-
      ing CLASSPATH 451
  java ant task
    specifying without modify-
      ing CLASSPATH 451
aspectjtools.jar
  AspectJ tools library 439
  iajc ant task 448
    specifying without modify-
      ing CLASSPATH 450
aspectOf() 136
  control-flow-based associa-
    tion, and 136
aspect-oriented logging 153,
  156
  advantages of 156
  dependency reversal 156
  weaving 156
aspect-oriented programming
  See AOP 4
aspect-oriented resource pooling
  plug-and-play 208
  requirements 208
  template aspect
    See resource pooling tem-
      plate aspect 208
aspect-oriented thread
  pooling 226
-aspectpath option, ajc 444
  -injars option,
    combining 444
aspects
  abstract
    See abstract aspects

access control rule, and 139
access specification 56
association 122–136
  categories 122
  default association
    See default
      association 123
  implicit limiting of join
    points, and 132
  per-control-flow association
    See per-control-flow
      association 128
  scope 132
  state 122
  syntax 122
comparison with classes 56
consistent naming
  conventions 430
constructor 56
defining subaspect
  See subaspect 57
definition of 36
dissimilarity with classes 58
domination
  See aspect precedence 116
extending classes 58
extending restrictions 59
general form 55
implementing interfaces 58
inclusion of data members 56
inclusion of methods 56
inheritance
  example of 335
  precedence and 117
instance, accessing 124
instances
  accessing 135
  participant pattern,
    and 380
  percflow association
    example of 372
    transaction management
      example 372
  stateless aspects, and 382
  transaction context, as 369
instantiation
  capturing join point 375
  default association 58
  restriction 58
introducing default
  implementation 283

logging, using for
  See logging 146
maintaining state 122
mapping to Java class 41
multiple aspects 111
nested
  See nested aspects 56
nested inside a class, example
  of 361
parent types 56–57
per-object association
  See per-object
    association 125
precedence 111–122, 433
  avoiding coupling 116
  consistent naming
    convention 430
  explicit 115
  indeterminism 113
  inheritance, and 117
  logging, and 172
  member introduction 120
  Swing thread safety
    example 302
  usage style 116
privileged 139
  See also privileged
    aspect 59
state, maintaining 122
with data member, example
  of 333
with method, example of
  334
with nested classes, example
  of 334
aspectual interface
  participant pattern 274
aspectual recomposition 21
aspectual refactoring 426, 431
  conventional refactoring,
    comparison with 431
  normal usage, differences
    using 431
assert 230
  contract enforcement 230
  -ea option 233
  Jess, statement 419
asynchronous routing
  exception introduction
    pattern 311
  exception listener 311

exception-handling
    policy 311
atomicity
    transaction, and 357
auditing 324
    using logging 184
authentication 324
    AspectJ-based 333–336
    authorization
        prerequisite 337
    avoiding multiple login 334
    callback handler 329
    concern-specific exception,
        use of 335
    concrete aspect, example
        of 335
    conventional solution 329–333
    definition of 324
    developing subaspect 333
    just-in-time
        See just-in-time authentica-
            tion
    login scope 334
    property-based pointcut 270
    servlet session, as scope 334
    up-front login 354
authentication and authoriza-
    tion
    banking example 325–329
    separating join points 354
    fall back 354
authorization 324
    AspectJ-based 346–352
    authentication, as
        prerequisite 337
    concrete aspect 349
    conventional solution 336–
        345
    data-driven 352
    definition of 324
    enabling in a system 349
    multiple subaspects
        subject management 353
        use of 353
    policy file, example of 343
    routing of calls 348
    subsystem control 353
    wormhole pattern, and 256
authorization aspect
    dealing with checked
        exceptions 351

auto-commit mode 365–366
    transaction management,
        JDBC and 359
auxiliary characteristics
    participant pattern 270
AWT
    EJB programming restric-
        tions, and 191, 193
AWT thread
    See event-dispatching
        thread 288

B

backward-reasoning algorithm
    rule engine 412
banking system
    authentication and
        authorization 325
    business rule, example of 396
    check clearance system, sig-
        nificance of business
        rule 403
    core business logic
        implementation 396–
        401
    minimum balance rule 401
    overdraft protection rule 403
    overdrafts accounts 398
    persistence
        class diagram 358
    transaction management
        subaspect 374
    with rule engine 417–423
BasicPermission 338
before advice 83
    example of 39, 53, 82, 220
    exception throwing and join
        point execution 83
    throwing exception, example
        of 403
    usage of 83
before-and-after
    illustrating AspectJ's
        power 434
best practices
    business rules 420
    declare warning, use of 190
    policy enforcement, and 189
    public members 190
beta testing 432

binary operator 67
    type signature 69
bind
    Jess, statement 419
blank final variable 296
Blaze Advisor
    rule engine 417
blocking the caller,
    undesirability 298
build configuration 430
    correctness consideration 431
    deployment
        consideration 430
    development process 427
    policy enforcement 184
business rules
    airlines booking system,
        example of 395
    aspect
        template 395
    AspectJ-based
        mechanisms 394–396
    banking system, example
        of 396
    business objects, as facts 412
    changing nature 392
    context collection, need
        for 395
    current mechanisms 393–
        394
    definition of 392
    enterprise applications,
        and 392–393
    enterprise system, need
        in 392
    evaluating
        code tangling 392
    example of 392
    expression 393
    implementation
        choices 393
        overview 393
        steps 412
    JSR 94, and 393
    modularizing using
        AspectJ 415–417
    need for separation 392
    rule engine 412
    shopping cart, example
        of 392
    using rule engine 411

business-specific checked exceptions
    dealing with catching 267
business-specific exceptions
    dealing with 261
bypassing execution
    around advice, use of 373

C

C++ 183
    friend, access
        specification 188
C/C++ preprocessors 97
caching 235–241
    AspectJ-based 235–241
    deployment aspect, as 242
    development aspect, as 242
    feature change, caching
        example of 240
    growth management 241
    LinkedHashMap 241
    performance, finding
        bottlenecks 242
    per-object association 125
    resource pooling, difference
        from 235
    SoftReference, example
        of 241
    stylesheet 235
    using aspect 92
    validity consideration 240
    XSLT 235
call depth
    extra argument, using 367
    use in logging 170
    use in profiling 175
call stack
    wormhole pattern 258
call pointcut 74
    example of 214, 220, 291,
        299, 301, 304
    specifying method exception,
        example of 269
callback handler
    LoginContext, and 330
caller context
    current solution 257
    passing additional
        parameters 257
    thread-specific storage 257

    wormhole pattern 257
cflow pointcut 75, 383
    comparison with cflowbelow
        pointcut 76
    depiction using sequence
        diagram 76
    example of 75, 306
    transaction management,
        example of 371
    use in policy
        enforcement 192
    use in tracing aspects 159
    wormhole pattern, use in 404
cflowbelow pointcut 75
    comparison with cflow
        pointcut 76
    depiction using sequence
        diagram 76
    example of 75, 93
    top-level operation, capturing
        using 370
    usage of 77
    use in tracing aspects 159
characteristics-based crosscutting
    embedding pointcut in
        class 272
    enumerating join points 272
    participant pattern, and 270
checked exception 136, 260
    advice, restriction on 260–
        261, 264
    compiler errors 263
    current method 264
    dealing with, example of 262
    exception introduction
        pattern 260
    restriction, and overridden
        methods 261
    underlying logic, dealing
        with 261
class initialization join point 48
    comparison with object
        initialization 49
    pointcut syntax 74
    static blocks 49
CLASSPATH
    modification for AspectJ 439
-classpath ajc option 440
code review
    EJB programming
        restrictions 192

policy enforcement,
    using 182
code scattering 15–16, 426
    business rules, example
        of 394
    cause 16
    classification of 16
    complementary code
        blocks 17
    default interface
        implementation 282
    duplicated code blocks 16
    illustration 17
    JTA, and 388
    policy enforcement 182
    puzzle piece analogy 17
    resource pooling 206
    sign of crosscutting
        concern 429
    transaction management 368
code tangling 15, 426
    business rules 392
        example of 394
    cause 15
    code example 16
    crosscutting concern, sign
        of 429
    illustration 16
    logging 155
    policy enforcement 182
    resource pooling 206
    transaction management 368
collaboration flow
    participant pattern 276
commit
    database connection 366
common characteristics
    sharing of 270
    slow operations, example
        of 270
communicating failure
    transaction management 369
compiler warnings
    See -Xlint option, ajc 446
compile-time errors
    advice checked exception,
        and 264
compile-time declarations
    definition of 36
    inclusion in aspects 56

compile-time enforcement 180
  example of 180
  limitations 183
compiling
  source directories
    See -sourceroots option,
      ajc 441
  source files 441
concerns
  banking example 7
  composition of 8
  core
    See core concerns 4
  crosscutting
    See crosscutting concern 4
  definition of 7
  identification 8
  implementation 21
  process concerns 7
  role in software system 7
  separation
    See separation of
      concerns 8
  tangling 7
concern-specific checked
  exceptions 260
concern-specific exception
  authentication, use in 335
concern-specific runtime exception
  generic runtime exception,
    vs. 266
concrete aspect
  authorization example 349
concrete subaspect
  participant pattern 274
concurrency utility library 316
conditional check pointcut 80
configuration file
  authorization, role in 338
  example of 330
  java.security.auth.login.con-
    fig, specifying using 332
connection object
  transaction context, as 368
consistency
  transaction, and 357
consistent logging
  importance of 155
consistent naming
  convention 98

importance of 429
  example of 199
constructor join point 46
  call 46
  execution 46
  execution vs. call 47
  pointcut syntax 74
constructor signature 70
  example of 72
  similarity with method
    signature 71
  use of .. wildcard 70
context 87
context collection
  after returning advice 84
    example of 220
  after throwing advice 84–85
  business rules, need in 395
  caching, example of 92
  collecting field set value 80
  collecting return value 84,
    89
  collection exception
    object 80, 84–85, 89
  example of 40
  transaction management,
    example of 384
  using anonymous
    pointcut 87–88
  using args pointcut 80, 87
  using named pointcut 88
  using target pointcut 78,
    87
  using this pointcut 78, 87
control-flow
  concepts 75
  conceptual object 128
  thread of execution, and 128
  transaction
    management 368–369
control-flow association
  transaction management,
    example of 370
control-flow-based pointcut 75
  example of 75
conventional authorization
  issues 345
conventional logging 149
  consistency 155
  graphical illustration 155
  invasiveness 155

issues 154
  shortcomings 154
conventional profiling 175
conventional resource pooling
  code snippet 212
conventional transaction management
  committing at the top
    level 367
  disadvantages of 368
  passing the connection
    around 365
  using thread-specific
    storage 367
convincing
  management 435
  organization 434
  team 436
core business logic
  banking system, example
    of 396
  definition of 392
  modular nature 392
  stable nature 392
core concern 4
  capturing functionality 7
  consistent naming
    convention 429
  design phase 428
  implementation of 30
  implementation phase 429
  refactored code, importance
    of 429
  relativity 21
coupling
  database connection pooling,
    and 211
credentials
  authorization, checking
    for 336
crosscutting
  high-level example 37
  implementing using
    AspectJ 36–37
  viewing in ajbrowser 60
  viewing in an IDE 61
crosscutting concern
  business rules, example
    of 393
  capturing functionality 7
  client-side modularization 11

definition of 4
design phase 428
design/implementation
    mismatch 15
enterprise example 7
implementation 430
    designing aspects 430
    join point
            identification 430
    underlying technology,
        choosing 430
logging 154
modularization using
    AOP 12
modularization using
    OOP 11
need for additional
    methods 15
OOP shortcomings 4
pseudo code example 14
recognizing 428
rule of thumb 428
server-side
    modularization 11
tangling of data members
    15
tangling of multiple
    concerns 15
transaction management,
    example of 357
weaving 13
cryptography 324

D

-d
    ajc option 440
data introduction
    example of 121
    See member introduction 95
database connection
    identifying 216
    resource pooling, and 204
database connection pool
    capacity 217
    implementation of 216
    SimpleDBConnectionPool 21
        7
    timeout 217
database connection pooling
    aspect 211–223

changing pool
        implementation 215
fine tuning 222
registering connection, need
    for 213
resource creation join
    point 214
resource destruction join
    point 214
resource pooling template,
    mapping to 213
selective enabling 222
DatabaseHelper 358
data-driven authorization 352
    EJB, and 325
DBConnectionDescription 216
DBConnectionPool 212
DBConnectionPoolingAspect 2
    14
deadlocks 287
declarative form, EJB
    transaction management 357
declare error 97
    policy enforcement
        example of 186–187, 192,
            195
        transaction management
            example 374
declare parents 96
    example of 97
    Java inheritance rules 97
    restrictions 97
declare precedence 115
    abstract aspects 115, 119
    circular dependency 117
        enforcement usage 117
    common usage idiom 117
    dominating all aspects 116
    example of 115, 269
    example of multiple
        types 116
    logging, example of 220,
        332, 363, 408
    subordinating all aspects 116
    Swing thread safety, example
        of 302
    syntax 115
    use in logging 328
    wildcard, using 116
declare soft
    example of 319, 371

exception introduction pat-
    tern, vs. 335
    SQLException, example of
        361
    syntax 137
declare warning 97
    best practices, use in 190
    example of 180
    policy enforcement
        example of 186
        transaction management
            example 374
decorator design pattern 246
default association
    instance creation
        transaction management
            example 382
default interface
        implementation 281–285
    overriding 284
    partial 284
    multiple inheritance 284
    providing, idiom 281
DefaultTableModel 196
DelegatingThread 226
    implementation of 227
    need for 226
delegation pattern 282
deployment
    policy enforcement 185
-deprecation
    ajc option 440
design
    bloat 6
    limitations of techniques 6
    realization in hindsight 5
design pattern
    definition of 246
    idiom, difference 246
    language specificity, and 246
    object-oriented
        decorator 246
        factory 246
        visitor 246
    problem scope, and 246
    relationship with AOP 30
    use in design phase 430
design phase
    AspectJ, using 428
    core concern
            implementation 428

crosscutting concern 428
defining roles 428
detecting caller type
  call stack, using 406
  conventional methods,
    using 405
  wormhole pattern, using 405
development phase
  policy enforcement 184
developmental aspect
  policy enforcement 179, 184
distributed system
  tracing 157
distributed transaction
  management 387
doAsPrivileged()
  authorization, use of 338
documentation
  policy enforcement,
    using 181
domination
  See aspect precedence 116
durability
  transaction, and 357
dynamic context 101
  pointcut vs. reflection 101
dynamic crosscutting 34, 81
  definition of 34
  runtime policy enforcement,
    and 184
  See also advice 81
  static crosscutting, compari-
    son with 95
  use of pointcut 35
dynamic information
  logging 107
dynamic monitoring 176
dynamic profiling 432
dynamic proxies
  using 13–14
dynamic service-level
  monitoring 176

E

echo server
  EchoServer class 224
  thread pooling, example
    of 224
  worker class 224

Eclipse
  AspectJ compiler, relation
    to 440
  AspectJ integration 61
EJB
  2.0 specification 191
  authorization, and 325
  policy enforcement 191–195
  programming
    restrictions 191
    AWT, and 191, 193
    native library loading 194
    socket creation 194
    static fields 194
    System.in access 194
    threading 191
  transactions, and 357
EJB-lite framework 355
Emacs JDEE
  AspectJ integration 61, 440
empty pointcut definition
  idiom 280–281
enclosing context 102
Enterprise Resource Planning
  (ERP) 387
EnterpriseBean 192
ERP 387
error recovery aspect
  exception handling, and 261
evangelizing AspectJ 434
event-based programming
  comparison with weaving 24
event-dispatching thread 287
  improving UI responsive-
    ness, exclusion 315
  requesting operation 289
  Swing 195
  Swing policies 198
EventQueue.invokeAndWait()
  198, 289
  blocking caller 295
  InterruptedException 300
  InvocationTargetException
    300
  Swing thread safety, example
    of 293
  synchronous operations,
    example of 295
  worker object creation pat-
    tern, and 253

EventQueue.invokeLater() 198,
  289
  asynchronous operations,
    example of 295
  exception, and 311
  Swing thread safety, example
    of 293
  worker object, and 247
EventQueue.isDispatchThread()
  199, 300
exception handler join point 48
  pointcut syntax 74
exception introduction
  pattern 260–269
  chained exception 265
  checked exception 260
    wrapping of 265
  current solution 261
  declare soft, vs. 267, 335
  distinguishing concern spe-
    cific exception 267
  exception call stack
    understandability 266
  generic aspects 267
  getCause() 269
  initCause() 265
  need to capture all exception
    types, example of 372
  pattern template 265
  preserving exception
    type 265
  preserving exception
    specification 268
  propagating concern-specific
    exception 265
  propagating exception 265
  read-write lock pattern, use
    of 320
  runtime exception, use
    of 265
  SoftException 267
    propagating business-spe-
      cific exception 267
  summarily captured excep-
    tion, dealing with 268
  Swing thread safety, example
    of 312
  transaction management,
    example of 377
  unchecked exception,
    issue 265

exception-handling policy
grouping of calls 296
exception-handling strategy
change management, ease
of 312
exceptions
handling
combining operation, difficulty with 342
current solution 261
logging 163
using log4j 166
using the standard Java
toolkit 165
using System.err 164
softening 136–139
caution 139
effective code 138–139
execution vs. call
pointcut 138
under the hood 138
usage of 137
summarily capturing, example of 370
execution object pointcut 78
example of 78
execution pointcut 74
capturing constructor, example of 168, 385
capturing read operations,
example of 321
example of 159, 232, 306
existing build system
incorporating AspectJ 443
explicit aspect precedence 115
exposed join point
advice, on 82
Extensible Access Control
Markup Language
(XACML) 324
Extreme Programming
See XP 431

F

factory pattern 187, 246
field access join point 47
pointcut syntax 74
read access 47
write access 47

field read join point
pointcut syntax 74
field signature 72
example of 72
use of type signature 72
field write join point
pointcut syntax 74
field-get join point
getArgs(), and 104
field-set join point
getArgs(), and 104
final, and local classes 295
flexible access control
factory pattern, and 188
friend (C++) in Java 188
policy enforcement 187
shopping cart example 187
use of 187
Forte
AspectJ integration 61
friend (C++) 188

G

-g
ajc option 440
get pointcut 74
example of 186
getArgs() 104
example of 107, 168
field-get join point 104
field-set join point 104
handler execution join
point 104
primitive argument 104
getCause() 269
getConnection() 212
getDeclaringType()
example of 376
getKind() 105
example of 108
getResource() 205
getSignature() 105
example of 108, 199, 291,
328, 332
logging, example of 363, 408
use in logging 158, 168
getSourceLocation() 105
example of 108, 199
getStaticPart() 102, 104–105

getTarget() 104
example of 107
returning null 104, 108
static methods 104, 108
getThis() 104
example of 107, 168
returning null 104, 108
static methods 104, 108
getThread() method 226
GUI applications
See UI applications 313
GUI refreshing
responsiveness, and 314

H

handler execution join point
getArgs(), and 104
hasAspect() 136
hotspot
log() method interaction 150
HTML 236

I

iajc ant task
ajc compiler, and 448
ajc ant task, relation 449
aspectjrt.jar 448
specifying without modifying CLASSPATH 451
aspectjtools.jar 448
specifying without modifying CLASSPATH 450
aspectpath nested
element 453
compiling source files 448
creating aspect libraries 452
defining in build file 448
destdir attribute 449
incremental attribute 454
incremental compilation 453
injars nested element 452–
453
javac ant task, similarity 448
outjar attribute 452
sourceroots nested
element 449, 452–453
utilizing aspect libraries 453
weaving into JAR files 451
XnoWeave attribute 452

IDE
    crosscutting view 61, 434
    integration 61
    multiple aspect, viewing 433
idioms 277–285
    definition of 246
    design pattern,
        difference 246
    programming tips 277
if pointcut 80
    example of 80, 199, 223, 299
    nullifying advice, idiom 279
    removal of advice,
        warning 279
ILOG JRules
    rule engine 417
implementation phase
    AspectJ, using 428
    common practices 428
    core concern 429
implementation space
    one-dimensional 10
implicit limiting of join points
    refactor, warning 133
improving UI
    responsiveness 313, 314
incremental adoption
    policy enforcement, and 179
incremental compilation
    iajc ant task 453
incremental compilation mode
    See -incremental option,
        ajc 444
-incremental option, ajc 445
    sourceroots, need for 446
indentation
    concrete aspect 171
    example of 107
    reusable aspect 171
    use in profiling 175
indented logging
    IndentedLogging base
        aspect 171
    subaspect, example of 328,
        363, 375, 408
individual productivity
    improving, using AspectJ 434
infinite recursion
    avoiding 277–278
    avoiding, idiom 277
    avoiding using !within() 108

initCause() 265
initialization pointcut 74
    example of 107
-injars option, ajc 442
    -aspectpath option,
        combining 444
    -sourceroots and -outjar
        options, combining 442
    -sourceroots option,
        combining 442
inner class
    blank final variable,
        restriction 296
installing AspectJ 439
instance variable
    multiple subaspects, authori-
        zation example 353
interadvice precedence 119
    authorization, example of 349
InterruptedException 300
introducing compile-time errors
        and warnings 97
    example of 98
    restrictions on 97
    statically determinable
        pointcuts 97
    usage of 97
introductions
    definition of 35
    inclusion in aspects 56
    providing default implemen-
        tation, use in 281
    See member introduction 95
invasiveness
    transaction management,
        example of 366
inviting aspect
    participant pattern 274
InvocationTargetException 300
invokeAndWait() 196
invokeLater() 196
isolation
    transaction, and 357

J

J2EE
    transaction management,
        and 357
JAAS 261, 324
    authorization, using 337

callback handler 329
    J2SE 1.4 324
    login configuration file 329
JAAS-based authorization 337
Jakarta Commons Logging
        toolkit 173
JAR files
    creating
        See -outjars option, ajc 442
jar ant task 452
Java Authentication and Autho-
        rization Service
    See JAAS 324
Java byte-code specification
    AspectJ compiler, and 440
Java Expert System Shell (Jess)
    See Jess 417
Java Language
    Specification 296
java ant task
    aspectjrt.jar
        specifying without modify-
            ing CLASSPATH 451
    classpath nested element 449
    running AspectJ
        programs 449
Java Transaction API
    See JTA 357
java.awt.EventQueue 196
java.security.auth.login.config
    configuration file,
        specifying 332
java.security.policy
    policy file, specifying 344
java.sql.Connection 213
java.sql.DriverManager 219
java.sql.ResultSet 219
java.sql.ResultSetMetaData 219
java.sql.Statement 219
javac
    ajc, difference from 441
javac ant task
    compiling pure Java
        sources 452
    iajc ant task, similarity 448
JavaDoc 186
javax.jms.Session 246
javax.swing.SwingUtilities 196
javax.swing.text.Document 199
JBuilder
    AspectJ integration 61

JComponent 199
JDBC 211, 261, 358
JDBC 1.0 211
JDBC 2.0
    aspect-oriented resource
        pooling, interaction 215
    database connection
        pooling 215
    resource pooling 211
Jess
    assert statement 419
    bind statement 419
    defining facts, banking
        example 418
    defining rules, banking
        example 419
    derived facts, banking
        example 419
    interaction with Java
        objects 418
    knowledge base, storing
        into 418
    Rete algorithm, implementa-
        tion of 417
    rule engine 417
    rule expression
        LISP-like 417
    rule invocation 420
JessException
    Jess, unwrapping of 423
JIT compiler
    log() method interaction 150
JMS 203, 387
    queue 387
join point model 43
join points 43
    accessing information 101
    advice execution
        See advice execution join
            points 50
    associated context 43
    capturing aspect
        instantiation 375
    capturing using kinded
        pointcut 74
    categories 44
    class initialization
        See class initialization join
            point 48
    concepts 43
    constructor

        See constructor join
            point 46
    definition of 34
    demonstration example 50
    difference from pointcut 35
    enclosing context 102
    exception handler execution
        See exception handler exe-
            cution join point 48
    exposed 43
    field access
        See field access join
            point 47
    kind 102
    method
        See method join point 45
    multiple advice 114
    object initialization
        See object initialization join
            points 49
    object pre-initialization
        See object pre-initialization
            join points 49
    programmatic access 101
    sequence diagram
        illustration 43
    source location 102
    structural context 102
JoinPoint 102
    getArgs()
        See getArgs() 104
    getKind()
        See getKind() 105
    getSignature()
        See getSignature() 105
    getSourceLocation()
        See getSourceLocation() 105
    getStaticPart() method
        See getStaticPart() 104
    getTarget()
        See getTarget() 104
    getThis()
        See getThis() 104
    toLongString() 105
    toShortString() 105
    toString() 105
    use in logging 168
JoinPoint.StaticPart 102
    authorization, use in 347
    method parameters type,
        as 347

JoinPointTraceAspect
    example of 106
JOptionPane.showMessage-
        Dialog()
    asynchronous routing,
        issue 307
JRE 1.4 330
JSR 166
    concurrency utility library,
        and 316
JSR 175
    participant pattern, and 271
JSR 94 418
    business rules 393
JTA 357, 387
    AspectJ-based solution 387–
        389
    code scattering 388
    conventional
        implementation 388
    modularizing using
        AspectJ 388
    policy-enforcement, and 389
    transaction management 357
JTable 196
just-in-time authentication
    AspectJ-based 333
    conventional 331
    up-front login,
        difference 329

K

kinded join point
    getKind(), using 105
kinded pointcut 73
    definition of 73
    example of 73–74
    syntax 74
knowledge base
    Jess, and 418
    rule engine 412

L

legacy project
    AspectJ, using 432
legacy system
    policy enforcement, use of 373
    transaction management
        handling of issues 373

lexical arrangement
  advice precedence, example
    of 349
lexical scope
  concept 77
lexical-structure based
    pointcut 77
  example of 77
limiting join points
  Swing thread safety, example
    of 312
LinkedHashMap
  caching example 241
listener management
  swing thread-safety, and 288
local class and final
    variable 295
log analyzer 175
log()
  deducing the caller 150
  explicit invocation 154
  hotspot, and 150
  inefficiency 150
  JIT compiler, and 150
  logp(), difference from 150
  use in log4j 162
log4j 146
  policy enforcement, and 185
log4j.properties 162
logging 146, 156
  aspect precedence and 172
  aspect-oriented 153
  authentication and authoriza-
    tion example 328
  authorization example 342
  business rule, example of 408
  caching, example of 236, 239
  centralized control 156
  change management using
    aspects 159
  changing underlying
    mechanism 173
  consistency 155
  conventional 149
  debugging, and 146, 433
  example of 332
  indentation 107, 170
  instrumentation 150–151
  level 150
  method parameters 168
  modularization 156

multithreaded
  environment 173
  precedence between multiple
    logging aspects 173
  resource pooling, example
    of 219
  Swing thread safety, example
    of 291, 301, 306
  thread pooling, example
    of 232
  transaction management
    example 363, 375
  using AOP 12
  using for testing 174
  using OOP 11
logging idioms 167–174
logging toolkit
  advantages 149
  aspect-oriented logging, role
    of 156
  change of 155
  inadequacy 150
  log4j 146
  standard Java 146
login
  example use of 331
login configuration file 329
login scope 334
LoginContext 329
  example of 331
  initialization 330
logp()
  log()
    comparison with 160
    difference from 150
    vs., enforcing policies 179
  logging exception 165
  logging method
    parameters 170

M

maintenance phase
  AspectJ, using 432
  creating protection walls 432
  policy enforcement 184
makefile
  policy enforcement 180
matching field type 80
matching handler type 80

matching subclass join
    points 79
member introduction 95
  aspect precedence 120
  example of 95, 121
  interfaces, into 96
  per-object association, rela-
    tion with 125, 134
  reusable aspect 135
mentoring
  policy enforcement, using 184
MessageFormat class 170
metadata
  JSR 175, and 271
  participant pattern, and 271
method call tracing 157
  improving performance 160
  limiting scope 159
  log-level pre-check 160
method introduction
  business rules, example
    of 421
  example of 121, 402
  overriding base aspect intro-
    duction, example of 403
  use of introduced method,
    example of 403
method join point 45
  call 45
  execution 45
  execution vs. call 46
  pointcut syntax 74
method parameters
  logging 168
method signature 70
  examples of 70
  matching of modifiers 70
  similarity with constructor
    signature 71
  use of .. wildcard 70
  use of type signature 70
method tracing
  shopping cart example 158
  using log4j 162
  using System.out 158
  using the standard
    toolkit 160
modifying class hierarchy
  usage of 96
modularization
  authorization example 11

crosscutting concerns using
OOP 11
logging example 11
need for 11
using AOP 12
using EJB 12–13
using OOP 11
multiple aspects
example of 111
interaction of 433
undesirable behavior 113

N

named pointcut 65
context collection, example
of 228, 237
general form 65
using in an advice 66
native library loading
EJB programming
restrictions 194
negation operator 67
nested aspects 58
access specification 56
example of 188, 283
participant pattern, and 273–
274
policy enforcement, and 185,
189
nested class
inside aspect, example of 371
nested subaspects
example of 379
participant pattern, and 273
nested transactions 361
database commit 362
participant pattern, and 380
top-level methods 367
NetBeans
AspectJ integration 61, 440
network failures
handling using aspect 90
simulation of 91
networking
EJB programming
restrictions 194
NoAspectBoundException 136
nonmodularization
issues with 18–19
symptom of 15

nonrecursive calls
capturing 94
nullifying advice 279–280
alternatives 280
idiom 279
resource pooling
example 223

O

object initialization join
points 49
comparison with class
initialization 49
pointcut syntax 74
object pre-initialization join
points 49
pointcut syntax 74
object-oriented patterns
delegation pattern 282
object-oriented programming
AOP, relation to 11
strengths 7
weaknesses 7
operator
! 67
&& 67
|| 67
binary 67
precedence 68
use of parentheses 68
unary 67
use in pointcuts 67
optimization
using aspect 92
opt-in
participant pattern 274
org.aspectj.lang 104
org.aspectj.lang.JoinPoint
See JoinPoint 102
org.aspectj.lang.JoinPoint.Static
Part 105
See JoinPoint.StaticPart 102
org.aspectj.lang.reflect 104
org.aspectj.lang.SoftException
138
-outjar option, ajc 442–443
-sourceroots and -injar
option, combining 442

P

participant pattern 270–277
aspect instances, and 380
aspectual interface 274
collaboration flow 276
explicit participation 276
inviting aspect 274
overview 273
participant subaspect, example of 379
peripheral
characteristics 270
read-write lock pattern,
and 321
reversal of roles 273
template 274
transaction management
example of 379
use case 378
use of 369
UML class diagram 276
use case 378
warning 271
PATH
modification for AspectJ 439
pattern
thread-safety 287
percflow association 129
aspect instance, example
of 372
aspectOf(), and 136
example of 131
transaction management,
example of 370
percflowbelow association 129
aspectOf(), and 136
per-control-flow
association 128
alternatives 129
for transaction
management 128
reusable aspect 128
performance
architect's dilemma 241
resource pooling, improving
using 203
performance testing 432
performance-monitoring
aspect 432

peripheral characteristics
JSR 177 271
participant pattern 270
per-object aspect
association 125
aspect state 125
association lifetime 126
member introduction, relation with 125, 134
read-write lock pattern, example of 319
reusable aspects 125
sequence diagram 127
static-crosscutting, relation with 125, 134
usage of 125
personal productivity
improving use policy enforcement 200
pertarget association 126
example of 128
perthis association 125–126
example of 126, 319
read-write lock pattern, example of 319
persistence
banking system 358–364
plug-and-play
EJB programming restrictions 191
logging 177
profiling 175
resource pooling 203, 208
pointcut designator 65
pointcuts 65
abstract
See abstract pointcuts
access specification 56, 65
adviceexecution pointcut 74
anonymous and named 65
args pointcut
See args pointcut 80
argument 80
call pointcut 74
capturing based on return type
example of 304
capturing no join point 67
cflow pointcut
See cflow pointcut 75

cflowbelow pointcut
See cflowbelow pointcut 75
class initialization 74
conditional check 80
constructor call 74
constructor execution 74
context collection, example of 402
control-flow based 75
declaration 56
definition of 35
difference from join point 35
example of 39–40
exception handler 74
execution object 78
execution pointcut 74
field read access 74
field write access 74
get pointcut 74
handler pointcut 74
if pointcut
See if pointcut 80
initialization pointcut 74
kinded
See kinded pointcut 73
lexical-structure based 77
method call 74
method execution 74
named
See named pointcut 65
object initialization 74
object pre-initialization 74
operators 67
preinitialization pointcut 74
property-based 68
signature syntax 68
staticinitialization
pointcut 74
target pointcut
See target pointcut 78
this pointcut
See this pointcut 78
use in advice 83
use in static crosscutting 74
use with advice 35
using from another aspect
example of 301
wildcards 67
within pointcut
See within pointcut 77

withincode pointcut
See withincode pointcut 77
policy enforcement 179–201
application frameworks, and 181
call pattern detection 185
compile-time
See compile-time enforcement 183
conventional, problems with 182
core program behavior 184
current solution 181
definition of 179
deployment
consideration 184
detection tools, using 181
development phase 184
developmental aspect 179
documentation, as 181
documenting restrictions 181
EJB programming restrictions 191
flexible access control 187
implementation choices 183
JTA, and 389
library development 181
maintenance phase 184
overcoming adaptation resistance 200
overview 179–181
patterns 185–191
performance
implications 185
post-analysis 185
runtime enforcement
See runtime policy enforcement 183
schematic 180
Swing 195
transaction management, use in 373
using embedded code 181
warning vs. fixing 184
policy file
authorization, credential check 337
example of 343
post-analysis
policy enforcement, using 185

precedence control 115
  declare precedence,
    using 115
precedence rules 114
  advice 111
  after advice 114
  around advice 114
  aspect 111
  before advice 114
  graphical 114
  proceed() and 114
preinitialization pointcut 74
PreserveBusinessException
    aspect 269
privileged
  See privileged aspects 140
privileged aspects 59, 139
  caution 141
  incorrect usage 433
  testing phase 431
PrivilegedAction
  authorization, use of 337
  conventional authorization,
    example of 340
PrivilegedExceptionAction
  authorization, use of 337
  conventional authorization,
    example of 340
proceed()
  arguments to 85
  authorization example 348
  bypassing join point 85
    example of 214
  calling inside try block, exam-
    ple of 267
  example of 93, 214
  if(false), and 279
  resource pooling
    example 209
  return value of 85
  taking argument, example
    of 228
  transaction management,
    example of 370
  use of 83
  worker object, example
    of 299, 305
product development
  policy enforcement, and 184
profiling 175
  conventional 175

gradual focusing 175
plug-and-play 175
use in dynamic
    monitoring 176
programming
  idioms 189
  methodologies
    current status 6
    issues with current
      techniques 6
  practices
    policy enforcement 179
  tips
    idioms 277
property-based pointcuts 68
  participant pattern, and 270
protection against web site
    attacks 324
putConnection() 212
putResource() 205
putThread() method 226

Q

QA
  runtime policy enforcement,
    and 184
  using logging 174
queue
  JMS 387

R

reader threads
  read-write lock pattern,
    and 316
read-write lock pattern 316
  appropriate usage 316
  AspectJ
    implementation 318–
    321
  conventional implementation
    316–318
  conventional solution, inva-
    siveness of 318
  description 316
  exception introduction pat-
    tern, use of 320
  participant pattern, and 321
ReadWriteLock, concurrency
    utility library 317

realize
  Swing application, meaning
    of 295
ReentrantWriterPreference-
    ReadWriteLock
  concurrency utility
    library 317
refactored code
  core concern 429
refactoring 236, 426, 433
  AspectJ, using
    See aspectual
      refactoring 431
  base-derived aspect 298
refactoring aspect
  code sharing 402
reflection API 101–111
  class diagram 103
  dynamic information 102
  example of 106
  Signature interface 104–105
  SourceLocation interface 104
  static information 102
  static vs. dynamic
    information 102
  structural relationship 103
  UML class diagram 103
  using 106
reflective API
  See reflection API 103
  usage of 111
registerConnection() 212
regression testing
  logging, and 174
release()
  concurrency utility
    library 317
Remote Method Invocation
    (RMI) 137
RemoteException 137
repaint()
  swing thread-safety, and 288
requirement changes
  business rules 392
requirements
  accommodating new 6
resource destruction
  resource destruction join
    point 227
resource pooling
  advice 211

architect's dilemma, and 207
AspectJ-based
　See aspect-oriented
　　resource pooling 208
caching, difference from 235
class diagram 205
conventional, code
　snippet 206
database connection pooling
　See database connection
　　pooling 211
definition of 203
deployment aspect, as 242
development aspect, as 242
interface 205
invasiveness 207
issues 206–208
JDBC 2.0, and 211
performance
　finding bottlenecks 242
　improvement 203
replacing
　implementation 207
resource creation
　pointcut 210
resource destruction
　pointcut 211
role 205–206
sequence diagram 207, 210
switching on/off 207
transaction management,
　and 369
turning off 223
typical resource usage
　See typical resource
　　usage 203
resource pooling template
　aspect 209
concern-weaving 210
creating concrete
　implementation 208
database connection pooling,
　mapping to 213
implementation 209
participating entities 208
participating join points 208
pointcuts 208
resource creation
　pointcut 208
resource destruction
　pointcut 208

thread pooling, mapping
　to 227
ResourceDescription 205
ResourcePool 205
ResourcePoolingAspect 209
resource usage, typical 203–205
Rete algorithm
　Jess, and 417
　rule engine 412
Rete class
　Jess 421
return value
　worker object 296
return value management
　worker object creation pat-
　　tern, example of 300
reusability
　policy enforcement
　　aspects 184
reusable aspect
　exception handling 261
　read-write lock pattern 316,
　　318
reusable authorization
　aspect 346
revalidate()
　swing thread-safety, and 288
reversal of roles
　participant pattern 273
RMI (Remote Method
　Invocation) 137
roll back
　database connection 366
rule engine 393
　backward-reasoning
　　algorithm 412
　basic facts 413
　Blaze Advisor 417
　business objects as facts 412
　business rules, and 393
　core business logic, embed-
　　ding into 394, 411
　derived facts 413
　evaluation 396
　facts 412
　graphical illustration
　　behavioral 414
　　structural 413
　ILOG JRules 417
　implementing business rules
　　using 411

initialization 396
Java objects, as facts 412
Jess 417
knowledge base 412
overview 412
Rete algorithm 412
rule invocation 420
RuleML 412
rules 412
sequence diagram 413–415
working memory 412
RuleML
　business rules, and 393
　rule engine 412
run() method
　example of 224
　Jess
　　running engine 422
Runnable
　and worker object 247
　Swing thread-safety, use
　　in 289
　Swing, using in 197–198
　thread pooling 227
RunnableWithReturn
　transaction management,
　　example of 384
　use of 253, 299
　worker object creation
　　pattern 252
runtime policy violation
　logging 183
RuntimeException 136, 261

S

SampleLoginModule 330
scattering of decisions
　authorization example,
　　conventional 345
security API
　J2SE 1.4 324
Security Assertion Markup
　Language (SAML) 324
security concern 324
　auditing 324
　authentication 324
　authorization 324
　code scattering 325
　code tangling 325
　cryptography 324

protection against web site
attacks 324
separation of concerns 429
database connection
pooling 211
design/implementation
mismatch 10
design phase 10
house-building analogy 4
light-beam/prism analogy 8
multidimensional space 8
mutual independence 9
one-dimensional
implementation 10
orthogonality 9
robotic system example 4
software system example 4
through modularization 20
transaction management,
example of 357
sequence diagram
control-flow 76
join points 81
per-control-flow
association 130
per-object association 127
resource usage 204, 207
rule engine, AspectJ-
based 416
server-side applications
thread pooling 223
servlet 334
servlet session 334
set pointcut
policy enforcement, use
in 195
setAutoCommit()
transaction management,
JDBC and 359
shopping cart
business rule, example of 392
shopping cart example 147
showMessageDialog()
Swing thread safety, example
of 290
Signature
example of 328, 332, 363
signature pattern 68
constructor
See constructor signature
pattern 70

field
See field signature 72
method
See method signature
pattern 70
syntax 68
type
See type signature 68
Signature.getDeclaringType()
example of 376
Signature.toShortString()
logging, example of 408
Simple Rule Markup Language
(SRML)
business rules, and 393
socket 224
creation of
EJB programming
restrictions 194
socket connections
resource pooling, and 204
softening
See exception softening 138
SoftException 138
SoftReference
caching example 241
software system
as concern composition 7
-source
ajc option 440
SourceLocation 105
example of 108
-sourceroots option, ajc 441
-injars and -outjar options,
combining 442
-injars option,
combining 442
space/time tradeoff 207
special pointcut syntax, capturing no join points
example of 380
SQLException 265
standard Java logging kit 146
state
transaction management,
maintaining 369
stateless aspect
instances, and 382
static context 101
static crosscutting 34, 95
classifications of 95

definition of 34
dynamic crosscutting, comparison with 95
introducing compile-time
errors and warning
See introducing compile-
time errors and
warning 97
member introduction
See member
introduction 95
modifying class hierarchy
See modifying class
hierarchy 96
per-object association, relation with 125, 134
static fields
EJB programming
restrictions 191, 194
static methods
getTarget() 104
getThis() 104
statically determinable pointcuts
compile-time declaration 183
compile-time
enforcement 183
staticinitialization pointcut
example of 107
store()
Jess, storing facts 422
strongly typed languages 183
stylesheet 235
subaspect 57–58
authentication 333
example of 58, 125, 171,
251, 263, 281, 299, 301,
304, 308–309, 315, 319
participant pattern, use
of 273–276
transaction management 374
Subject
authorization, use of 337
example usage 333
Subject.doAsPrivileged() 348
Swing
event-dispatching thread,
and 195, 287
policy enforcement 195
need of 313
realized, meaning of 288

single-thread rule 287–290
    violation, use case 288
single-threaded,
        restriction 195
thread safety
    AspectJ solution 297–311
    asynchronous routing 291,
        295
    avoiding overhead 312
    conventional solution 293–
        297
    dealing with
        exceptions 311
    exception introduction pat-
        tern, use of 312
    exception-handling
        policy 296
    exempted calls 300
    hard-to-read code 290
    issues using pattern 289
    pattern 289
    policy enforcement 287
    return type consideration
        303
    return value
        consideration 291,
        295
    solution 289
    synchronous routing 291,
        295
    test problem 290
    worker object creation
        pattern 298
    worker object, and 247
SwingThreadSafetyAspect 299
synchronous routing
    non-void type 304
    Swing thread safety, explicit
        control 307
    worker object creation
        pattern 253
system evolution
    authorization example,
        conventional 345
System.err 163
    policy enforcement 185
System.in access
    EJB programming
        restrictions 194
System.out 157
    policy enforcement 185

T

-target
    ajc option 440
target pointcut 78
    context collection 87
        example of 228, 363
    example of 78, 121, 214, 220
    reflection, and 101
    static methods 78
    use of wildcard 78
taskdef ant task
    resource attribute
        defining AspectJ tasks 448
TCP/IP 203
    thread pooling example 224
Templates
    stylesheet 239
test cases
    creating using AspectJ 431
testing
    logging, use of 174
    using AspectJ 431
testing phase
    error reporting 432
TextCallbackHandler 330
    example usage 331
third-party aspects 117
third-party services
    use of dynamic
        monitoring 176
this
    advice, inside 124
this pointcut 78
    context collection 87
        example of 228, 383, 402,
        408
    difference from call
        pointcut 79
    difference from within
        pointcut 79
    example of 78, 123
    reflection, and 101
    restricting matched type,
        example of 403–404
    static methods 78
    use of wildcard 78
thisEnclosingJoinPointStatic-
        Part 101–102
    example of 103

thisJoinPoint 101–102, 105
    example of 52
    string representation 55
    thisJoinPointStaticPart, com-
        parison with 158
    usage of 83, 102
    use in logging 168
thisJoinPointStaticPart 101–
        102, 105
    as key in map 175
    example of 123, 291, 328,
        332, 343
    logging, example of 363, 408
    passing as method parameter,
        example of 347
    thisJoinPoint, comparison
        with 158
    usage of 102
    use in exception logging 164
    use in logging 158, 161
thread pool 230–231
    implementation,
        SimpleThreadPool 228,
        230
    ThreadPool interface 226
thread pooling
    destruction join point, non-
        obviousness 223
    improving UI
        responsiveness 315
thread pooling aspect 223–235
    active resource
        consideration 223
    AspectJ-based
        See aspect-oriented thread
            pooling 226
    aspect-oriented
        See aspect-oriented thread
            pooling 226
    fine tuning 234
    pool interface
        See thread pool 226
    resource creation join
        point 227
    resource pooling template,
        mapping to 227
    selective enabling 234
thread safety
    definition of 287
    patterns, for 287

read-write lock pattern
  See read-write lock
      pattern 316
threading
  EJB programming
      restrictions 191
ThreadLocal 129, 257
  logging, use in 173
  transaction management, use
      of 367
thread-local storage 129
  call depth, storing of 367
  logging, use in 173
  transaction management, use
      of 365
threads 226
  resource pooling, and 204
  resurrection 229
  waiting state 229
thread-specific connection
  transaction management,
      and 367
time-consuming tasks
  UI applications, issues
      with 313
timestamp
  use in profiling 175
top-level operation
  commit/rollback
      consideration 368
  determination of 367
  transaction management 368
  worker method, as 382
tracing 156
  indentation effect 53
  method call
      See method call
          tracing 157
  need for 156
  See logging 107
training 436
  policy enforcement,
      using 184
transaction management aspect
  exception handling, and 261
transaction management sub-
      aspect, example of 373
Transaction Processing (TP)
      monitor 387
transactions
  ACID properties 357

atomicity property 357
consistency property 357
context 382
  aspect instance, use of 369
  connection creation,
      avoiding 384
  connection object, forming
      of 368
  connection storage 382
definition of 357
durability property 357
integrity 362
  nested transactions 362
isolation property 357
management
  communicating failure 369
  conventional solution 364–
      368
  crosscutting concern,
      as 357
  declarative with
      AspectJ 357
  EJB, and 357
  explicit awareness, core
      concerns 368
  inconsistent state 357
  invasiveness 366
  legacy system, and 373
  multiple subaspects 379–
      382
  multiple subsystems 378–
      387
  property-based
      pointcut 270
  resource pooling, and 369
  roles
      storing connection
          object 382
      weaving commit and
          rollback 382
      thread-specific connection,
          and 367
  using per-control-flow
      association 128
nested 361
state management 372
Transformer
  multithreading issue 239
  stylesheet 235, 237
TransformerFactory
  stylesheet 235

try/catch
  exception introduction pat-
      tern, and 263, 265, 267
  transaction management, use
      in 369
type
  definition of 68
type signature 68
  example of 69
  example use in method
      signature 70
  package declaration 69
  subtype specification 68
  usage in other signatures 69–
      70
  use of wildcard 68
  using binary operator 69
  using unary operator 69
type signature pattern
  declare precedence, using
      in 116
  See type signature 68

U

UI applications
  improving responsiveness
      See improving UI
          responsiveness 313
unary operator 67
  type signature, and 69
unchecked exception 136
underdesign
  benefits 6
underlying logic
  exception, need to throw 261
up-front authentication
  AspectJ-based, using 335
up-front login 329
  protecting again unauthenti-
      cated access 336
UserTransaction 389

V

visitor design pattern 246

W

wakeupThread() method 226
weaver 22, 24

definition of 24
patching, difference from 30
using byte-code
    transformation 25
using source-to-source
    translation 24
weaving 4, 24
    abstract aspect 57
    AspectJ compiler 59
    behavior modification 34
    comparison with event-based
        programming 24
    definition of 24
    dynamic 25
    examples of
        pseudo code 26
        rules 26
        woven code 27
    example output 42
    into JAR files
        iajc ant task, using 451
        See -injars option, ajc 442
    just-in-time 25, 60
    logging example 156
    once-only restriction, ajc 443
    process overview 25
    resource pooling
        example 210
    rules
        definition of 23
        economical expression 23
        expression language 24
        role in crosscutting 33
        specificity 23
    static modifications 34
what-if scenario
    nullifying advice 279
wildcards
    * 67
    + 67
    .. 67
    consistent naming
        convention 429
    declare precedence, using
        in 116
    need for 67
    use in a type signature 68
within pointcut 77
    avoiding infinite recursion 53,
        108, 158, 164
        idiom 278

difference from this
    pointcut 79
example of 52, 77, 107, 159,
    312
limiting impact 427
limiting scope 186
    exception softening, exam-
        ple of 361
    resource pooling
        example 222
    restricting scope, example
        of 299
    usage of 77
    use in access control 187
withincode pointcut 77
    example of 77, 159, 189, 312
worker method 247
worker object
    anonymous class 248
    as context 254
    current solution 248
        drawbacks 249
    definition of 247
    direct invocation 254
    example of 299
    named class 248
    return value 252
        Swing, example of 296
    run() method, and 248
    Runnable, relation to 247
worker object creation
    pattern 247–256
    around advice 249
    authorization example 346
    authorization, advantages of
        using 346
    context collection 249
    example of 250
    getting return value 252
    improving UI
        responsiveness 313–314
    managing collected
        context 256
    overview 249
    passing worker to thread 251
    proceed() 249
        context management,
            and 256
        return value, and 252
        use of 251

return value management,
    example of 300
routing methods with return
    value 252
RunnableWithReturn 252
Swing thread safety 287, 298
synchronous routing 253
template 249
transaction context, and 382,
    385
transaction management,
    example of 378, 382
worker method, and 247
working memory
    AspectJ-based rule implemen-
        tation
        context collection 416
        setting of 416
    rule engine 412
wormhole pattern 256–260,
    384
    business rule implementa-
        tion, example of 405
    call stack 258
    callee pointcut 257
    caller pointcut 257
    caller type 260
    current solutions 257
    detecting caller type, example
        of 405
    example of 258
    graphical illustration 257
    implicit context 260
    overview 257
    passing context 257
    pattern template 258
    purpose 256
writer threads
    read-write lock pattern,
        and 316

X

-Xlint option, ajc 446
    modifying ajc shell script 446
    modifying ajc.bat 446
-XnoWeave option, ajc 444
XP 431
    AspectJ, using 431
    relation to AOP 28
XSLT 235